Liberty, Authority, Formality
Political Ideas and Culture, 1600–1900

Essays in Honour of Colin Davis

Edited by John Morrow and Jonathan Scott

imprint-academic.com

Collection and Introduction © John Morrow and Jonathan Scott, 2008
Essays © Respective authors, 2008

The moral rights of the contributors have been asserted.
No part of this publication may be reproduced in any form
without permission, except for the quotation of brief passages in
criticism and discussion.

Typeset by Open Digital Solutions
www.opendigital.co.uk

Published in the UK by
Imprint Academic, PO Box 200, Exeter EX55YX, UK

Published in the USA by
Imprint Academic, Philosophy Documentation Center
PO Box 7147, Charlottesville, VA 22906-7147, USA

ISBN 978-1845401351 (paperback)
ISBN 978-1845401429 (hardback)

A CIP catalogue record for this book is available from
the British Library and US Library of Congress

Contents

Preface		v
An Appreciation of Colin Davis by Dámaso de Lario		vii
Introduction by John Morrow and Jonathan Scott		1

I. Liberty

1. **Royalism and Liberty of Conscience in the English Revolution**   9
   by Glenn Burgess

2. **Authority and Liberty: Hobbes and the Sects**   29
   by William Lamont

3. **Toleration and the Godly Prince in Restoration England**   45
   by Mark Goldie

4. **England's Houdini: Charles II's escape from Worcester as a metaphor for his reign (1660-1685)**   67
   by Jonathan Scott

II. Authority

5. **How Oliver Cromwell Thought**   89
   by John Morrill

6. **Roger L'Estrange, Printed Petitions and the Problem of Intentionality**   113
   by Mark Knights

7. **Republicanism as Anti-patriarchalism in Henry Neville's *The Isle of Pines* (1668)**   131
   by Gaby Mahlberg

8. **Formality and Revolution: Carlyle on Modernity**   153
   by John Morrow

III. Formality

9. **Mobilisation, Anxiety and Creativity in England during the 1640s**   175
    by Mike Braddick

10. **The Uses of the Monarchy: A `Spanish Incident' in the Mid-Nineteenth Century**   195
    by Isabel Burdiel

11. **Settler Utopianism? English Ideologies of Emigration, 1815-1880**   213
    by James Belich

12. **A Colonial Way with Welfare?**   235
    by David Thomson

Conclusion

13. **Why *Homo Sapiens* had to be Saved by Culture**   253
    by Peter Munz

A Bibliography of the Publications of J. C. Davis   269
    compiled by Jocelyn Gamble

Contributors   275

Index   277

Preface

The career which began when J. C. (Colin) Davis enrolled as an undergraduate at Manchester University has included distinguished service at three New Zealand universities (Waikato, Victoria and Massey) and at the University of East Anglia. In all of these places he is remembered not only as an inspiring teacher and supervisor but as someone who thought hard and worked harder for the whole academic community of which he was part. Although the University of East Anglia benefited particularly from his capacity for academic leadership, the desire to relate the work of university historians to wider interests has been a feature of his entire career. So too has been the international scope of his own work and professional relationships within the English-speaking world and in continental Europe.

Preparation of this volume began in 2004 to mark Colin's retirement from his Professorship of English History at UEA the following year. Contributions were invited from friends, students and colleagues whose association with Colin extends to every stage of his career. The editors have been very fortunate in their contributors and wish to record their thanks to them. We all share an admiration for Colin's pioneering contributions to early modern scholarship as well as deep gratitude for his rich and generous engagement with the work of others. Those who have been his students and colleagues are proud to regard him as a friend. It is a matter of great regret that Peter Munz, who was responsible for appointing Colin to Victoria University of Wellington and provided strong support for him there, died while this volume was being prepared. The editors are most grateful to Anne Munz and Justin Cargill for their help in preparing Peter's essay for the press.

The editors also owe much to Mrs Jocelyn Gamble, the Executive Assistant to the Dean of the Faculty of Arts at The University of Auckland, for invaluable assistance in managing this project and preparing the typescript. The contributors know her email address at least as well as that of either of the editors. Jocelyn has also played a major role in researching and compiling the bibliography of Colin's work that appears here. Sandra Davis very kindly supplied some of the material for the bibliography. We are pleased to record our appreciation to Iain Hampsher-Monk for his help in facilitating publication and to Anthony Freeman of Imprint Academic and Frank Morrow of Open Digital Solutions for their role in producing this volume.

John Morrow and Jonathan Scott
Auckland and Pittsburgh

An Appreciation of Colin Davis

Dámaso de Lario

> ... there is no other path but the one in which we can recognize ourselves in every gesture and in every word: that of the obstinate loyalty to ourselves.[1]
>
> (José Saramago, *De este Mundo y del Otro*)

I find those words of the Portuguese Literature Nobel Prize winner José Saramago fitting to sum up Colin Davis's persona as a scholar, an academic, a teacher, a friend and a man of his time. Our paths crossed rather late in life, in 1993, three years after he took up his Chair of History at the University of East Anglia, Norwich, and only a few months after I had started my job as Cultural Attaché at the Spanish Embassy in London. As in the film *Casablanca*, that was the beginning of a long friendship that at the time (my London tenure lasted until 1998) allowed us to develop a number of projects together and later matured into a rich and creative personal and intellectual exchange.

Born in Yorkshire into a fisherman's family, Colin (J. C. in the academic literature) Davis trained at the University of Manchester, and after a short stint at the Foreign and Commonwealth Office — where he was destined to become a Russian expert — he took up an offer to teach at the University of Waikato, in Hamilton, New Zealand. Given that he subsequently made his name as a 'historian of political and religious thought and as a brilliant and provocative iconoclast', diplomacy's loss was certainly academia's gain.[2]

I have always wondered how much chance plays in a scholar's choice of the subject matter of his research and how much this is influenced by the scholar's own tenets. Or to put it perhaps in a more metaphysical way: are scholars attracted to the subject matters of their research or is it the other way around? To what extent can the scholar's tenets, in the long term, be

---

[1] 'no hay otro camino a no ser aquel en el que podemos reconocernos en cada gesto y en cada palabra, el de la obstinada fidelidad a nosotros mismos'. José Saramago, *De este Mundo y del Otro*, trad. B. Losada (Barcelona, 1997), p. 120.

[2] R. Hutton's review of J. C. Davis, *Oliver Cromwell* (London, 2001), H-Net Book Review, *H-Net: Humanities & Social Sciences Online*, August 2001.

affected by his or her research and also how can this be influenced by those tenets? In the case of history, E. P. Thompson had 'repeatedly insisted on the duty of the historian to "listen" to all of his sources, rather than merely giving shape to them', but the key issue, as Colin Davis put it, was whether that 'listening [is] done to inform one's perspective or according to one's perspective'.[3]

Given his analytical and argumentative capacity, his eye for detail and his ability to keep his sources 'at a distance', Colin Davis could have been a superb legal historian — to mention a discipline very close to my own intellectual interests. He chose instead a speculative area of history and there he centred first on 'the chimaera of utopian speculation'.[4] He did so because he discerned there something that appeared to have gone unnoticed to previous historians of political thought. The ideas of the 'ill-assorted few', as Davis described the early modern English utopians, 'stand at the fountainhead of a long and dominating political process ... [and] they help to reveal something fundamental about the nature of political idealism. The process ... is the growth of the centralised, bureaucratic, sovereign state with its impersonal, institutional apparatus'.[5]

Yet the history of the utopians as a whole, like that of the Levellers and of the Ranters, or the lives of Gerrard Winstanley, James Harrington or even Oliver Cromwell, to all of whom Davis has devoted a great deal of time and effort, is not the history of winners, in the mainstream sense of the word. But it fits with Colin Davis's ethos — hence the logic of the choice of his subject matter — and his radicalism without concessions. Thus his admiration for Christopher Hill did not prevent Davis from taking issue with him, and other 'fine radical commentators', for accepting 'as real a highly conservative and admonitory projection or myth from the 1650s' in a brilliant book where he proves that the Ranters were no more than 'a mythic projection'.[6] The same goes for John Morrill, with whom, in spite of a close personal friendship and a genuine appreciation for his work, Colin Davis maintains serious disagreements on the interpretation of the English Revolution.

In spite of his recognized contributions to the history of English

---

[3] See J. C. Davis, *Fear, Myth and History. The Ranters and the historians* (Cambridge, 2002), p. 137.

[4] J. C. Davis, *Utopia and the ideal society. A study of English utopian writing 1516-1700* (Cambridge, 1983), p. 8.

[5] *Ibid.*

[6] Davis, *Fear, Myth and History*, pp. x and 126.

political thought, which have stimulated reconsideration of 'the traditional categories in which historians had grouped Civil War radicals',[7] Colin Davis has never 'quite felt comfortable with the description of "expert", preferring to think of [himself] as a student. The difference is that what the years have given us is a confidence that we can derive an argument out of a mass of material and engage with its intellectual significance'.[8] And this is precisely one of Davis's distinctive features as a scholar: his constant quest for learning, through an argumentative approach to the sources, together with his efforts to make of history a useful tool for better understanding the world in which we live.[9] With this he combines a compassionate approach to his characters, no matter the severity of his historical scrutiny of their lives. He thus invites us to think of Cromwell 'rather more like ourselves, caught, most of the time, in the mess of the limitations of his society and therefore condemned to repeat what he has found to be the deficiencies of others';[10] or admits that Winstanley's life pattern was not a smooth one 'but then when does any life conform to a smooth pattern? — but partly because of that feels more authentic ... and it also helps us to understand more'.[11] He also suggests the possibility of a history of a radicalism which, 'while standing in a critical relationship to the status quo and seeking transformation, is not automatically coming to that task from a position of *radical* alienation', a difficult perception to pursue but one that would reward us with 'a richer and more human appreciation of the fitful impulse towards transformative change in our history'.[12]

It is unfortunate that lack of time and other commitments may prevent Colin Davis from bringing his work on liberty and formality together with studies of ideas of authority in Early Modern England 'to

---

[7] See note 2.

[8] J. C. Davis (hereafter JCD) to Dámaso de Lario (hereafter DL), letter of 11 January 2003.

[9] 'I have always felt that sense of standing on a shore with an ocean of knowledge unexplored before me', *ibid.*

[10] Davis, *Oliver Cromwell*, p. 9.

[11] JCD to DL, e-mail of 21 September 1999. Davis was at the time finding new archival information for his biography of 'Gerrard Winstanly 1609-1676', co-authored with J. D. Alsop, for the *Oxford Dictionary of National Biography* (Oxford, 2004-06).

[12] J. C. Davis, 'Problems (and Solutions?) in the History of English Radicalism', keynote speech delivered at the conference 'Rediscovering radicalism in the British Isles and Ireland, c. 1550-c. 1770; movements of people, texts and ideas', Goldsmith College, London, 21 June 2006, p. 20. Italics in the original.

show how the collapse of the ideas of formality and the transformation of the civic persona have left us with a serious crisis in the understanding of civic responsibility and citizenship'.[13] I very much hope that this *Festschrift* succeeds in closing at least part of the gap that the lack of implementation of that project would leave.

Colin Davis's intellectual preoccupations, which were shaped during his formative years as an academic at Victoria University of Wellington, also fashioned his commitment to the academic institutions of which he was part, and the role that he saw for himself as a teacher, particularly since taking up, at Massey University, his first chair. He summed it up poignantly two years before his retirement:

> I decided 20 years ago when I became a professor that I had a duty to do my best to maintain some quality in a higher education system which was being wrecked — and still is — by short term policies of politicians. On my good days, I think I may have held the tide back a little in my small area but after 20 years of constantly diminishing resources I see little hope for the system, either in the U[nited] K[ingdom] or N[ew] Z[ealand], left.[14]

Apart from J. C. Davis's involvement in his universities in New Zealand, that contributed to his sound academic career, he was instrumental not only in setting up the School of History at the University of East Anglia, Norwich, but also in making of it, at the turn of the last century, one of the top eight History Departments in the United Kingdom.[15] The latter recognition, together with the faster advancement than the national British average that that university had in 2001, was in good part due to the strategies and initiatives put forward by Colin Davis during his tenure as Pro-Vice-Chancellor for Humanities and Social Sciences. It was the second time that he had an appointment that was necessarily going to delay some of his work as an historian of English political thought, the core of his career. But he held the view that serving in managerial positions was an integral part of the duties of an academic.

The first time that Colin Davis was appointed Pro-Vice-Chancellor was during the inspirational, but rather short-lived, tenure of Dame

---

[13] JCD to DL, e-mail of 5 January 2004.

[14] JCD to DL, letter of 6 October 2003.

[15] The School of History of the University of East Anglia was amongst the eight Departments awarded the top rating (5*) in the 2001 Research Assessment Exercise.

Elizabeth Esteve-Coll as Vice-Chancellor of the University of East Anglia. It was during that period that, with Dame Elizabeth's full support, he and I devised a number of initiatives to bring his university and the University of Valencia — my *alma mater* — together and ultimately to bring closer the cultures of Britain and Spain.

One result was the involvement of the Sainsbury Centre for the Visual Arts of the University of East Anglia in some exhibitions of Spanish contemporary art, and the establishment of a minor in Spanish Studies (that did not prove to be popular enough to be maintained). But the success story was the Anglo-Spanish Seminar of Historical Studies — initially supported by the Cañada Blanch Foundation — that will soon be into its twelfth year and that, alternately in Norwich and Valencia, brings together distinguished historians of both countries around cross-border topics. A few years after that Seminar was started Colin Davis successfully elicited a grant from the British Academy to start a three year programme to encourage exchanges between Chinese and British historians.[16]

J. C. Davis has been a master at identifying original ideas and finding a way to make them fly. Another case in point was an Anglo-French Seminar on petitioning and political discourse in early modern society (1500-1700) that led him to prepare a bid to the Arts and Humanities Research Board 'to establish a centre for the historical study of petitions here [University of East Anglia] with funding for satellite activity at a number of other British and continental universities'.[17] At that time too he managed to make his university the lead institution in a consortium of British universities after successfully negotiating a deal with the University of Nanjing 'to assist their School of History in developing real archival research capability'.[18]

During my London years, from time to time, Colin Davis and I used to put some time aside to have a 'day out' together, preferably in some historical English village, and speak out our minds to one another. It was a wonderful intellectual exercise. Thus a conversation during a walk close to the sea at Blakeney made him think of 'the desirability of an international and interdisciplinary centre for the study of corruption and, in particular, its political, economic and cultural consequences', something that would need to be the embodiment of an international network of

---

[16] JCD to DL, letter of 5 November 2000.

[17] JCD to DL, e-mails of 21 December 2000 and 7 January 2001. The Seminar was held in Montpellier from 17 to 19 March 2000.

[18] JCD to DL, e-mail of 21 December 2000.

research programmes.[19] The first fruits of his persistence in this idea were a series of events at the University of East Anglia in 2003 on 'Re/Constructing Corruption'.[20] The follow-up to that was 'a volume to be published possibly by Cambridge University Press, a discussion going on between ourselves, Transparency International and Cambridge University to set up a national (U[nited] K[ingdom]) Centre for the study of corruption and a number of other things'.[21]

All of which is witness to the creative leadership of Colin Davis. Hence, and given his academic track record, it was legitimate for him to put himself forward as a candidate to succeed Dame Elizabeth as Vice-Chancellor of his university. He had the encouragement and the support of a number of influential academics but he was not part and parcel of the political establishment of the academic world. I have no doubt that the fact that, at the end, he was not appointed to the job was a personal and professional disappointment, to which J. C. Davis, loyal as ever to his academic institutions, responded by serving later, with Dame Elizabeth's successor, his second tenure as Pro-Vice-Chancellor. It is my personal view, however, that with his defeat as Vice-Chancellor his vision for the University of East Anglia as a research intensive university possibly vanished too, at least for a foreseeable future.

It is ironical though that subsequently two substantial academic opportunities in New Zealand came Colin Davis's way, a fact that testified to recognition of his stature as a scholar and as an administrative leader. But, in spite of their attractiveness, it was too late in time for him to consider a return even to academic arenas he knew extremely well.

Nonetheless, despite nearing retirement, the enthusiasm shown by Professor Colin Davis never waned. In 2005 Congregation honoured this dedication by awarding him with, not only the title of Emeritus Professor, but also one of four University of East Anglia Awards for Excellence in Teaching.[22] This was, without doubt, one of the highest rewards of his career. But his students have liked and respected him not only for being 'a popular and innovative teacher', and for 'the wealth of experience and infectious enthusiasm' brought to his subject by him,[23] but also because he

---

[19] JCD to DL, letter of 29 July 2001, p. 1.

[20] JCD to DL, letter of 12 July 2002 and attachment.

[21] JCD to DL, e-mail of 29 January 2003.

[22] 'Congregation 2005', Broadview Supplement August 2005, *Broadview. The Newsletter of the University of East Anglia* (August 2005).

[23] *Ibid.*

has always supported them through thick and thin, often well beyond his academic duties. This was a generosity that has also been at the base of Colin Davis's relationship with his colleagues, especially the younger ones to whom he has wanted to bequeath his visionary approach to the teaching of history.

Ten months before retiring he shared the news with me that a small group he had led in collaboration with the University of Hull had been successful in a bid for a significant grant

> to fund the first phase of the development of a 'virtual research environment' for the history of political thought 1500-1800. The money will be used to set up an on-line repository of resources (many of which are on-line in other forms) and to give us state of the art video conferencing facilities (which interface with the web based resources) for discussion, teaching and the formation of a closely integrated research community which will expand outwards from the two initial universities to others both in this country and overseas.[24]

The importance of that project was that it offered J. C. Davis's younger colleagues a way of overcoming the problem of scale in their specialism and enabling them to attract numbers of research students when he was retired.[25]

That project also highlights a preoccupation that runs through all of Colin Davis's projects and historical interpretations: inclusiveness. Teaching European history in the antipodes made obvious to him that he was talking about an entity — Europe — 'which had more in common than the differences which separated it' and made him feel the need for 'a global history which draws out European distinctiveness' as opposed to the nationalist histories in Europe.[26] Quite possibly that was at the heart of his Europeanism and of his dread of Euro-sceptical British governments. But it also informed his realisation, later in life, that democratising the European project is the only way of addressing 'the issues confronting the welfare/fiscal state within a democratic context of European nation states'.[27] To him, and to many a European citizen — continental or not —

---

[24] JCD to DL, letter of 10 October 2004.
[25] Ibid.
[26] JCD to DL, letter of 29 June 2005.
[27] JCD to DL, letter of 31 May 2005, p. 3.

the best hope for our children is a stronger Europe, held together by a shared regulatory framework, amongst other things, and with a common face to the rest of the world.

He saw that very clearly while spending a few days in Milan with his wife, Sandra. They were staying at a comfortable hotel across a square which every day filled up with east Europeans looking for employment in the black economy. The square was even fuller at the weekends as those people tried to have some sort of communal life. What Colin Davis thought he was looking at was

> the flesh and blood argument for a European constitution. The marginalisation of these people will produce more versions of what is happening in France now[28] and it is a European wide phenomenon. Either we have a European policy or we will have a far right backlash, but for effective European policy we need a European constitution.[29]

In its absence, and with the rising influx of immigrants from Africa and Asia, Europe might succumb to what Alan Ryan describes as 'appeals based on the irrational forms of identity — ethnic, racial, religious — rather than to appeals based on the rational forms — economic above all'.[30]

The French and the Dutch 'no's to that Constitution worried Colin Davis, but he has been perhaps more concerned by the Anglo-American relationship, 'the fatal choice of Blair', that has affected the long term vision which Tony Blair and Gordon Brown were initially committed to developing. This had the consequence that 'Britain now has a soft conservatism (New Labour) and a second conservative party which cannot decide whether to be soft or hard. Both are equally committed to an American relationship which undermines the experiment begun in 1997'.[31]

Davis's other major domestic concern is Britain's constitutional complacency, especially after Blair's Government was brought to task 'on the charge of misleading the public about the Iraq war'. Beyond issues of morality and governance what that revealed was the weakness of the

---

[28] He is referring to the violent riots that happened in the neighbourhoods of first and second generation migrants, mostly from the African continent, in the majority of French large cities in the second half of 2005.

[29] JCD to DL, letter of 6 November 2005, p. 2.

[30] A. Ryan, 'Cosmopolitans', *The New York Review of Books*, LIII:11 (2006), p. 48.

[31] JCD to DL, letter of 24 July 2005, p. 2.

British constitution in cases of possible abuse of executive power; 'it all comes back to the failure of the so-called English Revolution of the seventeenth century and the fact that the British have the least modern constitution in Europe!'[32]

History, again, is the tool that Colin Davis uses to assess the world in which he lives. It is a tool that has helped him to understand better his present, and to guide his students and readers into the same path. Chance, utopia and a powerful intellect were at the origins of his making as a successful scholar, academic and teacher. The human values nurtured at the household of his loving parents made him grow into a compassionate individual and an invaluable friend. Always faithful to his principles Colin Davis has thus reached the end of his professional life with the respect, recognition and affection that only men in full have. The serene harmony provided by his own family has played no small role in that.

We can only hope that, in the years to come, void of institutional professional duties, Colin Davis, master historian and observer of his time, will complete the unfinished histories he has in store with the radical scrutiny that has delighted his followers and energized his foes.

---

[32] JCD to DL, e-mail of 5 June 2003.

Introduction

John Morrow and Jonathan Scott

The essays in this volume are inspired by the seminal historical scholarship of J. C. Davis. During a prolific career as author and teacher Davis has transformed our understanding of early modern utopian literature and its contexts, and compelled students of seventeenth-century English history to re-evaluate the character and significance of movements and individuals who have had a prominent place in the historiography of the English Revolution. In place of previously established orthodoxies, Davis's analyses of groups such as the Levellers and individuals like Gerrard Winstanley and Oliver Cromwell have reoriented the inquiry around the contemporary moral themes of liberty, authority and formality.

Given the focus of Davis's research it is fitting that the initial centre of gravity of this volume lies in the rich and turbulent history of seventeenth-century England. Other essays, however, explore concerns which fuelled seventeenth-century discourses of liberty, authority and formality in different and later contexts. In so doing, the collection points to continuities and discontinuities in the political and intellectual histories of British, European and colonial societies from the seventeenth through to the late nineteenth and early twentieth centuries.

In the seventeenth century these themes demonstrate the degree to which the upheavals of the period were framed in terms of questions concerning the source, nature and scope of human authority. Claims to liberty and considerations of its basis, scope and implications were seen as important because they insulated individuals from the impact of contested human authorities, thus making it possible to pay due regard to the higher claims of Christian conscience. This conception of liberty was strongly positive because it stressed the need to preserve conditions under which human beings were best able to discern and follow the word of God. It had important implications for the way in which political, social and ecclesiastical authority was structured but it was not antithetical to authority as such. Rather, the issue was to identify the true nature of authority, the forms in which it was most appropriately embodied, and its relationship to liberty.

The first section of this volume consider a range of episodes during the Commonwealth and Restoration periods when the relationship between claims to liberty of conscience and issues of clerical and civil authority were brought into sharp relief. Glenn Burgess, William Lamont and Mark Goldie focus on arguments which sought to show that liberty of religious conscience necessitated a strong civil authority, often seen to require (as in Thomas Hobbes's writings) a sovereign endowed with an unquestioned and unquestionable monopoly of coercive power. In Hobbes's case, and those of the other Anglican writers discussed by Burgess, these concerns underwrote a commitment to royalism that did not preclude challenges to the Anglican supremacy and might be compatible with the promotion of liberty of conscience. Over the course of the seventeenth century the positions advanced here, a conjuncture of independency and erastianism, were adopted by those espousing a range of political, theological and philosophical views, and were embraced by 'royalists', 'independents' or 'Hobbesians'.

Arguments claiming a positive connection between liberty of conscience and civil power are identified in the writings of a diverse range of seventeenth-century figures including Michael Hudson, Jasper Mayne, Thomas Hobbes, William Walwyn and John Locke. They also played a significant role among Levellers and Muggletonians. Some formulations stressed that God's sovereignty precluded coercion by either clerical or civil powers while others (such as that of Hobbes) were concerned particularly to insulate both the civil power and the believer from the intrusions of clerical authority. Clerical influence was pastoral, not coercive, and sat within a framework in which liberty of conscience, strong divine power and strong civil authority coalesced.

But while clerical authority might be seen as an impediment to liberty of conscience, it was also presented as a means of giving effect to it. This position emerges from William Lamont's and Mark Goldie's examinations of Baxter and Owen. These writers saw liberty of conscience as a necessary condition for the creation of systems of parochial authority that instilled discipline resting on the defence of religious truth and reformation of manners. To these Presbyterian and Independent defences of clerical authority may be added those associated with the Anglican writers discussed by Burgess and Goldie. In all these cases the civil and spiritual spheres were seen as interdependent rather than being sharply separated, a position with a pedigree extending from Constantine to Oliver Cromwell to William III. Within this framework those who possessed clerical authority expected to enjoy the active patronage of Godly civil magistracy as they sought to further the work of reformation.

Anglicans, and also at times Presbyterians such as Baxter, saw a national church as a key component of this structure of interlocking and complementary authorities. As Lamont makes clear, Baxter valued national churches because they promoted Christian discipline. This conception relied upon the integrity of the relationship between the civil magistrate and the national church, one that was increasingly called into question by the policies and religious predilections of Charles II and his brother. Within a decade of the restoration of parliament and the Anglican church, Charles dispensed with the penalties attached to protestant and catholic nonconformity, thereby calling into question both the Anglican and parliamentary cornerstones of the restoration settlement as it had evolved, and rupturing the relationship between civil and clerical authority. Charles's policy sorely tested the loyalty of Anglican Cavaliers and also, as Goldie shows, presented Protestant Dissenters with a dilemma. While happy to secure the benefits of the King's Declaration of Indulgence, they declined to endorse the exercise of prerogative that gave rise to it. At the same time, however, Charles's actions might be seen in relation to a long-standing tradition of 'magisterial' Puritanism that looked to the Godly prince to promote or at least facilitate the path of reformation.

Jonathan Scott's consideration of the escape motif in Charles II's portrayal of his early, pre-restoration career provides a distinctive perspective on the implications of that monarch's tenderness towards the consciences of his nonconformist and Roman Catholic subjects. Charles was determined to exercise liberty of conscience in religious matters and cast off the fetters of parliamentary government. He utilised the authority he possessed as head of state and supreme governor of the church to subvert the Act of Uniformity (1662) and to free himself and his non-Anglican subjects from the religious implications of the supremacy of the Church of England. Scott shows how the thematic links between personal liberty and Catholicism were dramatised in narratives of Charles's escape to France after the Battle of Worcester which highlighted the help he received from local recusants. This escape was re-enacted figuratively when Charles as king looked to Louis XIV to preserve his religious and political liberty and to help him reunite his rebellious kingdom with Roman Catholic Christendom.

Because Charles's policy threatened Anglican hegemony it raised questions about the legitimation and the delegitimation of structures of moral and political authority. Such questions figured prominently in early modern discourses of Christian liberty. They became acute when social and political disruption challenged the courage and perspicuity of those who felt obliged to weigh human authorities in the light of their perceptions of

God's judgement. When claims to obedience were evaluated on this basis, they tended to be seen as contingent rather than fundamental. At the same time however, the search for legitimation consequent on radical change gave rise to a concern to identify alternative human authorities.

In the second section of this volume John Morrill addresses this issue by examining Oliver Cromwell's engagement with the Bible. He shows how Cromwell's reading, remembering and ruminating upon that sacred text invested him with the authority necessary to legitimate the decisive role he played in a revolutionary situation where other loci of authority – both personal and institutional – had been discredited. It was precisely this process, and context, which two centuries later attracted the sympathetic attention of Thomas Carlyle. John Morrow's essay explores some of the implications of Carlyle's reading of Cromwell's history, thought and impact as heroic. Carlyle analysed the ideational and moral context of collapsing traditional authorities by means of a theory about modernity and formality which illuminated not only the English but also the French revolution. Most strikingly, Carlyle recovered Cromwell's experience textually, editing the speeches and writings analysed by Morrill with personal commentaries relating his biblical exegesis to the requirements of the situation which confronted him.

The interplay between text-as-authority and the legitimation of sources of civil and clerical power is equally important in Gaby Mahlberg's study of Henry Neville's *Isle of Pines* and Mark Knights's consideration of petitions and other subscriptional declarations issued by Roger L'Estrange. These writers published anonymously in genres which, being located in a borderland between fact and fiction, posed interpretative problems for contemporary readers and historians. Mahlberg argues that Neville's bawdy dystopian island fiction owed its form to its author's wish to provide his readers with a critical political statement that would be licensed for publication despite the sensitivities of a recently restored monarchy grappling with the implications of England's humiliating defeat at the hands of republican Holland in 1667. Neville's satire was a serious hostile commentary on a regime that was represented as privileging procreation over politics, morality and even defence of the realm. Textually the satire focused on the absurdity of royalist attempts to legitimate the restored monarchy by appealing to a theory of biblical patriarchalism which looked even less plausible after 1660 than it had before 1640.

Although L'Estrange was a royalist, in the body of material analysed by Knights he relied not upon the textual authority of the Bible, or the writings of Anglican divines, but on the claims to authority that were peculiar to subscriptional genres. Knights shows how an appeal to authority on these grounds became problematic when L'Estrange condemned the use of this genre by the Crown's opponents and when his deployment of it could be shown to rest on false claims about the authorship of these petitions and appeals. This raises the question of what L'Estrange himself believed to be the authority of these texts and why, politically, he considered them indispensable.

In the final section of this volume the theme of authority is investigated in relation to institutional forms. As in the cases of liberty and textual authority this question could become acute in circumstances of social and political change. Michael Braddick identifies the phenomenon of mobilisations in the context of a prolonged crisis of institutional authority. While the Scottish Covenanters's response to Charles I's policies had generated a new focus of moral and institutional authority, the reaction in England was diverse and fragmented at both national and local levels. English mobilisations were limited collective alternatives to the path of personal biblical inspiration chosen by Cromwell. Like Cromwell, however, they incorporated modes of explanation that gave precedence to divine authority. Mobilisations were pressure points through which public anxiety and engagement were expressed, and on the basis of which new institutions and cultural forms could be created. In this sense they played a significant role in the creative processes which were integral to the revolution.

When the seventeenth-century English monarchy faced a legitimation crisis this owed much to alternative contemporary views of the implications of divine authority. By contrast, those facing the monarchical regime that emerged in Spain in the wake of the Revolutionary and Napoleonic wars resulted from the influence of liberal forces in politics, society and the economy. Isabel Burdiel explores the tensions that emerged in mid-century Spanish politics as a result of attempts to fuse traditional values and forms associated with absolute monarchy with new, liberal conceptions of politics, gender and honour. During the reign of Isabel II (1830-1868) these could not be sustained in the face of intense political rivalry between the Liberals and their parliamentary opponents, the financial opportunism that engulfed the royal family and the Queen's own reputation for libertinism.

Burdiel's account highlights a failure to forge a stable conjuncture of traditional and modern values in a context of rapid underlying social and economic transformation. James Belich and David Thomson show how these concerns resurfaced in the new world as settler societies sought to forge, or adapt, social ideologies that would underpin new forms of institutional authority. Belich's treatment of this theme is framed by the massive, largely voluntary, demographic shifts which underlay the generation of 'neo-Britains' in the nineteenth century. Migration to these new settlements was facilitated by technological development and motivated in part by a range of perceived material advantages resulting from a move from high density urban societies to low density rural environments. In addition, however, the new social forms of settler society were legitimated by appeals to folklore memory of a lost world of rural plenty and personal independence.

The issue of independence was also crucial in relation to the question of poor relief which vexed nineteenth-century European states under demographic pressure. As David Thomson shows, settler societies exhibited a determination to leave mechanisms such as the English Poor Law — which signified poverty, crowding and dependence — behind them. Their implementation in the colonies would spell the end of the dream of a low population density `utopia' and replicate the intrusive systems of old world personal and institutional authority. Ironically, however, what replaced these was far from simply the settler social idea of self-improvement. To build and sustain new world societies capable of realising such a vision demanded massive government investment. This made these colonies big government societies beyond previous European experience and required systems of institutional formality appropriate to states with distinctive conceptions of their role.

The concluding essay by Peter Munz offers an overarching perspective on this volume's central themes of cultural authority and self-definition. For Munz, following the later Wittgenstein, cultures (`Forms of Life') are discursive communities in which the meaning of words derives not from any external point of reference but rather is learned by participation in that community. By Munz this is deduced from what is known of the neurological basis of human communication. This conclusion is compatible with other Cambridge-associated methodologies of discourse analysis visible in this collection.

Part I
Liberty

Chapter 1

Royalism and Liberty of Conscience in the English Revolution

Glenn Burgess

John Aubrey has left us a well-known and often-quoted story intended to capture the flavour of Thomas Hobbes's sometimes sardonic religious views. Hobbes was walking along the Strand in company with a divine, and they came upon a beggar. Hobbes,

> beholding him with eies of pity and compassion, putt his hand in his pocket, and gave him 6d. The divine saw his chance to sally forth against the philosopher of self-interest, and asked him:
> 'Would you have donne this, if it had not been Christ's command?'
> 'Yea,' sayd he.
> 'Why?' quoth the other.
> 'Because,' sayd he, 'I was in paine to consider the miserable condition of the old man; and now my almes, giving him some reliefe, doth also ease me.'

Readers of Aubrey in the most familiar modern edition, that of Oliver Lawson Dick, will not know the identity of Hobbes's companion; but Aubrey in fact identified him as Jasper Mayne.[1]

Mayne was, like Hobbes, a client of the Cavendish family. A minor dramatist, he was also the author of several pamphlets during the 1640s, that provide striking anticipations — or echoes — of the language with which Hobbes sought to return the English polity to peace. Though he has scarcely been noticed by historians, Mayne is valuable to us in at least two ways. First, he enriches our understanding of the intellectual context in which Hobbes's ideas were formed; and, second, he brings our attention to the fact, largely ignored, that Hobbes was not the only royalist in the English Revolution whose religious ideas challenged Anglican convention,

---

[1] Andrew Clark, *'Brief Lives', Chiefly of Contemporaries, Set Down by John Aubrey*, 2 vols (Oxford, 1898), 1, p. 352.

and not the only royalist who *might* be considered a proponent of toleration, or of liberty of conscience.

The unexpected and hidden dimensions of royalist thought that will be explored in this essay illustrate a central claim of Colin Davis's work. The English Revolution was not a struggle *between* authority and liberty; it was, instead, a struggle in which all participants claimed to understand the true nature of authority, and the best way of combining it with the maximum possible degree of freedom. Much of Davis's own work has been concerned with radicals, showing us how much they were concerned to constitute 'true magistracy', to impose godly discipline, and to find liberty at least as much in a willing submission to God's will as in a 'liberal' freedom from the constraints imposed by rulers.[2] Colin Davis's recent approaches to the study of radicalism have emphasized its concern with the 'transformation of rule', a formulation that releases it from the tired polarity of liberty *versus* authority.[3] But there is another side to this. Just as those radical and parliamentary thinkers who defended their cause in the name of 'liberty' were not thereby rendered the enemies of 'authority', so those royalists who defended the authority of Charles I were not thereby rendered the enemies of 'liberty'. Indeed, they were as capable of exploring the implications of a 'neo-Roman' theory of liberty as those parliamentarians and Levellers identified recently by Quentin Skinner as the intellectual driving-force of the English Revolution.[4]

I

The early defences of Charles I, from the period 1642-3, have been most discussed by historians. Prominent in that discussion has been the

---

[2] J. C. Davis, 'Gerrard Winstanley and the Restoration of True Magistracy', *Past & Present*, 70 (1976), pp. 76-93; J. C. Davis, 'Against Formality: One Aspect of the English Revolution', *Transactions of the Royal Historical Society*, 6th ser., 3 (1993), pp. 265-88; J. C. Davis, 'Religion and the Struggle for Freedom in the English Revolution', *Historical Journal*, 35 (1992), 507-30; J. C. Davis, *Fear, Myth and History: The Ranters and the Historians* (Cambridge, 1986).

[3] J. C. Davis, 'Afterword: Reassessing Radicalism in a Traditional Society: Two Questions' in Glenn Burgess & Matthew Festenstein (eds), *English Radicalism 1550-1850* (Cambridge, 2007), pp. 330-71.

[4] Quentin Skinner, 'Rethinking Political Liberty', *History Workshop Journal*, 61 (2006), pp. 156-70; cf. Condren's remarks on the problematic assumption that 'republicanism' is something to be associated with 'radicalism' in early modern England: Conal Condren, 'Afterword: Radicalism Revisited' in Burgess & Festenstein (eds), *English Radicalism*, pp. 327-33.

body of ideas known — not altogether happily — as 'constitutional royalism'. Its chief points were developed in the public statements crafted largely by Sir Edward Hyde from February 1642, and taken up in pamphlets produced by Anglican clergymen like Henry Ferne, and by members of the Tew Circle (Dudley Digges, Sir John Spelman, and others). These royalists scarcely formed a coherent intellectual grouping, and the grounds on which they justified the view of English monarchy foisted by Hyde on his king varied widely. They did, however, share a wish to defend and reconcile two key principles: that sovereign kings were not accountable to their subjects, and that kings were obliged to respect the rule of law.[5]

By 1644, though, there was still no end in sight to the Civil War, and, worse, clear signs that the issues at stake were beginning to change. Royalist political writers responded to this situation, in some cases developing a harder line. It is, indeed, tempting to suggest that as Charles's fortunes declined over the decade, the claims made for him in pamphlet debate became ever more elevated, stopping just sort of deification with the posthumous *Eikon Basilike*. Tempting though the view is, it is not entirely correct. Royalist thought in the later 1640s certainly tended to exploit a starker insistence on divine right, but this was not always pushed to absolutist lengths. Though some historians have suggested that royalism showed a pattern of 'increasing absolutism ... as the 1640s wore on' many royalists still wished to defend the essentially moderate and legal character of the king's authority.[6] Griffith Williams, for example, made an important distinction between different senses of 'absolute', in effect distinguishing a legally-limited 'absolute' monarch from an arbitrary one:

> Therefore as some Kings are more restrained by their lawes then some others, so are their powers the lesse absolute; and yet all of them being absolute Kings and free Monarchs, are excepted from any account of their actions to any inferiour jurisdiction.[7]

---

[5] David L. Smith, *Constitutional Royalism and the Search for Settlement, c.1640-1649* (Cambridge, 1994); Robert Wilcher, *The Writing of Royalism 1628-1660* (Cambridge, 2001), chs. 4-5; B. H. G. Wormald, *Clarendon: Politics, History, and Religion 1640-1660* (Chicago, 1976).

[6] John M. Wallace, *Destiny His Choice: The Loyalism of Andrew Marvell* (Cambridge, 1968), p. 14.

[7] Griffith Williams, *Jura Majestatis, The Rights of Kings both in Church and State: 1. Granted by God 2. Violated by the Rebels 3. Vindicated by the Truth* (Oxford, 1644), p. 146.

The most interesting developments in royalist political thought of the later 1640s, though, relate to the relationship between politics and religion. These have been under-explored by historians. The search for settlement after the first Civil War, combined with the gradual emergence from the Westminster Assembly of proposals for change to the doctrine and government of the church, confronted royalists with a problem. To what degree was it possible to reach accommodation with the religious demands of parliament or army as the price for restoration of royal authority? Charles I himself toyed with the possibility of settling with his Presbyterian opponents by agreeing to a temporary imposition of Presbyterianism in England, and he toyed with offering his Independent opponents some degree of 'liberty to tender consciences' (though, just as importantly, he also toyed with playing these different groupings off against one another, casting doubt on the sincerity of his commitment to any of the concessions proposed).[8] It is apparent that in the years 1646-7 there was considerable discussion in Royalist-Anglican circles of these matters.[9]

One who devoted considerable energy to hammering out an Anglican political position in response to the events of the 1640s was Henry Hammond. He wrote a number of key tracts that state what he took to be the orthodox position of the Church of England, and together they amounted to a sustained critique of the political thought of England's war of religion. There were two key planks to his position. First, he argued that Christianity was an entirely pacific and non-violent faith, eschewing any claim that its purposes might be advanced by the sword. Accepting peace as a paramount political value meant, as well, that Christians were never disturbers of the civil polity, whether it was pagan or Christian, and never engaged in active resistance.[10] Second, episcopacy, though not directly

---

[8] Sir Charles Petrie (ed.), *The Letters, Speeches and Proclamations of King Charles I* (London, 1935), pp. 208-10; S. R. Gardiner (ed.), *Constitutional Documents of the Puritan Revolution 1625-1660*, third edition (Oxford, 1906), pp. 313 (12 May 1647), 347-8 (26 December 1647, Engagement with the Scots); Gardiner, pp. 286-7 (21 January 1645), 327 (9 September 1647); Richard Cust, *Charles I: A Political Life* (Harlow, 2005), pp. 420-38 summarises Charles's various negotiating positions during the 1640s.

[9] J. W. Packer, *The Transformation of Anglicanism 1643-1660, with Special Reference to Henry Hammond* (Manchester, 1969), pp. 175-6; *State Papers Collected by Edward, Earl of Clarendon*, 3 vols (Oxford, 1767-86), 2, esp. pp. 265-8.

[10] Henry Hammond, *Of Resisting the Lawful Magistrate upon Colour of Religion* (London, 1643, second edition, Oxford, 1644); also Hammond, *Of the Reasonableness of Christian Religion* (London, 1649), pp. 53, 98-102; Hammond, *To the Right Honourable, The Lord Fairfax and His*

instituted by Christ, was nonetheless an apostolic institution, and there could be no benefit in abandoning it to implement the Presbyterian proposals of the Westminster assembly. As far as he was concerned, the reference in the Solemn League and Covenant to following the model of the 'best reformed churches' could be taken as a reference to the episcopalian Church of England. Change could only be for the worse, and would, in addition, produce a church government less compatible with the monarchical character of the polity.[11]

Though expressed moderately, Hammond's position was less accommodating than it looked. It amounted, in effect, to the voice of authority demanding obedience. In arguing that all Christians were bound to loyalty to the church and commonwealth as by law established, Hammond left little room for accommodation with his opponents, and his ideas amount therefore to the cry, 'be reasonable — and obey'. Though proclaiming Charles's 'inclinations to peace' and his wish 'to make the way back to your Throne by none but Pacifick means', Hammond did not have a satisfactory recipe for the re-establishment of peace.[12] Beyond the fine words, what was missing in Hammond's works, falling through the gap between his commitment to peace and his commitment to episcopacy, was the question of religious toleration. While it is clear that Hammond did not accept the legitimacy of religious persecution, he was nonetheless more uncompromising than his tone and language would suggest.

The gap left by Hammond was filled by other royalist Anglicans, some more willing than he to contemplate changes to church government to accommodate Presbyterian demands, others willing to consider the acceptance of toleration as a route towards pacifying the country again. It is the latter development that is of interest here. Not surprisingly, many royalists were unwilling to take toleration very far. Griffith Williams, bishop of Ossory from 1641, is an interesting example, moving towards a very limited liberty of conscience quite early in the decade. Well known as a defender of royal authority by divine right, Williams was also keen to

Councell of Warre (London, 1649), esp. pp. 18-19; Glenn Burgess, 'Was the English Civil War a War of Religion? The Evidence of Political Propaganda', *Huntington Library Quarterly*, 61 (1999), pp. 173-201.

[11] Henry Hammond, *Considerations of Present Use Concerning the Danger Resulting from the Change of Our Church Government* (Oxford, 1644), esp. p. 13 for use of the Covenant.

[12] Henry Hammond, *The Christian's Obligations to Peace and Charity Delivered in an Advent Sermon at Carisbrooke Castle, Ann. 1647, and Now Published with IX Sermons More* (London, 1649), quotation from Ep. Ded., dated 16 September 1648.

defend the king's authority as supreme governor of the church. Christian kings, however, had also a second duty peculiar to themselves, a duty '[t]o preserve true religion, and to defend the faith of Christ, against all Atheists, Hereticks, Schismaticks, and all other adversaries of the Gospell, within their Territories and Dominions'.[13] Nonetheless, he noted that 'if Kings cannot perswade their Subjects to embrace the true Faith, they ought not to cut them off, so long as they are true Subjects'.[14] He was willing to allow a (grudging) toleration for religious diversity while giving no ground to the 'anabaptist' rebels of the 1640s.

Williams was clear that toleration was an 'exemption' — he came to the subject through a discussion of the king's power to dispense from ecclesiastical laws — and there was no suggestion either that religious diversity was a good thing, or that there was any *duty* compelling kings to be tolerant. Furthermore, it was to be strictly a *private* privilege, with no allowance for the public exercise of another faith. Toleration was essentially a matter of political prudence.[15] Williams discussed in turn the situation of Jews, Turks, Papists and Puritans — infidels, heretics and schismatics. The general principle advanced was that 'where the greater distance is from the true religion, there the lesser familiarity and neernesse should be in conversation, and the *greater* distance in communion'. Nonetheless, it was legitimate, though scarcely mandatory, to allow even infidels some tolerance. Papists, part of the same catholic church as protestants, had an even greater claim to toleration, while schismatics certainly were to be treated not as '*deadly* enemies' but as 'weake friends'. There was a qualification: schismatics were deserving of toleration provided that 'they proceede not to be turbulent and malicious'. When they did turn malicious, schismatics were more dangerous than all the others, who professed their religion peaceably.[16] Thus toleration was to be granted or with held 'not so much in respect of the *meliority* of their religion, as [in] their peaceable and harmelesse habitation among their neighbours without *rayling* against their faith, or *rebelling* against their Prince'. By this measure the puritans of the 1640s, though their religion was in itself tolerable, could make no claim to be tolerated. They deserved repression even more than the seditious presbyterians, suppressed by Elizabeth, and

---

[13] Williams, *Jura Majestatis*, pp. 48-9 (also p. 13).

[14] Griffith Williams, *The Discovery of Mysteries: or, The Plots and Practices of a Prevalent Faction in this Present Parliament to Overthrow the Established Religion* (Oxford, 1643), p. 71.

[15] Williams, *Jura Majestatis*, pp. 106-7, 113.

[16] *Ibid.*, pp. 107-11.

attacked in James's *Basilikon Doron*. Catholics were much more loyal to the king than they.[17] This distinction enabled Williams to defend the king's willingness to accept the support of Catholics even against his protestant enemies, but it did not provide much basis for accommodation.

The same cannot be said of Michael Hudson's *Divine Right of Government* (1647). Though an extreme defender of the king's temporal authority, Hudson was a critic of Charles I's religious policies. He began to write in order to defend the freedom of the conscience from political authority in the belief that the sacrilegious usurpation of the king's authority undertaken by Parliament was God's punishment of the King's sacrilege in usurping divine authority. In secular matters, kings had 'an absolute, and unlimited power, over both our estates and persons'.[18] But the situation was very different with regard to the king's authority in ecclesiastical and religious matters. Hudson was adamant that nothing could ever legitimate the active resistance or rebellion of subjects. Nonetheless, he drew tight limits around the king's authority in the spiritual sphere. He argued for restrictions on royal authority that arose from the fact that God had reserved certain matters to his sole authority, or to that of conscience. The question was to determine what things were '*extra regalia*, and Metapoliticall matters', in which the king could exercise neither his judicial nor his legislative authority.[19] The proper sphere of political authority extended over 'only the Externall duties of the Morall law, consisting in the right use of the Externall blessings of nature'; it extended not at all over 'intrinsecall acts of the soule'.[20] Political government existed under the covenant of works, the requirements of which, unlike those of the covenant of grace, could be known through nature by all. It followed that, 'though Heathens cannot be good Christians, they may be good Kings', and therefore 'Evangelicall duties [known only to Christians through revelation] cannot be directly and *per se* the object of Politicall Cognizance, or the subject of any positive Law or Statute, generally obligatory unto all persons'.[21]

The matter did not end there. Although evangelical duties could not be the direct object of political authority, they could be the indirect object. Any king who was a Christian was bound in conscience to make laws that ordered the worship of God in ways that the king believed proper, though

---

[17] *Ibid.*, pp. 111-13.
[18] Michael Hudson, *The Divine Right of Government: 1. Naturall and 2. Politique*, (n.p., 1647), p. 170. There are occasional hints of qualifications to this. See pp. 96, 118, 135-6.
[19] *Ibid.*, p. 141.   [20] *Ibid.*, pp. 144-5.   [21] *Ibid.*, pp. 150-51.

he was forbidden altogether from making laws 'in matters of faith and doctrine'.[22] Laws made to regulate religious worship, however, bound only those who agreed with him:

> But for other persons, who are not of the same perswasion concerning the Religion of these Evangelicall duties, but beleeve the practise thereof to be superstitious and dishonourable to God, and another forme of worship to be the onely acceptable service unto him ... . The enforcement of such a conformity by the Magistrate in Evangelicall worship and service in such persons contrary to their consciences, must necessarily render him guilty, not onely of their sinnes ... but also of sacrilegious intrusion upon those sacred prerogatives which God hath reserved wholly unto himselfe.[23]

This is a theory of liberty of conscience directly in the line that runs from William Walwyn to John Locke. Any attempt to impose beliefs or forms of religious observance upon another person were a direct intrusion upon that person, and, more importantly, upon the sacred prerogatives of God. All evangelical duties were beyond the sphere of political authority 'because conscience is the onely law and rule whereby the merits of these duties are to be judged', and anyone compelled to participate in religious worship against his conscience was compelled to sin.[24] A compulsive national church was therefore inevitably an illegitimate thing. The king shall not:

> By any positive Lawes and Statutes, determine what points shall be Orthodox, and what Hereticall: neither may he under the sanction of any personall, or pecuniarie mulct, or penalty, enjoyne his Subjects to professe and sweare such Creeds, and Articles of Faith and Religion, as those Laws shall make Orthodox: or by virtue of those Lawes punish any of his subjects, who out of conscience doe professe themselves of another different Faith and Religion.[25]

It is worth noting that this view could be held by divine-right royalists and Levellers because of a structural similarity between their ideas. The political thought of both rested on a powerful sense of God's authority and the limits that this must place on all worldly authority. James Daly

---

[22] *Ibid.*, p. 159.   [23] *Ibid.*, pp. 152-3.   [24] *Ibid.*, p. 157.   [25] *Ibid.*, p. 159.

remarked of Weldon's *Doctrine of the Scripture* that it 'is so emphatic on God's direct dominion that human kingship itself is sometimes frowned upon'.[26] It is easy to cull from royalist writings statements that could as readily form the foundations of Leveller argument. Hudson himself, for example, rooted the human duty to respect other persons in the duty to respect God and his creation.[27] Robert Grosse argued, in a discussion of consent theory that no person 'seems to be the Lord of his owne members; much lesse of anothers', reminding us of the Leveller view that human beings were not even self-possessing individuals because God had ultimate ownership of their persons. He went on to state another axiom that could have been endorsed by the Levellers: 'it is a Maxime and Principle among the Lawyers, that no man can transfer more power upon another then he hath himselfe'.[28]

Not surprisingly, royalists and Levellers took this point in different directions. For the royalist, it was proof of the bankruptcy of consent theory: the power to kill, possessed by rulers, must come from God, for no human being naturally possessed it. For the Levellers, the axiom guaranteed that political authority must always be limited. But the similarity of foundation meant that both royalists and Levellers could readily develop a theory of liberty of conscience rooted in a strong sense of God's sovereignty over the human soul. Of course, rather more Levellers than royalists chose to develop such an argument. There was, nonetheless, a degree of affinity between divine-right absolutism and a theory of liberty of conscience.

One of the reasons why few royalists developed theories of liberty of conscience must be that their justifications of kingly power were so often inspired by fear of anarchy and disorder. Religious pluralism was widely taken to be a major cause of anarchy. But Hudson confronted this argument directly. Did 'preservation of the Common-wealth' require 'Uniformity in matters of Faith and Doctrine'? No. For a start, uniformity 'is more to be desired then hoped for'. But beyond that, differences of opinion amongst Christians were inevitable and beneficial. They led to 'better information and knowledge in matters of faith', and as a result 'Christians are always best principled in those points which are most controverted'. The argument that religious differences led to political instability was simply swept

---

[26] James Daly, *Sir Robert Filmer and English Political Thought* (Toronto, 1979), p. 175, n. 6.

[27] Hudson, *Divine Right of Government*, p. 62.

[28] Robert Grosse, *Royalty and Loyalty. Or a Short Survey of the Power of Kings over their Subjects and the Duty of Subjects to their Kings* (n.p., 1647), pp. 5-7.

aside, 'for to pretend a necessity of unwarrantable meanes, for the security of Church or State, is but to appeale from God to the devil for succour'. In any case, the magistrate may make laws to deal with heresy and division 'when they come to be of Politicall Cognizance, i.e. acts of violence and injustice, disturbing the peace of the Common-wealth'.[29]

Hudson's position reflects an acceptance, very rare in the seventeenth century, of religious pluralism as a beneficial thing. Equally remarkable was his rejection of the view that idolatry, especially papist idolatry, which could be identified by reason without the aid of revelation, ought to be repressed by the magistrate. For papists their own 'formes of worship, (how Idolatrous soever in the eyes of Protestants, yet) in their owne eyes appeare to be the onely service acceptable to God'. No coercion could be of use against such sincere errors, and it would therefore be unjust and inequitable for the magistrate to attempt it.[30]

One of the purposes of this extraordinary argument was to defend the autonomy of the clergy against the secular power. The office of minister 'is not subordinate, but of a different degree and nature from the office of Kings, both of them being the Anointed of God, and neither of them depending directly and properly upon the other'.[31] It was thus not only Catholics and Presbyterians who could undermine the foundations of the English church-state, which had rested since the 1530s upon committing to kings the jurisdiction of order within the church. The example of Hudson might suggest that in some circumstances the clericist views of the established clergy could imply a threat to the royal supremacy in the church.[32]

II

Jasper Mayne, Hobbes's interlocutor during his walk along the Strand, was another writer who can be placed in this context. He was, perhaps, less extreme than some of those already considered, but he expressed himself with a clarity and style that make his pamphlets some of the best of the period. Moreover, some of the points that he advanced are both startling and original, even if his overall stance on political matters was less so.

---

[29] Hudson, *Divine Right of Government*, pp. 162-4.
[30] *Ibid.*, pp. 166-9. [31] *Ibid.*, p. 169.
[32] Though this was not so before the 1640s: see J. P. Sommerville, 'The Royal Supremacy and Episcopacy "Jure Divino", 1603-1640', *Journal of Ecclesiastical History*, 34 (1983), pp. 548-58.

Mayne noted that king and parliament 'challenged to themselves the *Defence* of one and the same Cause', protestant religion and the liberty of the subject.³³ But it was easy to show, he hoped, that the claims of parliament to be fighting in such a cause were an empty pretence. For a start, the liberty of the subject was, contrary to their claims, a very limited thing. The rights of kings were laid down in 1 Samuel 8, from which it was clear that when the Jews sought a king, they 'divested themselves of two of the greatest *Immunities* which can belong to *Freemen, Liberty* of *person*, and *propriety* of *Estates*. And both these in such an *unlimited measure*, as left them not power, if their *Prince* pleased, to call either *themselves*, or *Children* or *any thing* else their *owne*.'³⁴

It is true that kings, like anyone else, were bound by the laws of God and nature; but nonetheless their best and their worst actions had the same authority. A king carried 'a *Jus* or *power* ... *unquestionable* by the *Subject*, to doe if he pleased *things unlawfull*'.³⁵

Mayne's mention of the laws as the 'partition' between the king's prerogative and the people's liberty, and his commendation of Judge Jenkins, might suggest that he was prepared in practice to allow some degree of limitation on the king. This seems to be so, even though these same laws were rather alarmingly described as '*Figures* in the *Dust* ... [at] the *Mercy* of the next *Winde* that blowes'.³⁶ Mayne did concede that the king's legislative authority was now exercised through parliament.³⁷ And he seemed to agree with the view that in all matters the king had 'but a regulated power', derived as 'a *Trust* committed by the *Lawes* of this *Kingdome*, for the Government of it, to the *King*'.³⁸ Nonetheless, it was obvious that the king had a pre-eminent power in making laws, and possessed rights of which he could not be deprived without his own consent.

Mayne's apparent political moderation was further revealed in his answer to the question whether resistance was justified 'supposing the *King* not to have kept Himselfe to that *Circle of power* which the Lawes have drawn about Him, but desirous to walke in a more *Absolute compasse*'. It all depended on 'the *Tenure* by which he holds his *Crowne*'. If, by election or contract, kings had been accepted only on certain terms, then some sort of resistance might be lawful. But none of this applied to hereditary princes,

---

[33] Jasper Mayne, *Ochlo-machia: Or, The People's War, Examined According to the Principles of Scripture & Reason* (Oxford, 1647), p. 2.
[34] *Ibid.*, p. 7.　　　　[35] *Ibid.*, pp. 7-8.　　　　[36] *Ibid.*, pp. 11-12.
[37] *Ibid.*, pp. 12-13.　　　　[38] *Ibid.*, p. 7.

who were bound only by their coronation oath, of which God was the judge.[39] Thus, the subjects of the English king had no right to defend with force the liberties given to them by law, though the liberties were real enough. Mayne added that, leaving aside ship money which was now abolished, the king had not obviously infringed the subjects's rights anyway.[40] Indeed, parliament's record of infringing liberties was much worse; and this alone made Charles 'the *first King* that ever took up *Armes* for the *Liberty* of his Subjects'.[41]

The second question Mayne tackled was whether religion could be a just cause of war. He began by stating at length the opinion of Grotius that if there was found a nation of atheists, it would be legitimate to use force 'to banish them out of the *World*'. This was because religion was essential to the maintenance of human societies. Laws might bind and make sociable the external man, but religion was needed to bind the inner. Mayne rejected Grotius's opinion.[42] In a startling passage, with few parallels at this time, he even hypothetically affirmed the sociability of atheists:

> Though I shall grant the saying of *Plutarch* to be true, that *Religion* ... [is] one (nay one of the firmest) *Bonds of Society*, and *supporters* of *Lawes*, yet I have not met with any *demonstrative* Argument, which hath proved to me, that there is such a necessary dependance of *Human society* upon *Religion*, that the Absence of the *One* must inevitably be the Destruction of the *other*. ... '[T]is possible that a Countrey of *Atheists* may yet have so much *Morality* among them, seconded by *Lawes* made by common agreement among themselves, as to be a *People*, and to hold the society of *Citizens* among themselves, And as 'tis possible for them, without *Religion*, so farre, for meere *utility* and *safeties* sake, to observe the *Law* of *Nations*.[43]

Still less could false religions be punished, for '*Idolatry*, though it be a *false Religion*, is yet as conservant of *Society* ... as if't were *true*'.[44] As for the true faith, since not all of that was rationally demonstrable in such a way as to compel the mind to assent to it, it 'would be unreasonable to make *Warre* upon mens *persons* for the reception of a *Doctrine* which cannot convince their minds'. Only if Christ came and performed miracles to convince us might refusal to accept the true faith be inexcusable.[45]

---

[39] *Ibid.*, pp. 15-16. [40] *Ibid.*, pp. 17-18. [41] *Ibid.*, p. 19. [42] *Ibid.*, pp. 22-24.
[42] *Ibid.*, pp. 24-25. [44] *Ibid.*, p. 26. [45] *Ibid.*, p. 27.

No distinctions were needed: war for defence of religion — any war, any religion — was wrong. All religion is '*Opinion* built upon *Authority*', and this can never be conclusive enough to deprive men of their liberty to believe whatever they wished. It was true, that a king had power concerning 'the *Outward* exercise of *Religion*'; and could judge controversies. But he was not infallible, and therefore his determinations were not 'Oracles'. The subject could never forcibly resist the prince; but equally, he could never be made to believe anything by the prince, and was entitled in religious matters to resort to passive obedience.[46]

Mayne's argument clearly rested on the assumption that the purposes and foundation of civil societies were purely temporal. They relied on principles of reason and utility, divine in origin, but accessible to all human beings. There could be no justification for insisting that they must have a particular religious complexion, for religion was a matter of internal belief. These arguments formed the basis for Mayne's suggestions, made in other writings, for settling the religious differences of the 1640s.

An earlier work had in its very subtitle expressed his central proposition: for 'taking away the distinction of government into ecclesiasticall and civill: and proving the government of the civill magistrate onely sufficient in a Christian Kingdom'. This work was addressed to parliament, and related particularly to the disputes over church polity between presbyterians and independents. It did not mark its author as a Royalist. '[A]ll power in a Christian Kingdom is in the same persons' — that included ecclesiastical authority. In support of this view, Mayne argued that a society needed only that government 'necessary for the wellbeing thereof, and any other is superfluous: but the government of the Civil Magistrate here is only necessary, *Ergo*, none else ought to be'.[47] Civil laws alone are sufficient to punish sin and error, for even heathen princes have suppressed many of them. Ministers of the church, indeed, altogether lacked coercive power: there *was* no power, in this sense, but civil. Indeed, Mayne claimed that after the advent of Christian princes, the church lost even the power to censure by excommunication. The only powers possessed by priests were 'to Preach and Baptize, and administer the Supper of the Lord', also to ordain elders and bishops, to marry, and in council to determine matters of controversy. Ministers should hope that the magistrate will take all ecclesiastical power fully into his own hands,

---

[46] *Ibid.*, pp. 30-31.

[47] Jasper Mayne, *The Difference about Church Government Ended* (London, 1646), title page, p. 2.

do away with ecclesiastical courts, and leave them free to perform their proper functions.[48]

In an Oxford sermon on the text 1 Corinthians 1:10, Mayne looked at the subject from the other end. The sermon was essentially a defence of sober learning against unlearned zeal and enthusiasm. In it Mayne avoided questions of right and law, but gave advice on how to seek unity and agreement. He rejected the idea that in normal circumstances anyone could claim divine inspiration. His argument thereafter rested on essentially sceptical foundations. All men should focus on what they had in common as both men and Christians. They should recognise that it was wrong to give one another abusive names, for 'God rather dwells in still, soft voyces'. Men needed to recognise that the differences between Calvinists and anti-Calvinists that led to schism were trivial, 'things as small as Cummin, or Anice'. In many cases, the differences that animated scholars were over things that could not be known.[49]

The only solution in such circumstances was to avoid schism, and to 'conforme our selves to the harmelesse (though to us unusuall) custome of the place'. Mayne recognised that the central difficulty lay in bringing men to be of one mind when there could be no infallible teachers for them to follow. The solution to the difficulty was to be discovered in 1 John 4:1. Men were instructed not to be credulous or to accept the truth of whatever any supposedly holy person said, and to weigh carefully whatever was said. Was it rooted in scripture? Did it inculcate proper Christian virtue? The answer left individual Christians to decide for themselves: Mayne told his congregation, 'I will not take upon me to be the Judge of Controversies, but you your selves shall be'.[50] There was no appeal to authority, even though Mayne (like Hammond) defended the sole legitimacy of a properly consecrated clergy,[51] because he had no trust in the capacity of any human being to apprehend with certainty religious

---

[48] *Ibid.*, pp. 2-3, 4-6, et seq, 10-11. The last of these powers had earlier been assigned to the civil magistrate, 11-12.

[49] Jasper Mayne, *A Sermon Concerning Unity & Agreement preached at Carfax Church in Oxford, August 9, 1646* (Oxford, 1646), pp. 6-11, 22-24, 33-34, 32-35.

[50] *Ibid.*, pp. 35, 52-54, 54-57.

[51] *Ibid.*, pp. 16-17. On this theme see also Mayne, *A Sermon Preached at the Consecration of the Right Reverend Father in God, Herbert, Lord Bishop of Hereford* (London, 1662), esp. pp. 34-42, in which Mayne declared himself 'not *Erastian* enough' to believe that anyone could exercise priestly functions without ordination by the laying on of hands (p. 39). Mayne, *A Late Printed Sermon against False Prophets, Vindicated by Letter from the Causeless*

truth.⁵² The function of the clergy was to guide and inform the individual Christian in his judgement, not to compel that judgement.

In all of this there were anticipations of Hobbes's discussion of heresy and the problem of religious authority. Others can be heard in Mayne's sermon on Ezekiel, 22:28, attacking those who invoked the authority of prophecy to justify their rebellion and sedition. Like Hobbes's, Mayne's analysis of the problem was rooted in his awareness of the human capacity for rhetorical redescription or *paradiastole*. Speech was, for Mayne, the thing that divided human beings from the beast; it was an essential support of human intercourse and commerce. But speech can be used deceitfully, to 'turne *Chrystall* into *Jet*'.⁵³ The capacity to describe good as evil and evil as good produced the feeling that 'there had been no such things in *Nature*, as *Right* or *Wrong*, *Justice* or *Injustice*, but only as *Holy men* would please to call them'.⁵⁴ By this means, false prophets had been able to:

> [deal] with the *publique Sinnes* of their *times*. *Rapines*, and *Oppressions* were *filed*, and *polisht*, into the softer names of *Just levyes* and *supplyes*. *Murthers* also and *Bloodsheds*, together with the *Cryes* of *Widdowes*, and *Teares* of *Orphans* were *smooth'd* and *glazed* into the milder appearances, perhaps, of publique *utility* and *necessity of State*.⁵⁵

In both Old Testament times and in seventeenth-century England, 'Arts were used to make bad projects seeme plausible'.

Aspersions of Mr Francis Cheynell (London, 1647), pp. 19-21 perhaps suggests why it was important to him that the church be defined in formal terms (by the apostolic succession).

⁵² Mayne returned to the subject of schism in a more careful but less interesting sermon of 1652: Jasper Mayne, *A Sermon against Schisme: or, The Separations of These Times.* (London, 1652).

⁵³ Mayne, *Sermon against False Prophets*, pp. 23-25. This emphasis on speech and language as the grounding for human sociability — and diversity — is found in Mayne's other works, see e.g. *Sermon Concerning Unity & Agreement*, pp. 26-29.

⁵⁴ Mayne, *Sermon against False Prophets*, pp. 7-8. Mayne's horror at this phenomenon is very evident — see pp. 11-12 especially. On Hobbes's concern with rhetorical redescription (*paradiastole*) see Quentin Skinner, *Philosophy and Rhetoric in Thomas Hobbes* (Cambridge, 1996), pp. 279-84, 317-26, 338-43.

⁵⁵ Mayne, *Sermon against False Prophets*, pp. 10, 14; also pp. 26-27.

Mayne followed this with a doctrine familiar to us from his later *Ochlo-Machia*. Religion can never be propagated by force. It must be spread only by persuasion because it was not a matter on which sufficient certainty could be obtained for anything else to be possible.

> In short, some things in the *Excellencyes*, and *Height* of the *Doctrines* of Christian *Religion* being no way *demonstrable* from *Human principles*, but depending for the *credit*, and *evidence* of their *truth* upon the *Authority* of *Christs miracles*, conveyed along in *Tradition*, and *Story*, cannot in a *naturall* way of *Argumentation* force *assent*. Since, as long as there is such a thing in men, as *liberty of understanding* all *arguments*, even in a *Preaching*, and *perswasive* way, which carry not *necessity* of *demonstration* in their *Forehead*, may reasonably be rejected.[56]

These themes — the diversity of human moral judgement; the reliance of Christianity on the testament of miracles; the recognition that this testament could not be first-hand but was a form of historical evidence based on our trust in the credibility of those authorities who informed us of the miracles — were all elaborated by Hobbes.[57] For both, the political danger of religion lay in the fact that it was hard to distinguish true from false speech in matters to do with the faith — 'he is ... thought to be the *holiest man*, who can lye most in a holy Cause'.[58] Mayne was less critical than Hobbes of the value of scholarship and the utility of University learning in helping towards a right understanding of scripture.[59] But like Hobbes, he stressed the priority of public over private interpretation. Addressing Cheynell, Mayne wrote:

> Your other *mistake* is, That you confound the *Spirit* of God speaking in the *Scripture* with the private *Spirit* (that is) *Reason*, *Humour*, or *Fancie* of the *person* spoken to. Sir, let that *blessed Spirit* decide this controversy between us. He sayes *that no Prophecie of*

---

[56] *Ibid.*, p. 16. Mayne, *A Late Printed Sermon againstt False Prophets* (London, 1647), p. 19.

[57] Hobbes stressed that the capacity to perform miracles was an essential mark of a prophet, and showed Christ to be a true prophet; Thomas Hobbes, *Leviathan*, ed. Richard Tuck (Cambridge, 1991), p. 257.

[58] Mayne, *Sermon against False Prophets*, p. 25.

[59] E.g. *Ibid.*, p. 28. It is typical of him that, when challenged by Cheynell, Mayne refused a public debate in English and proposed instead a debate in Latin before the Oxford divinity school. Mayne, *Late Printed Sermon*, pp. 5, 12, 13-14, 38-39.

the Scripture is of private Interpretation [2 Pet. 1:20]. That is, so *calculated*, or *Meridianized* to some select *minds & understandings*, that it shall hold the *candle* to them *only*, and leave *All others* in the *Darke*. But, if you will consent to the Comment of the most primitive *Fathers* on that *Text*, The meaning of it is; That as *God* by his *Spirit* did at first dictate the *scripture*, so he dictated it in those things which are *necessary* to *Salvation*, intelligible to all the world of Men, who will addict their minds to read it.[60]

The 'public doctrine' of the Church of England was defined by act of parliament in the 39 Articles.[61] While endorsing royal (and parliamentary) authority, Mayne denied any coercive authority to the church — even to the true and apostolic church.

III

Thomas Hobbes and Jasper Mayne inhabited overlapping intellectual worlds, but we should not suppose that the two of them thought identically. Their close acquaintance is usually dated to the period following Hobbes's return to Cromwellian England, especially after 1656 when Mayne was a chaplain to the earl of Devonshire, but it should be noted as well that Mayne had also succeeded Robert Payne as Newcastle's chaplain in 1639, a time when Hobbes was moving closer to the orbit of this particular branch of the Cavendishes.[62]

Mayne's thinking resembles Hobbes's in a number of particulars, even though he does not put the particulars together in the same way or as systematically as Hobbes. This could be a sign of Hobbes's influence, through conversation or writing, or reflect the wider intellectual orientation of the Cavendish world in which both men shared. Mayne's adherence

---

[60] Mayne, *Late Printed Sermon*, p. 46.

[61] *Ibid.*, p. 47.

[62] Wood notes that Mayne became the Devonshire chaplain in 1656 'so consequently to be a companion with Thomas Hobbes ... between whom there never was a right understanding' (Wood, *Athenae Oxonienses*, iii, 971-2). See also *Oxford Dictionary of National Biography*; Noel Malcolm, *Aspects of Hobbes* (Oxford, 2002), p. 95. On Hobbes and Newcastle see Lisa T. Sarasohn, 'Thomas Hobbes and the Duke of Newcastle: A Study in the Mutuality of Patronage before the Establishment of the Royal Society', *Isis*, 90 (1999), pp. 715-37; and Lisa T. Sarasohn, 'Was *Leviathan* a Patronage Artifact?', *History of Political Thought*, 21 (2000), pp. 606-31.

to the doctrine of the apostolic succession matches Hobbes's account of religion in *De Cive* rather than the more extreme views of *Leviathan*.⁶³ But in his discussion of atheism and his ruthless assertion that Christian commonwealths needed only a temporal power, Mayne went beyond the early Hobbes in ways that did foreshadow the later extremism of *Leviathan*. Though he wrote from a position within the true apostolic Church, he nonetheless provided the framework of an argument that made all churches into private associations to which the state might or might not give its approbation. As for Hobbes, matters of faith existed on an altogether non-political plane, and they could not interfere with men's political duties.

Perhaps the central concern shared by the two men was with the power and corruptibility of language. In 1664 Mayne published his translations of Lucian, which had been made in 1638, with a letter of dedication to Newcastle. The dedication defended Lucian as a rhetorical model, condemning along the way those preachers of the English Revolution who 'with a *Romantick* showre of words' gave their hearers 'a Text of Scripture transformed into a *Chaos*, pursued without just order, & stuffed with Bombast, & confusion'. It was little wonder that Lucian had his detractors in an age dominated by:

> a *canting Generation* of men, whose *Rhetorick* was as *rude, & mechanick* as their persons, [and who ...] *defile* the English Tongue with their *Republick* words, which are most *immusicall* to the Eare, and scarce *significant* to a *Monarchicall* understanding. Words which are the meer *Excrements* of Language; which proceeded from the late *Body politick* of this *Uncivilized Nation*, and were not allowed their legitimate *concoxion*, but broke forth into the World with *Brutishness*, and *Rebellion*. Coyned & minted by those *Seditious, Rump* grammarians, who did put their own *impressions* to the Kings *Silver*, and so committed *Treason* against their Prince, and their own *rude stamp* and sense to their *Goth* and *Vandall* words; and so committed *Treason* against His *good people. Quem penes Arbitrium est & Jus & Norma loquendi.*⁶⁴

---

⁶³ Richard Tuck, 'The Civil Religion of Thomas Hobbes', in Nicholas Phillipson & Quentin Skinner (eds), *Political discourse in early modern Britain* (Cambridge, 1993) ch. 6; also Tuck, 'Warrender's De Cive', *Political Studies*, 33 (1985), pp. 308-15.

⁶⁴ Jasper Mayne, *Part of Lucian Made English from the Originall in the Yeare 1638* (London, 1664), Ep. Ded. sigs A3v-A4.

Both Hobbes and Mayne were acutely aware of the dangers of religious language, and sought ways of immunising secular authority from the corrosive effects of rhetorical religions. In doing this, the two shared many views — an insistence that that was only one sort of authority (political); that churches did not wield any sort of political authority; a common Erastianism, and even the fearless view that there was no illegality that kings could not commit, even if they should not.[65] It is at least arguable that both of them developed, as well, some sort of theory of liberty of conscience, if only as an implication of their denial of any political or coercive authority to the clergy.[66]

There are, though, things that distinguished Mayne from Hobbes. His position was closer than Hobbes's to that taken in Newcastle's 1659 'Advice to Charles II'. Newcastle's strong support of the Anglican establishment is something that Hobbes cannot have found easy to stomach. He retained into the Restoration period the belief (most strongly articulated in *Leviathan*), that the claims of the Anglican clergy were scarcely less of a threat to the sovereign's authority than those of Presbyterians or any other clerics.[67] Newcastle, though, was a strong defender of the church. Like both Hobbes and Mayne, he was firmly Erastian. Every commonwealth has two parts, 'the state Civill, & The state Ecleseasticall' and 'iff Both thes states, or partes of the Body poleticke Bee not governd in Cheefe by one, & the same person, They cannot bee sayd to bee parts of the same Monarchy'.[68] But the Episcopalian government of the Church of England was perfectly

---

[65] On the last point cf. Glenn Burgess, 'On Hobbesian Resistance Theory', *Political Studies*, 42 (1994), pp. 62-83.

[66] A more controversial claim in relation to Hobbes — but for a variety of views see Alan Ryan, 'A More Tolerant Hobbes?' in Susan Mendus (ed.), *Justifying Toleration: Conceptual and Historical Perspectives* (Cambridge, 1988), ch. 3; Richard Tuck, 'Hobbes and Locke on Toleration' in Mary Dietz (ed.), *Thomas Hobbes and Political Theory* (Lawrence KS, 1990), ch. 8: Glenn Burgess, 'Thomas Hobbes: Religious Toleration or Religious Indifference?' in C. Nederman & J. C. Laursen (eds), *Difference and Dissent: Theories of Tolerance in Medieval and Early Modern Europe* (Lanham MA, 1996), ch. 8; Justin Champion, ''Le culte privé est libre quand il est rendu dans le secret': Hobbes, Locke et les limites de la tolérance, l'athéisme et l'hétérodoxie' in *Les fondements philosophiques de la tolérance en France et en Angleterre au xviie siècle* (ed.), Yves Charles Zarka, Franck Lessay, & John Rogers (Paris, 2002), pp. 221-253.

[67] Paul Seaward, ''Chief of the Ways of God': Form and Meaning in the *Behemoth* of Thomas Hobbes's, *Filozofski Vestnik*, xxiv: 2 (2003), pp. 169-88.

[68] Thomas P. Slaughter (ed.), *Ideology and Politics on the Eve of the Restoration: Newcastle's Advice to Charles II* (Philadelphia, 1984), p. 12; cf. Conal Condren, 'Casuistry to Newcastle:

compatible with this requirement. There was no need to look elsewhere, when:

> wee are already posest of an Eclesiasticall Government, Instituted by the Apostles, received And approved by the primitive christens, Establisht by the Princes, & parlements, of our owne kingdome, pretending To no power over the kinge att all, nor no power under the King, neyther, but from him, & by, him teaching active obedience, to all the Lawfull Comands of Lawfull authority, And passive obedience, even to those commands that are not Lawfulkl, so the Authority commanding them bee not unlawful.[69]

'[N]o Bishopps, no King', Newcastle said, echoing King James VI and I.[70] If he had discussed the matter of church government with Hobbes, he clearly had not listened too closely. But Jasper Mayne could well have told Newcastle something very similar to this.

There is no reason to suppose that there was a 'Cavendish' political line in any simple sense. Many of the views that Mayne and Hobbes shared could have derived from a variety of sources, including but not confined to one another. However, what we can learn from the conjunction of Hobbes and Mayne is that there is no need to step outside royalism to find a context for Hobbes's positive evaluation of 'independency' in church government.[71] As this essay has suggested, by the later 1640s royalists were showing a remarkable capacity to think through some fundamental assumptions about the nature of the English church-state. Colin Davis has reminded us that the intellectual eddies and flows of the English Revolution defy easy categorization and simplistic labelling. Royalist thought, too, needs rescuing from its stereotypes, and no one has done more than Colin Davis to show us how to go about such a task.

'The Prince' in the World of the Book' in Phillipson & Skinner, (eds), *Political Discourse*, pp. 177, 183-84.

[69] Slaughter (ed.), *Ideology and Politics*, p. 14.

[70] *Ibid.*, p. 15.

[71] Hobbes, *Leviathan*, ch. 47, p. 479. Jeffrey R. Collins, *The Allegiance of Thomas Hobbes* (Oxford, 2005); J. P. Sommerville, 'Hobbes and Independency', *Rivista di Storia della Filosofia*, 59 (2004), pp. 155-73; Sommerville, 'Hobbes, *Behemoth*, Church-State Relations and Political Obligations', *Folizofski Vestnik*, 24 (2003), pp. 205-22.

Chapter 2

Authority And Liberty: Hobbes and the Sects

William Lamont

Thomas Hobbes made the definitive case for the magistrate's authority in 1651. The case for liberty was made most eloquently by his enemies in the sects. 'Authority' and 'liberty' are here seen as polarised opposites which find their classic exposition in the mid-seventeenth century debate between the future Bishop of Oxford, Samuel Parker, and his Independent opponent, John Owen. Owen argued in 1667 that the Dutch owed their success in trade to their religious toleration. Parker's counter to this in 1670 was the claim that religious disunity produced commercial failure. To Owen the victory: the 'Commonwealth Principles' which he advocated would be guaranteed by the accession of Dutch William in 1688.

However, the defeat of Parker was not the defeat of Hobbes. This paper will make three claims. First, to see Parker as surrogate for Hobbes is as wrong as to see Owen as surrogate for the sects. Second, 'Commonwealth Principles' are elastic enough to be read in strikingly different ways by their champions, even when they agreed that William III's rule embodied them. Third, Hobbes would end up as the villain for some of these 'Commonwealth' apologists and the hero of others.

Why should we not read Hobbes into Parker? His *A Discourse of Ecclesiastical Polity* is soaked in Hobbes. When he summarises the contents of his fifth chapter we hear echoes of *Leviathan*:

> Religion is useful or dangerous in a State, as the temper of mind it breeds is peaceable or turbulent. The dread of Invisible Powers is not of itself sufficient to awe people into Subjection, but tends more probably to Tumults and Seditions. This largely proved by the ungovernableness of the Principles and Tempers of some Sects ... . How the Fanaticks of all Nations and Religions agree in the same Principles of Sedition. To permit different Sects of Religion in a Commonwealth is only, to keep up so many incurable Pretenses and Occasions of Publick Disturbance. The corrupt Passions and Humours of Men make toleration infinitely unsafe.

When we read the title of his chapter, however, we realise how far Parker is from endorsing Hobbes: 'A Confutation of the Consequences that some men draw from Mr. Hobs's Principles in behalf of Liberty of Conscience'. What he cannot forgive in Hobbes is his candour. Hobbes is the candid friend of strong government.

G. K. Chesterton once said that the candid friend is candid in everything — except, that is, in the pleasure he gets from being candid. Religion may be a cheat, says the future bishop, but 'they are the most mischievous Enemies to Government that tell the World it is so'.[1] When the anorexic Martha Taylor, in a celebrated case, was tested for the authenticity of her spiritual visions, debate raged as to whether she had passed excrement or urine. Hobbes was outraged: 'I think it were somewhat inhuman to examine of these things too nearly, when it so little concerned the commonwealth'. Parker's point is that nothing is too little to escape the magistrate's scrutiny — least of all the subject's excrement, as in the totalitarian dystopias of Swift and Orwell.[2] But for Hobbes all that matters is what concerns the commonwealth, and nothing matters more for that than the protection of the subject's liberty.[3] In the famous last chapter of *Leviathan* he shows how the Papal, Episcopal and Presbyterian knots on men's liberty were progressively dissolved until we are reduced 'to the Independency of the Primitive Christians to follow Paul, or Cephas, or Apollos, every man as he liketh best'. He explains why this sort of 'Independency' (and he is fully aware that there were other, very different, sorts of 'Independency' passing themselves off under that name) was indeed the best:

> First, because there ought to be no Power over the consciences of men, but of the Word it selfe, working faith in every one, not always according to the purpose of them that Plant and Water, but of God himself, that giveth the Increase: and secondly, because it is unreasonable in those, who teach there is such danger in every little Error, to require of a man endowed with reason of his own, to follow the Reason of any other man, or of the

---

[1] W. Lamont and S. Oldfield (eds), *Politics, Religion and Literature in the Seventeenth Century* (London, 1975), pp. 205-9.
[2] G. Orwell, 'Politics versus literature', *The Penguin Essays of George Orwell* (London, 1984), p. 377, on totalitarianism, Swift and the significance of the victim's ordure.
[3] D. Wootton, 'A perpetual object of hate to all theologians', *London Review of Books*, 17 (1995), p. 13.

most voices of many other men; Which is little better than to venture his Salvation at crosse and pile.[4]

Now this is the same argument, and written in almost the same words, as that which was advanced by the antinomian, William Walwyn, to make his case as early as 1641 for liberty of conscience:

> and therefore holds it unreasonable, to be forced to follow other men's Judgments and not his owne in a matter of so great importance as that of his salvation is.[5]

The convergence is striking and significant.

We are indebted to a major new study for showing us how illusory is the gap between Hobbes and the sects, and Walwyn in particular among them.[6] Walwyn is exceptional among radicals in accepting 'Antinomian' as an accurate self-description of his religious position, one who believes that all are 'justified freely by his grace through the redemption that is in Jesus Christ'.[7] In his apologia, *Walwyn's Just Defence*, he claimed that he had been freed from the anxieties induced by a gospel of works or determinism by 'that part of doctrine (called then, Antinomian) of free justification by Christ alone'.[8] But he is not exceptional among the sects in playing down his social status (Leveller Walwyn, son of a prosperous landlord and privately tutored, ranked above Hobbes, son of a parson) or his educational skills (Walwyn cited 'Plutarch, Seneca, Lucian, Thucydides, Montaigne and Pierre Charron, amongst others' in his *Walwyn's Just Defence*, whilst deprecating his own poor Latin). The 'Naylerite' Rich praised 'brave Hobbs' as well as Saltmarsh and Vane.[9] The Calvinistic Independent and Baptist ministers, Kiffin, Price and Rosier, when they renounced sectarianism, personalised it in the form of *Walwyn's Wiles*.[10] Their caricature of Walwyn had him jeering at Fast Days, sceptical about

---

[4] Hobbes, *Leviathan*, ed. Richard Tuck (Cambridge, 1991), pp. 479-80.

[5] J. R. McMichael and B. Taft (eds), *The Writings of William Walwyn* (Athens, GA, 1989), p. 57.

[6] N. McDowell, *The English Radical Imagination* (Oxford, 2003).

[7] *The Writings of William Walwyn*, p. 89.

[8] *Ibid.*, pp. 395-6.

[9] McDowell, *The English Radical Imagination*, pp. 10, 172.

[10] W. Lamont, 'Pamphleteering, the Protestant consensus and the English Revolution' in R. C. Richardson and G. M. Ridden (eds), *Freedom and the English Revolution* (Manchester, 1986), pp. 85-86.

hell, scorning prayers, and refusing to be intimidated by the Almighty. A few years on, they could have been publishing *Hobbes's Wiles*, making precisely the same charges against him.

John Owen was closer to Kiffin, Price and Rosier than he would ever be to Walwyn, and he was no more a surrogate spokesman for liberty therefore than Hobbes can be for authority. At first sight he would seem to have been ideally cast for that role. He was the man who took on Parker's (not Hobbes's) argument that religious toleration was bad for trade. He began his writing life as a Presbyterian minister and went on to become the leading spokesman for Independency (the least bad alternative, according to Hobbes). But did untying the Presbyterian knot mean an end to knots, or just to the Presbyterian one? He had made the 'liberty' case against Scottish Presbyterians in 1649. After the Restoration he argued for toleration when his fellow minister, Richard Baxter, sought 'comprehension' within a reformed National Church. From Hobbes's perspective, however, these differences are illusory. Scottish Presbyterians, English 'Baxterians' and Independents were alike in their pursuit of clerical discipline, but went about it differently. Owen poured scorn on 'professors' of religion who made a fetish about their liberty 'as they called it'.[11] He wrote in 1668 of 'the great use of magistracy in the world ... the terror of him that bears the sword'.[12] He saw pluralism as a vice, not a virtue. In 1681 he lamented the multiplicity of thoughts in men's minds: 'what a hell of horror and confusion it must needs be!' He would go on to argue that the 'design of conviction' was 'to put a stop unto these thoughts, to take off from the number, and thereby to lessen the guilt'.[13] The sects were under no illusions about Owen. This man was no friend to them. The Quaker Samuel Fisher even challenged Owen to a Latin boxing match to show off his superior education (if he chose to exploit it), while Henry Stubbe accused Owen of reneging on former 'liberty' beliefs in calling for State persecution of Quakers.[14]

In 1649 Owen answered his own question — did the civil magistrate have a duty to bring the people to the truth? — with this revealing reply: 'Were the precious distinguished from the vile, Churches rightly established, and church discipline so exercised that Christians were under some

---

[11] John Owen, *Evidences of the faith of God's elect* (London, 1695), p. 69.

[12] John Owen, *On Indwelling Sin*, (London, 1668), p. 270.

[13] John Owen, *An enquiry into the original, nature, institution, power, order, and communion of evangelical churches* (London, 1681), p. 116.

[14] McDowell, *The English Radical Imagination*, pp. 162, 178.

orderly view an easy finger would untie the knot of this query'.[15] Hobbes' easy finger untied that knot by arguing for 'Independency', by which he meant that there should be no power over men's consciences. Owen agreed that there could be no untying of knots without Independency but meant by this the unbridled assertion of clerical power over men's consciences — precisely the opposite of Hobbes' ideal. Yet Owen was ready (in 1660 at least) to concede a half-way house 'being in that confusion wherein we are'. In other words, the ideal scenario for Owen was a magistrate-ordered godliness, but in the present mess he would settle for second best: a toleration which at least would permit the exercise of discipline at the level of the congregation (New Independent was but Old Presbyter writ small?)

When Owen was first Cromwell's chaplain, the primary goal had seemed attainable. By 1658 he had settled for the internal discipline. He and his fellow ministers did their bit in distinguishing the precious from the vile (his personal contribution to the Independent ministers' Savoy Conference of that year). He helped in the removal of a magistrate not up to the job (Richard Cromwell) in 1659. And with the Stuart Restoration in 1660 toleration was the only way that godly discipline could get any sort of toe-hold. The Independent ministers had behaved no differently a decade earlier at the Westminster Assembly when they had stressed their nearness to their Presbyterian colleagues in their document *An Apologeticall Narration*. It was an affinity, like Owen's later, based on the exclusion of their separatist antinomian colleagues. And the greatest of them, Walwyn, in his *The Compassionate Samaritaine* of 1644, spoke for fellow malcontents in claiming that they had been 'left in the lurch'.[16] No wonder he would go on scorning the 'liberty' credentials of Independent ministers like Owen who, at the drop of a hat, would ditch their sectarian colleagues and find comfort in cohabitation with the magistrate.

The question that Owen had set himself in 1649 — did the civil magistrate have the duty to bring the people to the truth? — was one that a representative gathering of puritan ministers addressed at Whitehall in 1648. Their brief, precisely, was to decide 'whether the magistrate have, or ought to have, any comprehensive and restrictive power in matters of religion'. Colin Davis subjected the Whitehall Debates to a brilliant reading in a ground-breaking article in 1992. He found that the 'liberty' which they claimed to be seeking was liberty for, not from, the service of God. He

---

[15] John Owen, *Righteous Zeal encouraged by Divine protection* (London, 1649), p. 203.
[16] *The Writings of William Walwyn*, p. 102.

showed, in close analysis of the text, that the great majority of the members were searching throughout the debates for 'submission to Christ' and that 'liberty was only a preliminary to that act'. Where, though, could we expect in seventeenth-century England to find a puritan commitment to such a concept as freedom from, that is to say, to the assertion of an autonomous individual will? Davis answers, only in the antinomians, indeed in men like Walwyn whose gloss on 'Independency' we saw that Hobbes, for one, could relate to.[17]

I borrowed his argument (stole it rather) in showing that the Putney Debates, a year earlier than Whitehall, owed their seemingly incontrovertible linkage with 'liberty' not to the content of the debates themselves, but to their editor's 1938 choice of title (*Puritanism and Liberty*) and to astute packaging (two-thirds of the volume not about Putney at all, but consisting of excerpts from contemporary pamphlets which relate to the title). In a bizarre twist, J. D. Lindsay, in his updated introduction to the 1950 edition, carried A. S. P. Woodhouse's 1938 liberty thesis a stage further in recruiting Putney puritans into the ranks of premature anti-Stalinists. In fact, the fear of such men, at both Putney and Whitehall, of being swamped by antinomians, made them exceedingly cautious about embracing the very concept of liberty; it is even possible that the over-reaction of Cromwell and Ireton to An Agreement of the People on the first day at Putney owed something to the suspicion that Walwyn may have been its part-author.[18]

Owen, therefore, had not embraced liberty when he pointed up some of the commercial advantages of religious toleration. Like his puritan colleagues at Putney and Whitehall, he was an unreconstructed and impenitent champion of authority and discipline. Parker was not being paranoid in blaming Hobbes for the rise of liberty, only in claiming that it had infected the main ranks of nonconformity, and not just its antinomian fringe. With this perspective in mind it is possible to inject a cautionary note to our genuine welcome to four recent reassessments of Commonwealth politics. They are very different works, but some areas of agreement can be discerned. Cromwell's Instrument of Government confirmed a degree of religious liberty remarkable for early modern Europe. The godly 'had to compete for support in a religious marketplace

---

[17] J. C. Davis, 'Religion and the struggle for freedom in the English Revolution', *The Historical Journal*, 35, 3 (1992), pp. 507-30.

[18] W. Lamont, 'Puritanism, liberty and the Putney debates' in M. Mendle (ed.), *The Putney Debates of 1647* (Cambridge, 2001), pp. 241-55.

where liberty of conscience was guaranteed by law'.[19] The England of the 1650s — with its London coffee houses where newsbooks were read —marked 'a central place in the internal, as well as the more famous external, commercial development of the nation'.[20] The creation of a commercial society in the 1690s and beyond owed much to the early defenders of the English Commonwealth — 'the new generation of radicals who emerged in the 1650s' who understood that the powerful states in early modern Europe 'could only continue to protect liberty by embracing commercial society'.[21] The achievements in the governance of England after 1689 owe an incalculable debt to what the nation learned from the Dutch in fiscal, military, political and religious terms ('protestant liberty of conscience').[22] The implicit theme of the four studies is made explicit in the sub-title given to one of them: Pincus's 'Commercial Society and the Defenders of the English Commonwealth'. Defenders are named: Henry Parker, John Streater (in two of them), Henry Robinson, Marchamont Nedham and Algernon Sidney.

But there is a curious omission in all of them. None refers to one of the most famous contemporary defences of the Commonwealth which, like them, sees its fulfilment in the future reign of William III. Its author is no shrinking violet. 'Commonwealth' is written into the title of his work. He goes to great lengths in the text to define what the term means. But there is one profound difference from the other sources cited. His commitment to Commonwealth necessitates an attack on, not a defence of, Commercial Society. Is this why Richard Baxter's *A Holy Commonwealth* has been silently removed from the debate? Perhaps it is time to put it back.

Baxter's Commonwealth is neither republican nor Stuart — Oliver Cromwell, Richard Cromwell, or William III could head it. Its ideal was to reform the Reformation which Henry VIII had botched. Its programme was that of the Commonwealth preachers in Edward VI's reign. No wonder that Baxter regretted that England's best reign was its shortest. The

---

[19] A. Hughes, 'Religion, 1640-1660' in B. Coward (ed.), *A Companion to Stuart Britain* (Oxford, 2003), pp. 350-73.

[20] D. Hirst, 'Locating the 1650s in England's seventeenth century', *History* (July 1996), pp. 359-83.

[21] S. Pincus, 'Neither Machiavellian moment nor possessive individualism: commercial society and the defenders of the English Commonwealth', *American Historical Review*, 103 (1998), pp. 705-36.

[22] J. Scott, 'What were Commonwealth Principles?' *The Historical Journal*, 47, 3 (2004), pp. 591-613; Scott, *Commonwealth Principles: Republican Writing of the English Revolution* (Cambridge, 2004), pp. 353-57.

programme then and now was to build hospitals and schools, tax the rich, found new universities. Baxter's 1650s correspondence reflects his growing excitement with such projects. A letter from a fellow enthusiast, Abraham Pinchbecke, in 1653 shows their mutual recognition of the importance of the Commonwealth concept:

> doe not wee see in Common Weales how after ages perceiving the faileing of their people in the observation of some precedent laws doe ad remedies to such transgressions and new conditions to old laws, or make new laws where the other are imperfect, or the present condition of affaires require? and for invention have we not some whose braines have brought forth some new formes of government very rationall?"[23]

The end result would be, not a freer, but a more rational and disciplined society: a land fit for saints, not merchants.

Baxter had not started the Commonwealth as its advocate. After consulting his friend, Richard Vines, he refused to take the Engagement to the Commonwealth. Both saw behind Cromwell's professions of liberty only the mask concealing the antinomian beast. What changed Baxter's mind? His experience through the 1650s of putting his reforming ideals into practice in his Kidderminster parish was his education. The godly discipline which he set up there became the basis for his hopes of a Holy Commonwealth at first parish level, then through his Ministerial Associations at county, and ultimately at national, level. Baxter was won over to Cromwell by the freedom he was permitted to carry out his experiment. But there was a paradox here. That freedom was exploited to advance a programme of coercion. It was a clerical spy system which made the Kidderminster success possible. That was not how he would have expressed it, of course; he preferred to speak of 'the zeal and diligence of the godly people who thirsted after the salvation of their neighbours and were in private my assistants'. Michael Walzer quoted this very passage from Baxter's memoirs to show how wrong R. H. Tawney had been, in his *Religion and the Rise of Capitalism*, to make Baxter the spokesman for the coming world of bourgeois trust and contract — the harbinger of that 'Commercial Society' celebrated in their different ways in the four studies referred to above.[24] But Tawney's argument should not be misrepresented.

[23] Doctor Williams' Library, London, Baxter Correspondence, iv, fol. 43.

[24] M. Walzer, 'Puritanism as a revolutionary ideology', *History and Theory*, 3 (1963-4), pp. 63-65.

He is not saying that Baxter was a *willing* agent of change; only that, at least by 1670, he had been forced to recognise that he had to abandon his earlier dreams of Holy Commonwealths. That was when he withdrew that book and asked that henceforth it should be treated as *non scriptum*.[25] Three years later his *A Christian Directory* becomes the model for clerical diffidence and self deprecation.[26] He there presents himself as the Holy Fool, stumbling into political and social matters which were well beyond his competence to assess. This loss of nerve had a general implication. The treason of the clerk, in Tawney's reading of Restoration England, was when ministers like Baxter gave up believing in discipline.

The discipline about which Baxter had written in the 1650s, and which he practised in Kidderminster, had never been sectarian. He started from the premise that 'ordinarily the same persons are fit to be members of Church and Commonwealth'. That sounds like godly elitism — a revolution of the saints. After all, the majority of the people are ungodly: that was why Baxter did not believe in democracy. Yet Baxter's Holy Commonwealth was neither minority nor democratic rule. He recognised that a National Church had not only its 'members within' but those without. His Kidderminster success had been built upon the catechising of his parishioners, but it had been no less important in his County Association of Ministers and ultimately in their extension across the nation. There was a 'ripening' process by which 'catechumens' were brought into Church membership. Beyond them, but more distantly, were those who had been excommunicated and neighbouring infidels, all who came under the aegis of a true 'National Church'. A 'Christian Commonwealth' owned none as *Civis* but he who was fit to be a Church member, yet there were many 'meer subjects' who were nevertheless entitled to look to the State for the protection of their lives and possessions. The protector was the godly magistrate, and what a relief (if, in Baxter's case, belatedly) when he found him in Oliver Cromwell! That discovery owed much to the appointment of John Howe, Baxter's puritan ministerial friend, as Cromwell's chaplain. Baxter could (and did) push in private correspondence with Howe the reforming ideas which were to surface in his public writings. When Howe continued to serve as chaplain to Richard Cromwell, the links became even closer (the son had no regicide past to hide).

Baxter's *A Holy Commonwealth* of 1659 embodied his vision of an

---

[25] Richard Baxter, *A Holy Commonwealth*, ed. W. Lamont (Cambridge, 1994), pp. 251-2.
[26] Richard Baxter, *A Christian Directory* (London, 1673).

active magistrate and a reform-minded ministry.[27] What wrecked these hopes? One cause was the political intrigues of John Owen and the Wallingford House conspirators against Richard Cromwell. This was a conviction which Baxter's editors expunged from his posthumous memoirs. But a more profound answer was in the poisonous ideology which motivated them: in a word: 'Liberty'. Its classic exposition was Sir Henry Vane's *A Healing Question* of 1656. It was there, according to Baxter, that Vane had argued that 'Liberty' was the key to 'the good old cause'.[28] But Baxter believed that 'Liberty' to preach up 'Popery, Mahometanism, Infidelity and Heathenism' was the same 'Libertinism' which had disfigured Laudianism before the Civil War. He spelt out the consequences: 'a man that would deny the life to come, or revile Christ and the Scripture, or teach men to worship Mahomet, or the Sunne and the Moon, if he have liberty, and a plausible tongue, may look to have Disciples'. Liberty plays havoc with family hierarchies and military discipline: 'it is the loosing of the Dragon, and not the liberty of the Saints'. To stop the magistrate from intervening in matters of faith and worship is to deliver 'all the fruit of our Labours, Prayers and Victories into the Papists hands'. Nor is it a defence of the Instrument of Government to say that 'liberty' as an ideal is not extended in its provisions to 'Popery and Prelacy'. Baxter's point is, that once liberty is accepted as its overarching principle, then Papist exemption from it, for instance, will in the course of time seem unreasonable and discriminatory. For his part Baxter is sure that 'the farre greatest part of the godly in the land', which is his *vox populi*, 'abhorre the thoughts of Liberty for the Masse, and for preaching up Popery, Mahometanism or Infidelity: Most of them desired the Acts for the Lords Day, which showed that they are for no such Liberty'.[29]

Baxter had to swallow these brave words of 1659 in 1670. We saw that Tawney believed that this capitulation was symbolic of a watershed which had been reached in puritan social thought. He had called puritanism 'the schoolmaster of the English middle classes' and then added 'it is a strange school which does not teach more than one lesson'. The two lessons that puritanism taught, he argued, were collectivism and individualism — or, in the words of the fourth chapter of *Religion and the Rise of Capitalism*, 'A Godly discipline versus the religion of trade'. The Baxter of 1659 incarnates

---

[27] Baxter, *A Holy Commonwealth*, p. 131.

[28] Sir H. Vane, *A Healing Question* (London, 1656), in W. Scott (ed.), *A Collection of Scarce and Valuable Tracts ... of the Late Lord Somers*, 13 vols (London, 1808-1815), 6, pp. 303-13.

[29] Baxter, *A Holy Commonwealth*, pp. 18, 23, 26, 27, 32, 34, 35.

the first: Holy Commonwealths, clerical overseeing, catechizing. The Baxter of 1673 incarnates the second: freedom of the market, passivity of the magistrate, deference of the clergy. Baxter best champions the latter three principles in his *A Christian Directory*. This is the most cited Baxter tract in Tawney's book. He makes it stand as the representation of that profound generational shift in Restoration England, when divines stopped criticising the acquisitive society and became its accomplice. Tawney called the rules which Baxter had set out in his 1673 tract subtle and sincere but 'like seeds carried by birds from a distant and fertile plain, and dropped upon a glacier ... were at once embalmed and sterilized in a river of ice'.[30] What Tawney failed to recognise was that the ice had begun to melt for Baxter at least by 1686 (when his prison apocalyptic researches revived old aspirations for godly magistracy) and certainly after 1688, when change of dynasty made these practical politics. This was the turn-about which neither Baxter nor Tawney had foreseen.

The accession of a Protestant ruler in William III reawakened Baxter's yearnings for a Cromwellian 'Holy Commonwealth'. His 1691 pamphlet, *A National Church*, outlines a rigorously prescriptive programme of reform. Baptism would not be the 'infant ceremony' it now is, but one where parents were taught to *know* what was meant by entering their children into a covenant. The scandalous would be kept out of the Sacraments. The universities would be purged until there were only 'godly careful tutors'. Religious toleration was not an absolute right; it depended on the will of the lawgiver. There must be 'a wise and godly King that must be the principal means to accomplish all this'. Whether it was, as in 1659, Richard Cromwell, or, as in 1689, William III, was a matter of supreme inconsequence: Commonwealth and monarchy were complementary, not contradictory, terms. Only one thing would destroy a 'National Church': 'Sins of Injustice and Unmercifulness, especially Rich Men's oppression of the Poor, Landlords grinding their Poor tenants, Justices and Lawyers unrighteous in Suits and Judgments, are sins threatened by the Prophets as the forerunners of Destruction'.[31]

This was the vision which inspired Baxter's angry last posthumously published testament in the same year, *The Poor Husbandman's Advocate*. For nearly three hundred years it survived only in manuscript, having almost certainly been suppressed by his literary executors Daniel Williams and Matthew Sylvester for its social radicalism. It was found in the Baxter

---

[30] R. H. Tawney, *Religion and the Rise of Capitalism* (London, 1926), pp. 211-6.

[31] Baxter, *Of National Churches* (London, 1691), pp. 49-70.

archive by his biographer, F. J. Powicke, who published it in 1926 – perhaps appropriately in the year of the General Strike – but too late for Tawney, whose Scott Holland Memorial Lectures (later to be published as *Religion and the Rise of Capitalism*) had been delivered in 1922.

Baxter had seen this neglected work as his contribution to the debate about 'Commonwealth'. Those who equate it with 'Democracy' are called 'ignorant Sots' – he had said as much in *A Holy Commonwealth*. Baxter remained a Commonwealth advocate in both periods, even if in 1691 he was prepared to offer an alternative 'National Church' title. Contemporaries whom he respected, like John Selden and Sir Matthew Hale, and before them Grotius, knew what the word 'Commonwealth' meant, whereas 'the Ignoramuses seem not to know that the common welfare is so essentially the *Terminus* of the Policie, that to exclude it is to dissolve all the Policie, Kingdom and State'. Fifth Monarchists had propagated their fantasies of a future thousand-year rule of Christ on earth and missed the actual achievements of Christian magistracy. 'Would they have the Churches have the full power of Church discipline, to separate the precious from the vile?' Baxter had asked and then answered himself – that is precisely what happens when the right Protestant ruler is in charge. We saw that Owen in 1649 had said that he was all for magistracy if the godly discipline was secured. Why then had he not recognised what Richard Cromwell's magistracy had offered in 1659? Even worse, Baxter suspected that Owen was the man who had destroyed those hopes, and with them the Protectorate. Baxter voiced these suspicions in unpublished sections of his memoirs. Even in his most careful pamphlet, *A Christian Directory*, he had bad things to say about rack-renting landlords. But it was the prospect in 1691 of a recrudescence of 'the full power of Church discipline' which made the later admonitions anything but the toothless pieties of 1673.[32]

The point became clear in correspondence with his friend, John Humfrey. Both advocated National Churches, indeed Humfrey suggested the term to Baxter.[33] But they meant different things by it. Humfrey was thinking of an Erastian framework with the minimum of ministerial discipline.[34] But for Baxter the discipline was the *point* of a National Church:

---

[32] F. J. Powicke (ed.), *The Reverend Richard Baxter's last treatise* (Manchester, 1926), pp. 20, 21, 22, 38, 42, 43, 46, 48, 51, 52, 55.

[33] Humfrey's words were: 'This will make the book sell', Doctor Williams' Library, Baxter Correspondence, i, fol. 72.

[34] J. Humfrey, *Union Pursued* (London, 1691), p. 2.

Kidderminster writ large in 1691, as it had been (briefly) in 1659.[35] What stood in the way of a National Church? First 'Popery'. Baxter's proof that the two were mutually exclusive so impressed Coleridge in 1829 that he borrowed the term, as well as the argument, in the case that he made against Catholic Emancipation.[36] That Popery could have been included in Humfrey's National Church showed Baxter and Coleridge how he had missed the point. The second obstacle was antinomianism. It was Sir Henry Vane's libertinism which Baxter had rounded on in the additions to his preface in *A Holy Commonwealth*. Baxter had followed keenly the Antinomian Controversy in Vane's Massachusetts in 1637. He approved Governor Winthrop's use of the General Court to protect the interest of debtors from their merchant creditors. When the precipitant of the controversy, Anne Hutchinson, the wife of a merchant, challenged a gospel of works, most merchants supported her because, as James Henretta has argued, they feared a close regulation of their spiritual, as well as their economic, lives. But they lost, and Henretta claimed that Massachusetts Bay became 'an authoritarian state, a holy commonwealth on the model of Calvin's Geneva'.[37]

These American tensions were well known to Baxter. John Eliot, a witness against Anne Hutchinson in 1637, became Baxter's most faithful transatlantic correspondent. Eliot's *Christian Commonwealth* and Baxter's *A Holy Commonwealth* not only sound similar and were published in the same year (1659); they are fruits of a common commitment to a godly discipline.[38] When Baxter propagated his 'National Church' beliefs in 1691, another New England minister, Increase Mather, succeeded Eliot as his confidant.[39] Baxter told Humfrey of his wish that the world had 'more such Nationall Churches as New England is (if a Province may be called a Nation)'. In *The Poor Husbandman's Advocate* Baxter apologised for his copious citations of Scripture texts for good works, because of the need to

---

[35] Doctor Williams' Library, Baxter Treatises, vi, fols. 296-302.

[36] S. T. Coleridge, *On the Constitution of the Church and State*, ed. J. Barrell (London, 1992), p. 80; W. Lamont, 'The Two "National Churches" of 1691 and 1829' in A. Fletcher and P. Roberts (eds), *Religion, Culture and Society in Early Modern Britain: Essays in Honour of Patrick Collinson* (Cambridge, 1994), pp. 335-52.

[37] J. Henretta, 'The Protestant ethic and the reality of capitalism in colonial America', in H. Lehmann and G. Roth (eds), *Weber's Protestant Ethic: origins, evidence, contexts* (Cambridge, 1993), pp. 329-33.

[38] Doctor Williams' Library, Baxter Treatises, vii, fol. 7.

[39] *Ibid.*, fol. 301.

combat the influence from the grave of Anne Hutchinson's antinomian contemporary, Tobias Crisp. Crisp's posthumous works had been republished in 1690 to general acclaim — or so Baxter thought. Actually Baxter's revered friend, John Howe, had been one of twelve ministers who had done no more than sign a certificate attesting to the *authenticity* of eight additional sermons of Crisp which had been reprinted. This was not the same, as he later reassured Baxter, as *approving* the doctrines contained in them. He would be one of seven who subsequently dissociated themselves from these doctrines.[40]

How hard Baxter took this is reflected in the plea at the end of the sixth chapter of his manuscript for future readers to 'peruse the Texts that I have so largely cited, and then nothing but obstinate prejudice or contempt of Scripture, can keep you from abhorring this *Crispian, Anti-Christian Libertinisme*'.[41] Freedom was debased coinage to puritans like Baxter who saw it as synonymous with libertinism. It was objectionable in another way which Baxter addressed in that same unknown treatise. It was what Tawney had addressed in his own 1938 work, *Equality*, when he pointed out that 'freedom for the pike is death for the minnows'. Baxter had written his treatise for the minnows. For them he draws out the consequences of a free market. When the pike wants his taxes lower, Baxter is scathing: 'Who should pay money but those that have it? And who should pay dearer for the publike safety than they that have most to loose?' There is something obscene about the way society distributes its rewards: '*You* do but give your *money*; but poore men give their *lives* for the publike service by sea and land. While you sit warme at home out of fear and danger, they are night and day in suffering and peril'.[42] When Tawney saw puritans like Baxter as the tamed apologists for the new 'religion of trade' he grossly miscast them. We now can see that, at the end of his life, Baxter was a seventeenth-century Tawney.

Yet there *were* other puritans who did not feel this strong counter-pull of a 'godly discipline'. They were the antinomians, in Davis's helpful formulation, who wanted liberty *from*, not merely liberty *for*. That is to say, liberty from Calvin's Geneva, Winthrop's General Court, Baxter's catechising — and all of them ripe for the 'religion of trade'. The chance recovery of the papers of one such sect, the Muggletonians, throws light on this process.

This was a sect which began about the same time as the Quakers and

---

[40] P. Toon, *Puritans and Calvinism* (Swengel, PA, 1973), pp. 85-105.

[41] Powicke (ed.), *The Reverend Richard Baxter's last treatise...*, p. 56.

[42] *Ibid.*, pp. 51-52.

was thought to be extinct by the nineteenth century. Its papers were discovered in 1974 and are now deposited in the British Library in 89 volumes. They are the basis of the first full history of the sect, which has been recently published.[43] Their most influential thinker was Thomas Tomkinson (1631 - c. 1710). In his *Discourse Upon the Epistle of Jude* (1704) he taught fellow believers to put their trust in Hobbes, who told truths opposed by 'almost all sects and opinions', but not by the Mugletonians if Tomkinson had his way. And he did have his way. When Tomkinson quotes a long passage from *Leviathan* he adds 'So farre learned Hobbes'.[44] What others found shocking in Hobbes were platitudinous to followers of Reeve, Muggleton and Clarkson — namely, mortalism, materialism, praying as 'attributes of intention', an internal hell, devil and dreams as projections of fear, witches and sorcery as old wives' tales, contempt for priests, lawyers, doctors, dons and universities. Above all, there is respect for the magistrate. Tomkinson's *Truth's Triumph* of 1676 conveys all the horrors of a Hobbesian state of nature when bereft of that control and a no less passionate conviction that no windows should be opened into men's souls.[45] Tomkinson's genius was to be the first of his sect to recognise their affinities with Hobbes. They would have recognised the same enemies — like Baxter, for instance, who as early as March 1652 was urging Thomas Hill, the Calvinist Master of Trinity College, Cambridge, to put *Leviathan* to the flames.[46] Hobbes had thought Independency the least controlling of religions. Tomkinson could find no organised religion to match his ideals, but agreed with Hobbes that the Independents were 'more moderate' than 'most of the other churches'.[47]

Richard Tuck has made a convincing case that it was as late as the end of the 1640s, in his Parisian exile, that Hobbes decisively broke with Anglican orthodoxy on two crucial points of doctrine. One was an external hell. The other was the immortality of the soul. They were the two primary irrational fears from which both Hobbes and Tomkinson wanted to liberate mankind. From this perspective Tuck called *Leviathan* 'the greatest of the English revolutionary utopias'.[48] *Truth's Triumph* is another.

[43] Lamont, *Last Witnesses: the Muggletonian history 1652-1979* (Aldershot, 2006).
[44] British Library, Additional MS, 60198, fol. 6.
[45] British Library, Additional MS, 60190, fol. 27.
[46] Doctor Williams' Library, Baxter Correspondence, iii, fols. 272v-273.
[47] British Library, Additional MS, 60193, no foliation.
[48] R. Tuck, 'The civil religion of Thomas Hobbes', in N. Phillipson and Q. Skinner (eds), *Political discourse in early modern Britain* (Cambridge, 1993), pp. 120-138.

It was via Hobbes that a small sect from 'the world turned upside down' era was made serviceable for a very different age. In 1725 a Muggletonian, John Nicholls, wrote out in manuscript what he called his 'Hobbists Creed'. A few excerpts convey the flavour: 'I believe that God is almighty matter ... that it is to be decided by the civil power whether he created all things else ... that the prime law of nature in the soul of man is self-love'.[49] By the time of the American War of Independence Roger Gibson, a Muggletonian merchant bankrupted in the conflict, still hailed the war as the assertion of natural rights. He said of Muggleton's *A Divine Looking Glass* that 'Scepticks and Deists approve of it as the best System of Revealed Religion that ever they knew or heard of'.[50]

In 1679 Tomkinson had prophetically claimed the future economic advantages which would irresistibly flow from honouring liberty of conscience:

> then could men trade freely with one another and such as wher more conscionous than the Rest (being the onely Thriving people and the most wisest and Industreous of any) I say such would trade freely to the greate benefit of the Common-wealth and the Commonwealth and State would in noe land flourish but only in that where the magistrate punisheth upon the breach of the civil law and for nothing besides.[51]

The Hobbists Creed, and 'religion of trade' were now perceived as one and the same thing. For one sort of Commonwealth believer (the Muggletonians) no identification could be more desirable; for another sort (the Baxterians) nothing more repugnant.

---

[49] British Library, Additional MS, 60173, fol. 27v.
[50] British Library, Additional MS, 60234, fol. 73.
[51] British Library, Additional MS, 61093, no foliation.

Chapter 3

Toleration and the Godly Prince in Restoration England

Mark Goldie

I

By the Act of Toleration of 1689 English Protestant Dissenters achieved freedom of worship. But it was not the first time since the Restoration of monarchy in 1660 that the Dissenters had been liberated. Twice, in 1672 and 1687, toleration had been granted, but on those occasions it was the fruit of royal edicts, suspending the laws against nonconformity. The bestowal of liberty by means of Declarations of Indulgence posed profound dilemmas for Puritan consciences. Most Dissenters embraced the opportunity to worship openly, but most resisted royal pressure to defend the royal prerogative. This essay considers the few who were prepared to do so in 1672.

Because, in 1673, the House of Commons pronounced the Declaration unlawful, there has been a tendency to construe the episode as a constitutional clash between statute and prerogative.[1] Yet, while contemporaries undoubtedly raised the issue of the authority of parliament, the debate was more ecclesiological than secular. It had to do with liberty of conscience, the nature of the church, the authority of bishops, and the role of the supreme magistrate in the exercise of godly rule. This was an incident in England's long Reformation.

We first need to note the paradoxical circumstances of Restoration Dissent. The 'great persecution' was more the work of parliament than the crown. The Clarendon Code, enacted in the 1660s, was brutal: it not only enforced Anglican uniformity but also criminalised all rival religious meetings. Quakers and Baptists were jailed in their hundreds. The code culminated in the Conventicle Act of 1670, which Andrew Marvell memorably called 'the quintessence of arbitrary malice'.[2] It unleashed informers and

---

[1] A position restated in C. C. Weston and J. R. Greenberg, *Subjects and Sovereigns* (Cambridge, 1981), pp. 162-76.
[2] *The Poems and Letters of Andrew Marvell*, ed. H. M. Margoliouth, third edition, 2 vols (Oxford, 1971), 2, p. 314.

imposed crippling fines and sequestrations. Yet Charles II did not share the priorities of the Cavalier-Anglican establishment and sought conciliation. His motives were to assist Catholics and to appease Puritans. The fact that oppression was the work of parliament and liberty the gift of kings shadowed the debate over the Declaration. The deepest paradox was that some Puritans, who had been Parliamentarians during the Civil War, now defended royal ecclesiastical supremacy.

The Declaration was not unprecedented. Charles had attempted this device in 1662, but had withdrawn at the behest of parliament. The furore in 1672-3 was far greater. In 1670 he obtained a proviso in the Conventicle Act protecting his 'supremacy in ecclesiastical affairs'. In Scotland, in 1669, he secured a Supremacy Act, sacked an archbishop, and issued an Indulgence to Presbyterians.

The English Indulgence was issued on 15 March 1672. Under it, prosecutions were suspended and licences issued to Dissenters to allow meetings at stated venues, while Catholics were permitted to worship in private houses.[3] Some 1600 licences were issued, mostly to Presbyterians and Independents (as Congregationalists were still called), and to a few Baptists; the Quakers refused to apply, but were left alone. Eleven months later the king was forced to summon parliament to finance his Dutch war. The Commons speedily resolved that 'penal statutes in matters ecclesiastical cannot be suspended but by act of parliament', and on 7 March Charles cancelled the Declaration.[4] His Cabal ministry collapsed, and two of its leading members, the Earl of Shaftesbury and the Duke of Buckingham, scuttled toward the opposition. The king had buckled under the wrath of parliament, and thereafter he became a prisoner of the Cavalier Anglicans.

In public debate the topic of toleration had ignited earlier, in 1667, after the fall of the earl of Clarendon and the advent of the Cabal, a ministry anxious to amend the Clarendon Code. Attempts at legislative 'comprehension' (the readmission of moderate Puritans to the Church) and 'indulgence' (toleration of sects beyond the pale of the Church) had prompted a formidable national controversy. Sir Charles Wolseley published *Liberty of Conscience* (1668), the Independent John Owen ('Cromwell's pope') issued *Truth and Innocence Vindicated* (1669), the

[3] For the text see J. P. Kenyon (ed.), *The Stuart Constitution* (Cambridge, 1986), pp. 382-3. The fullest account remains Frank Bate, *The Declaration of Indulgence, 1672* (London, 1908).

[4] *Commons Journal*, 9, p. 252; *Lords Journal*, 12, p. 540; Historical Manuscript Commission, *9th Report, House of Lords*, p. 25.

Quaker William Penn his *Great Case of Liberty of Conscience* (1670), and John Milton, *Of True Religion* (1673), while John Locke drafted his earliest essay for toleration (1667).[5] From the Church's side, there appeared Simon Patrick's (un-) *Friendly Debate* (1668) and Samuel Parker's vitriolic assault on nonconformity and defence of the state's right to impose uniformity, *A Discourse of Ecclesiastical Politie* (1670), to which Marvell retorted with *The Rehearsal Transpros'd* (1672).[6] Claims for the rights of conscience were abetted by *politique* or 'reason of state' arguments on behalf of the economic utility of tolerating the 'sober industrious trading part of the nation'. In these debates, the *means* by which toleration might be achieved, whether by parliament or prerogative, were subordinate to the larger question of the desirability of toleration as such. Indeed, one argument in defence of the Declaration was precisely its irrelevance to the larger issue: no earthly authority could legitimately abridge the rights of conscience or suppress Christian ministry, so the Declaration merely allowed what parliament wrongly prohibited. This amounted to a recourse to natural law to justify legal nullification: parliament's laws were void, because they breached the laws of God and nature. 'The act of parliament is against the command of God: the king permits what God bids'.[7]

Subsuming the Declaration under the general cause of religious toleration could not, however, meet the need specifically to defend the crown in apparently violating statutes. A more sustained legitimation of prerogative toleration was called for, and four advocates stand out. Bulstrode Whitelocke was a Puritan lawyer, a former Parliamentarian, a member of the Republic's Council of State, and a lord in Cromwell's Upper House. In 1663 he responded to a request from the king to give a positive opinion on the crown's right to grant indulgence in religion. His memorandum was redrafted in 1672 but published posthumously in 1687 as *The King's Right of Indulgence in Spiritual Matters*, now to defend James

---

[5] See Gary De Krey, 'Rethinking the Restoration: Dissenting cases for conscience, 1667-1672', *Historical Journal*, 38 (1995), pp. 53-83; De Krey, *London and the Restoration, 1659-1683* (Cambridge, 2005), pp. 100-7, 122-3.

[6] For Parker and Marvell see, most recently, Jon Parkin, 'Liberty transpros'd: Andrew Marvell and Samuel Parker' in Warren Chernaik and Martin Dzelzainis (eds), *Marvell and Liberty* (Basingstoke, 1999).

[7] John Humfrey, *The Authority of the Magistrate about Religion* (1672), p. 28; cf. Richard Baxter, *Sacrilegious Desertion* (1672), p. 47; Philip Nye, *The King's Authority in Dispensing with Ecclesiastical Laws* (1687), pp. 14, 30; Nye, *A Discourse of Ecclesiastical Laws* (1687), pp. 9-10. For the nullity case see De Krey, 'Rethinking', pp. 79-80.

II's Declaration.[8] Philip Nye was an Independent minister who had opposed a Presbyterian settlement in the Westminster Assembly in the 1640s and had been prominent under Cromwell. Though committed to a conception of the church as a federation of voluntary gathered congregations, he also defended civil ecclesiastical governance, the duty of the magistrate to protect and regulate a gospel ministry. He was licensed under the Declaration. His tract, *The King's Authority in Dispensing with Ecclesiastical Laws*, was also published posthumously in 1687, but composed in 1672.[9] As the publishing history of Whitelocke's and Nye's works shows, their arguments were pertinent throughout the Restoration, and 1672 but one occasion for their iteration. Henry Stubbe was an idiosyncratic publicist with an intellectual trajectory which ran from Independency to Islam, via friendship with Hobbes and polemics against the Royal Society. His Puritan anticlericalism metamorphosed into a proto-Enlightenment ideal of civil religion. In 1672 he was paid by the king's minister Lord Arlington to defend the Dutch war, and his *Further Justification of the Present War* (1673) included a vindication of the Declaration.[10] Finally, John Humfrey was a minister who eschewed denominational partisanship in the 1640s, yet took Presbyterian ordination and was ejected in 1662 because he refused to accept its invalidity. Though he was licensed as a Presbyterian in 1672, he disliked the label. He campaigned persistently for comprehension of moderate nonconformists. In the backlash against the Declaration, he was briefly jailed. His key work

---

[8] British Library, Add. MS 21099, 'The King's Right to Grant Indulgence in Matters of Religion Asserted'. See *Oxford Dictionary of National Biography*; Ruth Spalding, (ed.), *The Diary of Bulstrode Whitelocke, 1605-1675* (Oxford, 1990), pp. 663-4; Spalding, *The Improbable Puritan: A Life of Bulstrode Whitelocke, 1605-1675* (London, 1975), pp. 237-8, 279. The tract is often attributed to Arthur Annesley, Earl of Anglesey. See Annabel Patterson and Martin Dzelzainis, 'Marvell and the Earl of Anglesey: a chapter in the history of reading', *Historical Journal*, 44 (2001), pp. 703-26, at 710n.

[9] *Oxford Dictionary of National Biography*. Nye pursued his themes in several further tracts: *The Lawfulness of the Oath of Supremacy* (1662, 1683), *The Best Fence Against Popery, or, A Vindication of the Power of the King in Ecclesiastical Affairs* (1686), *A Discourse of Ecclesiastical Laws, and Supremacy of the Kings of England* (1687).

[10] This drew on unpublished papers by him: 'An Inquiry into the Supremacy Spiritual of the Kings of England', 'The History of the Spiritual Supremacy', and 'An Answer unto Certain Objections Formed Against ... the Declaration': National Archives, SP 29/275/220-2. See James Jacob, *Henry Stubbe, Radical Protestantism and the Early Enlightenment* (Cambridge, 1983), ch. 6.

was *The Authority of the Magistrate about Religion* (1672).[11] These four authors did not adopt identical stances. Whitelocke and Nye were closest, the former citing works by the latter.[12] These two were concerned especially with a legal-historical defence of the royal ecclesiastical supremacy. So too was Stubbe, though he belongs among 'freethinkers' rather than Dissenters; even so, there was an affinity between Puritan and Hobbesian anticlericalism. Humfrey's concerns were distinct, directing his attention primarily to the relationship of the Declaration to his conception of the church.

II

That the king had violated statutory law was unquestionably a key claim of opponents of the Declaration. Lord Keeper Bridgeman was sacked for refusing to seal the Declaration. In the Commons' debate on the Declaration on 10 February 1673, MPs railed against the breach. When the king initially stood his ground, the Commons retorted that he was in danger of 'altering the legislative power'.[13] The frankest summary comes from the Venetian ambassador, who reported that it was said that the king acted 'arbitrarily concerning religion' and 'intended to destroy the authority' of parliament.[14]

A classic, later, exposition is Gilbert Burnet's in his *History of His Own Time*: parliament saw that 'popery and slavery lay at the bottom' of the Declaration.[15] Yet we need to be wary of retrospective Whiggery, in which events were subordinated to a narrative of 'popery and arbitrary power'. To be sure, this narrative arguably was born in 1673, in the form that would dominate the remainder of the Restoration, and this had much to do with the sudden eruption of fear of France.[16] But it was not the sole

---

[11] *Oxford Dictionary of National Biography*; see Conal Condren, *George Lawson's 'Politica' and the English Revolution* (Cambridge, 1989), ch. 12.

[12] Whitelocke, *The King's Right of Indulgence* (1687), pp. 3, 50.

[13] See Anchitell Grey, *Debates of the House of Commons, 1667-1694*, 10 vols (1763), 2, pp. 15ff; William Cobbett, (ed.), *The Parliamentary History of England*, 36 vols (1806-20), 4, pp. 518ff.

[14] *Calendar of State Papers Venetian, 1671-2*, p. 225.

[15] Gilbert Burnet, *History of His Own Time*, 2 vols (1724-34), 1, p. 346.

[16] The terms of debate were dramatically changed by Peter du Moulin's *England's Appeal* (March 1673), which forged the association between a pro-French foreign policy and the threat of popery. See K. H. D. Haley, *William of Orange and the English Opposition, 1672-1674* (Oxford, 1953).

perspective in 1672-3, and it was rapidly improvised. Burnet's own account reveals the adventitious nature of the new rhetoric. Churchmen, appalled at Charles's Declaration, cast about for arguments to destroy it. Anti-popery naturally was one, and illegality another. 'Now the pulpits were full of a new strain: popery was everywhere preached against, and the authority of the laws was much magnified'. About the Scots, Burnet was yet more pointed: 'the episcopal party, that were wont to put all authority in the king, as long as he was for them, began to talk of law. They said, the king's power was bounded by the law.'[17] Marvell likewise accused English church leaders of stirring up the pulpits. 'Upon the publication of the Declaration [they] deliver orders ... to beat up the pulpit-drums against popery.' Churchmen, he said, had been wrong-footed, for the authority of the civil magistrate, which Parker so dogmatically defended against the Dissenters, was now used 'to a purpose quite contrary to what [he] had always intended', so that Parker was now 'terribly angry with the king'.[18] Shaftesbury, too, held that the alarm about popery was cynically got up by the bishops, who sent their 'emissaries the clergy' into the pulpits; he pointed out that the Declaration allowed Catholics no more liberty than had been customarily permitted them.[19]

It was a short step from churchmen preaching against popery to MPs trumpeting the laws as the bulwark of Protestantism. The 'constitutional' point was an artefact of the Commons' debates of 1673, and it played an insignificant role in the pamphleteering of the preceding months. It is striking that the future Whig, Shaftesbury, would defend the Declaration as late as 1675. In longer Whig hindsight, of course, the 'constitutional' point would render the Declarations of 1672 and 1687 the principal causes of the condemnations of the royal 'dispensing' and 'suspending' powers that were enshrined in the Bill of Rights of 1689. Yet even Lord Macaulay, who wanted to call the Declarations 'despotic', conceded the legal ambiguity of the crown's position, and allowed that it was because the prerogative was used for an abhorrent purpose, to promote popery, that rejection

---

[17] Burnet, *History*, 1, pp. 308, 283.

[18] *The Rehearsal Transpros'd*, in *The Prose Works of Andrew Marvell*, ed. Annabel Patterson, Martin Dzelzainis, N. H. Keeble and Nicholas von Maltzahn, 2 vols (New Haven, 2003), 1, pp. 123, 175. For an assault on the popish implications of the Declaration see William Lloyd, *A Seasonable Discourse* (1673).

[19] *A Letter from a Person of Quality* (1675) in John Locke, *An Essay Concerning Toleration and Other Writings*, ed. J. R. Milton and Philip Milton (Oxford, 2006), pp. 344, 343. Locke is often credited with a share in this tract.

of it became a constitutional principle.[20] The English 'constitution' was always an artifice generated by political and religious contingencies.

As several historians have shown, a weight of legal opinion held that the crown had a power to dispense with laws *pro bono publico*, a fact recognised in the Bill of Rights which, in condemning the dispensing power, added the caveat, 'as it has been assumed and exercised of late'.[21] For centuries the crown had issued dispensations, '*non obstante*' ('notwithstanding') laws to the contrary, to exempt individuals from ecclesiastical and economic legislation. It is true that the Declaration was charged with a more fundamental, wholesale suspension of laws, and the Bill of Rights would enter no caveat concerning the 'suspending' power. Yet the Declaration did not assert any claim to suspend laws, only to suspend the execution of laws, arguably a significant distinction. The crown's defenders urged that the Declaration was not a legislative act of repeal, but an executive act of mitigation of penalties. Accordingly, it fell within the crown's conventional prerogative of clemency. The crown routinely pardoned criminals and ameliorated the severity of punishments, without any suspicion that this nullified the laws. To pardon a traitor was not to repeal the law of treason. The Declaration should therefore be construed as an act of general dispensation. There was plausibility in this notion that the Declaration suspended penalties, not laws, for this was precisely what the Toleration Act of 1689 would later do, for its proper title is 'An Act Exempting their Majesties Protestant Subjects, Dissenting from the Church of England, from the Penalties of Certain Laws'. It was not a toleration act so much as a statutory indulgence.[22]

The crown's Dissenting supporters took up this theme. Whitelocke defined the Declaration as 'a relaxation of punishment', 'a grant of the prince's clemency, by which a subject is freed from punishment'.[23] Shaftesbury likewise insisted that the 'executive power [must be] fully

---

[20] Lord Macaulay, *The History of England*, 2 vols (London, 1889), 1, pp. 108-9.

[21] See especially Lois Schwoerer, *The Declaration of Rights, 1689* (Baltimore, 1981), pp. 59-64; Paul Birdsall, '"Non Obstante": a study of the dispensing power of English kings' in Carl Wittke, (ed.), *Essays in History and Political Theory* (Cambridge, MA, 1936); Caroline Edie, 'Tactics and stratagems: parliament's attack upon the royal dispensing power, 1597-1689', *American Journal of Legal History*, 29 (1985), pp. 197-234; E. F. Churchill, 'The dispensing power of the crown in ecclesiastical affairs', *Law Quarterly Review*, 38 (1922), pp. 297-316, 420-34.

[22] As also into a draft bill of March 1673 to allow the king to suspend the execution of statutes for five years: Historical Manuscript Commission, *9th Report, House of Lords*, p. 25.

[23] Whitelocke, *King's Right*, pp. 2, 53.

enabled to mitigate, or wholly to suspend, the execution of any penal law'.[24] Nye had a chapter headed, 'Our Relief is from the Jurisdiction and Power in his Majesty, to Dispense and Exempt', and he held that the Declaration only 'remit[ted] the penalty or punishment'. He distinguished legislative from executive power: all that was at issue was the executive power of 'mitigating, exempting, dispensing, licensing, pardoning', out of mercy or equity, or for the public good in exigent cases. Nobody supposed, he said, that laws should always be 'executed in their full rigour'. Discretion and prudence should govern enforcement, and ordinary experience showed that magistrates never attempted to enforce every statute. They did not do so against Catholics, against whom there was a battery of savage laws. They did not do so, he lamented, against profanity and immorality. To single out the Dissenters for plenary enforcement was a misguided and vindictive piece of penal policy.[25] In these arguments there emerged a strong Puritan 'antiformalist' concern that the civil magistrate should pay more attention to enforcing laws against licentiousness than against nonconformist worship. 'Holy living' mattered more than the formalities of religious rituals and rubrics.[26]

In light of the argument for executive suspension of penalties, the Dissenters justified the Declaration as an act of royal mercy. In some cases, this evoked highflown paeans of gratitude. The egregious verses of the Presbyterian poet Robert Wild achieved notoriety, if only because made risible by rival Anglican versifiers.

> So great, so universal, and so free!
> This was too much, great Charles, except for thee!'[27]

Slight though the panegyric mode seems, the accent on clemency as a cardinal virtue of princes ran deep. The early-modern penal regime was one of harsh laws but also of selective enforcement, and the role of mercy

---

[24] Shaftesbury, *Letter*, in Locke, *Essay*, pp. 341-2.

[25] Nye, *King's Authority*, pp. 2-3, 10-11, 19; cf. Nye, *Discourse*, pp. 2-3, 21, 23.

[26] The Puritan concern with the failure to punish immorality was strong: Nicholas Lockyer, *Some Seasonable and Serious Queries* (1670), p. 12; Henry Stubbe, *Further Justification of the Present War* (1673), p. 67. The anti-formalist theme is richly illuminated in J. C. Davis, 'Against formality: one aspect of the English Revolution', *Transactions of the Royal Historical Society*, 3 (1993), pp. 265-88.

[27] *Dr Wild's Humble Thanks for his Majesties Gracious Declaration* (1672), which provoked a series of poetic responses.

was large. Clemency was the theme in the formal addresses of thanks to the king, such as that of John Owen, as well as in remarks in surviving diaries of preachers, who, like Thomas Jolly, was simply grateful 'for what the Lord had done by the king'. Whatever the 'secret springs' of the Declaration, wrote Matthew Henry, for the 'poor Dissenters' it was a return to 'life from the dead, and gave them some reviving in their bondage'.[28]

The principal voice of the Church against the Declaration was the archdeacon of Totnes, Francis Fullwood.[29] He did not argue that the Declaration was illegal. On the contrary, he accepted the case for suspension rather than repeal, and maintained thereby that the Declaration offered limited concessions and remained consonant with the laws for uniformity. He read the Declaration in ways favourable to the Church, in order to draw its sting. 'The Declaration doth directly ... acknowledge that the Church of England is established by law'. The Declaration states that the Church is the 'standard of the general and public worship' and is to be 'preserved, and remain entire in its doctrine, discipline, and government'. To 'indulge' or 'tolerate' is not to approve or establish. The king had not sanctioned Dissent but merely permitted it, out of clemency and reason of state. 'In this Declaration the king doth not command anything contrary to the statutes'; he 'doth not ... uncommand or unenjoin anything which the law properly commands or enjoins'. Nothing in the Declaration warrants 'separations, or alter[s] their evil nature'. Through the course of several tracts, Fullwood, a passionate enemy of the Declaration, declined to argue that it was illegal: what roused his wrath was the 'sin' of Dissenting schism.[30] His position would be echoed by post-Revolution high churchmen, who argued that the Act of Toleration did not *authorise* Dissent, but merely showed clemency to schismatics.

Both friends and enemies of the Declaration construed it as a threat to the Church of England and its bishops, rather than to parliament and legislators. The Declaration is 'an extreme weakening of the Church of England

---

[28] Bate, *Declaration of Indulgence*, pp. 92-93, and appx 5; *The Notebook of Thomas Jolly*, ed. H. Fishwick (Manchester, 1894), pp. 10-11; Matthew Henry, *The Life of the Rev. Philip Henry*, (ed.), J. B. Williams (London, 1825), p. 128; *Calendar of State Papers Domestic, 1671-2*, pp. 332, 355, 527; cf. John Salkeld, *The Resurrection of Lazarus* (1673); *Vindiciae libertatis evangelii* (1672), pp. 7-14.

[29] Francis Fullwood, *Toleration not to be Abused* (1672); *The Doctrine of Schism* (1672); *Humble Advice* (1672); *The Necessity of Keeping our Parish Churches* (1672).

[30] Fullwood, *Toleration*, pp. 13-14, 17.

and its episcopal government', wrote John Evelyn.[31] 'If this Declaration signifies anything, the Church of England signifies nothing', said Edward Vaughan.[32] Just as Fullwood tried to mitigate the threat to the Church, so the more conciliatory Dissenters took the same tack, insisting it was absurd to suppose that the Declaration undermined the Church, for it remained secure in its wealth, privileges, benefices, and jurisdictions. Not only had the king said that the Church remained the 'rule and standard', but also he had styled the Dissenters' assemblies 'conventicles', not churches, and their pastors 'teachers', not ministers; the Dissenters were furthermore forbidden to preach against the doctrine and discipline of the Church.[33] And, indeed, Dissenters complained that licences were refused for public places like guildhalls and disused chapels.[34]

Other Dissenters, however, were more aggressive and saw the Declaration as a salutary restraint upon ecclesiastical tyranny. In the pamphlets of 1672 the greatest passions were aroused over ecclesiastical and not legislative power. Humfrey was glad that the king's 'kind act' would 'nettle' the churchmen; he spoke of 'episcopal bigots' worshipping their 'god of ... uniformity': 'blind, obstinate, perverse'. Stubbe wrote of the 'modern dictators of ecclesiastical policy'.[35] Owen rehearsed the 'severe and destructive penalties' by which the prelates pressed conformity 'to the utmost punctilio'. The king's 'noble' disposition toward indulgence ought not to be 'sacrificed to the interests of any one party' and to the cruelties of 'ecclesiastical censures'.[36] The Conventicle Act was a special source of animus. Nicholas Lockyer, formerly chaplain to Cromwell, asserted that the Act was driven 'by the bishops and their corrupt interest' and that parliament succumbed to doing the 'drudgery

[31] *The Diary of John Evelyn*, ed. E. S. De Beer (London, 2006), p. 515.

[32] Grey, *Debates*, 2, p. 21.

[33] Nye, *King's Authority*, p. 46; Stubbe, *Further Justification*, pp. 64-68; cf. *The Judgement of a Good Subject* (1672); Nye, *Discourse*, p. 23.

[34] *Calendar of State Papers Domestic, 1671-2*, pp. 372, 381-2.

[35] Humfrey, *Authority*, pp. 10-11, 14, 37; Stubbe, *Further Justification*, p. 69. However, for Stubbe's *politique* defence of a national clergy as a check on popular anarchy, see *Rosemary and Bayes* (1672), pp. 18-19; Jacob, *Stubbe*, ch. 6. A sub-theme in these debates was the notion that a ruler needed either a clergy or a standing army to overawe the people, and that the former was preferable. Stubbe argued so. The *Letter* (1668) suggested that toleration would require a standing army, pp. 5, 9. Bishops Morley and Sheldon feared the king might displace their influence with an army: John Miller, *After the Civil Wars* (Harlow, 2000), p. 211.

[36] John Owen, *Works*, ed. W. H. Goold, 15 vols (London, 1966), 13, pp. 519-22, 534-5, 523.

of the bishops'. He vilified 'the prelatical interest', 'the bishops' cruel courts ... backing the Common Prayer with armies'. Would that parliament had legislated instead against 'the sordid ignorance, pride, sloth, debauchery and covetousness of the clergy'. Lockyer's tone was agonistic and exilic. The Dissenters were as the Israelites, in bondage under Egyptian taskmasters; they cried to God for deliverance and, by the hand of a king, were succoured.[37] Robert Wild pointed to the resentment of 'angry churchmen', now that 'their younger brother Joseph go[es] in [a] coat of divers colours'. Religion had been 'rescued from informing laws', and each Sunday the furious Anglican clergy 'spit' as they utter the prayer for the monarch. 'Thy canting tribe, be gone.'[38] The king's contribution to this anticlerical assault was to allow publication of Marvell's *Rehearsal Transpros'd*, as a rebuke to Parker's attack on the Declaration.[39]

The anticlerical animus had become intense after the fall of Clarendon and was encouraged by the Cabal ministers, Buckingham, Arlington, and Ashley (the future earl of Shaftesbury). During Buckingham's ascendancy in 1667-9 there was much sabre-rattling against the hierarchy. Charles himself encouraged enmity against the bishops. 'The king', wrote Burnet, 'was much offended with the bishops' and professed to be 'disgusted at the ambition, covetousness, and the scandals of the clergy'.[40] Pepys recorded that government ministers 'vilify the clergy', that the ministers 'will sacrifice the church' and that 'the bishops must certainly fall, and their hierarchy'. There was talk of expropriating episcopal wealth, as the Puritans had done in the 1640s, and of reducing bishops to taking 'salaries out of the Exchequer', in other words turning them into dependent civil servants.[41] Among Shaftesbury's papers there survive two memoranda, dating from about 1670. One rehearses arguments that ecclesiastical jurisdiction lies in the monarch and not the clergy. The other proposes that the king should 'recover' his ecclesiastical supremacy by appointing a Vicar-General to govern and reform the

---

[37] Lockyer, *Some Seasonable*, pp. 11-16.

[38] *Dr Wild's Humble Thanks*; Wild, *A Letter* (1672), p. 4.

[39] Historical Manuscript Commission, *7th Report*, p. 518; Patterson and Dzelzainis, 'Marvell and Anglesey', p. 708. Parker's coded attack on the Declaration occurs in his Preface to *Bishop Bramhall's Vindication* (1672).

[40] Burnet, *History*, p. 258.

[41] *The Diary of Samuel Pepys*, ed. Robert Latham and William Matthews, 11 vols (1971-83), 8, pp. 532, 584, 587, 596; 9, pp. 1, 36, 45, 347, 448, 473, 485; *Calendar of State Papers Domestic, 1667-8*, p. 238; 1668-9, p. 320.

church, and 'chastise ... that clergy which hath so much opposed his conduct of late'.[42]

III

The Declaration was held to derive its legitimacy not only from the general prerogative of clemency but also from the special authority of the royal ecclesiastical supremacy. The location of the supremacy had remained deeply ambiguous since the Reformation. That ecclesiastical authority did not lie with Rome was clear enough; where it lay within Protestant England was opaque. Several claims had been advanced: royal, parliamentary, episcopal.[43] Parliament had frequently legislated for religion, but, equally, monarchs had personally governed in religion, for they had issued directions for preachers, injunctions and articles of visitation, and given authority to church canons. The Declaration referred to the 'supreme power in ecclesiastical matters, which is not only inherent in us, but hath been declared and recognised to be so by several statutes'. The prime authorities were the statutory Oath of Supremacy and the monarch's title as 'supreme governor' of the Church. The defenders of the Declaration paraded precedents for the exercise of personal governorship, citing instances of long accepted royal exemptions of persons and groups from religious laws. The most prominent examples were the liberties granted, since Queen Elizabeth's time, to 'stranger' churches, the Huguenot, Walloon, and Dutch. In London, Norwich, and Canterbury there were flourishing congregations of non-Anglican worshippers, exempt from parish and episcopal authority. Likewise, the permission granted since Cromwell's time for Jewish worship. Moreover, Elizabeth had indulged Catholic priests, and in 1586 issued an instruction to suspend enforcement of the recusancy laws. On the Puritan side, she had been lenient over Prayer Book rubrics, to ease vestiarian objections. Monarchs had allowed Catholic chapels for their consorts, and most of the seventeenth century had seen leniency in the enforcement of anti-Catholic laws. The history of the royal ecclesiastical supremacy was therefore one of royal 'exemptions, licences, faculties,

---

[42] National Archives, PRO 30/24/6B/427 and 430. One is endorsed by Locke, who has sometimes erroneously been said to be the author.

[43] See Jacqueline Rose, '"Kings shall be thy nursing fathers": Royal ecclesiastical supremacy and the Restoration church', *Historical Research* (forthcoming).

dispensations, *non obstantes*'.⁴⁴

For Whitelocke, the context to which this argument belonged was anti-papal. He placed the supremacy within a grand survey of royal curbs upon papal and prelatical pretensions down the centuries, by French, Spanish, and Hungarian kings as much as by English, signalled especially in their right to make bishops. Kings everywhere, at least those who understood their proper estate, had conferred the pastoral insignia upon bishops, in defiance of the papacy. The tradition of Gallican anti-papalism is prominent here, Whitelocke citing the Pragmatic Sanction of 1438, and the fifteenth-century conciliarist theorist Jean Gerson. The English Henrician repudiation of Rome became, not a pivotal moment, but one incident among many, and no break with antipapal tradition. Henry VIII had followed Henry II, who challenged Becket, and Edward III, who outlawed *praemunire*. Curiously, in this mindset there was a strong sense of the continuity of Christendom, not radically disrupted by the Reformation and its theological differences but, rather, divided much earlier, over jurisdiction, between papalists and anti-papalists. It was an argument directed toward the subordination of priestly pretensions generally. What mattered about the crown's supremacy was that it was *lay* and *secular*, and to deny it amounted to clerical and popish usurpation.⁴⁵

This 'magisterial' strain in English Puritanism, its faith in the godly prince as the agent of pastoral reform, was deeply ingrained, though the Restoration saw its final phase, for it would give way, on the one hand, to despair at the Stuart propensity to embrace popery, and, on the other, to the argument, embraced initially by Independents and by Locke, that the state had no business in religion. The magisterial theme has been called the theory of 'Protestant imperialism', and it was present in the thinking of Marvell and Richard Baxter.⁴⁶ It was influenced by Foxe's *Book of Martyrs*, which set the suffering of the Protestant martyrs in the context of England's providential mission to overthrow papal monarchy. Whitelocke

---

⁴⁴ Whitelocke, *King's Right*, *passim*; quotations at p. 41; Nye, *King's Authority*, pp. 10, 19-21, 25, 40, 60-64; Burnet, *History*, p. 347; cf. Nye, *Discourse*, pp. 14, 35-37; Grey, *Debates*, 2, p. 14; Churchill, 'Dispensing Power', p. 423.

⁴⁵ Whitelocke, *King's Right*, pp. 22-34; Stubbe, *Further Justification*, p. 32.

⁴⁶ William Lamont, *Richard Baxter and the Millennium* (London, 1979); Lamont, *Marginal Prynne* (London, 1963), chs 7, 11; Lamont, 'The religion of Andrew Marvell' in Conal Condren and A. D. Cousins (eds), *The Political Identity of Andrew Marvell* (Aldershot, 1990). Prynne's final work had been the thousand page *Exact Chronological Vindication [of the] King's Supreme Ecclesiastical Jurisdiction* (1665-6).

invoked the Foxean *translatio Christi*: the transmission of Christianity to England by Joseph of Arimathea, who planted a fragment of the Cross at Glastonbury. This in turn validated the *translatio imperii*, the repatriation of the imperial sovereignty that the medieval papacy usurped. The iconic figure of the Emperor Constantine stood as the principal emblem of the godly prince. Defenders of the Declaration regularly invoked Constantine. Stubbe wrote that Charles II 'revives the primitive policy of Constantine'.[47] Other early Christian emperors were cited too, for the Declaration was said to be 'exactly consonant with the edicts of Theodosius the Great'.[48]

Some defenders of the Declaration went further and asserted the quasi-sacerdotal character of kingship. Whitelocke argued that 'the king is a mixed person', ecclesiastical as well as lay; Stubbe that Charles 'acteth like a bishop'.[49] Whitelocke held that originally the offices of king and priest were identical and only with the passage of time had the priesthood become a distinct caste. Adam instructed his sons to make sacrifices to God; Noah, Abraham, and the patriarchs were priests as well as lay leaders; Moses, Joshua, David, and Hezekiah sacrificed at the altar; Deborah was prophetess as well as queen. The early Christian emperors, particularly Constantine, had summoned and presided over Church councils. Anglo-Saxon kings had exercised sacerdotal office: Edgar and Canute had made canons and instructed and admonished the clergy. When sacerdotal functions were delegated by kings to priests, the latter were apt to believe that these offices belonged inherently and exclusively to themselves: this misconception was the mainspring of priestly pretensions. This argument took sustenance from the sages of the common law, in their admonitions against the jurisdiction of the church courts. Whitelocke cited Sir John Davies for the view that jurisdiction over marital and testamentary matters had once belonged to the civil courts until usurped by the ecclesiastical.[50] Shaftesbury's memoranda argued that ecclesiastical jurisdiction fundamentally lay not 'in the clergy but magistracy', that princes 'entrust' bishops with it, 'as favours derived to them from the crown', and that they 'might have given it (if they had so pleased) to justices of the peace'. It was 'a great mistake' to hold that 'all the power in scriptures given to the

---

[47] Stubbe, *Further Justification*, pp. 32-35, quotation at p. 32.

[48] Stubbe, *Further Justification*, pp. 59, 67; cf. Humfrey, *Authority*, pp. 124-6; Grey, *Debates*, 2, p. 15. On 'Constantinian Christianity' see Jacob, *Stubbe*, chs 6-7.

[49] Whitelocke, *King's Right*, pp. 32, 35, 37; Stubbe, *Further Justification*, p. 32; cf. Stubbe, *Rosemary and Bayes*, p. 3.

[50] Whitelocke, *King's Right*, pp. 18-20, 25-27, 31, 37.

Church was construed of the clergy'.[51]

Whitelocke did not confine his argument to the Judaeo-Christian dispensation, for he broadened it into a universal anthropology. The Greek, Persian, and Chaldean rulers had been priest-kings, and Aristotle wrote that, anciently, kings sacrificed to the gods. The pagan Roman emperors 'joined the pontifical authority with the caesarian power', and 'our British kings were supreme over the Druids'.[52] There was special point in appealing beyond the Christian dispensation. Faced with a king like Charles II, it was important to intimate that godly magistracy may be exercised by a less than godly monarch. A favourite citation was of King Cyrus. In the Book of Chronicles, this Persian conqueror of Babylon invited the Jews to rebuild the temple at Jerusalem. Thus, even a heathen prince could be God's instrument.[53] It was an impudent instance, but lent credibility to the general case, by diminishing the apparent naivety of the Dissenters' lauding of Charles, for there was an acknowledged irony in praising godly princes in the presence of a libertine monarch. The Cyrus motif would become even more popular in 1687 when Dissenters thanked the Catholic James II for his Declaration.

In pursuit of a universal anthropology of sacral kingship, the defenders of the Declaration moved beyond the ambit of anti-papal Puritanism. The tradition of 'Protestant imperialism' would find a future after all, transmuted into Enlightenment theories of civil religion and critiques of priestcraft.[54] There are parallels with Hobbes, whose account of religion, and deflation of all priestly pretensions, can be construed within the frames both of Protestant imperialism and Enlightenment anticlericalism. Stubbe admired Hobbes, and his defence of the Declaration stands poised between those readings. Neither he nor Whitelocke dared cite Hobbes, but their case for the godly prince recollects the frontispiece of *Leviathan*, where the prince carries the sceptre in one hand and the pastoral staff in the other. They referred instead to John Selden, whose impact on English anticlericalism was considerable.[55] That Hobbes could be useful to the Dissenting cause, though not publicly admitted, was clear to one

---

[51] National Archive, PRO 30/24/6/430.

[52] Whitelocke, *King's Right*, pp. 20, 25.

[53] 2 Chronicles 36:22-3; Ezra 1:1-4, Isaiah 44:28; Humfrey, *Authority*, pp. 13, 97; Wild, *Letter*, p. 6; *Vindiciae*, p. 11.

[54] See Mark Goldie, 'Priestcraft and the birth of Whiggism' in Nicholas Phillipson and Quentin Skinner (eds), *Political Discourse in Early Modern Britain* (Cambridge, 1993).

[55] Whitelocke, *King's Right*, p. 69; Stubbe, *Further Justification*, pp. 33, 38.

contemporary, the Huguenot emigré Louis du Moulin, whose conviction was that 'all church power is popery' and who prayed that 'toleration will be the downfall of the hierarchy'. Du Moulin had earlier published in defence of Cromwell's religious settlement. He was never much interested in 'constitutional' questions: his priority was saving the secular commonwealth from churchmen. He drew upon the Erastian tradition of Marsilius, Grotius, Selden, and Hobbes, and argued that since it was never in the interests of churchmen to diminish their own power, God had chosen lay philosophers as instruments in the evangelical task of stripping naked the priestly Whore of Babylon. He wrote to Baxter that, as to the truth about church power, God had 'strangely discoursed [it] ... first to Erastus, a physician ... laying open the grand cheat of ecclesiastical jurisdiction ... and, which is a greater shame to the ecclesiastical order ... hath permitted that men [as] ill-principled as Grotius and Selden, yea Hobbes as bad as can be, should come nearer the truth than many good men'.[56]

A more cautious case was presented by Humfrey, who was careful to say that kings are not priests, but equally clear that kings have pastoral responsibilities. Kings are earthly 'keepers of the Tables', tasked with 'protecting', 'promoting', and 'disciplining' the Church. As they command in civil things for the good of the commonwealth, so they command 'in ecclesiasticals for our spiritual edification'. Monarchs are obliged to ensure that the people are instructed and the Word preached. Humfrey's task was delicate. He must show that, despite the king's ecclesiastical power, the king must not coerce people of tender conscience. He deplored Parker's crushing of liberty of conscience by right of the magistrate. He insisted that to defend the Declaration is not to defend the state's coercive authority over the externals of religion, for the Declaration is permissive. It is Parker who has 'fallen in with Mr Hobbes' and with those who teach there is 'no God but Leviathan only'. (Hobbes was variously interpreted in this controversy: here the reading is of an intolerant, rather than du Moulin's anticlerical, even tolerant, Hobbes.) Humfrey had also to disabuse critics who accused him of being excessively permissive in his tolerance: a godly Quaker should be indulged, he held, but not people who spurn godliness altogether, for 'the magistrate may punish those that keep from church out of irreligion'.

---

[56] Dr Williams' Library, London: Baxter Letters 5, fos. 192 (c. March 1670); cf. *Calendar of the Correspondence of Richard Baxter*, comp. N. H. Keeble and Geoffrey F. Nuttall, 2 vols (Oxford, 1991), 2, p. 85. For du Moulin, see Mark Goldie, 'The Huguenot experience and the problem of toleration in Restoration England' in C. E. J. Caldicott, H. Gough, and J-P. Pittion (eds), *The Huguenots and Ireland* (Dublin, 1987), pp. 175-203.

Humfrey's acknowledged guide was Grotius, chiefly the *De imperio summarum potestatum circa sacra* (1648) but also *De jure belli* (1625). Grotius provided the acceptable face of the theory of the godly prince, and Humfrey's enthusiasm for 'that learned and judicious man' was considerable. Unlike Hobbes, Grotius had been careful of distinctions. The prince was but the 'civil' head of the church and not the 'constitutive', and was concerned only with 'external regiment'.[57] In Humfrey, the claims of private conscience and the powers of the godly prince were finely balanced.

IV

For the Presbyterians, who were the most conspicuous body among the Dissenters, a principal anxiety of conscience in 1672 concerned the issue of schism. They were committed to the principle of a national, uniform church, and were hostile to separatism. In this, they shared the ecclesiology of the Anglicans, and were heirs to the non-sectarian Puritanism of Elizabethan times. They saw themselves as belonging to the Church of England, and only for particular and temporary reasons detached from it. Since their ejection in 1662, most Presbyterian ministers had striven to avoid separation, by attending parish churches and by holding their religious meetings 'out of church time', so as to avoid setting up 'altar against altar'. They were sensitive to the charge of schism and distinguished themselves from the 'independency' of the sects. Their hopes for reform rested more on comprehension within the Church than toleration outside it.

Yet now the king invited them to take out licences for independent congregations. It was not the royal prerogative, but fear of the 'sin of separation' that weighed heavily. Baxter, the doyen among them, was reluctant to take out a licence, because he demurred at the requirement to state what denomination he was of, 'the name of some sect'. But he finally made an application, refusing to denominate himself. He was, he said, 'merely Christian', though 'Protestant' in repudiating Rome, and no 'Presbyterian', for he did not reject episcopacy in its pure 'primitive' form. Only on these terms did he 'humbly crave his majesty licence to preach the gospel, with a *non obstante* to my nonconformity'.[58] The same tension is visible in the

---

[57] Humfrey, *Authority*, pp. 38-40, 44, 67, 103, 128; on Grotius, pp. 36, 40, 43, 95, 128-9; cf. pp. 23, 34-35, 97, 129; *Vindiciae, passim*.

[58] Baxter, *Correspondence*, 2, p. 140.

diary of Philip Henry: 'the danger is ... lest the allowing of separate places help to overthrow our parish order, which God hath owned ... We are put hereby into a trilemma, either to turn Independents in practice, or to strike in with the conformists, or to sit down in former silence and sufferings'.[59]

Not all Presbyterians took such a firm line against separatism. A younger generation of ministers was prepared to be less deferential toward the national church. The experience of ejection and persecution schooled them in quasi-independency, and they were prepared to entertain a denominational future outside the Church. One reason why the king issued the Declaration was that his advisers detected a growing rift in the Presbyterian ranks. Sir Joseph Williamson reported that the younger ministers, nicknamed the 'Ducklings', were at odds with the older, the 'Dons', for they wished to reorientate the Presbyterians: some 'Presbyterians are growing to Independents'. The Dons included Baxter, William Bates, and Thomas Manton, while the Ducklings numbered Vincent Alsop and Samuel Annesley.[60]

Anglican churchmen eagerly exploited the Presbyterians' dilemma. They charged that by accepting the Declaration they had become sectarians. A sheaf of tracts chorused the accusation of schism and separation, and, because Baxter took out a licence, the Dons were not exempt. Fullwood was quick to point to this 'sacrilegious desertion' by the 'prelate of nonconformity'. In his *Doctrine of Schism*, he had little to say about the prerogative, for the 'general question' was 'whether it be lawful for the presbyters to refuse communion with our parish churches, and to gather themselves into distinct and separate churches'. He complained of the 'rash and sudden' manner in which the Dissenters established new congregations, or 'anti-churches', in open competition with parish churches. Presbyterians had long taught, he pointed out, the unity of church communion, but were now reneging.[61] A principal strategy of the Anglicans was to demonstrate that the Presbyterians of the 1640s had been deeply hostile to toleration. They reprinted extracts from Presbyterian tracts, and it was not difficult to assemble a parade of Puritans who had vilified the sects. This was the main thrust of Fullwood's *Toleration not to be Abused*. 'They stated toleration intolerable'. Therefore, 'to gather them-

---

[59] *Life of Henry*, pp. 128-9.

[60] *Calendar of State Papers Domestic 1671*, p. 496; 1671-2, p. 28. See Robert Beddard, 'Vincent Alsop and the emancipation of Restoration Dissent', *Journal of Ecclesiastical History*, 24 (1973), pp. 161-84.

[61] Fullwood, *Doctrine of Schism*, pp. 2-3, 32-40, 102, 107; cf. Fullwood, *Humble Advice*.

selves into distinct and separate congregations is a practice unlawful in the judgement of the Presbyterians themselves'.[62]

Independents, Baptists, and Quakers had reason to be suspicious of the Presbyterians as double-dealers. These groups had no interest in comprehension and so were more ready to cleave to the religious pluralism that the Declaration offered. The more radical the Puritan, the more likely they were to accept the Declaration. (This phenomenon would be especially pronounced in 1687 when the Quakers became the most enthusiastic supporters of James II's Indulgence.) Their fear was that, if comprehension were achieved, then the Presbyterians readmitted to the Church would quickly behave just as they had done in the 1640s: they would be as anti-tolerationist as their Anglican brethren and seek to suppress the sects. In fact, some churchmen were already in this position, for they were former Presbyterians who had accepted the re-establishment in 1662. Fullwood was one such, his arguments for 'Anglican' uniformity essentially those of his earlier Presbyterian self: old Calvinist ecclesiology could easily look like Anglican 'high churchmanship'. Similarly, some supporters of the Church were willing to countenance comprehension since, by neutralising the Presbyterians, it would make the suppression of the sects easier. The Anglican Edward Seymour told the Commons in 1668 that he was 'for comprehension ... and so an end of nonconformity'.[63]

All this poses a large, unresolved question about the Presbyterians. When and how did they detach themselves from their intolerance of the 1640s? This is both a sociological question about their institutional transition from 'church type' to 'sect type', and an ideological one about their embrace of tolerationist principles. Humfrey, for one, remarked of the generation of the 1640s that 'they are dead', and he was clear that, though he distinguished two sorts of Dissenter, and though he wanted comprehension for his own sort, he embraced indulgence for others, and deplored

---

[62] Fullwood, *Toleration*, pp. 2, 6, 9, 11; cf. Fullwood, *Doctrine of Schism*. The theme was taken up by Parker in his Preface to *Bramhall's Vindication*, and in several anonymous tracts: *Indulgence unto Dissent* (1673); *Toleration Disapproved* (1672); *The Nonconformist's Plea for Uniformity* (1674); *Speculum Baxterianum* (1680; written 1672).

[63] *Parliamentary History*, 4, p. 416. See Richard Ashcraft, 'Latitudinarianism and toleration' in R. Kroll, R. Ashcraft, and P. Zagorin (eds), *Philosophy, Science, and Religion in England, 1640-1700* (Cambridge, 1992). Ever alert to reasons of state, Stubbe suggested that the Declaration might force the Presbyterians back toward Anglicanism. 'Being indiscriminately mixed in such a loathsome company and character [as the sects], may operate upon the minds of many to abate of their preciseness' (*Further Justification*, p. 64).

the treatment of the Independent Owen and the Baptist William Kiffin.[64] Yet it is not clear that others were as forward as he. Baxter averred that 'it was the toleration of all sects unlimitedly that I wrote and preached against'.[65] And Adam Martindale remarked that 'I did so little like an universal toleration, that ... if the king had offered me my liberty, upon condition that I would consent that papists, Quakers, and all other wicked sects should have theirs also, I think I should never have agreed to it'.[66]

One answer to the accusation of schism was to put the case for the Declaration in pastoral terms. Presbyterians argued that in taking out licences they offered no challenge to the unity and structure of the established Church. Rather, they augmented the Church's provision for preaching and its mission to inspire godliness in their common flock. Parishes, they urged, were often undermanned and overstretched, a condition exacerbated by the scandal of clerical pluralism and absenteeism. For Puritan clergy to supply an additional afternoon sermon in a populous city parish, or a meeting for worship in an outlying rural hamlet, was nothing so dramatic as 'schism' or the 'setting up of a new religion', but merely an addition to the Church's evangelical mission. We do not, wrote Humfrey, gather congregations out of competition, strife, or vainglory, but because there is a spiritual hunger. Philip Henry likewise justified his use of the Declaration by arguing that 'he looked upon himself but as an assistant to the parish ministers'.[67] This 'semi-parochialism' acquired plausibility from the evident fact that in the cities people 'gadded' to sermons, going in search of preachers who suited them, regardless of parish boundaries and denominational identities.

It was possible to extend this pastoral argument by suggesting that the Indulgence amounted to an informal comprehension. According to Humfrey, by licensing ministers, the king 'does incorporate them as integral parts ... with those of the parochial constitution, into the church national'. Presbyterian congregations thereby became quasi-parishes, their ministers having 'the same authority as the parish priest'. 'Those particular assemblies, having the authority of the supreme head of the church, equally with the parish churches, they are manifestly constituted thereby parts of the church national'.[68] This was Baxter's view: licensed congrega-

---

[64] Humfrey, *Authority*, pp. 11, 96.

[65] Richard Baxter, *Reliquiae Baxterianae* (1696), 3, p. 131.

[66] *The Life of Adam Martindale*, ed. Richard Parkinson (Manchester, 1845), p. 198. Nonetheless, he took out a licence.

[67] Humfrey, *Authority*, pp. 25, 56; *Life of Henry*, p. 132; cf. Baxter, *Sacrilegious Desertion*, pp. 11-12.

[68] Humfrey, *Authority*, pp. 24, 27. The point is made in De Krey, *London*, p. 122.

tions are 'parts of the parish church' and their preachers were 'chapel curates'.[69] He devoted his *Sacrilegious Desertion* (1672) to pressing the pastoral case: this was a tract prompted by the Declaration, but his worries had nothing to do with prerogative, parliamentary authority, or even the royal supremacy, and everything to do with avoiding the sins of schism and separation.

The Declaration of Indulgence indubitably provoked a crisis of conscience among the Dissenters, but it was a crisis in ecclesiology, in theories about the nature of Christ's church and the proper role and limits of the godly prince.

---

[69] Baxter, *Sacrilegious Desertion*, pp. 35, 91; cf. *Life of Henry*, p. 129.

Chapter 4

England's Houdini: Charles II's escape from Worcester as a metaphor for his reign

Jonathan Scott

What we want is born of what we want to get away from.[1]
(Adam Phillips, *Houdini's Box: on the Arts of Escape*)

I

In *Houdini's Box: on the Arts of Escape*, Adam Phillips considers four great escapists. These people achieve their sense of freedom, or of self, in the process of escaping some place of confinement. Such people have two characteristics of particular interest. One is that in order to achieve their desired experience of escaping, equal ingenuity is necessary in constructing the circumstances of imprisonment from which it is their destiny to flee. The second is the element of repetition necessarily introduced by this compulsion: there is no such thing as a Houdini who only escaped once.

Neither historians nor contemporaries seem to have been concerned that from the moment of his return to the throne of his ancestors Charles II told and retold the story of his escape from the Battle of Worcester in 1651. That famous oak tree was or became a symbol of Englishness, inspirational of rural pubs and real ale. The most important early published account was a *History*, not of escape, but *of His Sacred Majesties most Miraculous Preservation*.[2] Charles was not fleeing *from* his Kingdom, but laying the basis for restoration to it. Yet when, twenty years later, at the darkest moment of his reign, the King dictated his own account of the escape to Samuel Pepys, his emphasis was quite different.[3] And that emphasis,

[1] Adam Phillips, *Houdini's Box: On the Arts of Escape* (London, 2001), p. 6.
[2] [Thomas Blount], *Boscobel; or the Compleat History of His Sacred Majesties Most Miraculous Preservation*, third edition (London, 1680); *Boscobel ... The Second Part* (London, 1681).
[3] *An Account of His Majesty's Escape from Worcester, dictated to Mr. Pepys by the King himself* [October 3rd and 5th, 1680], reprinted in Allan Fea, *After Worcester Fight* (London, 1904). The shorthand manuscript is in the Pepys Library, Magdalene College, Cambridge MS 2141.

particularly upon the King's saving relationship to France and to Roman Catholicism, explains the policies which led to the crisis of 1678 to 1683. These narratives may be used to question the master narrative of English restoration itself as one of closure and return. Getting the King out of exile was easy; it would be another matter getting exile out of the King. An alternative script is that after Worcester Charles really did succeed in escaping the country which had murdered his father, and that this escape was continually re-enacted.

This is to return to a theme of unrivalled importance for the reign of Charles II which has been less well-served by the new generation of restoration historiography than by its predecessors.[4] French influence upon England reached a peak during this period not only because of Louis XIV's creation of a new European superpower, but also as a result of the French personal experience, family ties, and religious and political inclinations of the restored English king.[5] According to one biographer it was the 'consistency ... determination ... even stubbornness' with which 'Charles pursued ... his aim of aligning England closely with France' which suggests that this policy 'was based on a more than rational assessment of England's purely foreign policy interests'.[6] To these qualities we may add dogged deviousness and breathtaking recklessness: from this master of the ministerial shuffle, royal zig-zag and U-turn we find an unexpected taste for the kamikaze dive. By 1681 England was a client state of Louis XIV's new *imperium*.

The most serious crisis of this king's reign, from 1678 until 1683,

---

[4] Leopold Von Ranke, *A History of England Principally In The Seventeenth Century*, 6 vols (Oxford, 1875), vols 3-4; Keith Feiling, *British Foreign Policy, 1660-1672* (London, 1968). Compare various contributions to the *Albion* vol. 25, no. 4 (1993), and see p. 620; and Tim Harris, *Restoration: Charles II and his Kingdoms, 1660-1685* (London, 2005). France was incomparably more important to this King than either Ireland or Scotland. In *England in the Reign of Charles II*, 2 vols (Oxford, 1955) David Ogg discussed all three kingdoms, their new world colonies and their European contexts.

[5] Jonathan Scott, *England's Troubles: Seventeenth Century English Political Instability in European Context* (Cambridge, 2000), pp. 166-176.

[6] Paul Seaward, 'Charles II (1630-1685), King of England, Scotland, and Ireland', *Oxford Dictionary of National Biography* (Oxford, 2004). According to William Temple the Treaty of Dover took the Dutch by surprise. 'They could not imagine a Conjunction between England and France for the ruin of their State; For, being unacquainted with our Constitutions, they did not forsee how we should find our Interest in it'. William Temple, *Observations Upon the United Provinces of the Netherlands* (London, 1673), p. 242.

resulted directly from these policies. During its course Charles II and the restored Stuart monarchy survived an upheaval replete with imagery of the English civil wars and perceived by contemporaries as '41 again'. Charles' first accomplishment was in riding out this storm, and so avoiding the fate of his father. In addition, however, some historians have gone so far as to suggest that this crisis was the belated making of Charles II. From its midpoint they have detected a royal resolution conspicuously lacking from the first twenty years of his reign. In this confrontation with a series of intransigent Houses of Commons, there were limits to what the King was prepared to do to secure co-operation. Unlike his father he did not surrender key prerogatives. He stated in March 1681: 'Men ordinarily become more timid as they grow old: as for me, I shall be, on the contrary, bolder and firmer and I will not stain my life and reputation in the little time that perhaps remains for me to live.'[7]

Charles I had abandoned his right to dissolve the Long Parliament following a successful Scots invasion. In July 1679 Charles II also faced a Scots rebellion commanding sympathy in both the House of Commons and the City of London.[8] The defeat of these rebels by the Duke of Monmouth helped to retain royal control over the summoning and dissolution of parliaments. The consequent accomplishment for which historians praise the King is his political escape.[9] It would contribute a valuable additional perspective to acknowledge the extent to which the crisis from which escape proved necessary had been of the king's own making. The Houdini of English kingship was equally the architect of his own imprisonment. It would be still more illuminating to discern, behind both of these feats, Houdini's second footprint of repetition. Between 1678 and 1683 the entire country was plunged back into the fears, and the memories, which it had been the purpose of Restoration to banish. What did this calamity owe to the policies of a king from whose mind the experiences of war, of regicide and of exile could never be erased?

---

[7] Quoted in Antonia Fraser, *King Charles II* (London, 1979), p. 397.

[8] Algernon Sidney, *Letters to Sir Henry Savile* in *Sydney on Government*, ed. J. Robertson (London, 1772), p. 43; Jonathan Scott, *Algernon Sidney and the Restoration Crisis, 1677-1683* (Cambridge, 1991), pp. 149-53.

[9] A dissenting view is Hutton, *Charles II: King of England, Scotland, and Ireland* (Oxford, 1991), pp. 401-2.

II

To identify the King as sole author of the restoration crisis would be an exaggeration. That upheaval was driven by fears, resulting from European and local circumstances, with a long history.[10] Yet to describe the King's own role in reigniting these fears is to dissent from an older account of this crisis. According to this Charles II was, as it were, the innocent victim of a political mugging. The real culprit was his brother James Duke of York, of whom the King remarked wittily that he 'lacked both the religion and the good sense of Henry of Navarre'.[11] In 1673 parliament's new Test Act outed the heir to the throne as a Roman Catholic. It was a short step from here to the ignition of public fears of popery by Titus Oates in 1678, and to the attempts to exclude James from the succession to the throne which became the focus of confrontation between the House of Commons and the crown from 1679 to 1681.[12]

Yet all of these events were consequences of this crisis, not causes. The Test Act was one consequence of a sharp parliamentary confrontation of royal policies which had been formulated in 1667-70 and announced in 1672. These included Charles' second attempt to declare a Declaration of Indulgence, for Roman Catholic as well as protestant dissenters, from the Act of Uniformity of 1662. This was accompanied by a Declaration of War, in alliance with Catholic France, upon the protestant United Provinces. When, in November 1680, the House of Commons published an *Address to His Majesty* recounting the causes of the crisis by which the nation had become engulfed, its focus was not upon the succession but upon 'the Attempts of the Popish Party, for many years last past ... not only within this, but other your Majesties Kingdoms, to introduce the Romish, and utterly to extirpate the true protestant religion'.

> After some time [these Jesuits] ... became able to influence matters of State and Government ... the continuance or Prorogation of Parliaments has been accommodated to serve their purposes ... . Ministers of England were made Instruments ... to

---

[10] Scott, *England's Troubles*, chs. 7 and 16.

[11] F. S. Ronalds, *The Attempted Whig Revolution of 1678-81* (Urbana, 1937), p. 118, note 58.

[12] This account is given by J. R. Jones, *The First Whigs* (London, 1961) and criticized by Scott, *Restoration Crisis*, esp ch. 3.

> make War upon a Protestant State … to advance and augment the dreadful power of the French King.[13]

Fear of a revived threat of popery and arbitrary government focused public attention upon all manifestations of popery at the court of Charles II, of which the religion of the heir to the throne was one.[14] To explain the resulting crisis we need to explain the revival of these apprehensions. For the genesis of the Declarations of Indulgence and of War of 1672 we must look to the dramatic reorientation of English foreign policy of 1667-1670.

In 1668 England had joined, in the Triple Alliance, a protestant project for the containment of France. In the Treaty of Dover (1670) Charles II abandoned this agreement for an alliance with France itself, with one objective of destroying the United Provinces. In the accompanying secret treaty, which was not a very good secret, the King being forced to deny the existence of any 'secret articles of dangerous consequence',[15] Charles undertook to support Louis XIV's European ambitions, in exchange for annual pensions; to follow the attack on the Netherlands with an announcement of his own Roman Catholicism; and to convert his whole kingdom to that religion, using 'six mille [French] hommes de pied, s'il est besoin'.[16]

Comments John Miller: 'Now that he was firmly established as the king of a strongly anti-Catholic country, the idea of [Charles] turning Catholic would seem bizarre to the point of lunacy'.[17] Indeed the first person to perceive that to an innocent bystander these policies might appear to have emanated from an asylum was Charles himself. Colbert de Croissy informed Louis XIV:

> He … told me … he [supposed] that … I considered that he and those to whom he had confided the conducting of this business were crazy to claim to be capable of re-establishing Catholicism in England; that … everyone apprised of the kingdom's affairs and

---

[13] *The Humble Address of the Commons in Parliament Assembled, Presented to His Majesty, Monday 28th Day of November 1680* (London, 1680), p. 76.

[14] Scott, 'England's Troubles: Exhuming the Popish Plot', in Tim Harris, Paul Seaward and Mark Goldie (eds), *The Politics of Religion in Restoration England* (Oxford, 1990); Andrew Marvell, *The Growth of Popery and Arbitrary Government* (Amsterdam, 1677).

[15] *His Majesties Gracious Speech to both Houses of Parliament Jan 7 1674* [O.S.], p. 6.

[16] M. Mignet, *Negociations Relative A La Succession D'Espagne Sous Louis XIV*, vol. 3 (Paris, 1842), p. 190 and pp. 187-97 in general.

[17] John Miller, *James II* (London, 1991), p. 60.

of the disposition of its people had to have the same thought; however ... [for various reasons], he hoped that with the support of your majesty this great undertaking would have a favourable outcome.[18]

What was going on?

Approaching his own conversion in 1668 James had discussed it with Charles 'knowing that the King was of the same mind'. There followed a meeting on 25th January 1669 with the Duke of York, Lords Arundel and Arlington, and Sir Thomas Clifford. The King explained

> How uneasy it was to him not to profess the Faith he beleev'd, and that he had call'd them together to have their advice about the ways and methods fittest to be taken for the setteling of the Catholick Religion in his Kingdoms, and to consider of the time most proper to declare himself; telling them ... That he was to expect ... many and great difficultys in bringing it about, and that he chose rather to undertake it now, when he and his Brother were in their full strength ... than to delay it till they were grown older ... . This he spake with great earnestness, and even with tears in his eyes ... . The Consultation [concluded] ... that there was no better way for doing this great work, then ... with the assistance of his Most Christian Majesty.[19]

Our only account of this meeting derives from James, who had an interest in talking up his brother's pro-Roman Catholicism.[20] Yet every aspect of the project thus described is verified by the record of the subsequent treaty negotiations. There is much additional evidence of Charles' longstanding interest in a 'reconciliation' with Roman Catholicism and a 'stricter alliance with France then there has hitherto been'.[21] What the

---

[18] Mignet (ed.), *Negociations*, p. 102.

[19] J. S. Clarke, *The Life of James the Second*, 2 vols (London, 1816), 1 p. 422; see also James MacPherson (ed.), *Original Papers; Containing the Secret History of Great Britain*, 2 vols (London, 1775), 1, pp. 48, 50.

[20] Ronald Hutton, 'The religion of Charles II' in Malcolm Smuts (ed.), *The Stuart Court and Europe* (Cambridge, 1996), p. 234.

[21] On the King's campaign for a 'stricter alliance' between 1663 and 1669 see Arthur Bryant (ed.), *The Letters, Speeches and Declarations of King Charles II* (London, 1935), pp. 142, 150, 163, 165, 181-3, 223-4; and Ruth Norrington (ed.), *My Dearest Minette: The Letters between Charles*

treaty negotiations make clear, alongside sharp bargaining over French subsidies, is that wheras Louis primary interest was English assistance in the war on the United Provinces, that of Charles concerned French support for 'Catholicity'.[22] Throughout the negotiation English documents began with the matter 'de plus Important ... Le Roy de la grand Bretagne estoit convaincu de la verite de la Religion Catholique et resolu de se declarer Catholique et de reconcilier avec l'Eglise de Rome'.[23] This conversion was to be the centerpiece of a dramatic reorientation of Stuart religious, political and foreign policy to establish a 'paix, union, vraye confraternite' and 'confederation perpetuelle' with France which would secure the future of the monarchy and dynasty.[24] In this connection I must disagree with Ronald Hutton's characterization of the most important letter from Madame to her brother as confining its 'arguments to international power politics ... [with] nothing about any spiritual yearnings'.[25] Henrietta argues that 'the matter' of England's relationship with Holland 'takes on a different aspect because you have need of France to ensure the success of the design about R. [religion], and there is little likelihood of your obtaining what you desire from the King except on condition that you enter into a league with him against Holland.' It hopes that 'This war is not likely to be of long duration ... and far from injuring the design you have touching R. it will perhaps give you the means of executing it'.[26]

In August 1670 Louis relayed to Charles the transcript of a conversation which had taken place at Versailles between Marshal Turenne and the exiled English republican Algernon Sidney. Sidney opined:

II and his sister Henrietta, Duchesse d'Orleans (London, 1996), pp. 156-82, 210-11. Ranke, *History*, 3, p. 495 emphasises that the religious project was driven not by James but 'the King himself'.

[22] Mignet, *Negociations*, vol. 3, pp. 7-8, 100-6, 115-24, 128, 132, 187-97. As specified in the draft treaty (p. 118): 'Le roi de la Grande-Bretagne, etant convaincu de la verite de la religion catholique, et resolu de se declarer catholique et de reconcilier avec l'eglise de Rome, croit que, pour faciliter l'execution de son dessein, l'assistance du roi tres-chretien lui pourra etre necessaire.'

[23] Paris, Ministere des Affaires Etrangeres, Archives Diplomatique, Correspondence Politique Angleterre, 95, pp. 235-6; also 241, 247-8, 258-9.

[24] *Ibid.*, p. 229. For the shared perception of a continued English republican danger see Colbert to 'Sire' [the King] 19 August 1669, pp. 57-58.

[25] Hutton, 'The Religion of Charles II', p. 234.

[26] Norrington (ed.), *Minette*, pp. 163, 165, 166, 210.

> that the [English] Presbeterians and independents would never rest ... until they had liberty of conscience ... that they had less hatred for the Catholic religion than for the government of the bishops ... that in consultation with the heads of the various sects and some measure of liberty of conscience, the King of England would have nothing to fear from them; on the contrary he would be able to depend upon their fidelity.[27]

These opinions are almost identical to those of the King himself, confided to Colbert nine months earlier. Charles' religious hopes rested upon the fact

> que les presbyteriens et toute les autres sects avaient encore plus d'aversion pour l'eglise anglicane que pour les catholiques; que tous ces sectaires ne respiraient qu'apres la liberte de l'exercice de leaur religion; que pourvu qu'ils l'obtiennent, comme c'est son dessein de leur accorder, ils ne s'opposeront point a son changement de religion.[28]

The King replied to Colbert agreeing with Sidney and repeating his belief 'that by giving [this liberty] to others, they will not take it ill accordingly when he also takes it for himself'.[29] That we should, in this context, understand the *Declaration of Indulgence* issued in 1672 as intended precursor to His Majesty's own declaration of conversion seems clear.[30] No wonder the Convention parliament made it a 'Felony' to say of 'the King ... *that he is a Papist, or popishly affected*'.[31] It has been remarkably obtuse for historians to ascribe the resulting fear of popery to hysteria when there was indeed a real popish plot, masterminded by the King.

The early years of Restoration had gone swimmingly, with the Earl of Clarendon managing the political process, and the Duchess of Castlemaine

---

[27] Du Roy a Colbert, 29 July 1670 (my translation).

[28] Mignet, *Negotiations*, p. 102.

[29] London, National Archives 31/3, Baschet transcript no. 125, 4 August 1670.

[30] 'That ... Charles did for a time seriously, even enthusiastically, entertain the idea of announcing his reconciliation to the Catholic church is perhaps the most rational interpretation of the events surrounding the secret treaty of Dover.' Seaward, 'Charles II'.

[31] Edward Hyde, *The Continuation of the Life of Edward Earl of Clarendon*, 2 vols (Oxford, 1760), 1, p. 427.

massaging the King.³² However by 1667, with London devastated by plague and fire, and the regime's first war ending in humiliation, the honeymoon was over. Part of Charles' motivation for Dover was to take revenge against the Dutch.³³ This does not, however, explain its religious clauses, or the king's indifference to the probable domestic reaction to this cynical destruction of a key protestant ally.³⁴ One reason for the King's insensitivity to the fears of his subjects may be that he had fears of his own. Fear not only of popery, but for the security of monarchy, had been a constant of seventeenth century English politics.³⁵ How much more reason for this was there in the mind of a King, once a hunted fugitive, then penniless exile, whose father had been publicly murdered by the people over whom he now reigned? 'We are bound to *honour* our Kings and Princes ... and how have we done it? *Murder the Father! Banish the Son!*'³⁶

Nobody during the 1660s took the durability of re-established monarchy for granted. The defeat of 1667 did little to diminish such anxieties in the mind of the King in particular. Towards the end of his life Charles gave Sir Henry Shere an account of 'that Great Calamity' of the Dutch raid on Chatham

> with Soe feeling a Sense of ye Misfortune ... That a Stranger to the Story would ... have Guessed It to have just then hapned; soe lively and lasting an Impression had that fatall Success made in his Majesty's Mind ... [A]s his ... Matie ... observed to me ... the People on the Occasion of ... [that] Attempt ... were frighted almost out of their Obedience, and the Successe of that action threatened even a Convulsion of the State.³⁷

---

³² This was, according to the laws of politics rather than physics, a cause of friction between the King and his Lord Chancellor. As Clarendon unwisely informed his master in early 1667: his 'Excess of Pleasures ... had already lost very much of the Affection and Reverence the Nation had for him'. Hyde, *Continuation*, vol. 2, pp. 262-3 (and 258). See also A. Browning (ed.), *Memoirs of Sir John Reresby* (Glasgow, 1936), p. 35; and Gilbert Burnet, *History of My Own Time*, ed. Osmund Airy, 2 vols (Oxford, 1847), 2, p. 482.

³³ Miller, *Charles II*, p. 194. Mignet, *Negotiations*, pp. 7-8 sets this antipathy in wider contexts.

³⁴ Scott, *England's Troubles*, pp. 172-176; for an alternative explanation see Hutton, 'The making of the Secret Treaty of Dover', *Historical Journal* 29, 2 (1986). In *Charles II*, vol. 2, p. 601 David Ogg emphasizes Louis XIV's own confessional motives for signing the treaty.

³⁵ Scott, *England's Troubles*, pp. 62-65.

³⁶ Francis Gregory, *David's Returne From His Banishment* (Oxford, 1660), pp. 11, 14.

³⁷ National Maritime Museum, Greenwich, REC/6 Item 24, pp. 343-4, 353.

This may explain why, when he was forced in 1673 to withdraw the Declaration of Indulgence, and to pull out of the war, Charles spoke as if he had narrowly escaped a rebellion. When parliamentary anger intensified over unabated French military expansion Charles asked Louis why he couldn't give up a town or two to save him from his father's fate, or from being 'chased from his kingdom' again.[38] As alarm mounted Charles refused to change course because his opponents were out to 'take over the government' and so he could not abandon France as 'the only security he has'. Hence one of the most remarkable royal protestations, from any period, to Ruvigny, that Charles 'alone was standing up for France's interests, against his entire kingdom'.[39]

There is thus every reason to see behind the remarkable reorientation of royal policies inaugurated in 1667 the shock of military defeat and a resulting desire for security in alliance with France. The Secret Treaty promised French military support for the English monarchy against parliament and people 'should they rise against it'. Nor within this context were the religious, political and military aspects of the alliance strictly separable. Thus the Marquess of Normanby ascribed the King's throwing 'Himself into ye hands of a Roman-Catholick Party, so remarkable of late for their Loyalty' to 'his being tir'd ... with those bold Oppositions in Parliament' and thereupon 'lulled ... asleep with those inchanting Songs of Soveraignty and Prerogative'.[40] In all respects Charles had been here before. Indeed, since the year in which he began to receive annual pensions from Louis was 1652,[41] the secret Treaty did not so much inaugurate a new financial relationship as reanimate an old one.

The subsequent crisis of 1678-83 was precipitated by revelation to the House of Commons of letters documenting Charles' continuing secret relationship with Louis. Amid the ensuing uproar Charles dissolved his 17 year old Cavalier parliament. So much for the King as author of his own captivity. How did he escape?

---

[38] Miller, *Charles II*, pp. 219-20.

[39] *Ibid.*, p. 244. Burnet records (*History*, 2, p. 471): 'Ruvigny told me [Charles] desired that all ... the French ... naval [plans] might be sent to him; and he ... stud[ied] them with concern and zeal. He shewed ... how they ought to be corrected, as if he had been a viceroy to France, rather than a king that ought to have ... prevented [them]'.

[40] Pepys Library MS 2142, ff. 2-3.

[41] 192,000 livres a year; the dowager Queen Henrietta Maria a further 72,000. Edward Corp, *A Court in Exile: The Stuarts in France, 1689-1718* (Cambridge, 2004), p. 4.

III

In September 1680 Charles II faced the most dangerous moment of his reign. A year previously, when the second 'exclusion' parliament was elected, Charles had refused to allow it to meet. Rather he preferred to trust, for over a year, to his preogative powers of prorogation, and face the unwelcome accompanying necessity of extreme financial retrenchment. This Long Prorogation provoked the petitioning campaign of 1679-80 which produced the first visible polarisation within this crisis, between petitioners (for the meeting of the parliament) and 'abhorrers' (of those petitions). Thus reappeared what Henry Neville called the two 'infamous factions' which had earlier led the country into civil war.[42] In January 1680 the petitioners were confronted by Charles with the remark: 'I admire [that] gentlemen of your estates should animate people to mutiny and rebellion!'[43]

It was the view of abhorrers not only 'That petitioning for the sitting of the Parliament is like 1641', but that it was intended 'to bring his Majesty to the block, as his Father was brought'.[44] This view could only have been reinforced by the result of elections held in June 1680 to the shrievalty of the City of London. In 1641 loss of the City government, beginning with the shrievalty, had helped to seal Charles I's fate. Now again victory went to two radical opponents of the crown, one a notorious republican. In the words of Secretary Jenkins 'th[is] election ... is a parallel line drawn to that of 1641-2'.[45] In the analysis of York: 'This looks as if London would set up for a Commonwealth.'[46]

It was beneath these thunderclouds that in late September 1680 the royal coach departed the capital. Ronald Hutton has remarked that 'It did not seem to occur to [the King] that, with political tensions rising as Parliament approached, he might forgo the pleasures of Newmarket.'[47] On the contrary, for the Houdini of English kingship, this was precisely the moment to escape. For Charles, indeed, Newmarket appears to have

---

[42] Caroline Robbins (ed.), *Two English Republican Tracts* (Cambridge, 1968) p. 16.

[43] Quoted in Miller, *Charles II*, p. 329.

[44] A. Grey, *Debates in the House of Commons*, 7, pp. 380, 389-91; Roger North, *Examen* (London, 1740), p. 542.

[45] Quoted in Henry Sidney, *Diary of the Life and Times of Charles II*, 2 vols, R. Blencowe (ed.) (London, 1843), p. 87.

[46] MacPherson (ed.), *Original Papers*, p. 112.

[47] Hutton, *Charles II*, p. 393.

offered an escape not simply from London but from kingship. As John Reresby recorded: 'The king was ... soe great a lover of the diversions which that place did afford, that he lett himselfe down from Majesty to the very degree of a country gentleman.' And what more appropriate thing to do, upon arrival, than to ask Samuel Pepys to transcribe His Majesty's own master escape narrative?[48] As we have seen, this was hardly the King's first account of his escape from the battle of Worcester in 1651. On the contrary, on this and related subjects His Majesty became a crashing bore.[49] It is surely significant, however, that Charles chose this moment to commit for the first time to writing his own version of these events. Such an impression is reinforced by a comparison of his version with other accounts.

Published tales of His Majesty's 'strange and wonderful escape' had appeared early in the reign.[50] It was in August 1660 that the king instructed Thomas Blount to 'continue and perfect that history of his wonderful preservation, after the battle of Worcester'.[51] He ordered those involved to furnish Blount with their accounts, and gave Blount rights of monopoly over their publication. The resulting *Boscobel* was first published in 1662, and republished in 1680. Another early account intended for publication was that of Francis Windham, an assistant in the King's escape, written 'by especial command from his Majesty ... immediately after the King's return into England.' This was presented to the King but the decision to publish was not taken until, again, 1680, the intention then being 'that the implacable Enemies of this Crown may be forever silenced and ashamed'.[52]

What significance are we to attach to the King's decision in this same year to give his own version of a story already being publicly told by two others? One answer is Windham's: that it was the Monarch's intention to ashame 'the implacable Enemies of this Crown'. Once before they had

---

[48] Reresby, *Memoirs*, p. 259.

[49] Burnet, *History*, 2, p. 469: 'Wilmot, earl of Rochester said he wondered to see a man have so good a memory as to repeat the same story without losing the least circumstance, and yet not remember that he had told it to the same persons the very day before'.

[50] John Danvers, *The Royal Oake, Or, An Historicall Description of The Royal Progresse, wonderful Travels Miraculous Escapes ... of his Sacred Majesty Charles the II*, fourth edition (London, 1660), Title Page; *A true Narrative and relation of His Majesty's Miraculous Escape from Worcester* (London, 1660), reprinted in Allan Fea, *The Flight of the King*, second edition, revised (London, 1908).

[51] *Calendar of State Papers Domestic 1660-1661*, p. 149.

[52] Quoted in Hannah Smith, 'Images of Charles II', dissertation for the M.Phil in Historical Studies, University of Cambridge, 1998, p. 68.

attempted to destroy this King, having already killed his Father, but had failed. In this formulation Charles' purpose was twofold: to remind the public of the real and continuing danger; and to advertise his own proven powers of survival. This makes the dictation to Pepys an early act in that orchestrated political reaction described by Roger North (and John Dryden) as a 'second Restauration'.[53] In his darkest political hour, the King may have been attempting to reassure not only, or even primarily, the public, but himself. Yet we should not be surprised to discover in this unusual personal intervention a deeper insight into the King's own reading of the issues.

In Blount's account we find both elements already mentioned, duly emphasised. These are the implacable malice, and wickedness, of the King's enemies 'the fanatics'; and the King's own extraordinary powers of survival. These latter are due to his Majesty's personal qualities, to the help of his friends, and to the exemplary assistance of God Almighty. This is

> the wonderful history of a great and good King, violently pursued in his own dominions by the worst of rebels, and miraculously preserved, under God, by the best of subjects … . The admireable providence of Almighty God … never appeared more miraculously than in this strange deliverance of his majesty from such an infinity of dangers, that history itself cannot produce a parallel … there was no kind of misery (but death itself) of which his majesty, in this horrible persecution, did not in some measure, both in body, mind, and estate, bear a very great share; yet such was his invinceable patience in his time of tryal, such his fortitude, that he overcame them all.[54]

If we turn to the King's own rendition of this story we find two very remarkable departures from this plot. The first is the criticism levelled at those royal troops at Worcester who failed to 'stand by me agt. ye Enemy'.[55] In this extremity of his personal fortunes, Charles resolved to seek his salvation alone rather than tie his fate to 'men who had run

---

[53] See quotes in Scott, *England's Troubles*, p. 434.
[54] Blount, *Boscobel* (London, 1894), pp. 114, 116.
[55] Pepys Library MS 2141, p. 5: 'we had such a No of beaten men with us (of ye Horse) that I strove as soone as ever it was dark to get from them. And though I could not get them to stand by me agt. ye Enemy, I could not get ridd of them now I had a mind to it.'

away'.⁵⁶ Here Charles' assertion of control over his own escape contrasts sharply with Blount's emphasis upon the role played in His Majesty's preservation by 'the best of [his] subjects'.⁵⁷ It also places more emphasis upon what became the most important judgement Charles had to make. Hunted, in a republican military state, who could he trust?

It is the King's answer to this question which is, in its context, no less amazing than the secret treaty of Dover, as well as in perfect conformity with that document. It was 'Roman Catholics' that 'I chose to trust ... because I knew they had hiding holes for priests, that I thought I might make use of in case of need'.⁵⁸ There was Richard Penderall, 'an honest man'. There was another

> 'honest gentleman, Mr Woolfe ... [who] had hiding-holes for priests; Mr Pitchcroft ... a very honest gentleman ... and Roman Catholic ... Major Careless ... a major in our army ... a Roman Catholic also ... a very honest fellow, whose name was Pope ... [who] had been a trooper in the King my father's army ... and other Catholics, including Father Hodlestone, and Mrs Hyde'.

Finally there was 'Sir John Preston and his brother', the latter to become a Jesuit and to earn a mention in Titus Oates' 1678 narrative of the Plot.⁵⁹

Thus after his own abilities, and the assistance of God, Charles owed his escape almost entirely to that persecuted English religious minority who had suffered even more during the seventeenth century than Kings.⁶⁰ Let us now remember that this narrative emerged during a political emergency ignited by a belief that the English state and government had become infiltrated by 'Jesuitical counsels'. By the end of 1680, amid the ferment created by this apprehension, 24 Roman Catholics had been publicly hanged, drawn and quartered. The Court's official response to this situation was to deny the slightest sympathy with popery. To accuse Charles's narrative of failing to sing from this same hymn sheet would be a spectacular understatement.

One might see His Majesty's decision in 1651 to throw in his lot with

---

[56] 'The King's Own Narrative' in *His Majesty Preserved ... King Charles II's Escape After the Battle of Worcester Dictated to Samuel Pepys by the King Himself* (London, 1954), pp. 17-19.

[57] This is also a theme of Danvers' *Royal Oake*.

[58] 'The King's Own Narrative', p. 21.

[59] *Ibid.*, pp. 26-8, 31.

[60] Cf. again Danvers, *Royal Oake*, p. 2.

a 'knot of midland recusants'[61] as a reaction to his recent persecution by the Scots kirk. Yet it was not taken in an English experiential vacuum, as the reference to a trooper in his father's army reminds us. One reason given by Charles II for his 1662 Declaration of Indulgence was the military loyalty shown by 'those of the old religion' toward his father.[62] Earlier, in exile Charles's religious relationships at the Louvre, in Catholic Germany, and with the Papacy had given his protestant courtiers coniptions.[63] In 1654 in Cologne he promised a papal nuncio toleration for English catholics if he was restored, and an Irish Jesuit in his service, Peter Talbot, hinted his Majesties' willingness to convert. Burnet claimed that 'Before Charles left Paris he changed his religion'.[64] The Marquis of Halifax also believed that Charles lost his veneration for the Church of England in Paris, and that 'after the first Year or two he was no more a Protestant ... when he came into England he was as certainly a *Roman Catholick*, as ... a Man of Pleasure; both very consistent by visible Experience'.[65]

In 1663, following the failure of his first Declaration he commented to the French ambassador that 'no other creed matches so well [as Catholicism] with the absolute dignity of Kings'.[66] In November 1670 at a secret meeting with another papal nuncio Charles reiterated his determination to reward the loyalty of his Catholic subjects.[67] It is true that in 1653 Charles reacted furiously to his mother's attempts to convert his brother the Duke of Gloucester, reminding her that her husband had died for the Church of England. But these letters offer much more convincing evidence of panic about potentially fatal damage about to be done to the prospect of restoration than of zeal for the protestant cause. The following year Talbot

[61] David Underdown, *Royalist Conspiracy in England 1649-1660* (New Haven, 1960), p. 53.

[62] *The Popish Plot, Taken from Several Depositions Made before the Parliament* (1678), in W. Scott (ed.), *Scarce and Valuable Tracts ... [of] the Late Lord Somers*, 8, p. 59.

[63] George Warner (ed.), *The Nicholas Papers vol 1: 1641-1652* (London, 1886), pp. 296-7, 284, 299-301, 305.

[64] Burnet, *History*, 1, p. 133. See also 2, p. 472: 'No part of his character looked wickeder ... than that he was professing to be of the Church of England ... yet secretly reconciled to the Church of Rome'.

[65] George Savile, Marquis of Halifax, *A Character of King Charles II* in *The Works of Sir George Savile* (ed.), N. Brown, 3 vols (Oxford, 1989), 2, pp. 484, 486.

[66] Hutton 'The Religion of Charles II', pp. 230, 232.

[67] Ranke, *History* vol. 3, pp. 503-4 and 395-8. Ranke concludes that after 'his sojourn[s] in France, Belgium, and Catholic Germany ... Not only his convictions ... but also his sympathies belonged to Catholicism' (p. 495).

assured the nuncio, plausibly enough, that Charles' intervention 'had been necessary to avoid alienating English public opinion and that Charles had not been sincere in it'.[68]

Of this King the Earl of Halifax remarked: 'he did not perhaps think so much of his Subjects as they might wish'.[69] Indeed, as we have seen, he thought that royalists were incompetent, and the rest were rebels, and he had some basis in experience for these opinions. No wonder if, rather than depend upon his parliaments, Charles preferred to accept a political dependence upon France.[70] 'The Kings Own Narrative' thus makes very good sense of the Franco-Catholic context of this crisis, and of His Majesties's stances throughout his reign.

To turn finally to Charles as author of his escape, we need to note an aspect of the context for this crisis which has not yet been mentioned. This was the rupture in Anglo-French relations which followed the marriage treaty between Mary Stuart and William of Orange in late 1677.

IV

Remarkably, when the Restoration crisis was triggered by the revelation of Charles' secret correspondence with France, this was orchestrated by the French ambassador.[71] The French objective was to topple the architect of the Stuart-Orange marriage alliance, Danby, and to punish Charles for using Danby to apply pressure for an increase in his French pension. It was following this rupture that the King was thrown into financial as well as political dependence upon a series of hostile parliaments which he could not control. Facing isolation, as his father had in 1640, his initial response was to resort to those arts of compromise, and apparent policy reversal, by which his reign had hitherto been sustained. There followed new parliaments, new ministers, and a new expanded privy council, accompanied by loud denunciations of popery and apparent co-operation with investigations of the plot.

In the view of His Majesty's opponents, for the second time this century the government had succumbed to the lure of popery and arbitrary government. This was as evident in the court's personalities as in its

---

[68] Hutton, 'The Religion of Charles II', pp. 232-3.

[69] Halifax, *Character*, p. 493.

[70] Burnet, *History*, 2, pp. 471-2.

[71] Scott, *Restoration Crisis*, pp. 113-4.

policies, including a pro-catholic, pro-French King, a catholic heir, a French catholic mistress and 'arbitrary' chief ministers in England and Scotland. After a decade of misuse of the royal prerogative of summoning, dissolving and proroguing parliaments in exchange for French pensions, there was now no cure for this condition but a preparedness to give to parliament unimpeded power to prosecute these twin afflictions until they had been eradicated.

For the King, on the other hand, such a view simply confirmed the revival of a plot of a different kind, the assault upon royal power which had emerged during the 1620s and eliminated the monarchy by 1649. This could be seen in attempts by the House of Commons, in alliance with the City of London, to appropriate all the levers of royal power. These included control of foreign policy, the appointment of ministers, the integrity of the succession, and the royal prerogative governing the meeting of parliaments.[72] As the King said to John Reresby:

> I know it is said that I intend the subversion of the religion and government ... to lay aside Parliaments ... But ... thos that say it the most ... would subvert the government themselves and bring it to a commonwealth again.[73]

In 1651 rescue had come in the shape of a boat from 'Pool' carrying 'sea coal' which had conveyed His Majesty to France. Now again Charles sent for the political equivalent of the same vessel. In June 1679 he had warned ambassador Barillon that Louis 'must decide whether he wanted a republic or a monarchy in England. If he did not support the royal authority actively ... nothing would prevent parliament from taking over control of foreign affairs and everything else'.[74] Barillon concurred that 'the Affairs of the Crown were low, and just lapsing into the total Arbitrariment of the Commons'.[75] Yet it was not until December 1680 that Barillon warned Louis: 'I do not think a republic in England would be in the interests of France. One saw by experience how powerful the nation

---

[72] All of these powers were put under serious pressure by the government's opponents between 1679 and 1681. See Count D'Avaux, *The Negotiations of Count d'Avaux*, 4 vols (London, 1756), 1, pp. 62-63.

[73] *Memoirs of Reresby*, pp. 111-2.

[74] J. J. Jusserand, *Recueil des instructions donnes aux ambassadeurs et ministres de France, vol XXV, Angleterre* (Paris, 1929), p. 271.

[75] North, *Examen*, p. 529.

became under such a united government'.⁷⁶

It was the consequent restoration of French support which allowed Charles to dispense with parliaments, and then with the crisis more generally. A royal proclamation announced the end of parliaments for the time being, and there followed that systematic recovery of royal control known as the loyalist reaction. Among the 'fanatic' plotters executed in 1683 were several ex-soldiers of the New Model Army. As the king asked Barillon: 'how was he to spare men who would not have spared him had he fallen into their hands?'⁷⁷ They would not have spared him, he could have added, in 1651, or 1683.

Once again Charles had taken refuge not in the professed loyalty of his supporters, but in his own resources and the support of European catholicism. Moreover the political consequences of these decisions were not trivial: 'The Stuarts paid a high price for their pensions.'⁷⁸ From 1681 Louis XIV issued instructions concerning the work of English ambassadors on the continent and claimed authority over diplomatic visits to England from abroad. As the whig reply to the King's proclamation remarked:

> Let us then no longer wonder, that the time of dissolving our Parliaments, is known at Paris sooner than at London ... the reasons ... given for it, were formed there too.⁷⁹

On February 6th, 1685 Charles made his last escape and best. The day before he had been received into the Roman Catholic Church by Father John Huddleston, veteran of his Worcester flight.

V

If the ketch which spirited Charles to safety in 1651 was called the *Surprise*, that which returned him to England in 1660 might have been called *Unbelievable*.⁸⁰ One purpose of Restoration as political theatre was to

---

[76] National Archives, London, Baschet Correspondence no. 143, p. 291.
[77] Quoted by Ranke, *History of England*, 4, p. 188.
[78] Stephen Baxter, *William III and the Defense of European Liberty, 1650-1702* (New York, 1966), p. 174.
[79] *Vindication of the Proceedings of the Two Last Parliaments* (1681), in *State Tracts of the Reign of Charles II* (London, 1689), p. cxxxvii.
[80] Underdown, *Conspiracy*, p. 55; *The Diary of John Evelyn*, ed. Esmond de Beer (Oxford, 1955), p. 244.

deny the fact of dynastic interruption. Though it claimed to be restoring the King to the exercise of monarchical powers possessed from the moment of his father's execution, the reality was one not of continuity, but brutal truncation. In Charles I we have the last in a line of English royal anti-Houdinis, who did not escape. Another Restoration strategy was to control, and if possible cancel, political memory. While his Act of Indemnity and Oblivion (1660) forbade subjects to speak 'any way tending to revive the memory of the late differences, or the occasion thereof', his Majesty's own account of his escape, endlessly repeated, underscored the reality.

Boscobel was one contribution to the theatre of return: return of the lawful monarch; of the native son. It was 'our Choyce, *but in* God's hand, to *bring back* our David, King *of* England, *to his* Jerusalem'.[81] Yet following his exile how much of the David his subjects desired, and perhaps needed, remained to be recovered? Perhaps we must consider an alternative script: that after 1660 Charles's escape was not simply a story, or memory, but also a fact. In the words of Halifax, again: 'His Wit was better suited to his condition *before* he was restored than *afterwards.*' Certainly for the rest of the reign following the fall of Clarendon in 1667, the trajectory of the King's religious and political policies, as well as of his emotional life, lay in flight toward France.

To accept that Charles really did escape, and kept so doing, might help us to perceive other Restoration realities. Against the myth of monarchical continuity there is the fact that English monarchy had to be reconstructed, over a long period, upon part-republican administrative foundations. Against the myth of national self-containment this reconstruction was made to stick only by imported (quasi-French, Dutch and Hanoverian) materials. Within this process Charles II was, like his brother, part of the problem rather than of the solution. For him the real return was not to England, which he had successfully escaped, but to that spectacular court where James II would live out the rest of his days.

When a magician climbs into a box which is then sawn in half by his assistants, everybody knows what is supposed to happen next. How can he subsequently emerge in one piece? One thing about which all biographers agree is that 'There remains something elusive and tantalising about Charles II'.

---

[81] Gregory, *David's Returne*, Preface.
[82] Hutton, *Charles II*, p. 458.

> He remains ... a set of strongly marked characteristics with a cold void at the centre of them. He was a monarch who loved masks, whether of ceremony, of role-playing, or of intrigue. Behind those coverings, something was always missing.[82]

Perhaps what was missing from the box was Houdini himself.

Part II
Authority

Chapter 5

How Oliver Cromwell Thought[1]

John Morrill

The scholarly community owes many debts to Colin Davis, not least for his forthright and at times fearless reporting on his encounters with the past. His attempt to penetrate into the mind of Oliver Cromwell has been as rewarding and powerful a contribution as anything he has done. His demonstration of how *little* we know of Cromwell's faith and practice was at once stunning and influential. He has reclaimed Cromwell from the denominational straitjacket into which well-meaning Victorians had placed him. We owe to Colin a much clearer sense of Cromwell's antiformalism, his liturgical informality, his unsystematic soteriology, his lack of doctrinal coherence, and the overarching providentialism at the heart of the accounts he gave of his journey in faith. Colin refers to, but perhaps does not bring out sufficiently, Cromwell's Biblicism. This essay seeks to complement not to correct Colin's account of Cromwell's religion.[2]

I

Historians have recently rediscovered an account of Oliver Cromwell's election as MP for Cambridge in 1640 that contains a startling nugget of information relating to the 1630s:

> It was the hap of Richard Tyms ... to be at a conventicle (as he usually every Sunday rode to the Isle of Ely to that purpose, having a brother who entertained him in his course) where he

---

[1] I am grateful to David Smith, Ariel Hessayon, Grant Tapsell and the editors of this volume for comments on this essay.

[2] J. C. Davis, 'Cromwell's Religion' in John Morrill (ed.), *Oliver Cromwell and the English Revolution* (Harlow, 1990), pp.181-208; J. C. Davis, 'Against Formality: an aspect of the English Revolution', *Transactions of the Royal Historical Society*, 6th ser., 3 (1993), pp. 265-88; J. C. Davis, *Oliver Cromwell* (Oxford, 2001), ch.6.

> heard this said Oliver [Cromwell], with such admiration, that he
> thought that there was not such a precious man in the nation.³

Most of the account from which this is drawn is verifiable and accurate. So we have to face the likelihood that Oliver Cromwell was a lay preacher in an underground church and this changes our sense of the trajectory of Cromwell's religious radicalism. It deepens the significance of the letter Cromwell wrote in 1635, referring to the Bishops collectively as 'the enemies of God His Truth',⁴ a dangerous phrase to put into a letter that would be left lying around in a tavern or inn in central London waiting to be collected by a man who had in fact migrated to New England.⁵ Cromwell was putting his ears, if not his life, on the line by such fearless language.⁶ All this makes his precocious encouragement of officers and soldiers to stand up and testify much easier to understand.

Ten years later, we can eavesdrop on the private journals of a German ambassador, Hermann Mylius, twiddling his thumbs in London. In 1652, he recorded that

> In the king's chapel at Whitehall, General Cromwell sat today
> with his family in the same pew which was formerly used by the
> King and his children. Colonel Hugh Peter ... armed in a sword,
> dressed in military regalia, preached, and this is common; anyone
> may step up, when he wishes, and deliver a sermon.⁷

Cromwell's assumption of the royal pew more than a year before he (with such shows of reluctance) became Head of State is instructive; but Mylius's testimony that Oliver condoned and encouraged lay preaching well into

---

³ [J.Heath], *Flagellum*, third edition (London, 1665), pp. 14-18. I am grateful to Dr Andrew Barclay for showing me how much of the lengthy account of the Cambridge parliamentary election from which this is drawn, can be verified. Tims did indeed have a brother who was a tenant farmer close to Cromwell in St Ives in the 1630s; and this Tims did inherit the tenancy after his brother's early death.

⁴ Thomas Carlyle (ed. rev. S. C. Lomas), *The Letters and Speeches of Oliver Cromwell*, 3 vols (London, 1903), 1, p. 79.

⁵ John Morrill, 'Cromwell, Oliver (1599-1658)', *Oxford Dictionary of National Biography* (Oxford, 2004), www.oxforddnb.com/view/article/6765.

⁶ By the time he wrote William Prynne had lost his ears for seditious libel after trial in Star Chamber.

⁷ Leo Miller (ed.), *John Milton and the Oldenburg Safeguard* (New York, 1985), p. 41

the 1650s is also important. This paper will examine Cromwell's self-confidence as preacher and as Man of the Word.

II

Soldiers did step up to preach at the great Army Prayer Meetings of which we have records especially in the years 1647-9 — in the course of the meeting at Windsor in April 1648 when Charles I was branded a Man of Blood against whom God would have vengeance at human hands, in late November 1648 as they again asked for guidance about putting him on trial, and in the spring of 1649 when Cromwell was persuaded to take the Irish command at a prayer meeting which also produced a device for selecting the regiments which were to go to Ireland.[8] Following heated exchanges over the applicability of Acts chapter 1, the biblical account of the drawing of lots to select Matthias as the twelfth apostle after the suicide of Judas Iscariot, a small boy was called upon to pull out of a box the names of the regiments that were to serve.[9]

What happened at these prayer meetings is clear. The officers (and in the second half of 1647 the adjutators) sat in silence praying for guidance. They browsed their Bibles, or they let the scriptures they knew by heart swirl around in their minds, until a connection was made between the text and the scriptural-historical situation described in the text and their own current situation. And out of the silence came an exploration and an explication of that connection; an articulation of the existential sense of God's working through scripture to reveal his will to his chosen instruments.

The most dramatic example of this is the prayer meeting on the second morning of the Putney Debates — that is 29 October 1647. William Clarke's record is dominated by an extraordinary meditation by Goffe, based on the Book of Revelation chapter 17, in the course of which he showed how English Kings had overthrown the power of Antichrist in the person of the Pope, only to assume the trappings of Antichristian power themselves. He then said: 'let us inquire whether some of the actions that we have done of late, some of the things we have propounded of late, doe

---

[8] William Allen, *A faithful memorial of that remarkable meeting ... at Windsor Castle, in the year 1648* (London, 1659). See I. Gentles, *The New Model Army in England, Ireland and Scotland 1645-1653* (London, 1991), pp. 245-6; P. Gaunt, *Oliver Cromwell* (Oxford, 1996), pp. 92-93, and S. R. Gardiner, *History of the Great Civil War*, 4 vols (London 1892), 4, p. 235.

[9] C. H. Firth (ed.), *The Clarke Papers*, 4 vols (London, 1891-1901), 2, pp. 208-9.

not crosse the worke of God in these particulars; because in our proposing of thinges we doe indeavour to sett uppe that power that God would not sette up again'. This is startling talk. But it is followed by a long exegesis of the Book of Numbers, chapter 14, in which God deserts those who *anticipate* his will, take the law into their own hands to do what they believe God intends: 'Let us not now in a kinde of heate run uppe and say, "wee will goe now;" because itt may bee there is a better opportunity that God will give us.'[10] In the short term, this passionate (half-hour?) outburst seemed to leave the assembly cold. I have suggested elsewhere that it lit a slow fuse in the heart of Oliver Cromwell.[11]

Cromwell made a series of interventions in the debate on 1 November, and in each the weight of Colonel Goffe's meditation on Revelation and the Book of Numbers became more evident. He began by arguing that this was not the time or the place for the Army to decide on a negative voice in the King or in the Lords. That belonged either to a Parliament chastened and made wiser by the army's remonstrations or it belonged to a Parliament elected under new and better electoral rules.[12] Following Allen's call for all to keep an open mind on the King's future and following Sexby's meditation on the words of Jeremiah: 'we find in the worde of God: "I would heal Babylon but shee would not be healed". I thinke that wee have gone about to heale Babylon when shee would not',[13] Cromwell returned to Goffe's words, and went into a dramatic and clearly extempore meditation on the series of testimonies given forth as a result of the day of prayer.

> Truly wee have heard many speaking to us; and I cannott butt thinke that in many of those thinges *God* hath spoken to us ... . I cannott see butt that wee all speake to the same end, and the mistakes are onely in the way. The end is to deliver this nation from oppression and slavery, to accomplish that worke that God hath carried on in us ... . We agree thus farre.

---

[10] *Ibid.*, 1, pp. 282-5.

[11] John Morrill and Philip Baker, 'Oliver Cromwell, the regicide and the sons of Zeruiah' in Jason Peacey (ed.), *The Regicides and the Execution of Charles I* (Basingstoke, 2001), pp. 20-21; John Morrill, 'Rewriting Cromwell : A Case of Deafening Silences'. *Canadian Journal of History*, 38:3 (2003), pp. 20-21.

[12] Firth, *Clarke Papers*, 1, pp. 376-8.

[13] *Ibid.*, pp. 376-8.

From this basis, he argued that God may have revealed his wrath against Charles I, but that does not mean that 'God will destroy these persons [i.e. kings in general] or that power'.[14] Furthermore, God had clearly shown that they must not 'sette uppe' or 'preserve' kings where it threatens the public interest. But God had not yet made plain whether it would be hazardous to the public interest to 'goe about to destroy or take away' king and Lords or whether 'it would be [more] hazardous to retain them'. His plea is not to rush to judgement on this issue; after all, he had been notably reluctant to back adjutator calls for a march on London at the time of the crisis of Parliament-Army relations in June and July 1647. He had in fact a temperamental reluctance to act precipitously.[15]

All this gives us the key to Cromwell's politics over the next fifteen months: an ever-greater conviction that God intended Charles I to be struck down, and a continuing uncertainty about when and how that would be done and about the extent of his and the army's agency. This anger against a King who was duplicitous and willing the nation back into blood, the principal author and progenitor of the Second Civil War, can be seen to mount steadily; and Cromwell's public and private letters are a chronicle of his introspective search for the connection between God's actions in the history of His first chosen people of Israel, and of His new chosen people of England. In a sense Goffe's meditation at Putney took fifteen months to reach fruition.[16]

We have no record of Cromwell contributing to any of the prayer meetings, but given his background as a fiery lay preacher, his encouragement of others, and his willingness to deploy exactly the hermeneutics of prophetic preaching in the 1650s (as we will see), there is little reason to doubt that this is an accident of the fragmentary surviving evidence. But it does help us to understand the stream-of-consciousness letters rooted in biblical reflection which were concentrated in the years 1648-1653.

---

[14] *Ibid.*, p. 379.

[15] Davis, *Oliver Cromwell*, pp. 23-28 is especially good on Cromwell's prudence during the crises of 1647.

[16] Morrill and Baker, 'Zeruiah', pp. 22-32; J. F. Wilson, *Pulpit in Parliament: Puritanism in the English Civil War 1640-1648* (Princeton, 1969), pp. 198-214, offers an admirable account of the distinction between 'prophetic and apocalyptic eschatologies', one unpacking God's plan and an open future, the other making clear exactly what God was intending to do. Cromwell's was clearly a prophetic message; Allen's *A faithful memorial* (1659) is the only account of the Windsor Prayer Meeting in late April 1648 and Clarke never kept more than an abbreviated account of the prayer meetings referred to in his papers.

Particularly important are a series in 1648 that are saturated in reflections on the book of Isaiah and from the epistles. In a particularly revealing letter to Oliver St John, he suddenly burst into a passionate aside: 'This scripture hath been much stay to me: read it; Isaiah eighth, [verses] 10,11,14;- read all the chapter.'[17] The relevant passage, in the King James Version, runs:

> Take counsel together, and it shall come to nought; speak the word, and it shall not stand: for God is with us. For the Lord spake thus to me with a strong hand, and instructed me that I should not walk in the way of this people ... and he shall be for a sanctuary, but for a stone of stumbling and rock of offence to both the House of Israel from the Lord of Hosts, for a gin and for a snare to the inhabitants of Jerusalem.

We do not know whether Cromwell had a Geneva Bible with its marginal glosses.[18] If he did, the gloss on verse 14 was 'he will defend you who are his elect and reject the rest, meaning Christ against whom the Jews would stumble and fall'. All the leaders and great ones will be swept away, but a godly remnant will survive.[19]

'This scripture' seems to have been haunting Cromwell three months earlier in June 1648. In an outburst in the middle of a letter to Fairfax full of nitty-gritty military matters as he swept through South Wales, he wrote:

> I pray God teach this nation ... what the mind of God may be in all this, and what our duty is. Surely it is not that the poor godly people of this Kingdom should still be the objects of wrath and anger, nor that our God would have our necks under a yoke of bondage; for these things that have lately come to pass have been the wonderful works of God; breaking the rod of the oppressor, as in the day of Midian, not with garments much rolled in blood but by the terror of the Lord.[20]

This passage draws on Galatians, on Acts and on the Second Letter to the Corinthians, but the central image with its reference to the breaking of the Midianites is from the book of Isaiah, just after the verses he cited to

---

[17] Carlyle/Lomas, *L&S*, 1, p. 350.

[18] For his use of different translations see below pp. 10-11 and note 27.

[19] For the glosses in the Geneva Bible, I have used http://bible.christiansunite.com/gen.cgi

[20] Carlyle/Lomas, *L&S:* 1, p. 321.

Oliver St John.[21] And the reference to the day of Midian invokes the story of Gideon, the farmer who had been called from the plough to lead the armies of Israel. He winnowed the armies, reducing them to a compact force of Israel's russet-coated captains and he destroyed the Midianites and harried their fleeing army for 200 miles as Cromwell did after Preston. He then executed the Kings of the Midianites, denying them quarter because they had shed innocent blood on Mt Tabor. Having refused to take the crown himself he returned, loaded with honours, to his farm. It is not surprising that Cromwell found this a powerful story and suitable to his condition in 1648. Indeed his account of the battle of Preston, written the day after and sent to Speaker Lenthall, reads less like other accounts of the battle than it does of the Biblical account of Gideon's defeat of the Midianites at Ain Harod. This sense of the godly remnant being charged by God with great things sustained him through the crisis of the autumn of 1648. Reflecting, in a letter to Robert Hammond on 6 November, a full month before Pride's Purge, and in clear keen anticipation of it, Cromwell wrote of the actions of those he took to be his allies in Scotland:

> A lesser party of a Parliament hath made it lawful to declare the greater part a faction, and made the Parliament null, and call a new one, and to do this by force … . Think of the example and of the consequences, and let others think of it too.[22]

Cromwell was working out his own destiny in relation to God's plan, and God was no democrat. He had worked through a godly remnant in the days of Isaiah and he could and would do so again. This is the essence of other remarkable letters Cromwell wrote to Robert Hammond in the course of 1648, pleading with him to discern God's providential hand in current affairs. One paragraph alone in a letter of 25 November has 24 citations from eleven biblical books, with especial focus on the Epistle of James [ch.1 vv 2-6] with its exhortation to christians 'to ask in faith, nothing wavering — for he that wavereth is like a wave of the sea driven with the wind and tossed' and from Romans 8:1-6, with its great cry that, freed from the law, the true Christian must look beyond present deprivations to the presence of the Holy Spirit. Life in such a situation, say both St Paul and Cromwell, is life beyond hazard. In the fifteen months that straddled the period from the Putney Debates to the Regicide, Cromwell's letters contain constant meditations on

---

[21] Isaiah 9:4.
[22] Carlyle/Lomas, L&S, 3, p. 391 (supplement 35).

scriptures that are of a piece with the practice of army prayer meetings.

At no other point of his life are Cromwell's letters so bible-rich as in the period from Putney to Pride's Purge.[23] Striking by contrast is the relative sparsity of biblical references in his letters in the years 1640-7 or during his Irish campaigns of 1649-50. Few of his letters survive for the period from the Battle of Worcester (3 September 1651) to the establishment of the Protectorate, and during that period biblical references are confined to his private letters to family and old friends. After that, most of his public letters were drafted for him and we find little of interest for this paper. But at that point we can focus on his public utterances as Lord Protector that were in part political harangues, in part homilies.

III

The following sections will explore Cromwell's personal letters to close family and friends; and letters to public figures that he could be certain would be publicly shared, and in many cases printed. We then move on to the more problematic surviving accounts of his speeches.

On 13 October 1638 Cromwell — a man of 39 — wrote to his cousin, an 18-year-old newly married to Oliver St John, the rising star of the legal profession, and launched into a classic conversion narrative explaining how he had been 'a chief, the chief of sinners' [1 Timothy 1:15], but that God had called him 'out of darkness' despite his unworthiness not because he had earned any special merit by his way of life. As a result, his 'soul is with the congregation of the firstborn' (Jesus Christ [Hebrews 12:27]). It has all the hallmarks of a letter of encouragement to one who seems to have confided that she was 'in a dry barren wilderness where no water is' [Psalm 63:1]. And it is a letter saturated in Biblical language. In a letter of around 800 words there are thirteen different quotations or paraphrases from five different psalms, three New Testament epistles, the 2nd Book of Samuel, and three separate allusions to the Gospel of John.[24] None is developed, each

---

[23] If we take the 51 letters for 1648 contained in Carlyle/Lomas, *L&S* (vol. 1, letters 52-85 and supplements 26-39 [including 36/1-4]), 12 contain biblical references or allusion. Many of the others are brief military orders. Most of the twelve are to Thomas Fairfax and Thomas Hammond (private) or William Lenthall or the Scottish Commissioners (public). On the relative reliability of the various editions of his words, see John Morrill, 'Textualizing and contextualizing Cromwell', *Historical Journal*, 33 (1990), pp. 629-39.

[24] R. S. Paul, *The Lord Protector* (London, 1955), pp. 399-400.

resonating into a cavernous silence of the soul. It is hardly likely that he adopted this rhetorical strategy to impress his young cousin. He is surely seeking to root his own experience in that of the people of God; to universalise his experience of the power of God's grace to batter its way into stubborn hearts. At its heart is the assertion that although he had been 'a chief, the chief of sinners', 'he who hath begun a good work in me would perfect it in the day of Christ' [Philippians 1:6]. Most striking is the assertion, the bolder because it is not a direct allusion to Scripture, that Cromwell 'if here I may honour my God either by doing or by suffering, I shall be most glad'.[25] Here was Oliver, suffering from acute bronchitis and bouts of malaria, and languishing in a hateful job as estate manager for the Dean and Chapter of Ely, with scant opportunity to be *doing* the Lord's business. This is the coiled-spring effect of which I have written elsewhere, the waiting in suffering until the Lord showed how be could serve by doing: in the Long Parliament, in the New Model Army, in the act of Regicide, as Lord Protector.[26]

This letter teaches us one more thing. Cromwell was quoting from memory, and was mingling not only from the Geneva and King James versions, but also the Coverdale Version of the Psalms (as prescribed in the Book of Common Prayer).[27] This reinforces the idea that Cromwell not only attended a local parish church until 1640 and had all his children baptised there,[28] but was influenced by the language of its liturgies. More important is the evidence of this letter, which sets the scene for the remaining twenty years of his life, that he knew much of the bible by heart. But the mingling of translations suggests not learning by rote, but relentless and repeated

---

[25] Robert Paul speculates (*Lord Protector*, pp. 99-100), that this draws on Philippians 4:11 [sic for 10] – 'that I may know him and the power of his Resurrection, and the fellowship of his sufferings, being made conformable unto his death'; but I think this is a bit of a stretch.

[26] John Morrill, 'A liberation theology? Aspects of Puritanism in the English Revolution', in Laura Lunger Knoppers (ed.), *Puritanism and its Discontents* (Newark, Delaware, 2003), pp. 39-45.

[27] Paul, *Lord Protector*, pp. 399-400. Paul shows that Cromwell sometimes cites the King James version, sometimes the Geneva Translation, and sometimes conflates the two. But he does not notice that Cromwell also sometimes draws on the Coverdale translation of the psalms, which Cromwell could have known from the services laid down in the Book of Common Prayer.

[28] All Cromwell's children were baptised in the parish churches of Huntingdon. Since Cromwell was so involved in raising money for Dr Walter Welles's lectureship in Godmanchester, he may have worshipped there or in St Ives in the 1630s, but we have no evidence of attendance at or participation in any parish church after the early 1630s; Morrill, 'Early Life' in Morrill (ed.), *Oliver Cromwell*, pp. 22-36.

rereading. Other examples of Cromwell's intense engagement with the Bible include Hugh Peter's testimony that Cromwell spent the whole night of 13th October 1645, the eve of his storm and massacre of the garrison of Basing House, with its Catholic chapel packed with images, meditating on psalm 115 with its exaltation in the destruction of idols;[29] Edmund Ludlow's testimony that at his meeting with the Lord General in 1650, Cromwell 'spent at least an hour in the exposition of psalm 110', with its clear Regicidal message;[30] Samuel Carrington's testimony that at the end of his life Cromwell 'caused one of his gentlemen often to read the tenth chapter of Matthew and twice a day himself rehearsed the 71 Psalm'.[31] (Matthew 10 concerns the commissioning of the Apostles, and Jesus' predictions of the difficulties they will face; psalm 71 is a psalm of consolation — 'cast me not off in the time of old age ... when I am old and greybearded ... forsake me not'). On the battlefield of Dunbar he is reported to have repeated psalm 68 over and over again: let God arise, let his enemies be scattered: let them also that hate him flee before him. The battle won and with the pursuit to come, he halted the whole army to sing psalm 117 ('O praise the LORD, all ye nations: praise him, all ye people. For his merciful kindness is great toward us: and the truth of the LORD endureth for ever. Praise ye the LORD').[32]

The Protestant Bible consists of 67 books, 40 in the Old Testament and 27 in the New.[33] At some time of his life Cromwell cited a great majority of them (at least 34 of the former and 21 from the latter). But there are striking concentrations: if we take the quotations or allusions which are load-bearing, then one third were drawn from the Epistles, and one quarter from the psalms. Extracts from the major prophets (above all Isaiah), from the early books of the Old Testament (above all Numbers) and from the Gospels (especially John), each represent between 10 and 15 per cent. The remainder (less than ten per cent) come from the later Histories, the minor prophets, the Wisdom literature and the Apocalyptic books. The stories of

---

[29] Carlyle/Lomas, L&S, 1, p. 227.

[30] Paul, Lord Protector, p. 221; C. H. Firth (ed.), The Memoirs of Edmund Ludlow 1625-74, 2 vols (Oxford, 1894), 1, p. 243; PS 110:5 'The Lord at thy right hand shall strike through kings in the day of his wrath'.

[31] S. Carrington, The History of the Life and Death of his most serene Highness, Oliver Cromwell (London, 1659), p. 230.

[32] Paul, Lord Protector, p. 228.

[33] There is a useful and accurate display of the Books accepted by each of the great religious traditions at http://en.wikipedia.org/wiki/Books_of_the_Bible.

Moses, of David and of the primitive Church's struggles with paganism and pharisaical religion form the core of his scriptural meditations.[34]

Cromwell regularly encouraged members of family — by blood and marriage — to ponder the lessons of scripture. In the period 1648-50 he had persistent worries about his son and heir Richard. He wrote anxiously to Richard's father-in-law Richard Mayor asking him to take Richard in hand ('I wish he may be serious, the times require it').[35] And in one of his few surviving letters to his son — in which famously he encouraged him to read Raleigh's *History of the World* as 'a body of History, which will add much more to your understanding than fragments of story' — he also (and more emphatically) wrote:

> You cannot find nor behold the face of God but in Christ; therefore labour to know God in Christ, which the Scripture makes the sum of all, even life eternal. But the true knowledge is not literal or speculative, but inward, transforming the mind to it. It's uniting to, and participating of, the Divine Nature (2 Peter i.4): it's such a knowledge as Paul speaks of (Philippians the 3rd, 8, 9, 10).

Let the Word transubstantiate within you. This is of a piece with his letter to Oliver St John: take a passage of scripture, and meditate upon it until it takes over your life and guides your actions.[36]

When his son-in-law Charles Fleetwood was in Ireland, Cromwell wrote a series of letters baring his soul: a paean to the unconditional redeeming love of Christ in 1652,[37] an agonised, demoralised cry in August 1653 as the Nominated Assembly found itself in the Tower of Babel:

> Fain would I have my service accepted of the Saints (if the Lord will) but it is not so. Being of different judgements and of each sort seeking to propagate their own, that spirit of kindness that is to them all, is hardly accepted of any … . Yet it much falls out as

---

[34] This is based on my study of 24 letters across the course of his life from 1635-1656; and all his speeches to the Parliaments of 1653-8. About half of the references were recovered from the footnotes of Paul, *The Lord Protector* (but the rest by checking words and phrases in R. Young, *Analytical Concordance to the Bible*, eighth edition (London, 1979) and a variety of online Bible texts and concordances).

[35] Carlyle/Lomas, *L&S*, 1, p. 449 cf *ibid.*; 2, p. 451, 498; 2, p. 70.

[36] *Ibid.*, 2, pp. 53-54.

[37] Carlyle/Lomas, *L&S:* 2, pp. 258-9.

> when the two Hebrews were rebuked: you know upon whom they turned their displeasure.[38]

Rebuked by Moses, an interesting aside given that he was to be hailed as the new Moses when he became Lord Protector four months later: a new Moses who had led his people out of slavery under Pharaoh (Charles I) through the Red Sea (Regicide) into a trek across the Desert that would only end when the people learned true obedience to God. But here it is the Moses who has himself to flee to the desert that is evoked, a downbeat message that he further reinforces by the next sentence: 'Oh, would I had wings like a dove, would I, &c'. Fleetwood could be expected to provide the etcetera from psalm 55: 'for then I would fly away and be at rest. Lo then would I wander far off, and remain in the wilderness. I would hasten my escape from the windy storm and tempest'. Here we have evidence that Cromwell was not simply taking a back seat in the second half of 1653; he was expressing his yearning to be allowed to retire from public life. But lacking the wings of a dove, he must remain at the treadmill of duty.[39]

In his letters to Fleetwood, Cromwell is sharing his own interiorized engagement with gobbets of Scripture so far as they related to his own condition. But in letters to a number of other close friends (Thomas Fairfax in 1648,[40] Robert Hammond,[41] Oliver St John[42] and Thomas Lord Wharton over a longer period)[43] he strove to share his sense of biblical revelation in order to keep them on-side. His letters represent a virtual army meeting. The letter to St John on 2 September 1648 urging him to meditate on Isaiah chapter 8 is one; the letter to Hammond on 25 November 1648 urging him to study a range of Scriptures in order that he might 'seek to know the mind of God in all that chain of Providences, whereby God brought thee thither and that person [Charles I] to thee' is another. All the latter's biblical allusions are intended to bind Hammond fast to his duty to hold the King fast until a newly elected Parliament is ready to put him on trial.[44]

---

[38] *Ibid.*, pp. 307-8.

[39] For another passionate soteriological outburst to Fleetwood, from June 1655, rooted in I Corinthians, see *ibid.*, pp. 451-2.

[40] Carlyle/Lomas, *L&S*, 1, pp. 295-6, 317-24, 356-7, 372-5, 390-1.

[41] *Ibid.*, pp. 287-90, 302-4, 393-403; 3, pp. 383, 389-92, 431-2.

[42] *Ibid.*, pp. 350-1.

[43] *Ibid.*, pp. 353-4, 521-3; 2, pp. 119, 219; 3, pp. 285-6.

[44] Above, p. 108. For the letter, one of Cromwell's longest, see Carlyle/Lomas, *L&S*, 1, pp. 393-400. For its biblical content, see Paul, *Lord Protector*, pp. 406-10.

There is a particularly interesting set of letters to Philip Lord Wharton between 1648 and 1652. Wharton was a close political ally in the mid to late 1640s, a key member of the 'Independent' alliance; but he was one of those close allies from whom he became seriously estranged by the Regicide,[45] and one of the many he worked to bring back into the Commonwealth fold.[46] He made a special push to get these former allies back into active politics at the time of his departure for Ireland. Stop sulking, he told them: you do not agree with what the Army did; but it is over now, and you surely approve of my expedition to Ireland with the intention of crushing the rebels there.[47] He challenged Wharton with a particular biblical precedent.

> Be not offended at the manner of God's working; perhaps no other way was left. What if God accepted the zeal, as he did that of Phineas, whose reason might have called for a jury! What if God have witnessed his approbation and acceptance to this[48] also, not only by signal outward acts, but to the heart also? What if I fear my friend [you] should withdraw his shoulder from the Lord's work through scandals, through false mistaken reasonings.[49]

The reference to Phineas is to the story told in the Book of Numbers chapter 25, where Jehovah's wrath at the people of Israel for worshipping false gods, a wrath manifested in the sending of a plague that killed 24,000 of them, was stayed by the zeal of Phineas in skewering an Israelite man and a Midianite slave in mid copulation rather than dragging them before the judges. Verse 11 tells us that by his action Phineas 'hath turned my wrath away from the children of Israel, while he was zealous for my sake among them, that I consumed not the children of Israel in my jealousy'. Calvin's terse gloss on this verse is 'He was zealous to

---

[45] Sean Kelsey, 'Wharton, Philip, fourth Baron Wharton (1613-1696)', *Oxford Dictionary of National Biography* (Oxford, 2004), www.oxforddnb.com/view/article/29170; G. F. Trevallyn Jones, *Saw-Pit Wharton* (Sydney, 1967), ch. 13.

[46] Blair Worden, *The Rump Parliament* (Cambridge, 1974), p. 209; see also *ibid.*, pp. 67-70.

[47] A. Guerden, *A Most Learned, Conscientious and Devout Exercise* (London, 1649) offers an account of a supposed speech by Cromwell on the eve of departing for Ireland in which he addressed a group of sulky Independents. See John Morrill, 'Guerden, Aaron (c. 1602-1676?)', *Oxford Dictionary of National Biography* (Oxford, 2004), www.oxforddnb.com/view/article/65795.

[48] 'This' refers specifically to Pride's Purge.

[49] Carlyle/Lomas, *L&S*, 1, p. 521.

maintain my glory.'⁵⁰ Wharton was not impressed by the claims of Phineas Cromwell, and remained aloof from all the regimes of the Interregnum, although Cromwell continued to send him scriptural exhortations, and even tried to persuade him to agree to a marriage alliance between the families.⁵¹

IV

There is little difference between Cromwell's private and public rhetoric. When the spirit moved him, he hurled biblical citations at those he sought to persuade or to intimidate. At Putney Cromwell had crossed not one Rubicon but two on the banks of the Thames. The first was political: he had seen that Charles I was not to be restored. The question now was when, how and by whom he was to replaced. He was still not convinced that he should be put on trial. He was still not convinced that he had to die. He became committed to Charles' abdication in favour of one of his sons. But we can see the process of change beginning to happen on 1 November and we can see a trajectory of events through the lost days of Putney that completed that process. The silence of the record screams out at us that this was one of the great epiphanies of his life and it ended in Regicide and in the struggle to create a new England, and indeed a new world. The one surviving fragment of a Cromwell speech from the days after Clarke stopped transcribing his notes was biblical. Cromwell responded to a demand from Thomas Harrison that Charles was a man of blood and that 'they should prosecute him', by reminding the Council of the Army that as the case of David's refusal to try Joab for the slaying of Abner illustrated, there were pragmatic circumstances in which murder was not to be punished.⁵²

The second Rubicon-moment was rhetorical. From now on Cromwell did not keep his biblical ruminations to himself. He began to share them vicariously with all those with whom he was in contact. His letters in 1648 are saturated in reflections on the book of Isaiah and from the epistles. Yet, having pushed himself through the Regicide with the help of Scripture, he appears to have felt less need to justify his actions in

⁵⁰ The Genevan gloss is taken from http://bible.christiansunite.com/gen.cgi?b=Nu&c=25.
⁵¹ For other letters from Cromwell to Wharton, see Carlyle/Lomas, *L&S*, 1, p. 353; 2, pp. 119, 219; 3, p. 285.
⁵² Firth, *Clarke Papers*, 1, p. 417. For a full exegesis, see Morrill and Baker, [see notes 12 & 17], pp. 14-35, esp. pp. 21-22; Morrill, 'Rewriting Cromwell', pp. 553-78, pp. 567-72.

Ireland to himself and others by scriptural meditation. He invoked providence to justify his actions at Drogheda and Wexford, but not Holy Scripture. His *Declaration of the Lord Lieutenant of Ireland for the undeceiving of deluded people* (1 Jan 1650) is an incandescent rebuke to the Catholic clergy who had accused him of coming to Ireland to effect 'the destruction of the lives of the inhabitants of this island'. It is full of scorn against the superstitious, priest-ridden practices of popery, but only once does he burst out into biblical purple.

> *Your covenant, if you understood it, is with death and hell* [a], *your union is with Simeon and Levi!* [b] *Associate yourselves and you shall be broken in pieces; take counsel together and it shall come to naught* [c] For although it becomes us to be humble in respect of ourselves, yet we can say to you: God is not with you.[53]

This contains allusions to [a] Isaiah 28[54] [b] Genesis 49:5-7 [c] Isaiah 8 v.9. We will return to [a] in a moment. The reference to Simeon and Levi is to the sons of Joseph disinherited ('I will divide them in Jacob, and scatter them in Israel') because they had committed atrocities against peaceful neighbouring tribes. The second Isaiah quote [c] comes from the very chapter he told St John had 'made great stay with' him 15 months earlier.

But if the purpose and justice of his work in Ireland did not require any internal agony, his campaign against the godly Scots did. And in the second great concentration of letters wrestling with God's Word, Cromwell harangued the Scots and ruminated with the English public about the righteousness of his cause. In eight letters to the political and religious leaders of Scotland and to William Lenthall, the bible was always open in his mind.

In a famous challenge to the Commissioners of the Kirk on 3 August 1650, Cromwell beseeched them 'in the bowels of Christ[55] [to] think it

---

[53] The Declaration is printed in Carlyle/Lomas, *L&S*, 2, pp. 5-23. This quotation is at p. 7. There is an implied reference to Isaiah 51:17, 22.

[54] 'We have made a covenant with death, and with hell are we at agreement ... and your covenant with death will be disannulled and your agreement with hell will not stand; when the overflowing scourge shall pass through, and ye shall be trodden down by it.' (Isaiah 28: 15, 18).

[55] This comes from Philippians 1:8 ('For God is my record, how greatly I long after you all in the bowels of Jesus Christ') and is a favourite phrase, occurring at least seven times in his writings between 1638 and 1657.

104 *Liberty, Authority, Formality*

possible you may be mistaken.' Here he was, the General commanding an undefeated army of godly protestants confronting an even larger undefeated army of godly protestants. He had done his own thinking, and for them as well as for himself: 'I pray you read the twenty-eighth of Isaiah, from the fifth to the fifteenth verse'. They would have known what a stinging rebuke that was: for the passage describes how Jewish priests, drunk with strong wine, vomited over the altar of the lord. 'There is', Cromwell rammed home his message, 'a spiritual fullness that the world may call drunkenness … a carnal confidence upon misunderstood and misapplied precepts, which may be called spiritual drunkenness.'[56] Repeating what he had hurled at the Catholic clergy at the beginning of the year, he added, 'There may be a covenant with death and hell. I will not say yours is so. But judge if such things have a politic aim: to avoid the overflowing scourge, or to accomplish worldly interests.'[57] You may be, he is saying, as bad as the Irish Catholic clergy who had an indubitable covenant with death and hell.

His contempt for the arrogance and presumption of the Scottish clergy was powerfully reinforced a few weeks later when he was besieging Edinburgh Castle and the clergy holed up there refused his safe conducts to come out and preach in their churches on the Lord's Day, giving as their reasons their distrust of his persecuting spirit. They said that 'it savours not of "ingenuity" to promise liberty of preaching the gospel and to limit the preachers thereof that they may not speak against the sins and enormities of Civil Powers'. For good measure they haughtily told him that 'they have not learnt Christ as to hang the equity of their cause upon events'. Cromwell delivered an extraordinary 1500 word rebuke, wishing 'blindness had not been upon their eyes to all those marvellous dispensations which God hath lately wrought'; claiming that 'you err through mistaking of the scriptures' (a sentiment that must have induced a presbyterial red mist);

> you say you have cause to regret that men of civil employments should usurp the calling and employment of ministry … are you troubled that Christ is preached? … It will be found an unjust and unwise jealousy, to deprive a man of his natural liberty upon the supposition that he may abuse it. When he doth abuse it, judge [him]. If a man speak foolishly, you suffer him gladly because you are wise; if erroneously, the truth more appears by your convic-

[56] *Ibid.*
[57] Carlyle/Lomas, *L&S*, 2, pp. 79-80.

tion of him. Stop such a man's mouth by sound words[58] which cannot be gainsayed.[59]

V

Cromwell's speeches, unlike the letters, have been mediated through the hands of scribes and seventeenth-century editors. Such public utterances may be rhetorically insouciant (Cromwell pouring out his heart), or they may be cynically calculated to give an illusion of godliness. They are, by themselves and in comparison with the letters, less self-evidently the work of a sincere seeker after God's truth than of an embattled head of state. My own view is that they are evidence of his sincerity (not of his insincerity) but it is less easy to prove this than with the letters.[60]

The Kingship crisis of 1657 is a case in point. Did Cromwell turn down the kingship because he thought his army colleagues would prevent him from taking it or because he could not, in clear conscience, accept it? Cromwell, explaining why despite the power of the arguments used by those seeking to make him King ('I cannot take upon to refel [sic] those grounds, for they are strong and rational') finally made it clear he was not willing to accept.[61] He *could* not agree to take the title, he spoke of providential signs and concluded: 'I would not seek to set up that that providence hath destroyed and laid in the dust, and I would not build Jericho again.'[62] What God had destroyed (the walls of Jericho in the Book of Joshua, the House of Stuart in 1649) only God could restore. In a brilliant essay Blair Worden links Cromwell's refusal to a festering anxiety put there by erst-

---

[58] Grant Tapsell detects here a distinct pre-echo of the defence of 'sound doctrine' and the example of a good conversation to be found in clauses XXXV-XXXVI of the Instrument of Government.

[59] Carlyle/Lomas, *L&S*, 2, pp. 128-9. In the course of this harangue, he quotes from Numbers 11:26-27, how Moses had refused to silence two self-appointed prophets, Eldad and Medad, saying that 'he wished all Israel were prophets'. He was to put great emphasis on this last phrase at a crucial point in his speech to the Nominated Assembly on 4 July 1653: see below p. nn.

[60] Ronald Hutton, *Debates in Stuart history* (Harlow, 2002), pp. 93-131; Clive Holmes, *Why was Charles I executed?* (London, 2006), ch. 7; A. S. P. Woodhouse, *Puritanism and Liberty* (London, 1938), Introduction, p. 38, on which see the comment of Paul, *The Lord Protector*, p. 148.

[61] I. Roots (ed.), *Speeches of Oliver Cromwell* (London, 1989), p. 128 (13 April 1657).

[62] Roots (ed.), *Speeches*, p. 137.

while friends who accused him of the 'sin of Achan' — Achan's furtive covetous secreting of 'the accursed thing' in the booty taken at the sack of Jericho caused God to withhold further victories from Joshua. Was not Cromwell's pride and his coveting of fame and power the accursed thing that had caused his 1655 expedition to the Caribbean to fail? Worden's conclusion is that Cromwell's long rambling speeches during the kingship crisis 'indicate the difficulty of the decision and the strain which days of fruitless prayer created in him'. It was the Bible that came finally to his rescue.[63] There seems no need to see this as face-saving rhetoric for a decision forced on him by others. It was a decision forced on him by God.

The evidence of the letters, the circumstantial evidence of his long experience as a lay preacher and of prophetic speaking in prayer meetings, allows us to take the Biblical language of the speeches seriously. In his speech opening the 1st Protectorate Parliament, he began by citing Psalm 40: 'Many, O LORD my God, are thy wonderful works which thou hast done, and thy thoughts which are to us-ward.'[64] The passage he cites follows on from this suggestive verse: 'He brought me up also out of an horrible pit, out of the miry clay, and set my feet upon a rock, and established my goings.'[65] He then offered his own thoughts on the sermon that Thomas Goodwin had preached to the House before his own speech, about 'Israel's bringing out of Egypt through a wilderness, by many signs and wonders towards a place of rest' — just one of the times when he was likened and likens himself to Moses.[66] After laying out the theme of healing and settling, he returns to the Bible for a preacher's exegesis of the epistles of Paul to Timothy (2 Tim 3:1-2 and 1 Tim 4:1-2) and a little later the epistle of Jude.[67] Each is the biblical launching pad for a passage in which Cromwell reflects on their duties and responsibilities at this moment.

Five lunar months later, in dissolving the 1st Protectorate Parliament on 22 January 1655, Cromwell opens with a lengthy quotation from Psalm

---

[63] Blair Worden, 'Oliver Cromwell and the Sin of Achan' in (ed.), D. L. Smith, *Cromwell and the Interregnum* (Oxford, 2003), pp. 37-59, at pp. 57-59.

[64] Roots, *Speeches*, p. 29.

[65] The full passage he cites is exactly the translation in the King James Version, suggesting Cromwell had either prepared the text, or that it was tidied up prior to publication.

[66] Roots, *Speeches*, pp. 29-30. For discussions of Cromwell as Moses, see Laura Lunger Knoppers, *Constructing Cromwell: ceremony, portrait and print, 1645-1661* (Cambridge, 2000), pp. 155-7; Morrill, *Oliver Cromwell*, pp. 270-2.

[67] Roots, *Speeches*, pp. 31-33; Jude 1:22-23 ('and of some have compassion, making a difference: And others save with fear, pulling them out of the fire').

78 which contains a reproof that members have not hearkened to its challenge to 'set their hope in God and not forget the works of God'.[68] But the great biblical influence in this speech is the Epistle to the Hebrews, and especially chapters 8-12. He makes clear that his decision to dissolve Parliament was based on his discernment that 'the cause of God by the works of God, which are the testimony of God, upon which rock whoever splits shall suffer shipwreck',[69] and he then seeks to demonstrate that the failure of the Parliament to take up the clear mandates given to it had resulted in God driving them onto the rocks: 'he hath shaken and tumbled down ... everything which he hath not planted'. (Hebrews 12:27). This was not stuff that would convince anyone not already convinced; but it clearly convinced Cromwell himself.

In the longest of his speeches (17 September 1656), despite the predominantly secular tone as he defended his war with Spain and his controversial extra-legal actions, Cromwell offered an extended commentary on psalm 85, a passionate plea for God to remain willing to bless a people that remains unworthy; which he urged them to 'peruse [as] very instructive and significant'. He was to return to that psalm twice more in later speeches to the same Parliament'.[70] In his attempt on 25 January 1658 to keep the Second Parliament from hara-kiri, he pleaded with the members to mark what 'Paul saith to the Church of Corinth, as I remember: mark such as cause division and offences'.[71] Actually he is misremembering: it is Paul to the Romans 16:17, a sign that he was working from memory. But to the end, the Bible was not a way of adding rhetorical colour to his thoughts, but a springboard to them.

We will end with the remarkable speech he made to the Nominated Assembly on 4 July 1653, which needs a paper to itself, especially in the light of Robert Paul's suggestion that:

> the clue to interpretation is in Oliver's own claim that it was a 'charge' — the kind of commissioning given to a puritan minister at his ordination or induction to the pastorate. It is the practice on

---

[68] The Instrument of Government had specified a period of five months as the minimum time a parliament should sit. MPs were preparing a body of legislation, including a revised constitutional form on the assumption that five months meant five calendar months; Cromwell caught them unawares by interpreting the term to mean lunar months; Roots, *Speeches*, p. 58.

[69] *Ibid.*, p. 63.

[70] *Ibid.*, pp. 104-6, 170, 185; Worden 'Achan', p. 54.

[71] Roots, *Speeches*, p. 185.

> such an occasion for the procedure to follow a clearly-defined pattern, in which a review of the steps leading to the ordinand's 'call' and his acceptance, would proceed to the Charge or commissioning … . This is the pattern of Oliver's speech.'[72]

Cromwell began by a lengthy analysis of 'that series of providences wherein the Lord hath appeared, dispensing wonderful things to these nations from the beginning of our troubles to this very day'. Having concluded that 'truly God hath called you to this work by, I think, as wonderful providences as ever passed upon the sons of men in so short a time', he exhorted them 'to own your call, for it is from God'. At this point midway through a 3-hour speech, he turned to a series of extended biblical exegeses: Hosea 11:12; Exodus 32; Isaiah 41; Romans 12; Psalm 110 (the one he had spent an hour explaining to Ludlow); Isaiah 43; ending with Psalm 68 (the psalm on which he had meditated at Dunbar).[73]

> In my pilgrimage, and in some exercises I have had abroad, I did read that Scripture often, forty-first of Isaiah, 19: where God gave me, and some of my fellows encouragement as to what He would do there and elsewhere; which he hath performed for us. He said, He *would plant in the wilderness the cedar, the shittah*[74] *tree, and the myrtle and the oil tree; and he would set in the desert the fir tree, and the pine tree, and the boxtree together.* For what end will the Lord do all this? [verse 20] *That they may see and understand together that the hand of the Lord hath done this and the Holy One of Israel hath created it* — that he that hath wrought all the salvations and deliverances we have received. For what end! To see, and know, and understand together, that He hath done and wrought all this for the good of the whole flock. Therefore I beseech you — but I think I need not — have a care of the whole flock! Love the sheep, love the lambs; love all, tender all, cherish and countenance all, in all things that are good. And if the poorest Christian, the most mistaken Christian, shall desire to live peaceably and quietly under you — I say, if any shall desire but to lead a life in godliness and honesty, let him be protected.[75]

---

[72] Paul, *Lord Protector*, pp. 279-80, unfortunately not leading to any sustained analysis of Cromwell's choice of Biblical themes.

[73] Roots, *Speeches*, pp. 8-27.

[74] That is, the acacia tree.

[75] Roots, *Speeches*, p. 22.

Here is the authentic voice of the preacher, with its drawing of the listener into and then beyond the text. Here was as passionate a plea for religious liberty and tolerance as we find anywhere in his recorded words — the celebration of all the trees that rejoice in their togetherness as forest despite their variety and difference as trees. Above all, here is his call for the 'most mistaken Christian' to be protected. And then on he goes, pleading for the Assembly to take steps to promote public preaching and then on to the next text — psalm 100 verse 3 ('Thy people will be willing in the day of his power'),[76] back to Isaiah 43:21[77] and on to a plea as passionate as his plea for tolerance, his call for the Assembly to find ways to make the whole people fit to govern themselves, based around that phrase from Numbers 11:29 (which he had hurled against the Edinburgh presbyters in 1650): 'would all the Lord's people were prophets'.[78]

VI

Cromwell's obsessive Biblicism was discussed by Robert Paul in 1955, and by Blair Worden in 1985.[79] The focus of this essay is less on how his biblical allusions help us to understand what he meant, than on the process by which he came to take crucial decisions. When God's purposes were clear to him — as during the first civil war or in Ireland — he had little difficulty in deciding what was expected of him. But when God's purposes were more concealed — as over what to do with a King who would not accept God's judgement on him in battle, over how to reconcile his duty to the Army and to the Parliament that had created it, how to be sure that God was behind his undefeated army and not the undefeated Protestant army of the Scots, or *how* to move beyond the overthrow of the old tyrannies of the flesh into building a new commonwealth of the spirit, only prolonged meditations on the Scripture could help him. We are privileged to be able to listen in to some of the outcomes of those meditations.

It was from the bible that Cromwell developed his thinking about political forms;[80] it was in wrestling with scripture that he articulated his unresolved struggle to work out whether God's plan encompassed a

---

[76] *Ibid.*, p. 23.   [77] *Ibid.*, p. 24.   [78] *Ibid.*, pp. 24-25.
[79] Paul, *Lord Protector*, pp. 27-28, 39, 45, 148-9, 168-9, 221-2, 231, 274, 279, 300-2, 386, 397-9; Worden 'Achan', pp. 37-59.
[80] Firth, *Clarke Papers*, 1, pp. 369-71. I will discuss this speech of Cromwell's in the published version of my Ford Lectures at Oxford, provisionally entitled *Living with Revolution: the*

chosen people, a nation, or a godly remnant, His elect; and it was from the Bible that he learned that God was more concerned with ends than with means.[81]

And beyond that are legion questions about how Cromwell's Biblicism relates to that of others: of the members of the Westminster Assembly,[82] teasing out God's preferred ecclesiology from the New Testament; Thomas Hobbes, leery of the Old Testament, but still hooked on the New Testament as he explored the moral and religious duties of mankind;[83] William Dowsing, just one man who acquired, read and reread, feverishly annotating, sermons in which God's plan for the present was found encoded in the events of ancient Israel.[84] And all this in a world in which scholars were becoming painfully aware of the instabilities of the text in which God revealed himself: the Johannine comma[85] and other verses not in the earliest surviving papyri;[86] the claim that much of the story had been corrupted and changed by Ezra many hundreds of years after the events they described.[87]

This account does not confront the view of historians, beginning with Christopher Hill, who have seen Puritans as encountering the Bible as a subversive political text underpinning and legitimising social revolution.[88]

peoples of Britain and Ireland and the crisis of the seventeenth century in the chapter entitled 'The case of the army truly stated: adjutating revolution'.

[81] William Lamont, 'Oliver Cromwell and English Calvinism' in *Cromwelliana*, 1994, pp. 2-6; J. C. Davis, 'Against Formality'.

[82] R. S. Paul, *The assembly of the Lord. Politics and religion in the Westminster Assembly and the grand debate* (Edinburgh, 1985); Chad van Dixhoorn, 'Reforming the Reformation: Theological Debate at the Westminster Assembly 1643-1652', University of Cambridge PhD thesis (2004), in 6 volumes (soon to be published).

[83] Thomas Hobbes, *Leviathan*, enumerable editions since 1650, parts 3 and 4.

[84] John Morrill, 'William Dowsing, the bureaucratic Puritan' in J. Morrill, P. Slack, D. Woolf, (eds), *Public duty and private conscience in seventeenth-century England* (Oxford, 1992), pp. 173-203; John Morrill, 'William Dowsing and the administration of iconoclasm' in T. Cooper (ed.), *The Journal of William Dowsing : iconoclasm in East Anglia during the English Civil War* (Woodbridge, 2001), pp. 1-28.

[85] Rob Iliffe, 'Friendly criticism: Richard Simon, John Locke, Isaac Newton and the *Johannine Comma*', Ariel Hessayon (ed.), *Scripture and Scholarship in Early Modern England* (Aldershot, 2006), pp. 137-56.

[86] *Ibid.*

[87] Noel Malcolm, *Aspects of Hobbes* (Oxford, 2002), ch. 12.

[88] Christopher Hill, *The English Bible and the seventeenth-century revolution* (London, 1993).

Such readings were possible, as in the hermeneutics of a William Walwyn or a Gerrard Winstanley.[89] But Cromwell's reading was intense and immediate, a personal encounter between a man convinced he was a divine instrument and a God who spoke in a still small voice through his prophets and saints. What Cromwell believed may well be less important than how he came to believe it.

---

[89] For Walwyn and the Bible, see Lotte Mulligan, 'The religious roots of William Walwyn's Radicalism', *Journal of Religious History* 12 (1982), pp. 162-7; but set this against J. C. Davis, 'The Levellers and Religion' in Peter Gaunt (ed.), *The English Civil War: the essential readings* (Oxford, 2000), pp. 279-302. For Winstanley, see Andrew Bradstock (ed.), *Winstanley and the Diggers 1649-1999* (London, 1999), but set against J. C. Davis, 'Gerrard Winstanley and the Restoration of True Magistracy', *Past and Present* 70 (1976), pp. 76-93.

Chapter 6

Roger L'Estrange, Printed Petitions and the Problem of Intentionality[1]

Mark Knights

Petitioning and addressing were subscriptional genres with formal and informal rules. They were used both to construct and question authority, and implicitly claimed a liberty to do so. This chapter will focus on the petitioning, addressing, engaging and associating of 1659-60, activities that helped to articulate popular royalism and so aided the restoration of the monarchy.[2] In particular it will examine the deployment of these genres by one of the most prolific and interesting writers of the period, Roger L'Estrange. L'Estrange is perhaps best known for his work after the restoration as licenser of the press and for his polemic of the 1680s. The latter will indeed become part of the story.[3] But we shall also be concerned with earlier work, for in 1660, faced with a barrage of criticism from within royalist ranks, L'Estrange published a vindication in which he included over twenty petitions, addresses, declarations and other works which he had published anonymously immediately before and after the restoration of Charles II. These pieces, which might otherwise have remained unattributable, are highly revealing both about the nature of petitioning and other subscriptional genres; about the problems of print and textual authority; and about the difficulties of ascribing authorial intention.[4]

---

[1] I am grateful to Geoff Kemp, Gaby Mahlberg, Jonathan Scott and John Morrow for their very helpful comments and suggestions.

[2] For accounts of 1659-60 see G. Davies, *The Restoration of Charles II, 1658-60* (San Marino, CA, 1955); A. Woolrych, *England without a King 1649-1660* (London,1983); Woolrych, 'Introduction', *Complete Prose Works of John Milton*, ed. R. Ayers (New Haven, 1980), 7; R. Hutton, *The Restoration: a political history of England and Wales 1658-1667* (Oxford, 1985); R. Mayers, *1659: the crisis of the Commonwealth* (Woodbridge, 2004).

[3] G. Kitchin, *Sir Roger L'Estrange* (London 1913, reprinted New York 1971); P. Hinds, 'Roger L'Estrange, the Rye House Plot, and the Regulation of Political Discourse in Late-Seventeenth-Century London', *The Library*, VII, 3 (March 2002), pp. 3-35.

[4] In 1680 his publisher advertised that there were 'several discourses and pamphlets abroad in the world that passe for the writings of Mr Roger L'Estrange, wherein he never had any hand at all' (Kitchin, *L'Estrange*, p. 240). Geoff Kemp provides an accurate bibliography in

There appear to be fundamental inconsistencies in L'Estrange's position. First, the mobilisation of popular pressure and incitement to armed resistance that characterise his work in 1659-60 seems to sit oddly with his vigorous condemnation of petitioning in 1680 as rebellious and rabble-rousing. Was L'Estrange merely being hypocritical in disallowing his enemies what he had already allowed himself and his own side to do? And how could one judge if a petition was seditious or loyal? Second, as Geoff Kemp has recently highlighted, L'Estrange's work as a government censor who sought to restrict press debate seems in tension with his own prolific output.[5] Third, for all his black and white polemic he appeared to contemporaries to be an ambiguous, even dangerously enigmatic figure capable of appearing in different disguises; he was thus very difficult to read, or at least, he could be read in very different ways. To what or whom was he really loyal — himself, the king, the church, or, as his enemies suggested, popery or even Cromwell ('Nol's fiddler')? And, more generally, how can or could the printed works of such apparently ambiguous figures be accurately or properly interpreted, especially if, as in 1659-60, they deliberately impersonated the voices of others?[6] How did — or could — contemporaries decide on the motives and intentions of those who apparently used print to mislead? And if this was a problem for L'Estrange's age, can we as historians escape it? Trying to resolve these inconsistencies, ambiguities and paradoxes may help us to explore some significant problems about the nature of formality of genres, liberty of the press and textual authority in later seventeenth century England.

I

During the succession and constitutional crisis of 1679-1681 L'Estrange condemned popular petitioning. In early 1680, in response to mass petitions designed to pressurise the king into letting parliament sit, he published *A Seasonable Memorial in some Historical Notes upon the Liberties*

---

his 'The works of Roger L'Estrange' in Beth Lynch and Anne Dunan-Page (eds), *Sir Roger L'Estrange and Restoration Culture* (forthcoming). Peter Hinds is also reviewing L'Estrange's output 1678-1681 in a forthcoming book *'The Horrid Popish Plot': Roger L'Estrange and the Circulation of Political Discourse in London*.

[5] Geoff Kemp, 'L'Estrange and the Publishing Sphere' in Jason McElligott (ed.), *Fear, Exclusion and Revolution: Roger Morrice and Britain in the 1680s* (Aldershot, 2006).

[6] Marchmont Nedham and Daniel Defoe spring to mind.

of the Presse and Pulpit, with the effects of Popular Petitions. In it he argued that the civil war had been more the result of 'an Imposture th[a]n of a Confederacy' and that the imposture occurred when the people had been tricked by petitions, protestations, associations and covenants into sedition. 'The Faction made use of Petitions as common House-breakers do of screws; they got in little by little and without much noise, and so Rifled the Government.' He noted that most petitions, for all their rhetoric of humility, had a 'complaining part' that made them little more than a 'libell'; that many of the signatures on petitions were fraudulently obtained; and that petitions 'grew higher and higher, till they brought the King to the Block ... and the First Petition (how plausible soever) was the Foundation of all our Ruines'. Popular petitioning, for L'Estrange, was a key cause of the great rebellion. Its effect 'in our Case was no less than the destruction of Three Kingdoms; and let the Matter be what it will, the Method is a most necessary Link in the Chain of a Rebellion'. It was, he asserted, wrong 'for the Multitude to interpose in Matters of State', for the masses did not understand politics and 'the number of hands adds nothing to the Weight of the Petition; and serves only for Terrour and Clamour'. Indeed, he thought there was a 'natural transition from a Popular Petition to a Tumult'. Hence the civil war had been 'driven on, from First to Last, mainly by PETITIONS'.[7]

L'Estrange repeated these arguments in one of his best-selling tracts, *Citt and Bumpkin* (1680), which went through five editions by 1681, applying them directly to the mass petitioning campaigns of 1679-80 which had attracted large support in London.[8] The tract was a satirical dialogue between a City radical and a country petitioner about how their campaigns had been 'manag'd'. It alleged that clubs had been set up in the city and its suburbs to promote the petitions; that many signatures were invented; that in both the city and the country the dissenters (as allies of the papists) were 'great promoters of the petition';[9] and that many of its other promoters were hypocrites, motivated by ambition or money but invoking religion. At the end of the tract 'Trueman' (a thinly veiled L'Estrange) exposes the petitioners as 'Republicans and Separatists' and claims the petitions had been promoted 'by Falshoods' and 'fawning methods of popularity'. All power, Trueman asserts, was from God, not from the people; and the people could not rightly plead self-preservation, even against a tyrant.[10] A

---

[7] *A Seasonable Memorial* (1680), pp. 18, 21, 23, 36-37.
[8] M. Knights, 'London's "Monster" Petition of 1680', *Historical Journal*, 36 (1993), pp. 39-67.
[9] *Citt and Bumpkin* (1680), p. 3. [10] *Ibid.*, pp. 27, 29, 37-38.

second part of the dialogue, also published in 1680, attacked petitioning as part of the inventions, fictions and arts of popularity. To drive home his point L'Estrange also issued a graphic satire, *The Committee*, which depicted 'all the Rabble of Sects upon a consult joyntly petitioning & J[ack] Presbyter Chairman'.[11]

L'Estrange found himself bitterly attacked for having 'scandalously misrepresented all the late Petitions and the promoters of them' and there were complaints that his 'writings create Misunderstandings and tend to the Embroyling of the Kingdome'.[12] So intense was the pressure against him when parliament took up the matter in October 1680 that he fled abroad. But he also tried to vindicate himself in print. In *Discovery upon Discovery* (1680) L'Estrange refuted most of the wild stories that were circulating about him and, in order to show his loyalty to Charles II in exile, reprinted three pieces that he had published originally in 1659.[13]

This was not the first time he had published them as a vindication. Twenty years earlier, in June 1660, *L'Estrange his Apology* had gathered 21 pieces of print (including the three used in 1680) that had originally been published, anonymously, between Booth's rising in the summer of 1659 and the spring of 1660.[14] They included declarations, engagements, remonstrances and protests, often claiming popular support. For all his condemnation of popular 'Petitions ... Protestations and Associations', in 1660 and in 1680 L'Estrange, ironically, used those that he had penned himself in order to defend his royalist credentials. And their content and form was at odds with his later anti-populist, anti-petitioning stance.

---

[11] *The Dialogue betwixt Cit and Bumpkin Answered* (1680), epistle dedicatory, analyses the print. The suggestion that a Presbyterian plot lay under the Popish plot had been outlined by L'Estrange in his *Answer to the Appeal* (1679).

[12] *L'Estrange's Appeal* (1681), p. 2.

[13] For two replies see J. P., *Mr L'Estrange Refuted with his own Arguments* (1681), and L. Mowbray, *The Portraicture of Roger L'Estrange Drawn to the Life* (1681).

[14] *L'Estrange his Apology* (1660) included *The Declaration of the City to the Men at Westminster* (1659), Aug.; *The Engagement and Remonstrance of London* (1659), 12 Dec.; *The Final Protest and Sense of the City* (1659), [Thomason: 19 Dec.]; *The Resolve of the City* (1659), 23 Dec.; *A Free Parliament proposed by the City to the Nation* (1659), 3 Jan. 1660; *A Plain Case* (1660), 24 Jan.; *To His Excellency General Monck. A Letter from the Gentlemen of Devon* (1660), 28 Jan.; *The Sense of the Army* (1660), 2 Feb.; *The Citizens Declaration for a Free Parliament* (1660), 2 Feb.; *For his Excellency Generall Monck* (1660), 4 Feb. (this claimed to have been printed at Oxford); *Peace to the Nation* (1660), [Thomason: 14 Feb.]; *A Word in Season, to General Monck* (1660), [Thomason: 18 Feb.]; *Be Merry and Wise, or A Seasonable Word to the Nation* (1660),

II

As David Zaret has shown, petitions (and we can extend the argument to other forms of subscriptional activity) created a discursive space, and, when printed, invoked a sense of public opinion.[15] A dialogic process of petition and counter-petition widened public discussion and created a public sphere that was difficult to close. Petitions and similar genres sought to mobilise and give both identity and purpose to a community; and as a form of incorporated community voice they also offered a vehicle for questioning the legitimacy of institutional bodies such as parliament, which claimed to represent the people. Petitions, addresses, declarations, engagements, associations, appeals, protests, remonstrances and even letters, made representative claims of their own and created the sense of an imagined community. Governed by rhetorical formulae, some forms, like the declaration, protest and remonstrance, did away with the humility and supplications to higher authorities associated with petitions; rather they could assert, demand, threaten and even dictate. These features were exploited in 1659. Indeed, the capacity of petitions and associated genres to create rhetorically powerful counter-communities was recognised by the two groups ranged against the republic: the Presbyterians and the royalists. It is possible that the experience of 1659-60 convinced L'Estrange of the power of printed words, such that after the restoration he became both government censor (to restrict seditious words) and government polemicist (to produce loyal ones). As he remarked in the preface to his *Apology*, 'Let any man now shew me, by what other means than by the Press, 'twas

---

[Thomason: 14 Mar.]; *Rump Enough, or Quaerie for Quaerie* (1660), 14 Mar.; *No Fool to the Old Fool* (1660), 16 Mar.; *The Fanatique Powder-Plot* (1660), 24 Mar. [Thomason: 26 Mar.]; *A Necessary and Seasonable Caution, Concerning Elections* (1660), [Thomason: 24 Mar.]; *Sir Politique Uncased, or A Sober Answer to a Jugling Pamphlet* (1660) 27 Mar. [Thomason: 29 Mar.]; *Treason Arraigned in Answer to Plain English to his Excellencie the Lord Generall Monk* (1660) [Thomason: April]; *No Blinde Guides* (1660) [Thomason: 25 Apr.]; *Physician Cure thy Self* (1660), 23 Apr. [Thomason: 27 Apr.]. L'Estrange often shortened or even omitted the titles in the *Apology*, but the fuller version is given here. The *Apology* was issued with a variant title and was also republished as *A Short View of Some Remarkable Transactions* (1660).

[15] D. Zaret, 'Petitions and the "Invention" of Public Opinion in the English Revolution', *American Journal of Sociology*, 101 (1996), pp. 497-555; Zaret, *The Origins of Democratic Culture. Printing, Petitions and the Public Sphere in Early Modern England* (Princeton, 2000). For the wider literature on petitioning and associated genres see Knights, *Representation and Misrepresentation in Later Stuart Britain: Partisanship and Political Culture* (Oxford, 2005), pp. 114-5.

possible to Engage so many Persons, with so much Probability of good, and with so Little Hazzard of the Contrary.'[16]

The twenty-one reprinted texts included in the *Apology* merit close analysis, though there is room here only to highlight some of their key features. One is the repeated invocation of the threat of violence and another is L'Estrange's impersonation of the citizen voice in defence of civic rights which, he claimed, obliged a recourse to arms. *The Declaration of the City to the Men at Westminster* was published to coincide with the Presbyterian-led uprising in Cheshire in August 1659 and made no bones about what was needed.[17] Claiming to speak for the City of London, it warned MPs that 'if there be no other way left us than violence whereby to preserve our selves in our Just Rights, what Power soever shall presume to invade the Priviledge of a Citizen, shall finde 20,000 brave fellows in the Head on't'.[18] The use of print to provoke armed resistance was again evident in early December, when the army's heavy-handed suppression of a city petition led L'Estrange to believe that the apprentices were ready to riot. He printed a 'paper to quicken them', entitled *The Engagement and Remonstrance of the City of London*. In its original form the paper's subtitle claimed that it was signed by 23,500 hands, though this was silently omitted when it was republished in the *Apology*. It began with a remarkable assertion that 'as Citizens, wee are reduced to a necessity of Violence; and as Christians, obliged to the exercise of it; unless we will rather prostitute our lives and liberties, fortunes and reputations; nay our very souls and altars, to the lusts of a barbarous and sacrilegious enemy'.[19]

A third invocation of violence came in another broadside *The Final Protest and Sense of the Citie*. This defiantly proclaimed 'we have our swords in our hands' and 'we will by violence oppose all violence whatsoever which is not warranted by the Letter of the establish'd law'. L'Estrange made it clear that 'a sober and regular application to the authorities of the City, for redresse' of grievances had failed and that violence was therefore justified. Another broadside, *The Resolve of the Citie* pursued the idea that the restraint of the citizens had been stretched to breaking point once the common council had failed to redress grievances. It threatened: 'we have engaged and sworn the vindication of the city, and nothing can absolve us from the oath we have taken'. The citizens hoped for a peaceful resolution

---

[16] *Apology*, preface, Sig. B2v.

[17] Kitchin, *L'Estrange*, p. 46.

[18] *Discovery upon Discovery* (1680), p. 34.

[19] *Ibid.*, pp. 34-35.

but 'wash[ed] [thei]r hands of the consequences' if the magistrates failed to act. In this version, then, citizens were being loyal to the city and their rights, even if this meant violence, a position that by 1680 L'Estrange had totally rejected.[20]

1659-60 was not the first time L'Estrange had been associated with popular petitioning and armed association on behalf of the royalist cause. He had become embroiled in May 1648 in a furore about a petition from Kent's grand jury that had insisted on the king's rights as well as the people's liberties.[21] The petition had been suppressed and, L'Estrange claimed, he had consequently been invited to help the oppressed royalists in the county. In any case, he had penned a 'Letter Declaratorie' on behalf of the 'many thousands' who, he alleged, had subscribed the grand jury's petition. He had arranged for his letter to be 'dispersed and posted up' and then organised supporters into an 'Engagement' which obliged them 'to oppose effectually' anyone who disrupted the 'just and legall presentment of our humble desires to the two Houses of Parliament'. By his own admission he and his supporters 'betooke ourselves to our Armes, not to make good the Petition, but the Right of Petitioning'.[22] To advance the royalist cause, then, L'Estrange had vindicated the right of petitioning, and used it and its associated genres to mobilise and arm men to resist those in authority (albeit an authority whose legitimacy he did not recognise).

As we have already seen, L'Estrange claimed to represent others in both the Kent campaign and the 1659-60 ones. In the latter he was more than happy to foist and forge declarations that claimed to represent 'the sense of the city', as the title of one of his pieces put it. Indeed, he boldly denied that his texts were 'the Arrogant imposition of a single person'; rather they were 'the sense of a numerous and sober party'.[23] Yet the projection of royalist views as those of the majority did not pass unnoticed. One declaration 'of many thousand, well-affected Persons' who supported the Rump objected to 'the Cavaliers and malecontents

---

[20] *A Plain Case*, another of the republished tracts, argued that violence must meet violence [*Apology*, pp. 55, 57].

[21] His first known appearance in print, in 1646, took the form of a personal petition about his incarceration in Newgate for attempting a rising in King's Lynn. See *To a Gentleman, a Member of the Honourable House of Commons assembled in Parliament* (1646); *L'Estrange his Appeal from the Court Martiall to the Parliament* (1647).

[22] *L'Estrange his Vindication, From the Calumnies of a Malitious Party in Kent (relating to a Commotion there in May 1648)* (1649), unpaginated.

[23] *For his Excellency Generall Monck* in *Apology*, p. 65.

publishing without colour of truth, divers Declarations subscribed with the names of severall Persons who never knew of such Declarations or of their names put to them till they saw them in Print ... this is an old artifice of the father of lies'.[24] The question of the representativeness of such texts surfaced again in May 1660, this time from the loyalist side when the 'loyal-hearted' of Kent (where Roger had of course earlier been involved in royalist conspiracy) declared that 'many several petitions, remonstrances, declarations and other like addresses, framed or rather forged by a few disloyal, factious and seditious time-servers ... [have] been fathered, foisted, and obtruded upon us and presented and exposed to the open view and all the world in print, under our name and stamp' even though they were 'far from being the acts or from speaking the sense and desires of our more loyal county and city'.[25]

It was not just London that L'Estrange claimed to represent. In January 1660 he impersonated the 'Gentlemen of Devon'.[26] In a letter *To His Excellency General Monck* he ventriloquised for them, refuting the arguments used against re-admitting the MPs and arguing that public taxation could only be authorised by the nation's representatives in a free parliament. It is also possible that L'Estrange had a hand in *A Letter and Declaration of the Gentry of the County of Norfolk and the County of Norwich to his Excellency the Lord General Monck* (1660).[27] Whether such provincial declarations were inspired by these actions, or masterminded by Prynne, who has sometimes been seen as the common hand behind them, a number of other counties followed suit with similarly worded pieces.[28] Whatever the case,

---

[24] *A Declaration of many thousand well-affected Persons* (1660).

[25] *A Declaration and Vindication of the Loyal-hearted Nobility, Gentry and others of the County of Kent and City of Canterbury that they had no hand in the murder of our King* (1660).

[26] On 23 Jan. Monck addressed the Devon gentlemen, in response to an address in favour of a free parliament: *A Declaration of the Gentry of the County of Devon* (1660).

[27] L'Estrange had been brought up in Norfolk and took up arms at King's Lynn. His kinsman Nicholas L'Estrange was a prominent signatory of the declaration, along with three others from the L'Estrange family. The text of the letter reinforced the sentiments of Roger's *Letter from the Gentlemen of Devon*, calling for the readmission of secluded members and denying any obligation to pay tax without representation. The *Letter* was printed, with 45 names appended, though it declared to have 'many hundreds more', and a manuscript of the document exists, with about 1000 signatures. See *An Address from the Gentry of Norfolk* (ed.), W. Rye (Norwich, 1913), pp. 21-2.

[28] D. Ogg, *England in the Reign of Charles II* (Oxford, second edition, 1984), 1, p. 20. Addresses for a free parliament came from Suffolk, Leicestershire, Wawickshire, Kent,

L'Estrange's capacity to represent others knew no bounds. In the works reproduced in the *Apology* he impersonated the City apprentices, the army, a gentleman with the initials D. N and even, for satirical effect, a republican.

Impersonation was not the only sleight of hand in which L'Estrange indulged, for he also invented what he thought was necessary. Frustrated at the lack of direction among the forces ranged against the army, in early January 1660 L'Estrange published *A Free Parliament Proposed by the City to the Nation*, which attempted to promote an agreement, as he admitted later, 'under the notion of a thing already done'. He retrospectively dated the fictional proposal the 6th of December, the day after the army's bloody encounter with the petitioning apprentices. And he claimed that four commissioners, 'eminent both for honesty and fortune' had acted on behalf of the city and had dispatched copies of their petition 'throughout England and Wales'. He therefore urged the counties to choose 'two persons of known integrity' to liaise with them, for, he alleged, 'that paper which we commend to you, is already subscribed by many thousands of this city'. His broadside also printed a fictional reply to the commissioners, dated 3 January 1660, suggesting that their engagement for a free parliament had found unanimous favour in the country. Perhaps fearful of having his bluff called, L'Estrange said that the list of subscribers was available if required but that it was 'of more advantage and security to the Business in hand' for them to remain secret. Just as well, for this was pure invention.

He later also abandoned positions expressed in 1659-60 on presbyterianism, toleration and the memory of the civil war. The Presbyterians were, as the print of petitioning Jack Presbyter showed, one of his principal targets in 1679-80, when oblivion of civil war memories was far from his mind. Yet in early 1660, when the Presbyterians were pushing hard in print for a free parliament, L'Estrange had praised their chief polemicist, William Prynne, as 'the Honour of his age' and declared that he held Presbyterian royalists in 'more than Ordinarie Respect'.[29] Similarly he later abandoned earlier statements in favour of toleration and oblivion. Early in February 1660, when crowd activity was vital for maintaining political pressure, L'Estrange shot 'another bolt' from the press, advising Monck that 'in the case of differing Perswasions, [he] be pleased to form

Buckinghamshire, Cheshire, Shropshire, Staffordshire, Yorkshire and Oxfordshire, many of them signed by thousands of subscribers.

[29] *Apology*, p. 81. 'To those of the Presbyterian perswasion that truly love the King, I bear a more then Ordinarie Respect' (*Interest Mistaken or the Holy Cheat* (1661), dedication 'To the Good People of England' Sig. A*3).

such an expedient, that all may quietly enjoy and exercise their own opinions, so far as they consist with the word of God and with the publique peace'.³⁰ He also urged an act of oblivion and his name is to be found on *A Declaration of the Nobility and Gentry that adhered to the King, now residing in and about the City of London* (1660), which promised not to 'cherish any violent thoughts or inclinations to revenge against those who have been in any way instrumental' in the civil war 'and if the indiscretion of any bitter spirited persons transports them to expressions contrary to this our sense we utterly disclaim them'.³¹ His later journalism, however, was full of violent thoughts and he constantly dredged up the past against those who he saw as re-animating the good old cause.

L'Estrange's output in 1679-80 differed from that in 1659-60 in several ways. First, in 1659-60 he had sought to use mass petitioning and similar genres to mobilise and justify armed resistance and to animate popular pressure, whereas in 1679-80 he condemned mass petitioning and popular violence.³² Earlier he had articulated a set of citizen rights that he appeared later to reject. Moreover, as this impersonation of the citizenry suggests, he ventriloquized and created deliberate fictions, the type of 'lye' that he later condemned. Third, before his subsequent hostility to the Presbyterians and toleration he had supported them when it seemed pragmatic to do so; and though in 1660 he urged 'oblivion', he was later one of the most vehement in dredging up the past. Finally, he repeatedly used print to do these things, exploiting its potential to contest authority, mobilise and awe, even though he was later to condemn such activity. L'Estrange thus took established genres of subscriptional activity, associated with those who sought redress of grievance (or even, as with the Levellers, transformative change), to make them work for a return to monarchy.

Given the very different contexts of a struggle to restore monarchy in 1659-60 and a struggle to defend it in 1679-80, it might be thought understandable that L'Estrange's arguments and language changed whilst his loyalist intentions remained constant.³³ Indeed, loyalism might have justified the usage of otherwise distasteful genres. He might thus have shared the view of *A Happy Handfull or Green Hopes in the Blade; in*

---

³⁰ *Apology*, p. 64-65.   ³¹ *A Declaration*.

³² When impersonating the Devon gentlemen, L'Estrange had even claimed that 'the voice of the people (in this case) is the declaratory voice of providence' (*Apology*, p. 62).

³³ Under James II his loyalty led him to become a supporter of toleration, uneasily allying his pen with his erstwhile enemies. See L. Schwoerer, *The Ingenious Mr Henry Care, Restoration Publicist* (Baltimore, MD, 2001), pp. 193, 202, 218.

order to a harvest of the several shires (1660) that 'factious petitioning gave the beginning and loyal declarations must give the end to our miseries. But here is the difference, the first were made by the Scum, these by the cream of the nation'.[34] The republican regime was illegitimate and therefore popular pressure, public remonstrances and a recourse to arms were necessary to restore the legitimate ruler. His patriotic 'Design' was 'Honestly to serve my country'.[35] Loyal intention thus allowed him to break rules (of petitioning, of printing, of representing others) that he himself set out for the disloyal and which he rigidly sought to enforce and police. A good intent justified, even necessitated, the means, whether it be the frequent use of print, the articulation of rights of resistance or the invocation of the mob.

But his invocation of loyal intent had unintended consequences. In trying to establish loyalty and liberty, he opened himself to the charge of disloyalty and tyranny in the eyes of those who saw him as a fraud who conspired against the public good. Was he loyal and were his works loyal? How could one distinguish 'seditious' intent or 'design' from 'honest' or 'loyal' intent, when the definitions of seditious, honest and loyal depended on the standpoint of the viewer, when the words were rhetorical and polemical constructs, and when print could obscure the real intentions of an author? What was L'Estrange really trying to do through his print?

III

For L'Estrange's contemporaries there was a mismatch between his professed intention and the motive or effect of his writings. Whilst he saw himself as loyal, his critics suspected his honesty.[36] He admitted in the *Apology* that in 1660 he was 'suspected for an *Instrument* of *Cromwells*: his *Pensioner*; and a *Betrayer of his Sacred Majestie's Party, and Designes*'; and that his '*Scribling* gives a shrewd Offence'. He therefore vindicated himself by publishing his earlier anonymous printed contributions to the restoration and observed, 'I have not Publish'd any one Paper, but with a prime Relation to a Common good. As my Intent was Fair, so I demand, where

---

[34] *A Happy Handfull*, p. 5.

[35] *Apology*, p. 109.

[36] *A Caveat to the Cavaliers* (1661) stirred a controversy about the loyalty of those around the king and about L'Estrange's own loyalty.

the Effect was other of what I did?'[37] And he later claimed that his intentions were 'innocent'; he wrote, he said, to rectify or prevent misunderstandings not promote them; he could be acquitted of any 'ill meaning'.[38]

However, by 1680, when he again reprinted some of the earlier prints in another vindication, the discrepancy between alleged intention and effect was even harder for contemporaries to reconcile. Whilst L'Estrange continued to claim to speak for the public good, it was alleged in August 1680 that even the king found the effect of what he said divisive and silenced him.[39] Many others suspected that L'Estrange's intention was deliberately to divide the nation. One tract dismissed his vindications as attempts to 'palliate his Crimes and hide his Knavery, with this Cloak of Seeming Honesty'.[40] 'He has several disguises and shapes into which he puts himself, a meer Proteus to [d]elude the People, a juggling State Hocus Pocus'.[41] Using 'nothing but Sophistry', it is alleged, he hoped 'to blind the eyes of the people, and under the colour of a Protestant, set the Protestants together by the ears, to advance Popery'. He was 'the Speaking Trumpet of a designing Jesuit'.[42] 'Some there are that picture him with two Faces, the one looking forward toward the Protestant, the other toward the Popish Religion', while at the same time hypocritically exclaiming 'Oh! The Profuseness of the Press [and] carrying in his Hand either a Dialogue or a Letter to a Friend'.[43] ''Twill be hard to know him by his Pen, for he is not the same, nor writes the same things, nor wears the same face in 80 as he did in 50 or 51'. He misrepresented others, it was said, making 'use of Jesuitical spectacles which turns loyal men into comonwealthsmen' and belched 'out Lyes, Stories, Untruths, mixed with many Fables, Romances'.[44]

---

[37] *Apology*, preface, Sig. B2, 2v. cf. 'My Frequency of writing may perswade some that I'me [sic] in love with Scribbling; but what I now do, is no more then what I have ever done, when I believed my Duty call'd me to it', *State Divinity* (1661), p. 60. In 1661 L'Estrange condemned appeal to the common good as 'the common pretence of all seditious combinations': *Interest Mistaken or the Holy Cheat* (1661), epistle dedicatory: sig. A2.

[38] *L'Estrange his appeal* (1681), pp. 15, 19; *To the Right Honourable Edward Earl of Clarendon* (1661), p. 5.

[39] *Calendar of State Papers Domestic 1679-80* (London, 1915), p. 596.

[40] [C. Blount], *A Brief Answer to Mr L'Estrange his Appeal* (1680), p. 1.

[41] Anon, *An Hue and Cry after R. Ls* (1680), p. 2.

[42] Blount, *A Brief Answer*, p.1; anon, *The Character of Those two Protestants in Masquerade Heraclitus and the Observator* (1681), p. 1.

[43] L. Mowbray, *The Portraicture of Roger L'Estrange Drawn to the Life* (1681), pp. 3-4.

[44] *An Hue and Cry*, pp. 2-3; anon., *A New-years-gift for Towzer* (1682), p. 2.

He had a commission 'to say White is Black, and Black is White'.[45] He was 'not the Loyal person he pretends to'.[46] He and his fellow scribblers had 'no more Loyalty than what they are paid for'.[47] The 1659-60 and 1680 texts thus highlight the problems of loyalty, meaning and intentionality in an era of deliberately manipulative and misrepresentative print.

Even if L'Estrange's intentions were not clear to contemporaries, one solution for the historian is to say that we should not confuse (value-laden) *motive* with intention, and that we need not worry so much about the contemporary reaction, focusing instead on what speech act the author was *intending* to perform. In order to understand that, it might be argued, we need to recover what a person intended his audience to understand his writing to mean, and hence to focus on context. This is the position put forward by Quentin Skinner in a series of highly influential articles which he has since collected and thus restated (albeit slightly revised) in book form.[48] As Skinner puts it, 'the understanding of texts ... presupposes the grasp of what they were intended to mean and of how that meaning was intended to be taken'.[49] We might thus say that although his anonymous pieces in 1659-60 ostensibly advocated only a return of the secluded Members, we know, through our study of context, that this call was intended to restore the monarchy (despite the explicit denial of this in one of L'Estrange's texts and the possibility at least that he was the author of another text which seemed to disown the Stuarts if their return did not help the public good).[50] We could further suggest that

---

[45] Anon., *A Dialogue between a Monkey in the old Bayly and an Ape in High Holbourn* (n. d.), p. 2.

[46] *A Brief Answer*, p. 7.

[47] *The Character of Those two Protestants in Masquerade*, p. 2.

[48] Q. Skinner, *Visions of Politics. Volume 1: Regarding Method* (Cambridge, 2002). As with L'Estrange, therefore, earlier individual pieces are republished as a corpus. See also L. Mulligan, J. Richards and J. K. Graham, 'Intentions and Conventions: A Critique of Quentin Skinner's Method for the Study of the History of Ideas', *Political Studies* xxvi (1979), pp. 84-98; M. Bevir, *The Logic of the History of Ideas* (Cambridge, 1999). Skinner responds to post-modern critics in *Visions of Politics*, pp. 90-3, having already responded to earlier critics in 'Some Problems in the analysis of political thought and action', *Political Theory* 23 (1974), pp. 207-303.

[49] Skinner, *Visions of Politics*, p. 86.

[50] The letter to Monck said a return to monarchy was 'not ... the thing we contend for': *Apology*, p. 60. *A Letter Presented to his Excellency General Monck, by a Citizen, at his coming into London 3 Feb. 1659* claimed to be from one 'who is neither for a commonwealth, nor kingship, neither for Charles Stuart, nor for yourself, otherwise than they may conduce to the

the deployment of the discourse of citizen's rights was a deliberate 'move' since L'Estrange intended to persuade Londoners to act. We might also say that a second speech act was performed by the republication of the texts in 1660, and that here the intention was self-vindicatory. Republication in 1680 was a third act, again with the intention of self-vindication but also with the aim of buttressing royal power. Certainly, each context was different and does indeed shape our understanding of authorial intention.

Moreover, the contextualist position was also the one advocated by Roger L'Estrange himself when he confronted the issue of how to distinguish between a seditious and an honest petition. This question was in the air in 1659-60 but particularly important in 1679-80. In the latter year L'Estrange constructed a guide to enable readers 'to make a right Judgment upon a Popular Petition'. He suggested 'we should first consider the matter of it. Secondly the wording of it. Thirdly the manner of Promoting it. Fourthly the probable intent of it. And lastly, we should do well to consult History and Experience to see what effects such Petitions have commonly produced'.[51] He thus recommended examining a text's ostensible meaning ('the matter of it') and the words used to express that meaning ('the wording of it'), but also the 'intent' that could expose another meaning, and the effects of it, which could confirm suspicions about that other meaning. Using these criteria, he was sure of the 'evil intention' of the petitioners in 1680, since petitioning had already led once to civil war. The context of petitioning, the 'history and experience', suggested that the act performed by the petitions in that year was rebellious.

But, was rebellion the 'probable intent' of the petitioners or rather L'Estrange's polemical misinterpretation of their speech act? And what do we say about L'Estrange's repeated invocations in 1659-60 of the armed power of the people? Was his intention simply to use a set of ideas and words that he calculated as most likely to sway his audience, or did he

Good, Safety, Peace and Tranquility of the whole Nation'. It was published by H. B., possibly Harry Brome, L'Estrange's publisher who often used his initials in this way, It uses the relatively uncommon biblical word 'Horsleech' which is also found in *A Sober Answer to a Jugling Pamphlet* (*Apology* p.113); and compares magistrates to wolves, as L'Estrange did in *A Plain Case* (Apology, p. 56) and in his letter to Monck on 18 Feb, *Apology*, pp. 75-6. That he signed it 'J.B' is no disproof of authorship, since L'Estrange used the false initials 'N.D' that year on *Sir Politique Uncased*.

[51] *A Seasonable Memorial* (1680), p.18 (and enlarged on pp. 18-22).

really intend to justify popular resistance against an illegitimate regime, believing that the ends justified the means, even though he denied this reasoning to others? Was he never limited (in all senses) by the languages he deployed but free to use them only when occasion demanded? Did he also intend to argue for religious toleration and oblivion of the civil war? Can we say with any certainty what his intention was, beyond a desire to buttress the royalist cause?

Let us briefly examine some of problems about recovering authorial intention in relation to L'Estrange's 1659-60 writings. The first is basic since in their first incarnation we have a hidden author, whose work appeared anonymously and who also impersonated other voices.[52] Identifying the 'authorial' voice is thus rather difficult, since it is multiple and deliberately disguised; and we might easily (as both contemporaries did and historians have[53]) mistake L'Estrange's views for the voice of, say, the gentlemen of Devon or the citizens of London. Second, print allowed for, even facilitated, such manipulation and deliberate deceit, and was capable of mutability between editions and of being recycled (not necessarily by the author) in different contexts.[54] Even when irony and impersonation were not present, it is striking that only about 40% of printed titles carried the author's name.[55] Given this high level of anonymity, it may well be preferable, as John Pocock has suggested for other reasons, to analyse the

---

[52] The issue of Prynne's canon raises similar issues. In *The New Cheaters Forgeries* (1659) Prynne disowned *Mola Asinaria* (1659) and other works which had been published in his name 'by way of Irony' and 'derision'. The real author of *Mola* was Samuel Butler. But the pro-commonwealth *The Faithful Scout* no. 6 (27 May-3 June) nevertheless used *Mola* to reproach Prynne as a self-seeking Machiavellian. See Samuel Butler, *Posthumous Works* fourth edition (1732), pp. 225-6; Mayer, *1659*, p. 197.

[53] Thomas Rugg referred in his 'diurnal' to one of L'Estrange's City pieces as though it was credible; *Diurnal of Thomas Rugg*, p. 23 referring to *The Resolve of the City, 23 Dec 1659*, which he describes as a 'well pend thing'. Tim Harris, an excellent and careful historian, was sufficiently misled to quote from one of L'Estrange's bogus prints as though it is an actual reflection of the opinions of 23,500 citizens; Harris, *London Crowds in the Reign of Charles II: Propaganda and Politics from the Restoration until the Exclusion Crisis* (Cambridge, 1987), p. 44, citing *The Final Protest and Sense of the Citite* (1659). L'Estrange may have voiced the opinion of some Londoners, but the figure of 23,500 seems to have been fabricated.

[54] For an excellent discussion of deliberately misleading print see K. Loveman, 'Shamming Readers: Deception in English Literary and Political Culture', Cambridge PhD (2003).

[55] J. Barnard and D. F. McKenzie, with M. Bell (eds), *The Cambridge History of the Book in Britain, 1557-1695* (Oxford, 2002), 4, p. 792.

performance of a *text* as much as its author.[56] Third, the genres that L'Estrange was exploiting had conventions that we can contextualise and recover; and we need studies to map the rhetorics, conventions and forms of the remonstrance, the declaration, the proclamation, the engagement, the protest, the printed letter and so on. That suggests the need for a shift of focus, towards a history of discursive genres. Fourth, and here we might have L'Estrange's later re-publication especially in mind, we cannot ignore audience reaction, for the scope of any speech act is determined by the audience as much as by the speaker. If the motives and intentions of an author are constantly impugned by his enemies, then, as L'Estrange discovered, the range of speech acts that the author is capable of performing is limited for (and by) those readers, no matter what the author intended.

Finally, we will find it hard to pronounce on the sincerity of the use of any language. When in 1659-60 L'Estrange deployed the discourse of citizens and their rights, should we, given his later condemnation of such discourse, identify an intention simply to use whatever language would best mobilise popular royalism? Or did he deliberately and sincerely choose that language (of others available to him) because he intended to reinforce citizen power as the best security against the Rump? If writers take on languages as well as voices insincerely (and inconsistently) for polemical ends, how can we infer intention? We could say that the author was deliberately using a language that he believed would sway readers, and that the language of civic rights was one such. But that tells us more about the discourse and audience of 1659-60 than it does about authorial intention, and we can say relatively little about L'Estrange's sincerity concerning the values (including rights and popular violence) that such language conveyed.

Quentin Skinner is, of course, aware of some of the difficulties in recovering authorial intention. He admits to 'acute problems of interpretation in two main types of case. One is that we are confronted with hidden rhetorical codes such as that of irony'; another is when a writer issues an utterance but fails to make clear how exactly it is to be taken or understood. We might add other factors such as deliberate anonymity or impersonation; and conditions of partisanship that give words — such as loyalty or honesty — more than one meaning. Even so, Skinner suggests, recov-

---

[56] Pocock's method is thus rather different from Skinner's, despite their being frequently bracketed together as the 'Cambridge school'. See J. G. A. Pocock, *Virtue, Commerce and History* (Cambridge, 1985), pp. 4-7.

ering 'the context and occasion of utterances' will help us through. 'If we succeed in identifying this context with sufficient accuracy, we can eventually hope to read off what it was that the speaker or writer in whom we are interested was doing in saying what he or she said'. Crucially in these tricky cases, Skinner says, the 'fact that the intentions with which we act are always closely connected with our motives' helps; and 'ascriptions of intentionality can be further corroborated by examining the coherence of a speaker's or writer's beliefs'.[57]

Yet these two methodological aids fly in the face of his own very clear injunctions to *distinguish* between motive and intention, and *not* to expect or artificially construct consistency or coherence.[58] Indeed, if we use L'Estrange's motives to guide our interpretation of his meaning we become hostages to the rival versions of his designs pedalled by the author and his critics; and clearly he was not consistent in his advocacy of popular violence or petitions that sought to destabilise authority. Indeed, L'Estrange is rather unlike Bolingbroke, who provides Skinner with a model that is intended to have wider applicability for the study of the relationship between political action and language. For although like Bolingbroke L'Estrange adopted a Whiggish language that appears at odds with his Tory intentions, unlike Bolingbroke he renounced the limitations that consistent use of such language imposed.[59]

It may be the case, then, that where we have anonymity or deliberate ventriloquisation, where print culture enhances the abilities of authors to fictionalise, where ambiguous genres are used, where authorial motives have become the subject of partisan interpretation, and/or where polemical concerns shape writing and reader responses, that the recovery of authorial intention becomes a rather fraught exercise. We might, on the one hand, interpret L'Estrange's intentions as carefully timed interventions, acting in 1659-60 and again in 1679-80 to buttress monarchy by using the press and the language of civic rights to mobilise popular support for it; or on the other we could (along with his contemporary critics) see his vindications, his continual recourse to print, and his ambiguities as the carefully disguised acts of an opportunistic, self-advancing, professional

---

[57] Skinner, *Visions of Politics*, pp. 111-2, 114, 116, 119.

[58] *Visions of Politics*, pp. 67-72, 97-99. Consistency is nevertheless much more highly valued in Skinner, 'The Principles and Practices of Opposition: the case of Bolingbroke vs. Walpole' in N. McKendrick (ed.), *Historical Perspectives: Studies in English Thought and Society in Honour of J. H. Plumb* (London, 1974), pp. 98-99, 125.

[59] Skinner, *Visions of Politics*, pp. 111-2, 114, 116, 119.

dissimulator who deliberately sought to divide the people for his own or for conspiratorial (even crypto-catholic) ends. Can a theory of authorial intention encompass both? If it can, does it tell us very much? And if these are the difficulties raised by the 'minor texts' against which we measure the canon of great writers, is our yardstick inevitably a distorted one? These questions are not intended to suggest that trying to ascribe some authorial intentionality is wrong for, depending on the case, there can be significant advantage to be gained by adopting it. But, similarly, it may be less helpful in the murky, partisan and ambiguous world (far from unique to the restoration period) that I have been describing.

Chapter 7

Republicanism as Anti-patriarchalism in Henry Neville's *The Isle of Pines* (1668)[1]

Gaby Mahlberg

Henry Neville's *The Isle of Pines* (1668) is a story of travel, shipwreck and the survival and procreation of a man and four women on a lonely island in the Pacific. It is also one of the more enigmatic works of seventeenth-century republicanism. Though written by a well known politician and political thinker, and re-published as part of Thomas Hollis's republican canon, it has hardly received any serious treatment by historians of political thought or political scientists, despite its obvious concern with the state of nature, original societies and government.[2] Even Neville's biographer, Caroline Robbins, who studied the long-term continuities of the Anglo-American Commonwealth tradition, dismissed the fact that '[s]ome have found in the story a social moral', and described the work as having sprung simply 'from Neville's high spirits and Rabelaisian humour, writing to amuse himself'.[3] Similarly, Annabel Patterson's more recent book on *Early Modern Liberalism*, which deals extensively with Hollis's editorial efforts, does not even mention *The Isle*.[4]

Instead, a wide range of literary scholars have appropriated *The Isle* as travel literature, Robinsonade, Restoration satire and utopia.[5] They have

---

[1] I would like to thank Mark Knights, Andy Maclean, John Morrow and Jonathan Scott for reading earlier drafts of this article.

[2] *The Parliament of Ladies ... and The Isle of Pines,* (ed.) Thomas Hollis (London, 1768). One recent exception is Peter Stillman, 'Monarchy, Disorder, and Politics in *The Isle of Pines*' in Peter G. Stillman, Gaby Mahlberg and Nat Hardy (eds), '*The Isle of Pines* Special Issue', *Utopian Studies* 17.1 (2006), pp. 147-75.

[3] Caroline Robbins (ed.), *Two Republican Tracts* (Cambridge, 1969), p. 13.

[4] Annabel Patterson, *Early Modern Liberalism* (Cambridge, 1997).

[5] E.g. David Fausett, *Writing the New World: Imaginary Voyages and Utopias of the Great Southern Land* (Syracuse, 1993), esp. pp. 81ff; Harold Weber, 'Charles II, George Pines, and Mr. Dorimant: The Politics of Sexual Power in Restoration England', *Criticism*, 32 (1990), pp. 193-219; Pierre Lurbe, 'Une Utopie Inverse: *The Isle of Pines* de Henry Neville (1668)', *Bulletin de la Societé d'Etudes Anglo-Americaines des XVIIe et XVIIIe Siècles*, 38 (1994), pp. 19-32.

been more concerned with questions of genre, writing techniques, form and style than with any deeper historical and political significance of the piece. A notable exception is Susan Wiseman, who has engaged with issues of gender and patriarchal power in *The Isle* and located it in the ongoing seventeenth-century debate about political patriarchalism.[6] As Neville's Italian critic, Onofrio Nicastro, points out, while *The Isle* is a minor work of a minor author, removed from the high levels of theoretical and literary production, it is less superficial than first impressions suggest, addressing issues of more general importance.[7]

Neville's engagement with patriarchal power, the state of nature, and their religious implications reveal some key republican principles which must be linked to Neville's other works, in particular to his discourse on government, *Plato Redivivus* of 1680. It must also be read in the context of other republican works, such as John Milton's *Paradise Lost* of 1667, which similarly engages with the 'experience of defeat',[8] and Algernon Sidney's *Court Maxims*, the work of another disillusioned exile.[9] The *Court Maxims*, written in the Netherlands during the early 1660s, share Neville's frustration with Stuart patriarchalism, albeit without the satirical tone. They also share the Dutch context of *The Isle* which highlights the contrast between a successful republic and a declining monarchy. In short, *The Isle* must be read as part of a wider republican canon and placed firmly in its contemporary political and religious context. The purpose of this article is to re-appropriate *The Isle* for scholars of seventeenth-century republican thought and to re-appraise it as a work on politics and religion.

The author of *The Isle*, Henry Neville (1619–1694), was a republican who made his name as a pamphleteer, politician, and philosopher in a long career that connected the earlier and later halves of the seventeenth

---

[6] Daniel Carey, 'Henry Neville's *The Isle of Pines*: travel, forgery, and the problem of genre', *Angelaki*, 1 (1993), pp. 23-39; Karl Reichert, 'Robinsonade, Utopie und Satire im "Joris Pines" (1726)', *Arcadia*, 1 (1966), pp. 50-69; Max Hippe, 'Eine vor-Defoe'sche englische Robinsonade', *Englische Studien*, 19 (1894), pp. 66-104; Susan Wiseman, '"Adam, the Father of all Flesh", Porno-Political Rhetoric and Political Theory in and After the English Civil War' in James Holstun (ed.), *Pamphlet Wars: Prose in the English Revolution* (London, 1992), pp. 134-57.

[7] Onofrio Nicastro, *Henry Neville e l'isola di Pines* (Pisa, 1988), p. 7.

[8] The term is Christopher Hill's. See his *The Experience of Defeat: Milton and some Contemporaries* (London, 1984).

[9] John Milton, *Paradise Lost*, ed. John Leonard (London, 2000); Algernon Sidney, *Court Maxims*, ed. Hans W. Blom, Eco Haitsma Mulier and Ronald Janse (Cambridge, 1996).

century. After the English civil war and the execution of Charles I in 1649, Neville became a Member of Parliament and joined the new Commonwealth government and its Council of State. Angered and disappointed by Oliver Cromwell's expulsion of Parliament by military force in 1653, Neville joined the political opposition and became involved in plots against the Cromwellian Protectorate. From the mid-1650s at the latest, Neville also became an associate of the republican philosopher James Harrington, and aimed to implement part of Harrington's political programme during Richard Cromwell's Parliament in 1659. Neville was active in the political crisis of 1659-1660 and an exile in Italy in the 1660s. He contributed in print to the debates of the so-called Exclusion Crisis of 1678-1681, in which the parliamentary opposition aimed to exclude the Catholic James, Duke of York, from the succession to the English throne. He also engaged in the debate about religious toleration through his open defence of Catholics, strongly influenced by his Italian connections. He wrote satirical libels, a utopian travel narrative, a weighty political treatise, and even poetry. Neville has also been considered a possible translator of Machiavelli and author of a fictional letter vindicating him. His career was varied.[10] Yet, modern scholarship has focused only on specific parts of Neville's political activity and writing, such as his collaboration with Harrington or his contribution to the Exclusion Crisis.[11]

Some important aspects of Neville's thought and of early modern republicanism, however, have been lost in a historiography that has concentrated more on concepts of virtue and corruption, liberty and slavery, and political architecture than on what republicans were arguing *against*.[12] The focus on key moments and isolated concepts in the history of political thought, moreover, has ignored long-term continuities in English

---

[10] The main sources for Neville's biography are Robbins, 'Introduction', pp. 5–19; Anthony à Wood, *Athenae Oxonienses*, ed. Philip Bliss, 4 vols. (1813-1820), iv, cols. 410–11; Thomas Hollis's introduction to *Plato Redivivus* (1763), pp. 1–8; and the old *DNB* entry. More recently, see the entries on Neville in R. Greaves and R. Zaller, *Biographical Dictionary of British Radicals*, and in the *ODNB* by Nicholas von Maltzahn. See also Frances T. Kelly's forthcoming biography for the History of Parliament, and Gaby Mahlberg, 'Henry Neville and English Republicanism in the Seventeenth Century', PhD thesis, University of East Anglia, 2005.

[11] J. G. A. Pocock, *The Machiavellian Moment: Florentine Political Thought and the Atlantic Republican Tradition* (Princeton, 1975); Blair Worden, 'Republicanism and the Restoration, 1660-1683', in David Wootton (ed.), *Republicanism, Liberty and Commercial Society, 1649-1776* (Stanford, 1994), pp. 139-93; Nicholas von Maltzahn, 'Henry Neville and the Art of the Possible: A Republican Letter Sent to General Monk (1660)', *Seventeenth Century*, 7 (1992), pp. 41-52.

republican thought emphasised by Markku Peltonen, and of English republican practice as analysed by Patrick Collinson and Mark Goldie.[13] These continuities do not only manifest themselves in ideal state models, but also in a criticism of the monarchy and its theoretical underpinnings.

The Isle was written by a republican in exile against the increasingly authoritarian regime of the restored Stuart monarchy and the patriarchal political theory based on the Bible that was employed to defend it. It fuses a political and a religious dimension in its anti-patriarchal argument, underlining long-term continuities in republican thought from the early to the later seventeenth centuries and beyond, and focussing on republican criticism of the monarchy rather than 'government without a king'.[14] Finally, with its mockery of biblical literalism and defence of natural law theory it links Neville's republicanism to religious dissent and the scepticism so characteristic for the freethinking tradition of the 'radical' Enlightenment.[15]

Neville was not a systematic biblical exegete as Benedict de Spinoza or even John Locke, but his treatment of the Scriptures, especially of the Old Testament, reveals much both about his politics and his religion. *The Isle* thus also helps us to recover the much neglected religious dimension of early modern republicanism and its continued impact on post-Restoration thought.[16] This article focuses on Neville's republicanism as

[12] E.g. Pocock, *Machiavellian Moment*; Quentin Skinner, 'The republican ideal of political liberty', in Gisela Bock, Quentin Skinner and Maurizio Viroli (eds), *Machiavelli and Republicanism* (Cambridge, 1990), pp. 293-309.

[13] Markku Peltonen, *Classical Humanism and Republicanism in English Political Thought, 1570-1640* (Cambridge, 1995); Patrick Collinson, 'The Monarchical Republic of Queen Elizabeth I', *Bulletin of the John Rylands University Library of Manchester*, 69 (1987), pp. 394-424; the same, *De Republica Anglorum: Or, History with the Politics Put Back* (Cambridge, 1990); Mark Goldie, 'The Unacknowledged Republic: Officeholding in Early Modern England', in Tim Harris (ed.), *The Politics of the Excluded, c. 1500-1850* (Basingstoke, 2001), pp. 153-94.

[14] Cf. Zera Fink's definition of 'republic' in *The Classical Republicans: An Essay in the Recovery of a Pattern of Thought in Seventeenth-Century England* (Evanston, Ill, 1945), p. viii.

[15] J. A. I. Champion, *The Pillars of priestcraft shaken: The Church of England and its enemies, 1660-1730* (Cambridge, 1992); Jonathan I. Israel, *Radical Enlightenment: Philosophy and the Making of Modernity 1650-1750* (Oxford, 2001), pp. 447-56.

[16] See Champion, *Pillars of Priestcraft*; Mark Goldie, 'The civil religion of James Harrington' in Anthony Pagden (ed.), *The Languages of Political Theory in Early Modern Europe* (Cambridge, 1987), pp. 197-222; and for a different view Jonathan Scott, *Commonwealth Principles: Republican Writing of the English Revolution* (Cambridge, 2004).

anti-patriarchalism in *The Isle*, his views on the origins of government and natural law theory in relation to his scriptural criticism, and his emphasis on the necessity of laws for the ordering of a commonwealth, all of which are reflected in his later political treatise, *Plato Redivivus*. To understand the variety of different interpretations of *The Isle* we first need to look at the work itself and its historical and creative context.

The story of *The Isle* originally appeared in three parts, which were later put together and published as one pamphlet. The first part or 'core' text, licensed on 27 June 1668, is the narrative of the English bookkeeper George Pines, who suffered shipwreck in the Pacific Ocean while on his way to India in Queen Elizabeth's time.[17] He and four women, one of them a black slave, another his master's daughter, and two maids, saved themselves on a bowsprit and settled on a lonely island. Although they could hardly salvage anything from the ship, they wanted for nothing due to the richness of the island. They soon entered into sexual relations and generated offspring which had become so numerous after forty years that Pines decided to bring order into their colonial society by arranging marriages between the offspring of the different families, instructing them to have monthly Bible readings, and making his firstborn son, Henry, king over the others. Shortly before his death, Pines assembled his descendants again, numbering 1789, and divided them according to their mothers' names into the four tribes of the 'English', the 'Sparks', the 'Trevors' and the 'Phills'.

In the full version of the pamphlet, licensed on 27 July 1668, the first part is introduced by two letters from a Dutch merchant, and framed by a letter from a Dutch sailor, Henry Cornelius Van Sloetten. In this letter, which had also been published on its own, Van Sloetten tells us how he discovered the island in 1667, and what had happened to the English Pines between Elizabeth's time and the present.[18] Van Sloetten and his crew had been on their way to the East Indies when they lost orientation in a storm. They landed on the Isle where they found a number of naked people

---

[17] *The Isle of Pines, or, A late discovery of a fourth Island in Terra Australis, Incognita* (1668). For a full history of the text see Stillman, Mahlberg and Hardy (eds), '*The Isle of Pines* Special Issue', pp. 7-107. I shall be quoting from the *Utopian Studies* edition of *The Isle* throughout.

[18] The full version is *The Isle of Pines, or, A late discovery of a fourth island near Terra Australis Incognita by Henry Cornelius van Sloetten* (1668). The date 27 July is not precise. 'June' has simply been replaced by 'July' on the title page. The Stationers' Register has 4 July. Cf. Nicastro, *Isola di Pines*, p. 40. The letter on its own was published as *A New and Further Discovery of The Isle of Pines in A Letter from Cornelius Van Sloetten* (1668).

[19] Neville, *The Isle of Pines*, pp. 28-32.

speaking English, whose ruler, Prince William, the grandchild of George Pines told them the story of his people.[19]

As soon as George Pines was dead, and his son Henry succeeded, the growing population fell into anarchy. Political decay was followed by moral decay — as in the political maxim that Neville would describe in *Plato Redivivus*.[20] The country succumbed to debauchery, and one of the Phills, a descendant of the black slave woman, was executed for initiating political unrest. Having punished the offenders, Henry 'ordained' some basic, but harsh penal laws which kept the country peaceful till the arrival of the Dutch.[21] The Dutch came and explored the island, learnt about its people and customs and even built a palace for Prince William. But they also discovered that the people were unarmed and scared of their guns. When they were about to leave, another descendant of the black woman, who 'had ravished the Wife of one of the principal of the Family of the *Trevors*', caused an insurrection which William put down with Dutch assistance.[22]

The core text has left its mark most widely. Shortly after its first publication it was translated into Dutch, French, Italian, German and Danish, and copies also travelled to New England.[23] *The Isle*'s popularity is often attributed to the fact that most readers would have taken it at face value as a story of travel and adventure, maybe as a curiosity, but also as a promise of new social, economic and sexual opportunities abroad.[24] At first sight, *The Isle* looks authentic. As was customary for contemporary travel writing, Neville describes the climate and vegetation of the country, its resources, its animal population, as well as its people and their customs. He even reiterates an anecdote from a travel narrative on *The Golden Coast*, published three years earlier, in which the natives confuse a bagpipe with a living creature.[25]

---

[20] Cf. Henry Neville, *Plato Redivivus* (1681) in Robbins, *Two Republican Tracts*, p. 87.

[21] Neville, *The Isle of Pines*, pp. 39-41.   [22] *Ibid.*, p. 45.

[23] Worthington Chauncey Ford, *The Isle of Pines 1668: An Essay in Bibliography* (Boston, 1920); Fausett, *Writing the New World*, pp. 81, 84; J. C. Davis, *Utopia and the ideal society: A Study of English Utopian writing 1516-1700* (Cambridge, 1981), p. 25; Hippe, 'Vor-Defoe'sche Robinsonade', pp. 90, 102-4. See also 'The Publishing History of *The Isle of Pines*' in Stillman, Mahlberg and Hardy (eds), '*The Isle of Pines*', pp. 93-98.

[24] Reichert, 'Robinsonade, Utopie und Satire'; and Paul Ries, 'Die Insel Pines: Philosophie, Pornographie und Propaganda?' in Wolfgang Brückner, Peter Blickle and Dieter Breuer (eds), *Literatur und Volk im 17. Jahrhundert: Probleme populärer Kultur in Deutschland, Teil II* (Wiesbaden, 1985), pp. 753-76.

[25] *The Golden Coast, or, A description of Guinney* (1665), p. 80; cf. Neville, *The Isle of Pines*, p. 49.

Neville managed to fool the French scientist, Henri Justel, who wrote to the secretary of the Royal Society, Henry Oldenburg, at the end of July 1668 to enquire after 'the isle of Pines and your English Colony'.[26] A contemporary commentator suggested that the Hamburg merchants and seamen had also been taken in after reading the newsbooks and were most eager to find out more about the island;[27] and a German scholar discussed in a dissertation of 1674 whether the relations of Pines with the four women were legitimate and who was holding the sovereignty on the island.[28] Even religious zealots took an interest in *The Isle*, maybe intending to christianise the English Pines (although they already had some basic religion): a printer for the Society for the Propagation of the Gospel in New England was caught with an unlicensed copy of *The Isle* passing through his press in Cambridge, Massachusetts.[29]

Yet, while potentially enjoying the fact that he had managed to fool the world, Neville wanted his readers to break his code. For, at the same time that he was emphasising the truth of his story, he was also undermining his own claims to veracity in the tradition of earlier utopias. Neville introduced Van Sloetten's account with two letters from a real historical figure, the Dutch merchant Abraham Keek, to make it believable — a device borrowed from Thomas More's *Utopia* which begins with a letter of recommendation from More to his friend Peter Giles, in which he pretends to repeat a true story from the traveller, Raphael Hythloday, whose name means 'expert in nonsense' and was, of course, purely fictional.[30]

Similarly, Keek's first letter begins with the expected description of the island's location *'about 2 or 300 Leagues Northwest from Cape Finis Terre'*. Yet, it also admits *'that there may be some mistake in the number of the Leagues, as also of the exact point of the Compass'*, hinting at the account's fictionality.[31] Van Sloetten's narrative similarly ends with the claim that he has 'given ... a brief, but true Relation of our Voyage'. But he is also aware

---

[26] Justel to Oldenburg, late July 1668 in A. Rupert Hall and Marie Boas Hall (eds), *The Correspondence of Henry Oldenburg*, 13 vols (Madison, 1965-86), iv, letter 929.

[27] *Das verdächtige Pineser-Eyland* (Hamburg, 1668), fos. A4v.

[28] Nicastro, *Isola di Pines*, p. 6; Hippe, 'Vor-Defoe'sche Robinsonade', pp. 93-94.

[29] Ford, *Isle of Pines*, pp. 3, 5-6.

[30] 'Thomas More to Peter Giles, Greetings' in Thomas More, *Utopia*, (eds) George M. Logan and Robert M. Adams (Cambridge, 1989), pp. 3-7, and 'Introduction', pp. xi-xxviii, p. xi.

[31] Neville, *The Isle of Pines*, p. 26. Cf. contemporary travel works, such as *The Golden Coast*, pp. 7-8; *A Relation of Maryland* (London, 1630), p. 16; and *An Account of the Province of Carolina in America* ... (London, 1682), p. 5.

that some 'Nullifidians ... will believe nothing but what they see', again leaving it up to the reader to decide on the truth of the story.[32] *The Isle* is a 'utopia' because it is 'no-place', but it served as a vehicle of displacement onto which the problems of England were projected. While More's *Utopia* shows what England could and should be, Neville shows what it has become.

Indeed, the problem of a patriarchal ruler engaging in a promiscuous lifestyle while his country was divided and weakened by internal plotting and threatened to disappear into insignificance and oblivion abroad was rather close to home. George Pines is often identified as Charles II, whose numerous adventures with his mistresses were an 'irresistible ... target for satirists'. Charles's sex life not only worried his subjects because they associated it with 'civic irresponsibility, royal pride, or martial insufficiency', it also threatened the 'natural' hierarchy between the sexes. Charles's 'heterosexual promiscuity ... called [his male and royal identity] seriously into question', because his enslavement to his mistresses reversed 'traditional gender and social roles'.[33] His lack of patriarchal power meant political as well as sexual impotence, embodied in his barren marriage to Catherine of Braganza. Despite his promiscuous lifestyle, Charles seemed unable to produce a legitimate heir.[34]

Yet, critics of the crown not only perceived Charles as a failure in domestic politics, he also lacked skill in diplomacy. The sudden appearance of the Dutch on the Isle and their easy handling of the conflict has been linked to the English defeat in the second Anglo-Dutch war (1664-1667). Neville was watching from abroad, bemoaning the former greatness of England under the Commonwealth, while the republican Dutch carried the day and dominated the sea.[35]

It is not surprising that Neville used the travel narrative as a code to avoid government censorship in his politically precarious situation when commenting on English domestic and foreign policy from his Italian exile. While it is unclear how far Neville's contemporary audience was aware of the piece's political implications, it is safe to say his fictional techniques did not go unnoticed. The Oxford wit and notorious gossip, Anthony Wood, scribbled on his copy of the full version of *The Isle*, that 'when this was first

---

[32] Neville, *The Isle of Pines*, p. 26.
[33] Weber, 'Charles II', p. 196.   [34] *Ibid.*, p. 216.
[35] Lurbe, 'Une utopie inverse', pp. 28-9; Wiseman, 'Porno-Political Rhetoric', p. 150; Adam R. Beach, 'A profound pessimism about the empire: *The Isle of Pines*, English degeneracy and Dutch supremacy', *Eighteenth Century*, 41 (2000), pp. 21-36.

published 'twas look'd upon as a sham' — a pamphlet pretending to be something it was not.[36] Because encoded writing was so common the discovery of shams developed into a coffee-house game.[37] Travel narratives especially had always been open to exaggeration and fictional additions, so readers would naturally approach them with scepticism and suspicion.[38] Maybe Wood picked up on the parallels between Charles II and George Pines. But the political message also struck at a more abstract level, and doubts on the veracity of *The Isle* were also cast further afield.

A German critic wrote a thirty-two-page refutation of *Das verdächtige PINESER-Eyland / The Suspicious Isle of Pines* (1668), accusing its author of being a liar and show-off. He suspected 'Pines' to be a telling name, an anagram of the male reproductive organ, going on to criticise the many unbelievable coincidences which enabled George Pines and his company to survive on the island, such as the tinderbox, steel and flint to make fire, or the abundance of the place, as well as chronological inconsistencies.[39] Most importantly, he noticed, like others before him, that *The Isle* was a parody of the Biblical creation story.

A German translation of 1668 hinted at the parallels between the creation story and Neville's narrative by adding to the title of the pamphlet 'Vorbild der Ersten Welt'/'Model of the first World.'[40] The author of *Das verdächtige PINESER-Eyland*, who referred back to this edition, pointed out that the author of *The Isle* explicitly compared the island to paradise, that the climate was always temperate, that the people never fell sick, and that there was an abundance of everything.[41] More recently *The Isle* has been rediscovered as a criticism of patriarchal rule, a satire on 'royalist dreams

---

[36] [Henry Neville] *The Isle of Pines, or, A late discovery'*, by Henry Cornelius van Sloetten (1668).

[37] Katherine Loveman, 'Shamming Readers: Deception in English Literary and Political Culture c. 1640-1740', DPhil thesis, University of Cambridge, 2003, pp. 76-77, 32ff. On censorship and code, see Annabel Patterson, *Censorship and Interpretation: The Conditions of Writing and Reading in Early Modern England* (Madison, Wisc.,1984); and Lois Potter, *Secret Rites and Secret Writings: Royalist Literature, 1641-1660* (Cambridge, 1989). Nicastro agrees that *The Isle* was written in cipher. *Isola di Pines*, p. 154.

[38] Fausett, *Writing the New World*, p. 2; Loveman, 'Shamming Readers', p. 31.

[39] *Das Verdächtige Pineser-Eyland* (Hamburg, 1668), fos. A5r, A7r, A8r-v, B2v, B3r, B1v, B6v, B7r. Some other inconsistencies the author points out might be due to his reliance on a faulty translation.

[40] *Vorbild der Ersten Welt, Das ist: Wahrhafftige Beschreibung eines neuerfundenen Eylandes, genant Das Pineser Eyland ...* (n.p., 1668).

[41] *Das Verdächtige Pineser-Eyland*, fos. A8v.

of a primal patriarchy', and a history of 'origins'.[42] It was part of the ongoing debate about competing views on the origins of government and their consequences for political rule. The pamphlet plays on biblical motives, which loyal supporters of Crown and High Church employed to explain the origins of monarchy. If, as the book of Genesis claims, Adam was the first man, first father, and first monarch to whom God had entrusted the care of the earth and its creatures, then subsequent monarchs who had descended from Adam should equally rule their people like a father ruled his family. Thus patriarchal monarchy was presented as the one natural form of government. Ideas of family and state were closely intertwined.

Already in the early seventeenth century, it had been common to depict the family as 'a little commonwealth' and a microcosmic mirror-image of the state.[43] Families or households were the elementary building blocks of society and the smallest political and economic units, in which a father or household head exercised authority over his dependent wife, children and servants. All other social relations were governed by similar hierarchies and informal political agencies of class, gender, and age.[44]

Debate, however, arose between loyal monarchists and the opposition about how far the comparison between family and state should go and how far rights to political rule could be derived from it. The later James I claimed that a king had his position by divine right and became a 'natural Father to all his Lieges at his Coronation'.[45] Richard Mocket's dialogue on *God and the King* (1615), published to promote the Oath of Allegiance to James, went even further, claiming that the King 'receiuing his Authority only from God ... hath no superiour to punish or chastice him but God

---

[42] Cf. Weber, 'Charles II', p. 202, Wiseman, 'Porno-Political Rhetoric', p. 153, and Amy Boesky, '"Nation, Miscegenation: Membering Utopia" in Henry Neville's *The Isle of Pines'*, *Texas Studies in Literature and Language*, 37 (1995), pp. 165-84.

[43] William Gouge, *Of domesticall duties eight treatises* (London, 1622), p. 18.

[44] Gordon J. Schochet, *Patriarchalism in Political Thought: The Authoritarian Family and Political Speculation and Attitudes Especially in Seventeenth-Century England* (Oxford, 1975); Johann Sommerville, *Politics and Ideology in England, 1603-1640* (London, 1986), p. 27; David Underdown, *Revel, Riot and Rebellion: Popular Politics and Culture in England 1603-1660* (Oxford, 1985), p. 9; Michael J. Braddick, *State Formation in Early Modern England, c. 1550-1700* (Cambridge, 2000), p. 14.

[45] 'The Trew Law of Free Monarchies: or The Reciprock and Mutuall Duetie Betwixt A Free King, And His natural Subiects', in *James I and VI, Political Writings*, ed. Johann P. Sommerville (Cambridge, 1994), pp. 62-84, p. 65.

alone', and that his subjects' bond of obedience to him could not be dissolved.[46]

God and the King was originally directed against rebellious Catholics and ordered to be bought by every householder and to be studied in schools and universities. But patriarchal theory remained a popular justification for the monarch's political discretion under Charles I and well into the civil war period, when Parliament attempted to limit monarchical power in favour of Parliament. The writing of Sir Robert Filmer's *Patriarcha* dates back to the pre-civil war era. Although *Patriarcha* was not published until 1680, its manuscript may have circulated as early as 1628, but certainly by the 1640s.[47] However, Filmer also responded to the power struggle between King and Parliament with a number of published pamphlets re-asserting the monarch's authority, such as his *Anarchy of a Limited or Mixed Monarchy* (1648). In the *Anarchy* Filmer argued that, as neither Eve nor her children could limit the government of Adam, neither Parliament nor people could limit the powers of Charles.[48] Around the same time, in the late 1640s and early 1650s, Neville mounted his first anti-patriarchal attack with his *Parliament-of-Ladies* pamphlets, a series of satirical libels on a female assembly, which ridiculed the weakness of a monarch who had been overthrown by a Parliament refusing to play the role of his subordinate wife.[49] Thus, Neville's Restoration *Isle* was a continuation or revival of his anti-patriarchalism at the same time as patriarchal arguments were revived by the court to re-assert royal authority in the face of political opposition and religious nonconformity.

---

[46] [Richard Mocket,] *God and the King* (London, 1615 [1663]), p. 31.

[47] Schochet dates it in the early 1640s, in *Patriarchalism*, p. 116. Daly suggests a date between 1636 and 1642, in *Filmer and English political thought*, p. 4. Jonathan Scott, *Algernon Sidney and the Restoration Crisis, 1677–1683* (Cambridge, 1991), pp. 7, 208, and Richard Tuck, 'Communications: A New Date for Filmer's "Patriarcha" ', *Historical Journal*, 29 (1986), pp. 183-6, even think 1628 likely.

[48] *The Anarchy of a Limited or Mixed Monarchy* in Sir Robert Filmer, *Patriarcha and Other Writings*, ed. Johann P. Sommerville (Cambridge, 1991), pp. 131-71, p. 138.

[49] [Neville], *The Parliament of Ladies* (London, 1647); *The Ladies Parliament* (London, 1647); *The Ladies, a Second Time, Assembled in Parliament* (1647); and *Newes from the New Exchange* (1650). See Gaby Mahlberg, 'The Politics of Patriarchalism in 17th Century Pamphlet Literature', *Women's History Magazine*, 46 (2004), pp. 4-9; 'A Parliament of Ladies und die Öffentlichkeit des Privaten: politischer Diskurs im England des 17. Jahrhunderts' in Caroline Emmelius *et al.* (eds), *Offen und Verborgen: Vorstellungen und Praktiken des Öffentlichen und Privaten in Mittelalter und Früher Neuzeit* (Göttingen, 2004), pp. 229-47.

God and the King was republished in 1663 by Charles II's royal proclamation 'for the Instruction of all his Majesties Subjects in their Duty and Allegiance',[50] at the same time as the government was issuing repressive measures against dissent, excluding nonconformists from public office and forbidding unauthorized worship, which raised popular fears of uniformity and arbitrary government.[51] Patriarchalism 'remained a commonplace', although 'theoretical debate was muted' until the 1678-81 Exclusion Crisis, during which a number of Filmer's works from the 1640s were republished, and *Patriarcha* (1680) was published for the first time, soon achieving 'the status of official doctrine on royal power'.[52]

Based on a literal Bible reading Filmer fused ideas about the origins of government and political obligation. Government originated with Adam, who, as the first father of the first family, also became the first king and passed on his God-given monarchy through primogeniture to his eldest son and through him to all subsequent generations.[53] Children and subjects were by nature under the authority of their father and monarch and, therefore, unfree. '[C]ivil power' was 'by divine institution', assigned 'specifically to the eldest parent', while government neither depended on 'the choice of the people', nor on any 'pactions between kings and their people'.[54]

Filmer's account also responded to rival theories of natural freedom and an original contract between the people and their king. As men were

---

[50] [Mocket,] *God and the King*, title page [1663].

[51] E.g. *An Act for the well-governing and regulating of Corporations* (1661), 13 Charles II, c. 1; *An Act for the Uniformity of public prayers, and administration of sacraments, and other rites and ceremonies* (1662), 14 Charles II, c. 4; *An Act to prevent and suppresse seditious Conventicles* (1664), 16 Charles II, c. 4; *An Act for restraining Non-conformists from inhabiting in corporations* (1665), 17 Charles II, c. 2. Cf. Steven C. A. Pincus, *Protestantism and Patriotism: Ideologies and the making of English foreign policy 1650-1668* (Cambridge, 1996), p. 233.

[52] Susan Dwyer Amussen, *An Ordered Society: Gender and Class in Early Modern England* (Oxford, 1988), pp. 63-64; Filmer, *Patriarcha*, pp. xxvii-xxviii; and Julia Rudolph, *Revolution by Degrees: James Tyrrell and Whig Political Thought in the Late Seventeenth Century* (Basingstoke, 2002), p. 20.

[53] Elaborate genealogical tables visualising the line of descent from Adam via Noah, Abraham and Lot down to Jesus were commonly bound with the King James Bible and the Prayer Book. A 1612 edition, for instance, has *The Booke of Common Prayer ... with The Genealogies Recorded in the Sacred Scriptures ... With the Line of our Sauiour Jesus Christ obserued from Adam to the blessed Virgin Mary, and The Holy Bible* ...; similarly, *The Book of Common Prayer* (Edinburgh, 1633), is bound with *Genealogies, Apocrypha* and related pamphlets.

[54] Filmer, *Patriarcha*, pp. 6-7.

born into civil subjection and the monarch's sovereignty was indivisible, the king was the sole originator of laws. Filmer stressed the subordinate role of the House of Commons and denied its antiquity because admitting it as an original part of Parliament would increase its power. History demonstrated that the Commons had only existed since the Middle Ages and was therefore no essential part of the constitution.[55] The people and their representatives owed total obedience to the king. Patriarchal theory could be employed to strengthen monarchical power, which explains its popularity and contestation across the seventeenth century.

Opponents of patriarchalism, by contrast, could base their claims on the myth of the ancient constitution. According to this theory, parliaments, including the Commons, were ancient and had existed since time out of mind. Having developed out of the old Saxon assemblies they were an original part of the constitution and not dependent on the monarch. The king was obliged to take the counsel of his parliament. King, Lords and Commons acted as co-ordinate powers in the law-making process. How far the coronation oath also obliged the King to consent to laws was debatable. Moderate parliamentarians might argue that the King had a legislative veto, while Neville and other radical parliamentarians interpreted the coronation oath as a binding contract between ruler and ruled, obliging the king to consent to the laws the two houses had made, rendering the king subordinate to them.[56] The question was whether the king held absolute power over his subjects, or whether his power was limited by the law. The debate remained unresolved beyond Neville's lifetime, but the concern with patriarchalism provides a continuity in the political debates that has often been overlooked in a historiography focusing on ever smaller periods of time.

Neville's allusions to divine-right patriarchal theory are evident throughout *The Isle*. Not only does the island resemble a 'paradise', but the only man in the shipwrecked company immediately takes the lead over the women 'being now all their stay in this lost condition' and establishes male or paternal authority first over the women and later over his children and grandchildren.[57] The story is reminiscent of the biblical narratives of Adam

---

[55] Ibid., p. 54; See also Alan Craig Houston, *Algernon Sidney and the Republican Heritage in England and America* (Princeton, 1991), p. 77; J. G. A. Pocock, *The Ancient Constitution and the Feudal Law: A Study of English Historical Thought in the Seventeenth Century* (New York, 1967), ch. 7; Daly, *Filmer and English political thought*, pp. 48ff, 127, 144; and Schochet, *Patriarchalism*, pp. 116–17.

[56] Neville, *Plato Redivivus*, pp. 128-9.

[57] Neville, *The Isle of Pines*, pp. 33-34.

and Noah, which patriarchal theorists used to justify the natural subjection of the people to their monarch. In fact, 'Neville's satire... reads almost like a fictional adaptation of Filmer's [*Patriarcha*].'[58] The reference to Genesis is underlined by the fact that it takes George Pines and the women exactly seven days — as long as it took God to create the world — to establish themselves on the island.[59] Reference to Noah is made through the ship on which a little fraction of humankind has been saved to re-populate the earth.[60] Questions of polygamy and incest must be read in this context, because a limited number of people have hardly any other choice than to resort to incestuous relationships.[61] So George Pines stresses that he only let his offspring 'marry their sisters ... out of necessity', whereas later generations did so for 'wantonness'.[62]

While the issue of polygamy has received attention as a joke on contemporary suggestions that Charles II should take a second wife to provide an heir, the question of incest has been neglected.[63] Yet, it points to conflicts between a literal interpretation of the Old Testament and Christian doctrine. For, incest was a sin, yet God must have allowed it when creating only two people (or saving eight in the case of Noah and his family) from whom the whole of mankind was to descend.

This criticism of a literal interpretation of the Old Testament links directly back to one of Neville's works from the civil war period, *The Ladies, a Second Time, Assembled in Parliament* (1647), in which the female assembly asks the Presbyterian synod to explain the Scriptural passage that says 'and *Iudah* went in unto her, and lay with her, and why there is such a Tautology', and how it came 'to passe that *Lot* was able to performe the act of generation with his two Daughters ... and yet not know when they lay downe, nor when they rose up'.[64] Neville's irreverence towards the Old Testament contributed to his reputation as an atheist and inspired the accusation during the 1659 Parliament that 'he was more affected by

---

[58] Weber, 'Charles II', p. 202; cf Fausett, *Writing the New World*, p. 83.

[59] Neville, *The Isle of Pines*, pp. 34-35; Gen. 1:1-2:3. Scriptural quotes refer to *The Authorized Version of the English Bible, 1611*, ed. William Aldis Wright, 5 vols (Cambridge, 1909).

[60] Cf. Gen. 9:1.

[61] A. Owen Aldridge, 'Polygamy in Early Fiction: Henry Neville and Denis Veiras', *Publications of the Modern Language Association*, 65 (1950), pp. 464-72, and Nicastro, *Isola di Pines*, pp. 143, 146.

[62] Neville, *The Isle of Pines*, pp. 37, 39.

[63] Aldridge, 'Polygamy'; and Nicastro, *L'isola di Pines*, pp. 143, 146.

[64] *The Ladies, a Second Time*, p. 9.

reading Cicero than ... the Bible'.[65] Yet, Neville was not irreligious, he only disagreed with a High Church and Court interpretation of God's word.

Similarly, the allusions to the creation story, the population of the earth, and the origins of tribes and races in *The Isle* mock patriarchal ideology. After the first rebellion, King Henry gives the people a set of laws, loosely based on the Ten Commandments. Henry's first law against blasphemy is based on the third commandment, not to 'misuse the name of the Lord'; the second law, establishing the monthly assembly, is based on the fourth commandment to 'Remember the Sabbath'.[66] The third and fourth law against rape and adultery remind us of the seventh commandment against adultery, and the tenth against coveting 'your neighbour's wife, or ... maidservant'.[67] The fifth law against taking away one's neighbour's possessions also resounds the tenth commandment.[68] The sixth law resembles the first, yet replaces God by the governor, who the Pines should not 'defame or speak evil' of, and gives the governor a god-like position.[69]

Yet, Neville's religious laws might also reveal sympathies for religious Independency and nonconformity. The order to have the Bible read once a month inspires some basic Christianity and a loose religious bond, following Neville's republican ideal of a basic civil religion.[70] There are no priests on the island, and the informal meetings for worship recall those of independent congregations. The governor of the Isle wants a teaching of 'Christian religion', not protestant doctrine. Religion is to be based on the reading of the Bible so as to instil in them 'the true light of the gospel', the New Testament.[71] That is, the Old and the New Testament are in conflict.

Neville goes on to ridicule the direct line of descent from Adam to Jesus and its implications for patriarchal political theory in his description of polygamy, incest and moral decay. If the Bible has to be taken literally then all the rulers who claim their power directly from God must be the product of those morally objectionable relationships. If this direct line of descent is questionable, divine right monarchy looses its foundation. Thus,

---

[65] M. de Bordeaux to Cardinal Mazarin, February 27, 1659. See F. Guizot, *History of Richard Cromwell and the Restoration of Charles II*, 2 vols (London, 1858), 1, pp. 306-11, p. 308.

[66] Ex. 20:7-8. [67] Ex. 20:14, 17. [68] Ex. 20:17.

[69] Neville, *The Isle of Pines*, p. 40.

[70] Cf. Goldie, 'The civil religion of James Harrington'; and Martin Dzelzainis, '"T'was look'd upon as a sham": Henry Neville's *Isle of Pines*', paper presented at 'New Worlds Reflected: Representations of Utopia, the New World and Other Worlds, 1500-1800', a conference at Birkbeck College, London, 10 December 2005.

[71] Neville, *The Isle of Pines*, p. 38.

Neville's criticism of a literal reading of the Old Testament connects with the works of John Locke, Benedict de Spinoza and other contemporary freethinkers of the early Enlightenment, who doubted that 'the Bible ... is everywhere inspired and literally true', and argued that many of the Old Testament stories had to be understood metaphorically to be in 'accord with reason and understanding'.[72] Neville's Protestantism was therefore different from that of the Church of England, but also from that of other republicans, such as Milton, Sidney, Edmund Ludlow, and even James Harrington, in whose works we find 'providential and apocalyptic language'.[73] His understanding of the Old Testament is looking more forward to the eighteenth century sceptical tradition than back to Puritan zealotry.

Neville alludes to a number of key sections of the Old Testament frequently quoted by divine-right advocates. When the number of people has grown larger on the island, Pines divides them into tribes like the tribes of Israel, who descended from the sons of Jacob.[74] And Pines's narration ends with a formula borrowed from the benediction of Isaac, the father of Jacob, when he names his four tribes, 'whom God bless with the dew of Heaven, and the fat of the Earth'.[75] Even the names of Neville's characters are references to Scripture. Pines's closest wife is called Sarah, after the wife of the patriarch Abraham. She and George, named after the patron saint of England, are the parents of the tribe of English Pines or the English race.[76] They form the original family. Yet, as Neville would emphasise in *Plato Redivivus*, Abraham and Isaac 'were but ordinary fathers of families, and no question governed their own household as all others do'. Their paternal power did not extend further. Political patriarchalism was only a 'fancy ... first started, not by the solid judgement of any man, but to flatter some prince; and to assert, for want of better arguments, the divine right of monarchy'.[77] Pines's claim to government over the island was built on a fallacy.

Neville's final argument against patriarchal government, however, is not illustrated by the ridicule of a literal Bible reading, but by the marriage rituals of Indian rulers, which the Dutch captain learns about on his further journey. In India, the Brahmins ('priests or teachers') have the right of the

---

[72] Benedict de Spinoza, *Tractatus Theologico-Politicus* (London 1868), pp. 25, 26-27.
[73] Scott, *Commonwealth Principles*, p. 42.
[74] Gen. 35: 10-11.
[75] Neville, *The Isle of Pines*, p. 38; Nicastro, *Isola di Pines*, p. 126; Gen. 27:28.
[76] Nicastro, *Isola di Pines*, p. 125.   [77] Neville, *Plato Redivivus*, p. 86.

first night with the King's wife, so that the King cannot be sure about the paternity of his first child. Therefore, not his own descendants, but the sons of his sister succeed to the throne, 'as being more certainly known to be of the true Royal blood'.[78] Patriarchal rule and hereditary descent are absurd, because paternity can never be certain.

The full version of *The Isle* can be read not just as a parody of Biblical patriarchalism and scriptural literalism, but also as a dystopia or 'utopie inverse', a critical assessment of English politics and history and a story of decay from the Golden Age of Elizabeth's reign to the present.[79] The rule of Elizabeth was a high point in English politics, accompanied by military and naval power. With the arrival of the Stuarts this power turned into impotence with James I's refusal to fight a European war in the 1620s, followed by Charles I's failure to fight the same war successfully. Charles II's rule continued this Stuart tradition of military impotence which contemporaries often associated with his sexual antics.[80] Following the parable of the Stuart monarchs as that of the family of Pines the story of decay then leads on to theoretical issues about the origins and nature of civil government and interweaves with key issues from pre-civil war debates left unresolved at the Restoration.

When George Pines arrived on the island during Elizabeth's time, he found himself in '*Paradise*' 'the countrey so very pleasant ... full of pleasant fruits, and variety of birds ... and never colder then in *England* in *September*'.[81] Elizabethan England was like paradise before the fall, peaceful and prosperous. But with the patriarchal rule of the Stuarts things went downhill. Neville reflects on the Stuart period as one of court debauchery and government decay. 'Idleness and Fullness of everything' on the imaginary island caused Pines and his companions to give in to self-indulgence. Yet, he did not establish any other law than a vague exhortation to 'remember the Christian Religion'.[82] So with a growing population in the next generation 'those good orders' fell out of use and 'mischief began to rise ... [I]n multitudes disorders will grow, the stronger seeking to oppress the weaker, no tye of Religion being strong enough to chain up the depraved nature of mankinde'. Through a 'neglect of hearing the Bible read' and their 'sence of sin being quite lost ... they fell to whoredoms,

---

[78] Neville, *The Isle of Pines*, p. 46.
[79] Lurbe, 'Une utopie inverse.'
[80] I owe this point to Jonathan Scott.
[81] Neville, *The Isle of Pines*, p. 35.
[82] *Ibid.*, pp. 35, 38.

incests, and adulteries'.[83] The country entered civil war, and as in Neville's *Parliament of Ladies*, the moral transgressions of the people and their rulers are cast in sexual terms, as giving one's own private interest preference over the public.

Neville likens the story of the English civil war to that of the fall of man after tasting the forbidden fruit in paradise, playing on the same theme as Milton's *Paradise Lost* which had appeared a year earlier.[84] It is not accidental that he uses phrases like 'they soon *fell* from those good orders prescribed ... by my Grandfather', or 'they *fell* to whoredoms, incests, and adulteries'.[85] Nor is it accidental that the main culprit is John Phill, 'the second son of the *Negro-woman*' that came with George Pines to the island.[86] The blackness of the slave woman and her offspring is symbolic, combining the diabolical and uncontrollable in mankind with contemporary racial stereotypes.[87] The black slave is 'less sensible' than the other women and determined by sexual urges, which cause her to seduce Pines secretly as the devil in the shape of a snake seduced Adam and Eve. Yet, sexual relations between a white man and a black woman were perceived as unnatural, and Pines only 'lay with her ... in the night'.[88] John Phill, the product of this union, carried his mother's sin. After the civil war, he was 'proved guilty of divers ravishings & tyrannies', condemned to death, and 'thrown down from a high Rock into the Sea'.[89] This scene might allude to Charles I's trial for treason and execution as a tyrant after the civil war; and if John Phill stands for Charles I, then the laws made subsequently by the good ruler, Henry Pines, might allude to the laws of the Commonwealth, or, more abstractly, stand for the republican commitment to constitutionalism. If government does not arise from paternal power, it must grow out of a contract between ruler and ruled.

Although republicanism has often been disassociated historiographically from natural law theory Neville clearly embraced the idea of an original state of nature and war, which was ended by the creation of civil society by contract and the establishment of law. Neville's speculations in *Plato*

---

[83] *Ibid.*, p. 39.

[84] Milton, *Paradise Lost*, p. vii.

[85] Neville, *The Isle of Pines*, p. 39, my italics.

[86] *Ibid.*, p. 39.

[87] Cf. *Golden Coast*, p. 35, where black Africans are referred to as 'Moors, Moorens, or Negroes, a People of beastly living, without a God, Law, Religion, or Commonwealth'; and Boesky, 'Nation, Miscegenation', pp. 166, 169.

[88] Neville, *The Isle of Pines*, pp. 34, 36.   [89] *Ibid.*, p. 39-40.

Redivivus about 'the first government' being created out of 'necessity' are specifically Hobbesian.

> For every man by the first law of nature ... had, like beasts in a pasture, right to everything; and there being no property, each individual, if he were the stronger, might seize whatever any other had possessed himself of before, which made a state of perpetual war.

To end this 'perpetual war' the people resorted to a Lockean contract. Because of

> the fear that nothing should be long enjoyed by any particular person, (neither was any man's life in safety,) every man consented to be debarred of that universal right to all things; and confirms himself to a quiet and secure enjoyment of such a part, as should be allotted him. Thence came in ownership, or property: to maintain which, it was necessary to consent to law, and a government; to put them in execution.[90]

Government was based on consent and 'instituted for the good and preservation of the governed; and not for the exaltation and greatness of the person or persons appointed to govern'.[91] Most importantly, it was not patriarchal.

The parallels between *Plato Redivivus* and *The Isle* are striking. In *The Isle* the uprising of the Phills necessitates the first institution of laws and a government. As in *Plato Redivivus*, the people in the state of nature have fallen into war, and patriarchal power is not able to deal with the problem. George Pines as the father had been able to maintain authority over his wives and children, but in the second generation paternal power has lapsed, and order can only be established by laws. Yet, when the laws get out of use new chaos arises. The same is true for England in the 1680s, where 'the inexecution of the law' is one of the chief grievances Neville puts forward.[92] His emphasis is on the importance of constitutionalism, reminding us of Harrington's concern to make his *Commonwealth of Oceana*

---

[90] Neville, *Plato Redivivus*, p. 85. Cf. Thomas Hobbes, *Leviathan*, ed. C. B. Macpherson (London, 1968), ch. 14; John Locke, 'Second Treatise', ch. VIII, §§ 95-99, in *Two Treatises of Government*, ed. Peter Laslett (Cambridge, 1988).

[91] Neville, *Plato Redivivus*, p. 85.

[92] *Ibid.*, p. 145, cf. also pp. 126, 130.

an 'empire of laws and not of men'.[93] The need to make laws shows that patriarchal power on its own cannot grant stability, but that some structure needs to be instituted to enable the formation of civil society. After George Pines's death the patriarchal order disintegrates through the first insurrection of the Phills. The state of nature has turned into a state of war, which necessitates the making of laws and the first constitutional government. With the new laws put into execution by King Henry the country remains quiet for a while, but problems return under the next ruler, William — or the Restoration regime — and can only be resolved with the help of the Dutch.

The role of the Dutch is crucial because many English republicans and religious dissenters found exile in their towns during the Restoration. The Dutch merchant, Abraham Keek, whom Neville fictionalised as a letter writer, for instance, would house radical exiles from England during the 1680s and help them acquire the status of burghers of Amsterdam for their protection.[94] But Dutch religious freedom was also associated with economic strength. A closer English friendship with the republican Dutch would certainly have suited English republicans and dissenters as it might encourage religious toleration in England and an opening up of international trade.

Dutch strength as depicted in *The Isle* shows Neville's admiration for the republican neighbours as well as his concern for their superior power *vis-à-vis* English fiscal-military insignificance. This contrast evoked Neville's musings in *Plato Redivivus* about why England, once 'esteemed ... one of the most considerable people of the world', was 'now of so small regard, and signifie[d] so little abroad?'[95] From the age of Elizabeth the situation had constantly deteriorated (with the exception of the Interregnum, or the rule of King Henry), and the 'ship of state' had gone to pieces. The abundance of the island had made the Pines lazy and debauched, and although the large number of people on the island provided potential for wealth and economic growth as contemporary promoters of 'political arithmetic' tended to point out, they were not put to

---

[93] James Harrington, *The Commonwealth of Oceana* and *A System of Politics*, ed. J. G. A. Pocock (Cambridge, 2001), p. 8. Harrington adopted the principle from Aristotle and Livy.

[94] Scott, *Commonwealth Principles*, p. 50; Richard Ashcraft, *Revolutionary Politics and Locke's Two Treatises of Government* (Princeton, 1986), pp. 419-20; Richard L. Greaves, *Secrets of the Kingdom: British Radicals from the Popish Plot to the Revolution of 1688-1689* (Stanford, 1992), pp. 263, 410.

[95] Neville, *Plato Redivivus*, p. 79.

any use.⁹⁶ They did not produce anything, nor did they sell anything. The only leftovers from the former staple item of trade, manufactured cloth, were 'the Relicts of those Cloaths ... of them which first came hither', now worn by Prince William's wife.⁹⁷

Any economic potential had gone to waste under a succession of weak rulers who left a primitive country, populated through incestuous relationships, in which 'so many ... could speak *English*, and yet go naked'.⁹⁸ Nakedness was a symbol for the backwardness, primitivism and barbarism often ascribed to the inhabitants of foreign nations,⁹⁹ but it also refers to the Pines's lack of defence and implicitly to England's lack of fiscal-military strength after the Medway disaster of 1667. The English were both 'naked' and 'unarmed'.¹⁰⁰ So the Dutch defeated the insurrection with ease: 'for what could nakedness do to encounter with Arms?'¹⁰¹ Moreover, the Dutch are depicted as competent sailors and explorers, who survey the island, measure its size and explore its possibilities, while the English lack even the most essential tools, and live in little 'Huts ... made under Trees.'¹⁰² They never attempt to leave the island and have never seen 'a thing called a ship'.¹⁰³

Neville contrasts the republican Netherlands with the patriarchal monarchy of England, concluding that the patriarchal state is not conducive to trade, progress and military strength. Like Slingsby Bethel, he incites his readers to take the United Provinces as an example.¹⁰⁴ Patriarchal rule is not only ideologically unsound, it also does not encourage efficiency, as status and power rely more on birth than merit.

---

⁹⁶ E.g. John Graunt, Charles Davenant, William Petty and Gregory King. See also [Slingsby Bethel,] *The Present Interest of England Stated* (1671), p. 13; and [Philanglus], *Britannia Languens, or A discourse of Trade* (1680), p. 152. Cf. Nicastro, *Isola di Pines*, pp. 20, 126-7, 131-46; Aldridge, 'Polygamy in Early Fiction'; and Sandra Sherman, *Finance and Fictionality in the Early Eighteenth Century: Accounting for Defoe* (Cambridge, 1996).

⁹⁷ Neville, *The Isle of Pines*, p. 30.

⁹⁸ *Ibid.*

⁹⁹ Cf. *A Geographicall and Anthological Description of all the Empires and Kingdomes, both of Continent and Ilands in this terrestriall Globe*. (1634), pp. 3-4.

¹⁰⁰ Neville, *The Isle of Pines*, p. 42.

¹⁰¹ *Ibid.*, p. 45. Cf Harrington, *Oceana*, p. 98: 'What were two or three thousand of you, well affected to your country but naked unto one troop of mercenary soldiers?'

¹⁰² Neville, *The Isle of Pines*, pp. 31, 42-43, 41-42.

¹⁰³ *Ibid.*, p. 31.

¹⁰⁴ Bethel, *Present Interest*, p. 5.

The people's subordination to an absolute ruler stifles their development and weakens their productivity, and the power of their country.[105] The way out must be constitutional republican government in which laws, not monarchs, rule.

Neville's *Isle of Pines* reminds us that English republicanism was not confined to the Interregnum. Nor was it all about concrete forms of government, but also a response to tyranny, or a monarch's unreasonable claims to power. Neville's *Isle* thus belonged to the same anti-patriarchal tradition that would produce Locke's *Two Treatises of Government* (1689), Sidney's *Discourses Concerning Government* (1698), and Neville's own *Plato Redivivus* (1681). The antiquarian Thomas Hollis first emphasised this point when he re-published the core text of *The Isle* together with Neville's *Parliament of Ladies* in the eighteenth century as part of his republican canon and added a footnote referring to Locke's reflections on the royal prerogative in the *Two Treatises*.[106]

Hollis's re-publication effort bears witness to the ongoing rivalry between political ideologies of divine-right patriarchalism and contractarianism until well into the eighteenth century, and it reflects the resurgence of an old seventeenth-century debate during the 'American troubles' of George III's reign.[107] *The Isle* thus transcends its creative context in several ways. Neville's concern with patriarchalism connects the key phases of political conflict of the seventeenth century — the 1640s, the 1660s and the 1680s. Yet, Neville's mockery and criticism of the Old Testament as a basis for political rule also separates him from many other republicans of the mid seventeenth century and their apocalyptic language and links him more closely to a later generation of republican-minded religious freethinkers of the radical Enlightenment, such as those belonging to the circle of John Toland. Neville's innovative religious language might also have added to his appeal to later editors because it made his work more easily adaptable for an eighteenth-century Whig audience. With the help of his editors Neville's ideas of religious and political liberty would thus be relevant well beyond his lifetime.

---

[105] Cf. Quentin Skinner, 'A Third Concept of Liberty', *Proceedings of the British Academy*, 117 (2002), pp. 237-68, 258ff.

[106] [Neville] *The Isle of Pines*, p. 4.

[107] Cf. J. A. W. Gunn, *Beyond Liberty and Property: the Process of Self-Recognition in Eighteenth-Century Political Thought* (Kingston and Montreal, 1983), p. 169.

Chapter 8

Formality and Revolution: Carlyle on Modernity

John Morrow

I

Although Colin Davis's exploration of formalism and anti-formalism is focused primarily on the English Revolution, he suggests that the realignment of the formal and the informal may be a common, perhaps even a general feature of revolutionary situations.[1] This insight provides a starting point for considering Thomas Carlyle's widely read studies of the English and French revolutions, *The French Revolution: A History* (1837) and *The Letters and Speeches of Oliver Cromwell* (1845).

These works, part of a diverse output that embraced biography and pseudo-biography, history, literary, social and political criticism, were seen by Carlyle as contributions to a distinctive mission addressing the spiritual, moral and political needs of modern European societies. Carlyle's reading of a range of features of the contemporary world — political movements such as Chartism, working class and elite reactions to the rise of industrial society, English and Irish pauperism and the materialistic cast of the modern mind — was meant to demonstrate that European societies were still trying to come to terms with the requirements of a world in which the comfortable certainties of medieval culture were lost irretrievably. In a wide range of writings published from the 1820s through until the early 1850s Carlyle attributed these disturbing developments and the responses of legislators, social and clerical elites, men-of-letters, philosophers, prophets and promoters to a deep-seated malaise of mind and spirit and to a 'felt lack of faith' that exacerbated its dehabilitating impact. The age was 'at once destitute of faith and terrified at skepticism.'[2]

---

[1] J. C. Davis, 'Against Formality: One Aspect of the English Revolution', *Transactions of the Royal Historical Society*, sixth series, III (1993), p. 265.

[2] Thomas Carlyle, 'Sir Walter Scott', *Critical and Miscellaneous Essays*, 5, p. 46, cited hereafter as *CME*, *Works of Thomas Carlyle* (London, 1893-4); unless indicated otherwise all references to Carlyle's writings are to this edition, the 'half-crown edition'. For a recent account of the various stages of Carlyle's mission see John Morrow, *Thomas Carlyle* (London, 2006).

While Carlyle's response to the 'condition of England question' shared common ground with those advanced in a range of contemporary social and political criticism it was not directed by the spirit of nostalgia and conservatism which infused much of this literature. To the contrary, his writings were underwritten by a strongly progressive sense of the possibilities open to his contemporaries. If they were to take advantage of the situation, however, they would have to come to terms with the need to create a new formed world in place of the incoherent array of medieval vestiges and failed alternatives which littered the nineteenth century landscape. This challenge was a recurring *motif* in an account of modern European history as a process of far-reaching but incomplete cultural, social and political transformation.

In an early essay on historical writing, Carlyle glanced scornfully at Lord Bolingbroke's dictum that history was 'philosophy teaching by experience' because he objected to his predecessor's philosophy not to his didacticism. Carlyle saw historical writing as a vehicle for revealing the working out of God's purpose in the world. It would further this objective by inspiring modern readers to acquire the moral and psychological dispositions that would enable them to make positive contributions to the fulfillment of humanity's destiny; 'History ... is an Address (literally out of Heaven, for did not God order it all?) to our whole inner man.'[3] Carlyle rejected what he took to be conventional, enlightenment views on the progress of human society. These focused on *what* people understood and were dismissive of those aspects of past thought and practice that did not correspond with the products of the enlightened mind. Carlyle, by contrast, was interested in the emotional and moral dimensions of human understanding and belief. The key issue was authenticity in the act of believing. This reflected the moral character of the believer and had a bearing on the outcome of the belief because it provided a warrant for the quality of its object: 'No thought that ever dwelt honestly as true in the heart of man but was an honest insight into God's truth on man's part, and *has* an essential truth in it which endures through all changes, an everlasting possession for us all.'[4]

Questions concerning the quality of belief and its impact on the

---

[3] *Collected Letters of Thomas and Jane Welsh Carlyle,* ed. Charles Richard Sanders *et. al.*
(Durham, North Carolina, 1970), 7, p. 52. See also Thomas Carlyle, 'On History', *Critical and Miscellaneous Essays,* 2, pp. 253-5.

[4] Thomas Carlyle, 'Luther', *Heroes, Hero-Worship and the Heroic in History,* p. 111. Cited hereafter as *HHW.*

viability of systems of authority were central to Carlyle's understanding of the role that discourses of formality played in recovering the significance of modern European revolutions. The groundwork of his approach was laid in a work titled *Sartor Resartus*, published in 1833-4. *Sartor Resartus* was a strikingly original, largely fictional exploration of the condition of the modern European mind. After a spluttering debut in a periodical, this work secured an extensive readership which outlived its author; 70,000 copies were sold in the year following his death.[5] In *Sartor Resartus* Carlyle developed an elaborate metaphor likening forms to clothes which give distinct, culturally specific outward expression to the human spirit.

> All visible things are emblems; what thou seest is not there on its own account ... . Matter exists only spiritually, and to represent some Idea, and body it forth ... . On the other hand, all Emblematic things are properly Clothes, thought-woven or hand-woven; must not the Imagination weave Garments, visible Bodies, wherein the else invisible creations and inspirations of our Reason are, like Spirits, revealed, and first became all-powerful?

This metaphor, which was re-used in Carlyle's historical writings, extended to religious ideas, practices and institutions and to systems of political authority. The former were characterized as 'Church-Clothes': 'the Forms, the *Vestures*, under which men at various periods embodied and represented [to] themselves the Religious Principle ...'. Similarly, the network of authority and obedience which underwrote systems of criminal justice and the governmental apparatus on which they depended, could be represented by the regalia of the various actors in courts, legislatures and ruling councils. By portraying the authority of religious and political institutions in terms of the costumes of office-holders, Carlyle underlined the extent to which the efficacy of forms depended upon beliefs that were seen as being inseparable from them. When this connection was broken, human beings returned to a formless condition of 'Adamite' nakedness.[6]

If forms were to be embodiments or emanations of fundamental values that became objects of authentic belief, they had to be congruent with prevailing levels of intellectual and scientific understanding. At the same time, however, they had to be seen by the bulk of the population as spontaneously generated and sustained features of an integrated existence. Forms

---

[5] See Morrow, *Thomas Carlyle*, p. 213.
[6] Thomas Carlyle, *Sartor Resartus: The Life and Opinions of Herr Teufelsdöckh*, pp. 49, 147, 41-43.

which satisfied these requirements expressed some significant truth, gave essential support to human life and provided the basis of ordered, satisfying social relationships and the systems of authority which underwrote them. In this sense, as Carlyle put it, 'the formed world is the only habitable one.'[7]

Carlyle gave an account of such a world in *Past and Present* (1843), a work that celebrated the integrated culture of the high medieval period, contrasting this condition with what he took to be the chronically dislocated state of the modern world. The contrast highlighted the transitory nature of particular systems of formality. It was designed to prompt Carlyle's readers to seek earnestly for alternatives to medieval forms which had once been true but had become false. Some forms became false when they had outlived their time but were still treated as if they were valid representations of deep-seated beliefs. Others were advanced as alternatives to redundant forms but were incapable of satisfying the necessary conditions. These putative objects of belief were contrived and inorganic. They lacked any positive connections with prevailing levels of intellectual and scientific understanding and they also lacked the qualities necessary in emblems that convincingly represent to human beings the fundamental values that underwrite effective social and political authority. Even when false forms were not challenged openly, they corrupted the moral basis of society's institutional framework: 'Smooth Falsehood is not Order; it is the general sum total of Disorder. Order is *Truth* — each thing standing on the basis that belongs to it.'[8] As forms lapsed into falsehood, the sense of stability which characterised formed worlds gave way to prolonged and increasingly persistent moral uncertainty and instability. These periods were marked by sharp contests over particular forms, and intense debate on the deeper question of the role of formality in framing human thought, speech and action.

The inadequacy of false forms was signaled by the tendency for discourses of formality to become increasingly self-conscious. In more advanced stages of redundancy, adherence to past forms rested on manifest self-delusion. When those who challenged prevailing forms confronted the putative interests of political, social and ecclesiastical elites they were met by vigorous and sometimes brutal attempts to enforce conformity. These attempts were bound to fail since coercion could not generate conviction. In any case, true forms were natural and spontaneous expressions of the wholehearted belief on which viable systems of

---

[7] Thomas Carlyle, 'Cromwell and Napoleon', *HHW*, pp. 189-90.

[8] Thomas Carlyle, 'Luther', *HHW*, p. 139.

authority depended, not the basis of them.⁹ When formality became an end in itself, when individuals lived *for* the sake of forms rather than *in* and *through* them, the forms in question were false.¹⁰

In addressing issues of religious practice and church government, Carlyle placed a premium on independent judgment and was sharply critical of the claims of intermediaries to stand between humanity and God. He seems to have thought that while systems of religious formality may once have been useful, the time had come when fundamental issues of human existence could not be adequately expressed in this way. But while human authority had no role in matters of religious faith, it was central to maintaining social and political relationships that were compatible with humankind's obligations to God. Carlyle's views on this matter were emphatically illiberal and anti-democratic, resting on his commitment to the idea that effective and legitimate authority required hierarchical structures which reflected sharp differences in the intellectual, if not moral, capabilities of members of communities. These principles were embodied in the conventions and practices of particular societies, in the networks of formality in which these were expressed and institutionalised, but they were grounded in the deepest aspirations of the human spirit.

Although Carlyle did not see the English and French revolutions as parts of a discernable causal sequence, he thought they were both expressions of an admirable and active commitment to truth. Carlyle's treatment made it clear, however, that he believed they presented contrasting responses to the challenge facing those embarking on the hazardous but necessary journey from the medieval to the modern worlds. While the history of the French Revolution was largely salutary in terms of Carlyle's mission, he discerned great inspirational potential in the English Revolution.

II

Carlyle portrayed the outbreak of the revolution in France as a natural, and in this sense a justifiable, reaction against gross and prolonged failures of elite leadership.¹¹ He opened his study with an account of the general indifference that greeted the last illness of Louis XV in 1744, a

---

[9] *Ibid.*, p. 190.
[10] See Davis, 'Against Formality', p. 276 for this distinction.
[11] See Hedva Ben-Israel, *English Historians on the French Revolution* (Cambridge, 1968) for an excellent account of Carlyle's approach to this topic.

response which signaled the yawning gulf that had opened between the French people's inchoate sense of what they expected of their rulers and the Bourbons' understanding of their role. While Carlyle's account of the pre-revolutionary period in France focused on the failures of economic and political policy that had become conventional in histories of the revolution, his answers to the critical questions, what induced the French to push aside the authority of crown, church and nobility and why was the revolution so catastrophic, were framed by reference to the distinction between authentic and spurious formality. He argued that the crown's growing incapacity to perceive, let alone come to grips with, the challenges facing France, the manifest redundancy of the nobility, and the Church's commitment to ideas and practices that had no purchase on the modern world, created a situation where the practical and spiritual bankruptcy of the belief structures upon which authority depended was demonstrated more and more clearly.

Elite responses to the philosophy of the Enlightenment were an important part of this process because they indicated that the educated classes had renounced traditional objects of belief and, superficially at least, the possibility of belief itself. Carlyle contrasted a situation where the symbols attached to kingship and to the church represented 'realised ideals', with the condition of France in the early eighteenth century. This was an era of empty forms, a feature of

> decadent ages in which no Ideal either grows or blossoms ... . When Belief and Loyalty have passed away, and only the cant and false echo of them remains; and all Solemnity has become Pageantry; and the Creed of persons in authority has become one of two things: an Imbecility or a Machiavelism.[12]

Carlyle thought that the tendencies to false formality which characterized periods of transition were exacerbated by the impact of Enlightenment thinking among the upper classes of the country. Skepticism undermined belief and the forms of authority which were sustained by it. At the same time, however, it placed an increased reliance on the need to maintain and harden modes of formality as they seemed all that remained to hold society and the state together. Since these modes were false, subscription to them was inauthentic and insincere, demoralizing their proponents and damaging the moral consciousness of those who were subjected to them.

---

[12] Thomas Carlyle, *The French Revolution: A History*, 1, pp. 8, 9; cited hereafter as *FR*.

In France and elsewhere, this state of affairs provided the justification for the total overthrow of prevailing authority: 'Not *Hunger* alone produced even the French Revolution; no, but the feeling of the insupportable all-pervading *Falsehood* which had now embodied itself in Hunger, in universal material Scarcity, and Nonentity, and thereby become *indisputably* false in the eyes of all.'[13]

Carlyle saw extreme manifestations of false formality in eighteenth-century France as symptoms and harbingers of the utter collapse of French society. By the late 1780s clerical, political and social institutions and practices were but mere forms and were atomised by the revolutionary energy of the sansculotte:

> When ... Man's existence had for long generations rested on mere formulas which were grown hollow by course of time; and it seemed as if no Reality any longer existed, but only Phantasms of realities, and God's Universe were the work of the Tailor and Upholsterer mainly, and men were buckram masks that went becking and grimacing there, — on a sudden, the Earth yawns asunder, and amid Tartarean smoke, and glare of fierce brightness, rises SANSCULOTTISM, many headed, fire-breathing, and asks: What think ye of *me*?[14]

These forces, a visceral response to the inauthentic formality of the *ancien regime*, operated through a wide variety of agents in Paris and the provinces but their character was demonstrated most graphically by the Paris mob. While Carlyle deployed all his literary skill to portray the mob's hideously destructive passage across the stage of modern French history, he made it clear to his readers that it could not be merely dismissed with a shudder, as one would the terrifying monsters that stalk through nightmares. 'When so much goes grinning and grimacing as a lifeless Formality, and under the stiff buckram no heart can be felt beating, here once more, if nowhere else, is a Sincerity and Reality. Shudder at it; or even shriek over it, if thou must; nevertheless consider it.'[15]

The onset of the revolution triggered the complete collapse of French society and made a constructive political response to it virtually impossible. The Constituent Assembly's attempt to remake government by framing a constitution necessarily floundered because its members

---

[13] Carlyle, 'Cromwell and Napoleon', p. 194.
[14] Carlyle, FR, 1, p. 185.   [15] Ibid., p. 218.

possessed no set of shared beliefs and thus no basis for building the forms of the post-revolutionary world.[16] The Assembly's only real achievements were, in fact, part of the revolutionary process. It played a key role in destroying the vestigial structures of the old world and thus creating the conditions for the emergence of sansculottism as a hyperactive expression of 'disembodied anarchy', the antithesis of the formed world and the inveterate enemy of those who sought to create and inhabit such a world: 'The world of formulas, the *formed* regulated world, which all the habitable world is, — must needs hate such Fanaticism like death; and be at deadly variance with it. The world of formulas must conquer it; or failing that, must die execrating it, anathematizing it.'[17]

Attempts were made to escape from this situation, either by recourse to old forms or by trying to institute new ones. During the King's trial, for example, moderate elements within the Assembly tried to frame a process that was without precedent in terms of conventional legal forms. Carlyle described this exercise as an understandable but futile attempt to stretch old formulas to cover new practice. He contrasted this tragic recourse to what no longer had any meaning with the clear-eyed realism of Robespierre and Saint-Just.[18]

Among those who sought to cover the trial and execution of the King with comforting old forms was the party of the Gironde, a leading element in the first Legislative Assembly that met in October 1791. Carlyle noted that although the Girondins were men of talent with a capacity for 'working and shaping', they shaped 'alas not in marble, only in quicksand!'[19] Their devotion to forms was apparent in their faith that political and social authority in France could be re-made by appeals to constitutional principles that had no basis in reality and were directed towards the establishment of what Carlyle derisively referred to as a 'republic of respectability'. They sought to do so during a period (September 1792 to October 1795) when the anti-formal tide of sansculottism was in the full flood of its 'grandeur' and its 'hideousness', necessarily working 'not as a Regularity but as a Chaos; destructive and self-destructive.'[20]

For a time, this force appeared to be harnessed by the Jacobins. They used it to destroy the Girondins before falling victim to its remorseless appetite for destruction. Robespierre and his colleagues were prey to formalistic fantasies of their own, but Carlyle thought that they, of all the actors in the French Revolution, were best able to grasp the real significance of

[16] *Ibid.*, p. 188.   [17] *Ibid.*, p. 185.   [18] *Ibid.*, 3, p. 78.
[19] *Ibid.*, 2, p. 174.   [20] *Ibid.*, 3, pp. 2, 99.

sansculottism. Carlyle saw the revolution as a reaction against the prolonged failure of the French political and ecclesiastical establishments to address the legitimate demands of the ordinary people of France. These demands really came down to the requirement that government must be placed in the hands of those committed to bringing 'some glimmering of light and alleviation to the Twenty-five millions, who sat in darkness, heavy-laden, till they rose with pikes in their hands' and having the strength of character, will, and intellect to give effect to this requirement. The Girondins, playing only insincere lip-service to these demands and to the claim to moral equality that underwrote them, treated the ordinary people as instruments to be deployed in the pursuit of a middle class republic envisioned in terms of the mechanical formulae of parliamentary government.[21]

These formulae were disconnected from the realities of revolutionary politics and from the moral forces that had produced them. They were not the 'genuine substances' necessary to provide the basis for a sustainable order because they were as false in their own way as the redundant forms of the *ancien regime*.[22] But while neither Girondins nor Jacobins possessed the insight necessary to identify forms appropriate to the needs of modern humanity, Carlyle acknowledged that their urge to re-form the molten mass unleashed by the revolution reflected some level of understanding of the challenge facing society once the white hot forces of destruction had done their work. Before the process of reformation could begin in earnest, however, sansculottism would need to be tamed and the revolution brought to an end. This objective was secured by Napoleon Bonaparte, utilizing the military forces that the revolution had created to subject the motley anti-formal remnant to a salutary 'whiff of grapeshot'.

Napoleon's resolution on this occasion might have been seen as a harbinger of a heroic career that would have enabled France to begin to build a new moral, social and political order. It transpired however, that his undoubted talents were applied to the senseless and destructive pursuit of what in early nineteenth-century terms amounted to global supremacy, and to expropriating the 'semblances' to which the ruling classes of eighteenth-century France were so tragically wedded. By assuming the trappings of imperial majesty, allying himself by marriage to the Habsburgs, a dynasty that was a byword for redundancy, and coming to an accommodation with the Papacy, Napoleon sacrificed truth to a series of self-serving delusions: 'What a paltry patchwork of theatrical

---

[21] *Ibid.*, pp. 98-99, 105, 118.
[22] Carlyle, 'Cromwell and Napoleon', p. 188.

paper-mantles, tinsel and mummery, had this man wrapt his own great reality in, thinking to make it more real thereby!'[23]

Following Napoleon's final defeat in 1815, France remained trapped in a vacuum of unreality, completely unable to meet the challenge that he had failed to answer. The restoration of the Bourbons was a futile attempt to restore forms that had already been shown to be incapable of being objects of authentic belief to modern humanity. The Orleanist regime which replaced them in 1830 was a palpable sham practiced on the French people. Carlyle was scathing on the moral tone of restoration Paris — 'the hateful contrast between physical perfection and moral nothingness!' — and dismissed Charles X, the last Bourbon ruler of France, as a 'foolish old King'. The Orleanist regime which followed was no better. This 'system of inequities' was dispatched by Lemartine and his colleagues early in 1848 but the revolution otherwise proved a dawn of false hope, moving rapidly through all the Jacobin, Girondist and Napoleonic phases of its illustrious predecessor.[24]

III

By the time he wrote on the English Revolution, Carlyle had long ceased to subscribe to Christian orthodoxy. He saw in Puritanism, however, an approach to morality that reflected the element of truth that was present in all authentic statements of religion.[25] Morality rested on the sense of an underlying reality that was not the product of human will and provided the criteria for judging the ideas, institutions and practices of the formed world. While recognizing that 'church-clothes' had a role to play in representing the truths of Christianity to particular generations, Carlyle's sense of the relative unimportance of religious forms in the modern age is demonstrated by the fact that his treatment of Puritanism avoided any

---

[23] *Ibid.*, pp. 221-2.

[24] *CL*, 3, pp. 180-1; 5, p. 183; Thomas Carlyle, 'Louis-Philippe', *Examiner*, 4 March 1848; *Latter-Day Pamphlets*, p. 6.

[25] See Timothy Lang, *The Victorians and the Stuart Heritage: Interpretations of a Discordant Past* (Cambridge, 1995), pp. 122-38; John Morrow, 'Heroes and Constitutionalists: The Ideological Significance of Thomas Carlyle's Treatment of the English Revolution', *History of Political Thought*, XIV (1993), pp. 205-223; D. J. Trela, *A History of Carlyle's 'Oliver Cromwell's Letters and Speeches'* (New York, 1993); Blair Worden, *Roundhead Reputations: The English Civil Wars and the Passions of Posterity* (London, 2001), pp. 264-95.

discussions of theology or church government. He was aware that English puritans were concerned with such matters but he dismissed these aspects of the English Revolution (together with the legal and constitutional debates between King and parliament which preceded it) as regrettable signs that they had not shaken off some of the intellectual baggage of redundant religious formalism.[26] These passages in the English Revolution were part of the dead past, of no more fundamental interest to the historian than the ritualistic phantoms which exercised Archbishop Laud. By contrast, the underlying spirit of English Puritanism was presented as an important aspect of the living past, one that had relevance to Carlyle and his contemporaries.

This spirit was the most significant product of the Protestant Reformation. Luther's rejection of the hegemony of the Roman Catholic Church in 1517 was the culmination of a long train of intellectual, religious, spiritual and political developments which had undermined the forms by which medieval Christianity had been embodied. The response that greeted Luther's challenge over the course of the century that followed signaled emphatically that these forms had ceased to be objects of sincere belief. Carlyle stressed that Luther was not a conventional 'breaker of idols'. What was a stake in the Reformation (and in other contestations over forms) was not the worship of symbols as such, but the worship of symbols that were no longer capable of being believed. In such cases the object of worship was false, the act of worship insincere and the practice truly idolatrous: 'A human soul is seen clinging spasmodically to an Ark of the Covenant, which it half-feels now to have become a Phantasm .... It is equivalent to what we call Formulism, and Worship of Formula.'[27]

The earnest zeal of Protestantism in Germany was smothered after Luther's death by the intellectual formality of arid theological disputation. In Britain, however, it blossomed into 'Puritanism', a movement that Carlyle saw as a beacon of hope shining through the moral and spiritual confusion of the modern world. He credited his compatriot John Knox with propagating the seed of true reformation in Britain but he believed that its richest yield was 'English Puritanism'.[28] This way of thinking, one that was marked by a strong and consistent hostility to all manifestations

---

[26] Thomas Carlyle, *Oliver Cromwell's Letters and Speeches with Elucidations*, 1, pp. 93, 106; cited hereafter as *OC*.

[27] Carlyle, 'Luther', p. 113.

[28] Carlyle, 'The Portraits of John Knox', *CME*, 8, pp. 101-52. In his account of Cromwell's campaign in Scotland, Carlyle did not conceal his dislike of mainstream Presbyterianism and

of formality, gave the English Revolution its distinctive and significant character. It was the most important recent episode in a universal conflict which lay at the heart of the true history of the world: 'the war of Belief against Unbelief! The struggle of men intent on the real essence of things, against men intent on the semblance and forms of things.'[29] Carlyle acknowledged that the motto of the French revolutionaries — 'Liberty, Equality and Fraternity' — was an understandable response to the vacuum of moral and political leadership in eighteenth century France. In his later work on Puritanism, however, he used a strongly positive notion of liberty to explain the universal truth demonstrated by this movement: 'all men are, or else must, shall, and will become, what we call *free* men; — men with their life grounded on reality and justice, not on tradition, which has become unjust and a chimera!'[30]

Carlyle traced the anti-formalism of the Puritans to their understanding of the implications of humanity's subordination to God, adopting the clothes metaphor to frame the question that lay at its heart: 'Shall our life become true and a God's-fact, then; or continue half-true and a cloth-formula?' He noted with approval that Puritanism was underwritten by a clear, unequivocal belief that Christians had an overwhelming obligation to demonstrate a 'heartfelt conformity ... to the Maker's own Laws' and a determination to give these priority over systems of formality.[31] 'Mere formalism', the commitment to formality as a principle of human life, was seen as an impediment to the fulfillment of this obligation. Forms came between man and God, privileging rubrics over the unfolding realisation of God's intentions to the Godly. Carlyle thought that the Puritan position was epitomised by Oliver Cromwell's insistence on the need to seek divine guidance before acting and to consider carefully whether past actions appeared to have met with God's approval.[32]

In his edition of Cromwell's letters and speeches and in other writings on seventeenth-century English history, Carlyle related the positive features of the English Revolution to what he took to be the distinctive

---

its dogmatic formalism; see *OC*, 2, pp. 12-13, 20; 3, pp. 1-2, 19-20, 60, 164. This view accorded with Carlyle's family's commitment to a dissenting sect of Scottish Calvinism; see Morrow, *Thomas Carlyle*, pp. 3-4.

[29] Carlyle, 'Cromwell and Napoleon', p. 189.

[30] *Ibid.*, p. 191.

[31] Thomas Carlyle, *Historical Sketches of Notable Persons and Events in the Reigns of James I and Charles I*, ed. Alexander Carlyle (London, 1902), pp. 35, 42.

[32] Carlyle, 'Cromwell and Napoleon', p. 202.

virtues of the Puritan frame of mind. From the accession of James I the forces of anti-formalism and mere formality were in open conflict over a range of significant ecclesiastical and political issues. In the course of defending redundant forms, the Stuarts and their supporters weakened their position among the governing classes and demonstrated — directly to the Puritan elite and indirectly to the wider population — that they too had become mere 'semblances'.[33]

As prevailing forms became increasingly untenable, the Stuarts responded by making a cult of formality and bringing the coercive power of the state into its service. Carlyle saw this response as a further demonstration of their lack of moral and spiritual perspicuity. The falseness of this position was underscored by the widening gap between the elevated conception of monarchy promoted by James and the decadent reality of cavalier culture: 'Within high-stalking Formulas there walks a Reality fast verging towards the sordid. Hungry Valet-ambition, drunken Sensuality abound, on this hand; and on that, empty Hypocrisy not conscious that it is such.'[34]

James I's astuteness in theological disputation did not vouchsafe any insights into the meaning of Puritanism that would enable him to respond effectively to it. By blindly dismissing Puritan claims on the grounds that they challenged his authority, James prompted polarisation of the social and political elite. This misguided policy was pursued by Charles I and led to a situation in which 'the real heart of England', the impulse that connected the 'Eternal' to the temporal, came into increasingly open and sharp conflict with the traditional structure of political authority. As a result, the Puritans felt compelled to go beyond Luther's rejection of the 'hollow show of things' and to challenge what had become a 'false sovereignty', false because claims to political supremacy were in conflict with the requirements of divine law.[35]

Given Carlyle's aversion to displays of self-consciousness and his belief that these were indicative of falsehood or uncertainty, rather than earnest commitment, it is significant that he invited his readers to compare the public oath-taking and theatrical displays of surrogate religiosity in revolutionary France with the earnest proceedings of Scottish covenant-takers and English puritans. The quasi-religious pageantry of the festival of reason prompted absurdist images of an actress-deity, off-duty at home with her feet up in front of the fire. More generally, Carlyle observed that the theatricality of oath-taking was in inverse ratio to the veracity of oath-

---

[33] Carlyle, *Historical Sketches*, p. 55. [34] *Ibid.*, p. 56.
[35] *Ibid.*, pp. 35-40; 'Luther', p. 114.

keeping: 'no man or Nation of men, *conscious* of doing a great thing, was ever, in that thing, doing other than a small one.'[36]

Carlyle believed that Puritanism was an invaluable expression of a profound truth, but he did not regard it as a comprehensive one. Thus while the Puritans' strident anti-formalism was a natural, and in many ways an admirable, consequence of their understanding of their obligations to God, Carlyle described it as part of 'a confused struggle towards God's eternal Verity'.[37] This comment was directed at the exclusively anti-formal perspective adopted by many Puritans but it also reflected Carlyle's perception that the constructive role of Puritanism was impeded by the impact of this concern on the search for new forms. The Puritans' profound suspicion of forms, their 'naked formlessness', lead them to approach the task with a degree of self-conscious, agonizing scrupulousness that gave their anti-formalism a distinct air of rebarbative formality, engendering a degree of intolerance which was in sharp contrast with the more flexible and comprehensive position taken by Cromwell.

In recounting Cromwell's plea for recognition of the 'honest men' who served Parliament so well at the Battle of Naseby, Carlyle noted that this term embraced those vilified by the Presbyterian party as 'Schismatics', 'Sectaries' and 'Anabaptists' because they had not taken the Convenant. Such inclusiveness demonstrated Cromwell's attitude towards the narrow formalism of the Presbyterians and his practical commitment to an ideal of liberty of conscience that was above formulas.

> To Cromwell, perhaps as much as to another, order was lovely, and disorder hateful; but he discerned better than some others what order and disorder really were. The forest-trees are not in 'order' because they are all clipt into the same shape of Dutch-dragons, and forced to die or grow in that way; but because in each of them there is the same genuine unity of life … . Cromwell naturally became the head of this Schismatic Party, intent to grow not as Dutch-dragons, but as real trees … .[38]

Cromwell's policy as Lord Protector was informed by the same admirable attitude. Carlyle attributed to him the view that the term 'Saints' was

---

[36] Carlyle, *FR*, 2, p. 41.

[37] Carlyle, *Historical Sketches*, p. 35; 'Cromwell and Napoleon', pp. 189-90.

[38] Carlyle, *OC*, 3, p. 193. See Davis, 'Against Formality', pp. 278-9 on formalism and intolerance.

synonymous with 'Good Men' and praised the non-sectarian approach to church government reflected in the ordinances on the regulation of clergy promulgated in March and August 1654.[39]

Cromwell's capacity to negotiate the complexities of formality, distinguishing true forms from false ones and appreciating how necessary were the former to the settlement of the kingdom, marked him out as an archetype of political heroism. Figures worthy of the name were distinguished by their intuitive grasp of reality, their courageous engagement with its requirements in a given situation, and their earnest pursuit of the good of the state over which they ruled. In the particular circumstances of seventeenth century England, Cromwell's heroic status was demonstrated by his deeply sympathetic understanding of the essence of the Puritan spirit and its infusion of his political practice. Carlyle argued that perspicuity distinguished Cromwell from the main body of Puritans to whom he was fundamentally sympathetic and it justified the position of supremacy which he reluctantly assumed. In exercising his power, Cromwell had to contend with the inflexible anti-formalism that marked some Puritans' stance on religious issues and had the paradoxical effect of giving it the air of a formalistic cult. At the same time, however, the lingering hold of the constitutional formula that had played a significant role in pre-war debate prompted some Puritan leaders to raise questions about Cromwell's assumption of supreme power.[40]

Carlyle followed Cromwell's lead in taking a generally non-punitive view of these lapses, treating them with restrained, muted censure, tinged with pity and regret. He was far harsher in his treatment of those who resisted Cromwell's rise to power in the name of commonwealth and republican principles. These judgments were underwritten by strong views on the structure of effective systems of authority which echoed his hostile accounts of the constitution-mongering which was a feature of French politics in the 1790s. As in that case, it was closely connected to Carlyle's polemics against contemporaries who saw the perfection of parliamentary government as the cure for all Britain's ills.

Carlyle argued that the commonwealthsmen had been misled by the example of the Long Parliament into thinking that the now empty forms of traditional monarchy should give way to parliamentary sovereignty. In fact, the critical role played by that body in exposing the unreality of Stuart government and mounting a challenge to it, was due only to the impact of Puritanism on its leading members and on the military forces which they

---

[39] Ibid., p. 220; 4, pp. 6-7.   [40] Carlyle, 'Cromwell and Napoleon', p. 216.

deployed. While parliaments might provide sounding boards to which rulers might listen, they were incapable of governing effectively. Appeals to numbers, reliance on oratory and assumptions of equality were all incompatible with Carlyle's ideal of political heroism. When the shibboleths of parliamentary sovereignty were promoted as a challenge to Cromwell's position, they threatened to undermine the gains of the revolution and to frustrate any attempt to create political forms that would allow the Puritans and their countrymen to capitalize on them.

The pretensions of the Commonwealthsmen thus raised the specter that the false forms of Stuart kingship and Laudian prelacy would be replaced by the semblance of parliamentary sovereignty decked out in the clothes of antique republicanism. Carlyle was particularly dismissive of the Rump Parliament's attempts to establish a republic and indignant at its refusal to recognize Cromwell's claim to take a leading role in the English Commonwealth. It formed an 'Old Misrepresentative' bogged down by constitutional irrelevancies and divorced from the spark of Godliness that lay at the heart of English Puritanism. The Rump mistakenly believed that Cromwell's assumption of power in 1653 was a usurpation, a betrayal of its cause. In fact, Carlyle argued, Cromwell understood that the Puritan project could not be pursued by the Rump. It lacked any firm foothold in the Army and its appeal to constitutional and legal principle made no sense in the wake of the wholesale delegitimation entailed by the Revolution and the execution of the King. Carlyle presented Cromwell's dismissal of the Rump as an episode in the ongoing contestation of forms – 'The Reality ... swept the Formulas away before it' – but given the need to restore a formed world it was seen only as a step in a process which also involved a search for political and ecclesiastical forms to replace those which had long been in a state of atrophy and had finally been snuffed out.[41]

IV

Carlyle's analysis of discourses of formality in seventeenth-century England and eighteenth-century France provided a number of points of contrast that were significant in terms of his mission to his contemporaries. One set of issues concerned the impact of contested formality on the processes of large-scale social and political change. While Carlyle made it

---

[41] *Ibid.*, p. 213.

clear that he thought that the myopia of the Bourbons and the Stuarts meant that revolutions were inevitable in France and England, the course of pre-revolutionary development in each country differed significantly. In part this had to do with the character of those who persisted in clinging to traditional forms. Carlyle portrayed France as having sunk into a condition of decadence that affected the entire elite, and he attributed this to the shameful insincerity and rank disregard for the just claims of the people that accompanied its adamant insistence on maintaining the forms of the *ancien regime*. In the absence of authentic belief, the basis of authority simply evaporated, releasing on French society the full anarchic force of the sansculotte, sweeping away vestigial forms but also creating an environment that was unremittingly hostile to any attempt to re-form the world.

The situation in seventeenth-century England had been markedly different. Decadence was restricted to a small but visible section of the elite connected to the court. The leading champions of outmoded forms acted out of a sense of conviction which, while out of touch with reality, did not presage a state of complete moral collapse.[42] Carlyle was highly critical of James I's failings as a king, but noted that his views on the sanctity of monarchy were free of any taint of hypocrisy. His judgement on Archbishop Laud was similar: a rigid attachment to the forms of Anglican polity led Laud to excesses of judicial severity and was disastrous politically, but it was perfectly sincere. Carlyle's view of Charles I was far more hostile but by the time he came to the throne the moral fibre of the community had been stiffened by broadening and deepening Puritan influences.[43]

Thus while the intransigence of the English royalists was fatal to the Stuart dynasty it did not imperil English society, even when it had to contend with prolonged political conflict and civil war. As a result, the forces of sansculottism made only fleeting appearances during the English Revolution in Leveller and Digger episodes that were easily contained and had no significant impact on its character.[44] Carlyle claimed that from a very early stage in the contest between King and Parliament, the spirit of Puritanism had a strong hold on many members of the upper classes and formed a bond of sympathy between them and other earnest sections of the population. As early as 1624 when a concerted attempt was made to

---

[42] Carlyle, *FR*, 1, pp. 33-35.

[43] Carlyle, *Historical Sketches*, pp. 53, 281-8; 'Cromwell and Napoleon', pp. 197-8.

[44] Carlyle, *OC*, 3, pp. 119-22.

provide support for sound preachers across the country, it had become clear that Puritanism had attracted the support of the best minds and the most earnest characters in the kingdom.[45] The Puritan impulse subsequently found practical expression in the proceedings of the Long Parliament and then in the reformed parliamentary army that emerged in the early stages of the war. During the course of the war, Cromwell came to represent the essence of Puritanism, sympathizing with its fundamental principles but seeing quite clearly that its anti-formalism was only a stage, albeit a highly necessary stage, in the transformation of England.

In terms of its immediate outcomes, the English Revolution and its aftermath was not a great deal more promising than the French. Cromwell died without making significant progress in his search for new and appropriate forms. His successors were incapable of understanding this objective, maintaining a condition of tawdry moral equilibrium that did nothing to fit England for the challenges of the new world. They did manage, however, to stave off the slide into decadence that marked the history of eighteenth century France.

Carlyle occasionally made reference to the recent history of France in his 'condition of England' writings, noting in the closing volume of *The French Revolution* that the moral and material preconditions of sansculottism were present in nineteenth-century Ireland. This claim reflected Carlyle's view that while the destructive 'body' of sansculottism appeared in mortal agents such as the Jacobin Party, its 'soul' was the timeless repository of a force that was implacably hostile to false forms and committed to truth, sincerity, justice and human well-doing. The fate of the Girondins might thus serve as a warning to myopic middle-class reformers such as the philosophical radicals. In a similar vein, Carlyle drew attention to manifestations of sansculottism that threatened Irish society and had a damaging practical and moral impact on the English. He also insisted that if empty formality had not assumed Bourbon proportions, there was serious cause for concern at its impact on the effectiveness of British government, reducing the Foreign and Colonial Offices to mere 'protocolling establishments' and prompting a perverse vacuous bureaucratic pride, 'pedant darkness' asserting 'itself to be light', that ensnarled administration in red tape.[46]

---

[45] Carlyle, *OC*, 1, p. 45.

[46] Carlyle, *FR*, 3, 99, 266-7; *CL*, 9, pp. 69-70; *Latter-Day Pamphlets*, p. 72. The implications of England's misgovernment of Ireland for the 'condition of England question' were addressed in a chapter in *Chartism* (1939).

While the French Revolution had only a general and largely negative bearing on Carlyle's mission to his countrymen, he believed that the English Revolution was of direct and comprehensive significance for them. The Puritans provided an admirable model of moral rectitude that could be applied to conceptions of humanity's obligations that were not framed in terms of the theological forms that had exercised them. The revolutionary period had also demonstrated the advantages to the community when those who possessed rank and influence were endowed with moral and intellectual virtues of a high order. In this respect the Puritan aristocracy provided a salutary reminder of the shortcomings of modern elites: 'intellect stalks solitary like an Angel of Destruction through the World – Rank, a beautiful idiot, rolls placidly towards its doom.'[47]

Carlyle maintained that since Cromwell's death Puritanism had ceased to have a discernable impact on the intellectual, moral and political history of England. Indeed, historical works on the English Revolution were characterised by a complete failure to grasp its significance. Carlyle's studies of the period were produced with the intention of bringing Puritanism alive by recovering a heroic figure epitomizing the soul of the Puritan revolt against the false formality of the Stuarts.[48] This was less a matter of worshipping a great man than using an account of his character and achievements to restore living aspects of the past. For Carlyle, Cromwell's character and his approach to statesmanship provided an inspirational model for those who were still engaged in the search for forms which were appropriate to the needs of modern England. The Lord Protector's sharp reaction against the purveyors of malign notions of parliamentary government and democratic reform were related directly to nineteenth-century developments. More generally, the authenticity of Puritanism was an informative contrast to the myopia, unsettled skepticism and self-delusion of modern Britain. While much rested on the quality of leadership, the fact that Cromwell's achievements were set amid the wider context of Puritan culture in seventeenth-century England reflected Carlyle's belief that the effectiveness of heroic individuals was related closely to the diffusion of heroic qualities throughout the community. Similarly, the value of the lessons derived from the English Revolution depended on the 'nobleness' of modern readers.[49]

Thus the linking of anti-formalism and divine providence found in

---

[47] Carlyle, *Historical Sketches*, p. 233.
[48] Carlyle, *OC*, 1, p. 8.
[49] Carlyle, *Historical Sketches*, p. 36; *OC*, 4, p. 45.

seventeenth-century discourses was refocused in Carlyle's writings to emphasize heroic leadership and activism emanating from the divinity *in* humankind.[50] From this perspective, anti-formalism was one expression of the demand for authenticity. Another was the search for new forms deriving genuine authority from public belief. Carlyle believed that his contemporaries had much to learn from the English Revolution on the first of these matters as they faced up to the challenge of addressing the second.

---

[50] Thomas Carlyle, 'Signs of the Times', *CME*, 2, 240-7. See Davis, 'Against Formality', p. 283 for the seventeenth-century connection.

Part III
Formality

Chapter 9

Mobilisation, Anxiety and Creativity in England during the 1640s[1]

Michael Braddick

I

It has been conventional to discuss the social depth of political engagement in England during the 1640s in terms of allegiance. Despite the very high quality of the best work of this kind, however, there are persistent criticisms of this approach, particularly relating to the quality of the available evidence, and the dangers of determinism.[2] There is another difficulty, however: of reconciling 'ecologies of allegiance' with the fluidity of civil war politics. Analyses of allegiance tend to seek correlates for a fixed affiliation (royalist or parliamentarian) on the basis of a snapshot at a particular moment; and to supplement that with more qualitative accounts of receptiveness to the blandishments of one side or the other, again seeking social and religious correlates to explain differentials in receptiveness. We know, however, that there were more than two sides, that parliamentary and royalist causes shifted and were redefined, and that commitment to them was measured, conditional and carried varying degrees of conviction. Loyalty to the Crown in 1648 meant something quite different from royalism in October 1642, as John Lilburne among others could have pointed out.

Analyses of mobilisation — the attempt to influence or by-pass the formal institutions of government through appeal to opinion outside them — may be a better way forward than allegiance in understanding the social depth of political engagement. They have another significance too.

---

[1] Versions of this paper were presented at The Institute for Advanced Study, Princeton and at seminars at the Universities of Cambridge, Pennsylvania, Princeton, Sheffield and Yale. I am grateful to the audiences on those occasions and to the editors of this volume for their many helpful suggestions.

[2] David Underdown, *Revel, riot and rebellion: popular politics and culture in England 1603-1660* (Oxford, 1985); Mark Stoyle, *Loyalty and locality: popular allegiance in Devon during the English civil war* (Exeter, 1994); John Morrill, 'The ecology of allegiance in the English civil wars', reprinted in *The nature of the English revolution* (London, 1993), pp. 224-41.

Mobilisations were plural and overlapping, conflicting campaigns which evidently succeeded among the same local populations. They competed for control of standard languages and metaphors, and corroded the authority and legitimacy of the formal institutions of government. They caused much contemporary comment, most of it anxious and disapproving, but they also prompted creativity in the sense of new arguments or new ways of expressing them, and new means of communicating these arguments to wider audiences − intellectual, discursive and communicative innovations. They offer one way of considering the conditions of delegitimation of the institutions of English government, and a perspective on attempts to invest those institutions with a renewed legitimacy.

This bears on the larger themes of this volume and follows a lead from Colin Davis' work on the Ranters. Much attention has been paid to the existence or otherwise of a Ranter movement independent of the media 'sensation'; but much less to what that sensation has to tell us about revolutionary politics.[3] That sensation might be understood as one effort at mobilisation. It bears most closely on another of Colin's questions, however: 'why, of all the crises of seventeenth-century Europe, is it England's troubles which gave rise to a seminal debate on liberty and authority?'[4] What was the relationship between mobilisation, anxiety and this kind of creativity?

As Conrad Russell famously pointed out, England was the last of Charles' kingdoms to rebel and the only one with a sufficiently large royalist party to turn 'resistance into a large-scale civil war'.[5] It is paradoxical, therefore, that this Kingdom produced the most radical speculations about, for example, religious toleration, popular sovereignty or liberty. That paradox can be resolved, in part, through an attention to political process: specifically, the deliberate attempt to mobilize opinion outside the institutions of government in order to influence, in detail, proceedings within them; and then to mobilise men and resources to defend political positions with force. Initially this process was directed at parliament as pamphlets and petitions sold partisan positions to wider publics and were mobilized in order to push the Houses forward on specific policies. London's plural and sophisticated religio-political culture was crucial to this, as were the city's presses and crowds. In these campaigns, in London

---

[3] J. C. Davis, *Fear, myth and history: the Ranters and the historians* (Cambridge, 1986).

[4] J. C. Davis, 'Against formality: one aspect of the English revolution', *Transactions of the Royal Historical Society*, 6th series, 3 (1993), p. 266.

[5] Conrad Russell, *The fall of the British monarchies 1637-1642* (Oxford, 1991), p. 27.

and elsewhere, the local met the national: partisan positions were sold in terms of a common stock of images and metaphors for political life which communicated the larger meaning of both national and local political conflicts. This was not new: Lake and Pincus have recently argued for the existence of a post-Reformation public sphere of religious and political controversy, periodically activated in order to force Crown or Episcopal policy in a particular direction.[6] In late 1641, however, at a crisis point in negotiations over settlement in England rival mobilizations, intersecting with 'events', precipitated the collapse of parliamentary politics altogether.

There followed concerted attempts to use local institutions (quarter sessions, grand juries, assizes and the militia) for what were increasingly obviously partisan purposes. These developments posed a substantial challenge to the official view of these institutions as the embodiment of their local constituency — as the 'voice of the county' for example, or the local social and political order made manifest. As partisans sought to use the institutions of government in these ways it became clear that common terms of political debate had lost their shared meaning, that there was a crisis in the 'common sense system' of early Stuart politics. That created both anxiety and intellectual creativity; and this has to be understood in the context of the plurality and social depth of political mobilization in the aftermath of the Covenanters' revolution.

This is interesting in itself, of course, but it bears on civil war historiography in a more general sense. Emphasis on mobilization reveals a direct connection between the social depth of political engagement and the conditions which fostered intellectual creativity. It provides a sociological context in which to understand the legitimation and delegitimation of particular institutions; an insight into the conditions which provoked and enabled one of the most creative periods in English intellectual history. It is a modest step towards a deeper contextualisation of the history of political thought, 'of the links between words and action, or the constraints on action', as a means better to understand 'linguistically uniform partisanship, a war of words in which the adversaries inhabit the same linguistic context'.[7] In doing so it offers some explanation also for the extraordinary creativity of the English revolution: a revolution born out of civil war has less clear limits than one born out of Calvinist resistance theory.

---

[6] Peter Lake and Steve Pincus, 'Rethinking the public sphere in early modern England', *Journal of British Studies*, 42, 2 (2006), pp. 270-92.

[7] J. C. Davis, 'Political thought during the English revolution' in B. Coward (ed.), *A companion to Stuart Britain* (Oxford, 2003), pp. 374-96, at pp. 375, 393.

II

The problem of agreeing a post-Laudian settlement was by late 1641 acute.[8] Campaigns for 'Root and Branch' reform embraced a relatively broad coalition, and were pushed forward on the back of the rhetoric of anti-popery. By the time of the harvest recess in 1641 a counter-charge was gathering force, around the issue of religious decency, driven forward by anti-sectarian arguments. This represented the extension of a long battle about the identity of English Protestantism, caught between popery and Puritanism, but with anti-puritanism now largely refigured as anti-sectarianism.[9] Although these arguments are easy to track in print, they were expressed elsewhere too. The Protestation became a totem for those seeking further reform: in parliamentary debate it had been suggested that its commitment to protect the doctrine of the Church of England should be extended to include its 'discipline'. The suggestion was not taken up and by the summer of 1641 the Protestation was used as justification for attacks on the use of the prayer book and vestments.

In response a prayer book petition was mobilised in Essex, which may have been representative of a wider movement.[10] In the press an anti-sectarian scare was taking root, fuelled by John Taylor and, for example, the Adamite sensation — perhaps even more clearly than the Ranters a sensation rather than a movement.[11] During 1642, as iconoclasm and desecrations of the Prayer Book proceeded, pamphlets defended learned divinity and established discipline with reference to providential judgements. In Towcester, for example, it was 'attested by sufficient witnesses' that iconoclasts and desecrators of the Prayer Book had suffered appalling deaths; and in Mears Ashby a monstrous birth followed from a denunciation of the use of the sign of the Cross during baptism. These were political interventions: the Towcester pamphlet reprinted the House of Lords order

---

[8] For the following paragraphs see my 'Prayer Book and Protestation: anti-popery, anti-puritanism and the outbreak of the English civil war' (forthcoming).

[9] For the longer-term context see Peter Lake, 'Anti-puritanism: the structure of a prejudice' in Kenneth Fincham and Peter Lake (eds), *Religious politics in post-Reformation England* (Woodbridge, 2006), pp. 80-97.

[10] John Walter, 'Confessional politics in pre-Civil War Essex: prayer books, profanations, and petitions', *Historical Journal*, 44 (2001), pp. 677-701; Anthony Fletcher, *The outbreak of the English civil war* (London, 1981), ch. 9.

[11] David Cressy, *Travesties and transgressions in Tudor and Stuart England* (Oxford, 2000), ch. 15.

of January 1641 upholding worship according to the established laws.[12]

These appeals to Prayer Book and Protestation were not necessarily alternatives of course: they juxtaposed fears of popery and sectarianism to a population which was for the most part anxious about both. It is not difficult to find, for example, royalists hostile to popery and Catholic conspiracy, or parliamentarians hostile to the sects. The associated claims on behalf of parliamentary or Crown authority created divisions which did not map neatly onto these religious rhetorics. Just as order and reformation were not necessarily alternatives in most contemporary views of an ideal world, neither were the powers of the crown and the liberties of parliament.

The power of anti-popery had been boosted by the Irish rebellion, or at least by the ways that it was reported. From thence forward anti-popery was an obvious vehicle for attempts to secure control of the militia; as in the revelation of a 'gunpowder plot' in Derbyshire. A pamphlet published by John Thomas revealed the providential delivery from a plot to blow up a church during divine service, using barrels of gunpowder stacked in the cellars. Thomas was connected to other publishers promoting the image of John Pym and the dangers of active catholic conspiracy, and he seems to have had fairly direct connections with Pym himself. Certainly his publishing activities were related to parliamentary business – as in his publication of England's first newsbook.[13] The Derbyshire pamphlet appeared on the day that parliament considered the Militia Ordinance, and two days before John Hampden called for parliamentary control of the Tower of London. It offered graphic illustration of the need to disarm Catholics. Here, then, there was an identifiable group using an established image – of the gunpowder plot as an emblem of catholic conspiracy – to promote a particular policy; just as identifiable networks of gentry, clergymen and officeholders lay behind petitioning campaigns or the rival musters of 1642.[14] But these two issues – fear of popery and the exclusion of royal control over the militia – were distinct, and obedience to the

---

[12] Anon., *Wonderfull Newes: or, a true Relation of a Churchwarden in the Towne of Tosceter* (London, 1642); Anon., *A STRANGE and Lamentable accident that happened lately at Mears Ashby* (London, 1642).

[13] For Thomas and Pym see Joad Raymond, *The invention of the newspaper: English newsbooks 1641-1649* (Oxford, 1996), esp. pp. 109-10.

[14] See, for example, Walter, 'Confessional politics'; Peter Lake, 'Puritans, popularity and petitions: local politics in national context, Cheshire, 1641' in Thomas Cogswell, Richard Cust and Peter Lake (eds), *Politics, religion and popularity in early Stuart Britain: essays in honour of Conrad Russell* (Cambridge, 2002), pp. 259-89.

Militia Ordinance was more than a test of one's anti-popery, particularly after the issue of the Commissions of Array, when compliance with that meant non-compliance with the parliamentary ordinance. There are few correlations on a county basis between responses to rival petitioning campaigns and subsequent reactions to the rival musters. Certainly, anti-popery, even used in these creative ways, could not do the work being asked of it, to support constitutional and religious innovation.

These currents of opinion were not simply forces of nature. Behind the pamphlets, petitions and musters lay identifiable networks of printers, politicians and officeholders, trying to mobilise opinion behind their preferred solutions to the crisis. In doing so they deployed stock figures from a shared political culture but in a partisan way — to revert to received historiographical terminology they were attempting to introduce Politics into popular politics. Rival visions of the good life, and of how to achieve it, were expressed in terms of images, metaphors and discourses normally treated by historians as both popular, and (therefore?) non-partisan. Print was part of this, an adjunct to mobilisation, but in many ways it seems merely the fly paper on which wider discourses stuck.

Notoriously, however, print also acquired a life of its own. For example in the paper war of 1642 Henry Parker, sometime drafter of official declarations, was driven to articulate a radically new view of the English constitution, publishing this time as a private individual.[15] Here print made possible conversations which would otherwise not have taken place and, moreover, conversations in which escalating statements and rebuttals quickly sharpened and refined the positions. This too had practical consequences, as Bulstrode Whitelocke noted later in the year. Parliament had, he thought, 'slipped insensibly into this beginning of a civil war by one unexpected accident after another ... but from paper combats by declarations, notes, messages, and replies we are now come to the question of raising forces'.[16] In mobilising support among wider publics activists had made overlapping and contrasting demands on the basis of established languages of politics. They had been forced then to refine and defend these postures before a print audience, some of them coming to positions which were clearly not consensual, easily negotiable, or simple to ignore.

This process made the discourses of national politics available for

---

[15] Quentin Skinner, 'Rethinking political liberty', *History Workshop Journal*, 61 (2006), pp. 156-70, esp. pp. 165-8; and more generally, Quentin Skinner, *Liberty before Liberalism* (Cambridge, 1998).

[16] Quoted in J. H. Hexter, *The reign of King Pym* (Boston, Mass., 1941), p. 8.

appropriation in ways familiar from studies of popular politics across the early modern period. In the winter of 1640-41 petitioners made a connection between the decay of trade and the continuing failure of settlement, allowing them to petition in a traditional mode for relief but for directly partisan purposes. Thus, in January 1641, poor women in London assembled at the House of Lords seeking relief for their families, particularly their children who were threatened with starvation. Their solution was the exclusion of the Bishops from the House of Lords and the promotion of the campaign against popery; on this platform they jostled peers of the realm, including the Duke of Lennox, whose staff was broken by some of the women. Male petitioners on January 31 had distributed a printed version of their petition, with instructions about where to assemble, and to wear the petition as a mark of affiliation.[17] Weavers in the Stour Valley made a similar connection between their material grievances and a partisan position, as did petitioners around the country during 1641 and 1642.[18] The Waltham forest commoners who killed deer in the early summer of 1642 to assert their right of access to the forest, proclaiming that 'there was no law settled', were almost certainly claiming that the demise of prerogative courts meant that the unpopular regulatory regime of the 1630s in the forest was no longer enforceable, and a new settlement was required.[19] Lincolnshire rioters shifted their claims, to those of freeborn Englishmen and away from the piteous cries of humble supplicants; their opponents accused them less of sedition and more often of standing in the way of improvement intended for the good of the commonwealth. This social openness, and the possibilities for appropriation, may have contributed to gentry solidarity — in Suffolk for example, where divisions appear to have been papered over in the light of the uses being made of the crisis by the weavers in the Stour Valley.[20]

Analysis of these rival mobilisations offers a way into the instability of the politics of the 1640s, emphasising fluidity and a remarkable social open-

[17] Keith Lindley, *Popular politics and religion in civil war London* (Aldershot, 1997), pp. 130-7; David Como, 'Sowing sedition, raising riot: pamphlets, placards and street-politics, c. 1635-1645' (unpublished paper). The Protestation acquired a similar demonstrative significance.

[18] John Walter, *Understanding popular violence in the English revolution: the Colchester Plunderers* (Cambridge, 1999), esp. pp. 256-84; Fletcher, *Outbreak*, p. 223.

[19] C. Holmes, 'Drainers and fenmen: the problem of popular political consciousness in the seventeenth century' in Anthony Fletcher and John Stevenson (eds), *Order and disorder in early modern England* (Cambridge, 1985), pp. 166-95.

[20] *Ibid.*; C. Holmes, *The Eastern Association in the English civil war* (Cambridge, 1974), esp. p. 51.

ness. Such mobilisations characterise the politics of the 1640s, and were a symptom of the unclarity of the issues; they also by their very nature contributed to instability and fluidity. Mobilisation offers, therefore, a way of thinking about the depth of political engagement which supplements studies of allegiance. Mobilisations have a sociology, or a social history, but in analysing this we would be adding a sociology of networks and engagement to the existing structural sociologies — of class or political ecologies. This kind of analysis can also tend to accommodate calculation, appropriation and differing levels of (possibly tactical) engagement.

Print was important to these processes. Print could generalise particular incidents or grievances, giving them a national or even cosmic significance. It could accelerate mobilisation, as in the handbills scattered to encourage petitioning against the decay of trade on 31 January; and it could amplify particular campaigns, fostering the basis for common cause across regions where there was no institutional basis for mobilisation. So, for example, petitions mobilised on a county basis clearly made common cause across county boundaries, mimicking one another, using print to make their case a cause for the nation as a whole, and timed to impact on parliamentary deliberations.[21] Therefore pamphlets that we have are not examples of an autonomous popular politics inhabiting a completely separate cognitive realm. Instead they are evidence of attempts to mobilise opinion and support for particular measures through appeal to well-established tropes and metaphors: monstrous births, providential deliveries and so on. Print records these attempts for us, but the larger phenomenon of mobilisation was by no means restricted to print. However, print did have a particular significance in escalating, radicalising and refining the positions adopted in the ensuing debates.

III

The plurality of mobilizations in England contrasts sharply with the situation in Scotland. The Covenanting revolution was mobilized in ways that soon became familiar in England — through crowds, petition, print and then armed demonstration — but had dramatically different results. Offended by what they thought was contained in a new prayer book, an influential group of protesters organised first a petitioning campaign and

---

[21] Compare, for example, the timings of the delivery of provincial root and branch petitions and the dates of important parliamentary debates of the issue: Fletcher, *Outbreak*, pp. 92, 98-103.

then a national covenant. The latter bound all its signatories to stand together in defence of the true religion, and to stand with the King in the defence of the true religion. It was signed very widely indeed, in fact almost universally, and gave a clear historical and legal account of what the true Scottish religion was. The organisation of the campaign, and then of an army to defend this programme, gave rise to an unprecedented revolutionary body — the Tables. In a remarkable display of unity the Covenanters were able to create a manifesto for a national movement, mobilised by a new body and defended by force of arms in 1639 and 1640. This has some claims to being a near perfect expression of Calvinist resistance theory, although the public statements never quite admitted that that was what they were up to. But the covenant to God to defend the true religion was prior to the covenant to stand with the King in its defence, and in any case clearly offered at least the possibility that Charles was not defending the true religion. In effect an ungodly king was being resisted by another legitimate authority — the body of the Kirk and other earthly powers. Henderson's 'Instruction for defensive arms', for example, argued that if a superior magistrate issued an evil command then he removed himself from the line of divine hierarchy. A lesser magistrate might then act against him, effectively under the direct authority of God. While it was not clear who decided which commands were evil, the principle was clear enough: this was in line with (moderately) respectable resistance theory.[22]

This was not a popular revolt, but a legitimate action by lesser magistrates in the light of an obvious threat to the true church. It has been characterised by one modern historian as oligarchic centralism — an elite political movement, harnessing rather than unleashing popular feelings. Although the campaign was punctuated by crowd actions, there is a general willingness to believe that they were prompted, or at least exploited and mollified, by politicians close to the heart of government. This Covenanting revolution was remarkably successful, securing a climb down from Charles I on the substance of the issue and a tacit acknowledgement that he should deal with this revolutionary authority — the Tables — whose role was justified by the Covenant.[23]

In the Covenanting revolution Charles had been confronted with a positive vision of good government. In England he was confronted with negative reluctance to support a war. Many of Charles' English subjects

[22] David Stevenson, *The Scottish Revolution 1637-44* (Newton Abbott, 1973), pp. 133-7.

[23] For standard accounts see *Ibid*; Allan I. Macinnes, *Charles I and the making of the Covenanting movement, 1625-1641* (Edinburgh, 1991); Peter Donald, *An uncounselled king: Charles I and the*

were against prerogative power used to fight wars, and/or against the promotion of Laudian worship and Episcopal authority. Behind these negative positions lay numerous specific grievances, which did not necessarily amount to a defined and universal world view. These diverse complaints were converted into a positive platform by Pym and others, but as we have seen the radical measures promoted on the back of it evoked a reaction — others came to see this programme as a greater threat to church and constitution than the policies of the King.[24]

Political debate in England escalated with reference to a middle ground — defence of the state and church against a new challenge. Attempts to muster militias, take control of local stores of arms and to raise armies were justified defensively, in very similar terms. At Shrewsbury, as war was breaking out, the King pledged

> [to] defend and maintain the true reformed protestant religion established in the Church of England ... govern by the known law of the land, and that the liberty and property of the subject may be by them preserved ... and I do solemnly and faithfully promise, in the sight of God, to maintain the just privileges and freedom of parliament.[25]

The Earl of Essex had been commissioned to lead an army against him earlier the same month 'for the just and necessary defence of the protestant religion, of your majesty's person, crown, and dignity, of the laws and liberties of the kingdom, and the privileges of parliament'.[26] What really differentiated these positions was how they identified the threat — puritan populism or creeping popery. These were defensive coalitions, held together by fear. It was a clear contrast with the experience in Scotland where a single document was made to stand as an agreed vision of the past, informing an agreed vision of the future, and identi-

---

Scottish troubles, 1637-1641 (Cambridge, 1990); W. Makey, *The Church of the covenant, 1637-1651: revolution and social change in Scotland* (Edinburgh, 1979). For the wider context see Margo Todd, *The culture of Protestantism in early modern Scotland* (New Haven, 2002).

[24] Fletcher, *Outbreak*. Brian Manning, *The English people and the English revolution, 1640-1649* (Harmondsworth, 1976), esp. ch. 3, captures the rhetoric very well, although his analysis of the class basis for the 'parties' has been heavily criticised.

[25] Morrill, *Revolt in the provinces: the people of England and the tragedies of war*, second edition (London, 1999), pp. 52-53.

[26] *Ibid.*

fying the threat to that future.

A second contrast is institutional. In Scotland the discipline of the Kirk, particularly the Kirk sessions, offered an institutional basis for more or less unanimous mobilization around a clearly defined cause. This was co-ordinated at national level by a revolutionary body — the Tables — and supported in the General Assembly. In England control of existing institutions — parishes, grand juries, parliament — was contested, and there was no revolutionary body promoting a unified opposition to the Crown.

Glenn Burgess has observed that English radicalism during the 1640s was more rhetorical than theoretical.[27] Certainly the anti-Laudian alliance in England crystallized from diverse currents of opinion, which struggled for institutional expression in diverse fora. Plurality in the provinces produced shifting responses to changing questions. Plurality in the presses produced a rhetorical morass in which disputed terms like the constitution, order, law, custom and religion were often defined negatively, and control of institutions was often justified negatively, as a necessary defence in the face of a threat. But these conditions also offered opportunities for those with novel views to tout: because this was a less univocal response than that in Scotland, it was also more creative. In that context there was clearly theoretical radicalism too.[28]

There is no space here to consider the roots of the contrast in the religious and political cultures of England and Scotland, but it is worth noting that English government before 1640 depended to a considerable extent on co-operation, and that co-operation was conditional. What policies were pushed, and what visions of the good life informed them, varied from place to place and over time, so that the complexion of the poor law, the reform of behaviour and the prosecution of crime reflected the influence of local coalitions. These coalitions between ministers and officeholders, for example, were shifting and changeable — as for example in Dorchester after the fire. In the godly corner of the Stour Valley, many felt that the times had moved against them in the 1630s and chose to emigrate. This colouring of local government was supported and affirmed by patterns of patronage in the local church, of engagement with the church courts, and by Episcopal influence, creating no little diversity within the unity of the Church. Uniformity was a distant prospect and peace depended really on not trying to achieve it. Participation and engagement was informed by a

---

[27] Glenn Burgess, 'The impact on political thought: rhetorics for troubled times' in John Morrill (ed.), *The impact of the English civil war* (London, 1991), pp. 67-83, esp. p. 67.
[28] See, for example, Skinner, *Liberty before Liberalism*.

diversity of views about the true church and good government.²⁹ This plurality became obvious when engagement was sought over the construction of a new settlement after the collapse of the personal rule. It was then exaggerated and refined by mobilization and polemic.

English responses to the Scottish crisis produced a highly unusual radicalism from ingredients which were common to many conflicts in early modern Europe. Threats to the true religion as locally understood; concerns about the future of representative institutions, and problems arising from trying to govern multiple kingdoms were hardly unique to the Stuart kingdoms. However, some of the resolutions possible elsewhere were not possible in England. This could not resolve into a separatist movement, or result in partition or confessional separation, since these political conflicts did not follow territorial or ethnic divisions and represented a battle within a single church. Neither was deposition a serious possibility, although it was floated at various points, and the reversionary interest was unpromising. Instead, the English were locked into a debate about how to interpret apparently shared values, and for control of institutions universally agreed to have an important and legitimate role in religious and political life. England in the 1640s saw tremendous intellectual creativity because there was no obvious political exit, and no apparent hope of rhetorical solution. Instead new grounds were sought on which to construct secure knowledge of the social and political world. This situation arose from formal intellectual and institutional conservatism, which effectively locked political conflict in.

IV

These plural and conflicting mobilizations continued throughout the 1640s, and were accompanied by an escalating rhetorical battle.³⁰ Stiffening the sinews of the war efforts was an adjunct to, rather than alternative to, peace making — this was a process of armed negotiation. But each military and ideological escalation made the politics of the coalitions more compli-

---

[29] Michael J. Braddick, *State formation in early modern England c 1500-1700*. (Cambridge, 2000), pts 1-4; David Underdown, *Fire from heaven: life in an English town in the seventeenth century* (London, 1992); Frank Bremer, 'The heritage of John Winthrop: religion along the Stour Valley, 1548-1630', *The New England Quarterly*, 70:4 (1997), pp. 515-47.

[30] See Braddick, 'History, reformation and the cause: parliamentarian military and ideological escalation in 1643' (forthcoming).

cated. By defining the cause more closely, or even differently, these measures shifted coalitions and led to arguments within each camp about what the war was for. Each addition to the respective alliances — the Solemn League and Covenant, the Cessation, Montrose — created new sources of unease. Famously the debate about church government on the parliamentary side became the focus for arguments about what kind of war to fight and what kind of peace to accept. They became more fraught as victory approached, and still more divisive once it was achieved. After Marston Moor disagreements about who had won the battle intersected with the increasingly vituperative debate about independency, which had been escalating since the publication of the *Apologeticall Narration*, and was now taken to a new level by Thomas Edwards.[31] These mobilisations attracted varying degrees of commitment from among the same populations — it is difficult to measure popular 'allegiance' not least because the causes claiming allegiance shifted continuously.

The terms in which these mobilisations were mounted reveal political culture: the vocabulary of images, metaphors, rituals, assumptions and performances through which political negotiations are conducted; and the conventions, the grammar, governing their appropriate and intelligible use.[32] Pamphlets from the 1640s display a crisis of shared meaning. It was difficult to know what was going on, what it meant, or who to trust : a three-fold crisis, in fact.[33] Print reveals attempts to shift political 'common sense' — to change the grammar governing the use of these discourses, and to add to the vocabulary. This crisis also, therefore, fostered creative responses, and not only in print. The radical democratisation of the science, or art, of astrology, for example, bears testimony both to a real appetite for certainties, and a practical effort to satisfy that appetite. Institutions of government, and knowledge-making, had become dysfunctional and there is ample evidence of urgent and creative attempts to discover the will of God, manifested in nature or beyond nature.

Astrology may have been 'the most ambitious attempt ever made to reduce the baffling diversity of human affairs to some sort of intelligible

---

[31] Ann Hughes, *Gangraena and the struggle for the English Revolution* (Oxford, 2004).

[32] For this view of political culture see Michael Braddick, 'State formation and political culture in Elizabethan and Stuart England: micro-histories and macro-historical change', in R. G. Asch and Dagmar Freist (eds), *Staatsbildung als kultereller Prozess: Stukturwandel und Legitimation von Herrschaft in der Frühen Neuzeit* (Köln, 2005), pp. 69-90.

[33] Braddick, 'The English revolution and its legacies' in Nicholas Tyacke (ed.), *The English revolution and its legacies* (Manchester, 2007).

order'. It offered to unlock the secrets of social and political life, but also offered the key to personal life. Its promise was as great as political science, sociology and psychology combined; although it is not much celebrated by civil war historians, it was clearly meeting a huge demand in the 1640s. William Lilly's first almanac sold out in a week and the subsequent print runs were huge: 13,500 in 1646, reaching 18,500 by 1648. A decade later he was selling 30,000 copies each year. This was certainly not only a print phenomenon: at his peak Lilly also held 2,000 private consultations each year. There is another way in which Lilly was remarkable, however: in addition to reporting and interpreting signs of God's will, he published a self-help guide: *Christian Astrology*, still important for those trying to master these skills. Here was a demotic resource for interpreting God's purposes in the world, read in the book of nature — there were few if any similar successes in relation to the book of scripture, or of self-help manuals on how to read it. This seems to have answered a very widespread desire for secure knowledge and interpretative certainty.[34]

Astrology also generated a new institution — the Society of Astrologers — which served to legitimate truth claims in this area.[35] Most truth claims are taken on trust, and the corroded legitimacy of many institutions which had previously proclaimed what was going on and what it meant, clearly created a vacuum. Lilly's career and that of his great rival George Wharton, were clearly connected to the political crisis, and both wrote in ways that contributed directly to current political debate. But this was a creative response to the problem of truth, with a wide social resonance and implications well beyond the questions in hand.

Baconian attempts to read in the book of nature God's intentions in the world offered to satisfy similar anxieties, and were more closely connected with the direction of national political events. A key figure here was Samuel Hartlib, a protestant refugee from central Europe. He combined an interest in Baconian science — that is knowledge based on verifiable experience, and located within a coherent intellectual system — with an engagement with the educational ideas of Jan Komensky and with John Dury's promotion of protestant unity. Here the key issue was sound

---

[34] Keith Thomas, *Religion and the decline of magic* (Harmondsworth, 1980), chs. 10-12, esp. pp. 340, 348, 364. See also Ann Geneva, *Astrology and the seventeenth-century mind: William Lilly and the language of the stars* (Manchester, 1995); Bernard Capp, *Astrology and the popular press: English almanacs 1500-1800* (London, 1979); Patrick Curry, *Prophecy and power: astrology in early modern England* (Cambridge, 1989).

[35] Thomas, *Religion*, p. 361.

knowledge — of nature and of scripture — coherently organised and taught in a coherent way, to produce an educated, properly Christian population. A central element of these ideals was the communication of knowledge and experience, and Hartlib was himself a tireless letter writer and, when funds permitted, publisher. Accurate knowledge, and a method to understand its meaning, was also associated with the creation of institutions to authenticate truth: a college of experience in the utopian tract *Macaria* (and another college to consider doctrinal matters); the Office of Address in a later and more limited proposal. These hopes had a millenarian aspect too. Hartlib and many of his correspondents believed that in the Garden of Eden, before the Fall, Adam had enjoyed a perfect knowledge of creation. Through an active use of the resources around him, Adam was never hungry, or ill, and was at one with God's Word. Restoration of this knowledge of the natural world would help to prepare the way for the return of Christ and the Saints. This was an active and practical millenarianism, continuously concerned to make productive use of the environment.[36]

Here intellectual innovation was married to creative means of communicating ideas. Practical mobilization encouraged both intellectual and communicative creativity. These ideals were of potentially very wide appeal in the confused conditions of the 1640s, and Hartlib actively sought support for projects which embodied them. He publicised a number of practical projects through which he could promote this more effective use of God's bounty: the chemical manufacture of salt petre (essential ingredient of gunpowder, but also powerful fertiliser); setting the poor to productive work, making idle hands useful to the commonwealth; or promoting Atlantic trade, which would maximise use of natural resources, increase knowledge, and strengthen the commonwealth. Other projects included sponsorship of a woollen tank, testing torpedoes in the Thames, an interest in jam-making, bee-keeping and the cultivation of silk worms in Virginia. Behind it lay a single vision, of making full use of natural resources and political opportunities to edge the world back to a pre-lapsarian harmony with nature. Like astrology, this offered to lend meaning to the current confusion, and to offer a guide to truth in conditions which made it an elusive commodity. As a series of practical proposals, it was given impetus and public appeal by the political circumstances of the 1640s. Hartlib enjoyed minor but significant patronage from

[36] Charles Webster, *The great instauration: science, medicine and reform, 1626-1660*, second edition (Oxford, 2002).

the parliamentary regimes, and associates of his played important parts in, for example, the drafting of the navigation laws and the survey of Ireland following the English conquest during the 1650s.[37]

Hartlib was at the centre of a network of correspondents and fellow travellers, and promoted their shared vision in print. In those respects his efforts were like those of many other pamphleteers, mobilising and galvanising opinion, taking advantage of the press, and political opportunities, to promote a particular agenda. This is one way to contextualise the career of John Lilburne, whose particular grievances were generalised and amplified by print, and expressed in petitioning campaigns. He, Walwyn and Overton were probably allies in print before they met, and in the course of fighting their pamphlet battles they sharpened arguments about popular sovereignty which took them away from the boggy middle ground of much contemporary political debate. It was a social parallel to the equally universal appeal to nature. Like Henry Parker, the Levellers wrote, were challenged, and escalated their claims. Petitions were promoted not in the name of a county or borough, or of a particular interest group, but in the name of the people and they were promoting not a policy but a fundamental political theory.[38] In these campaigns discursive and communicative creativity were married quite closely to creative political and religious thinking, bearing directly on the course of the larger conflict.

Creative visions arising from debate in print were occasioned by rival mobilizations and became themselves the basis for practical mobilization. This further complicated the problem of achieving political settlement but also produced some surprising and important unintended consequences. The greatest success of the Hartlib circle, for example, was in the adoption of the Navigation Act. Benjamin Worsley, its probable author, was a close associate of Hartlib. He had a career in the Council of Trade through the interregnum and restoration, before handing over to John Locke. His economic thought is congruent with that of the rest of the Hartlib circle, and was expressed directly, and practically, in the Navigation Act. His immediate intention was to promote overseas trade and England's international position, but his motives were more radical and millenarian than is evident from a reading of the Act. In securing this practical step towards

---

[37] Ibid. For his patronage see C. Webster (ed.), *Samuel Hartlib and the advancement of learning* (Cambridge, 1970), p. 49; G. H. Turnbull, *Samuel Hartlib: a sketch of his life and his relations to J. A. Comenius* (Oxford, 1920), pp. 48-51.

[38] I am grateful to Nigel Smith for discussing these points with me.

the millennium, he was in alliance with Brenner's new merchant interest. The networks Brenner traced within the London merchant community reached into parliament, and were sustained by networks of religious fellowship. His new merchants were Independents, and likely to be sympathetic to the religious case made by Worsley and Hartlib. We might therefore see the Navigation Act as one of a series of successful mobilizations drawing on mercantilist and apocalyptic discourses, to promote a specific practical measure at an opportune moment. This can be uncoupled from a larger class analysis of the course of the whole revolution, without losing sight of Brenner's reconstruction of part of the sociology of this particular mobilization. We can also put God alongside mammon in this analysis.[39]

Attention to these mobilisations therefore intersects with the history of state formation. If the Navigation Act was an adventitious product of the revolution it was not randomly generated — we can specify both the basis for this mobilization and the contingent circumstances that made it effective. The 'necessities' arising from the war efforts broke through administrative and political constraints on tax-raising, and were tied to ideological campaigns to define and publicise the 'cause'. War-making was a political challenge in conditions of civil war, just as in the face of continental conflicts, and these mobilisations too are susceptible to close analysis.[40] Successful administrative innovation supported the development of a domestic arms industry and of the means by which to raise standing armies. After 1649, facing diplomatic isolation, the English government was able to transform its naval resources too, creating a navy far beyond the ambitions represented by the ship money reforms of the 1630s. This navy was supported by, and made possible the closer regulation of, a customs system, which began to appear to be both a tool of economic management and a revenue resource.

These new instruments of commercial and financial policy were of great interest to the new merchants, and also made them of interest to statesmen. They became fundamental to the Old Colonial system, although they were not what people had taken up arms to achieve.[41] As

---

[39] Thomas Leng, *Benjamin Worsley (1618-1677): commerce, colonisation and the fate of Universal Reform* (Woodbridge, forthcoming); R. Brenner, *Merchants and revolution: commercial change, political conflict and London's overseas traders, 1550-1653* (Cambridge, 1993).

[40] Braddick, 'History, reformation and the cause'.

[41] Braddick, *State formation*, esp. pp. 411-3; Scott Wheeler, *The making of a world power: war and the military revolution in seventeenth-century England* (Stroud, 1999).

Adam Ferguson had it:

> Mankind, in following the present sense of their minds, in striving to remove inconveniences, or gain apparent and contiguous advantages, arrive at ends which even their imaginations could not anticipate ... and nations stumble upon establishments, which are indeed the result of human action, but not the execution of any human design.[42]

The sociology of state formation rests on the same form of analysis as this sociology of mobilizations, and offers a way of connecting the history of this crisis with the long-term history of the state; and of connecting both to the remarkable discursive, communicative and intellectual creativity of this period.

V

Anxieties about what was happening, what it meant and who to believe were not restricted to print, but the surviving pamphlets do reflect that three-fold problem of truth-telling particularly clearly. Pamphleteers rapidly adopted the familiar techniques in all three areas: employing a plain style; discrediting opponents' claims by juxtaposing their claims with their actions; virtual witnessing and so on. These had analogues in some attempts to solve the problem of truth telling in practice: the Hartlib circle's interest in the communication of all knowledge independent of party or religious affiliation or the astrologers' rules of observation; the Baconian or astrological science of interpretation; and the validation of knowledge by institutions invested with cultural legitimacy (the Society of Astrologers or the College of Experience). These were attempts to take up the opportunities provided by the crisis in order to make some good out of it. In that sense they are like many other such initiatives, creating the luxuriant print debate with which many historians are familiar.

Mobilisation was a social and political phenomenon in itself, which attracted uneasy contemporary comment. Placing it at the heart of the political story gives social depth to politics while remaining sensitive to shifting political alignments. It also offers a way of resolving the paradox left us by Conrad Russell. The concentration here on the 1640s is deliberate

---

[42] Quoted in Braddick, *State formation*, p. 427.

— the constitutional experiments of the 1650s were only one strand of responses to a much wider crisis, which was not ended by the restoration.[43] Civil war, a product of institutional failure, preceded a revolution which was not expressed or contained in an institutional solution. An analysis of the mobilisation of support among wider publics is important to understanding this phenomenon and may also point towards ways of resolving another problem left by revisionism — the highly unusual English outcome from ingredients which were, apparently, common to much of Europe. But this analysis also suggests ways in which we might find that England was not like other European countries. There were differences of political circumstance, but also perhaps of political culture prior to 1640: the plurality of early Stuart religious and political life becomes crucial to an understanding of responses to the Covenanting revolution and the Irish rebellion.

More immediately, this analysis of mobilization suggests that an understanding of the openness of politics is important not just in its own right, but as part of the explanation for why parliament could not resolve conflict, and why civil war became revolution. Putting the Politics back in popular politics matters for our understanding of popular politics. Putting the importance of wider publics back into our account of the 1640s matters to our understanding of that crisis, its course and its consequences.

---

[43] For a similar view see Jonathan Scott, *England's Troubles: seventeenth-century English political instability in European context* (Cambridge, 2000), pt II.

Chapter 10

The Uses of the Monarchy: A 'Spanish Incident' in the Mid-Nineteenth Century

Isabel Burdiel

I

One of the great dilemmas in European political life after the series of revolutions in the late eighteenth and early nineteenth centuries was whether the monarchy would absorb the revolution or the revolution would absorb the monarchy. Contemporaries, perceiving this dilemma as a clash between the order and authority of tradition and revolutionary change, attempted to resolve it by means of constitutional monarchy, 'the almost natural framework' for the political stabilisation of liberalism in much of Europe.[1]

In Spain, after the frustrated experiments of 1812–14 and 1820–23, constitutional monarchy was consolidated during the reign of Isabel II.[2] For the Spanish Progressive liberal Joaquín María López, the evolution of

[1] P. Rosanvallon, *La Monarchie impossible: Les Chartes de 1814 et de 1830* (Paris, 1994), p. 46. For a review of the problem on a continental European scale, see Martin Kirsch, *Monarch und Parlament im 19. Jahrhundert* (Göttingen, 1999). I have offered an interpretation of the Spanish liberal revolution in I. Burdiel, 'Myths of failure, myths of success: new perspectives on nineteenth-century Spanish liberalism', *The Journal of Modern History*, 70 (1998), pp. 892–912. For the long-term consequences of the revolution, see J. Millán and M. C. Romeo, 'Was the liberal revolution important to modern Spain? Political cultures and citizenship in Spanish history', *Social History*, 29:3 (2004), pp. 284–300. As this essay is basically argumentative, I shall minimise the bibliographical references and concentrate on those that can be consulted in English.

[2] Isabel II was declared Queen in 1833 on the death of her father, Fernando VII, the last Spanish absolute king. She was three years old, and the regency was exercised by her mother, María Cristina de Borbón. Her uncle, the Infante, Don Carlos, invoked the Salic Law and absolutist orthodoxy and challenged her right to the throne, giving rise to a civil war (1833–40), which ended with the victory of the Isabellines supported by the liberals. The Queen herself came to power in 1843 and reigned until the revolution of 1868, which forced her abdication. She died in Paris in 1904. I. Burdiel, *Isabel II. No se puede reinar inocentemente* (Madrid, 2004).

the new regime would depend on the inevitable confrontation between Parliament and the Crown to control the political process:

> The real power in hereditary monarchies must necessarily be in conflict with the deliberating bodies ... the war may be lively or slow, muted or declared; it may be softened by moderation, dissimulated by hypocrisy, tempered or suspended by events; but it will soon come to an end and national representation will disappear or the monarchy will give way and be smothered.[3]

A good starting point from which to tackle the specific form that the conflict took in Spain during Isabel II's reign might be an analysis of the crisis in the mid 1850s. A popular rising at the time, known as the '1854 Revolution', put an end to the Crown's attempt to impose itself on Parliament with the support of the more reactionary sectors of the Moderate party. Since Isabel II's accession to the throne this party had governed on its own, casting the other political options, especially the very influential Progressive party, into hopeless opposition.[4]

Historians usually consider that revolution as a kind of delayed 'Spanish 1848' and see the following two years (the so-called *Bienio Progresista*) as the great lost opportunity to break the hegemony of the moderate liberalism characteristic of Isabel's entire reign. The emergence

---

[3] J. M. López, 'Lecciones de política constitucional' (1840) in *Colección de discursos parlamentarios, defensas forenses y producciones literarias*, 5 (Madrid, 1856–57), p. 77.

[4] Moderates and Progressives were both offshoots of the broad liberal movement that had fought against absolutism throughout the first third of the nineteenth century and succeeded in imposing a constitutional monarchy in the early 1830s. The differences between them were many and various. For our present purposes, two issues were decisive. The first had to do with the desire (or reluctance) to facilitate the political participation of the population by a gradual extension of suffrage, especially on a municipal level. The second issue was the possibility, or not, of an alliance with the privileged groups of the *ancien régime* and with the Crown which would (or would not) place the latter in a pre-eminent situation in the new liberal regime. The great dividing line lay between the Progressives' strict defence of national sovereignty (and therefore the primacy of Parliament) and the Moderates' desire to include the Crown in the definition of sovereignty of the nation through the concept of a sovereignty shared between Crown and Parliament (las Cortes) that would include an upper house where the old privileged class would be guaranteed representation. See I. Burdiel, 'The liberal revolution, 1808–1843' in J. Álvarez Junco and A. Shubert (eds), *Spanish History since 1808* (London, 2000), pp. 18–32.

of the 'social question' in Spain, with the first steps of the organised workers' movement and the incipient republican organisations, is assumed simply to have accentuated the panic of the 'respectable classes' which accompanied the conservatives' return to power in 1856. Seen from this viewpoint, the Spanish crisis in the mid-nineteenth century was no more than a further failure of the democratic social revolution heralded by the 'Spring of Nations' in Europe. That, more or less, is the route mapped out in V. G. Kiernan's influential and unsurpassed *The Revolution of 1854 in Spanish History*, encouraged by the texts that Marx and Engels published about the Spanish revolution in the *New York Daily Tribune* in August and September 1854.[5]

I am not setting out to replace Kiernan's interpretation with one that is radically different. I simply wish to use this brief period as a vantage point from which to analyse what, in my judgement, constitutes the underlying tension of the entire reign of Isabel II. I am referring to the confrontation between liberalism as a whole (going beyond its internal divisions) and the Crown. An allusion to this much more global conflict was made by Andrés Borrego (by then not a Progressive liberal but a Moderate) when he defined the 1854 revolution as

> an aspect, an accident, a step in the ongoing litigation between the monarchy and liberalism: a litigation that the genuine constitutionals, the enlightened minority, seek to adapt by assigning terms of agreement to it without having yet been able to wrest the weapons from the hands of those two fierce contenders.[6]

II

For Moderate liberalism, the coming to power of Isabel II in 1843 was an opportunity to put an end to the Spanish liberal revolution and seize control of the post-revolutionary scene from the Progressives. The central role assigned to the Crown in the design of the new regime was justified doctrinally by the need to strengthen executive over legislative power,

---

[5] The first edition of Kiernan's book was published by The Clarendon Press, Oxford, in 1966. The newspaper contributions by Marx and Engels appeared in K. Marx and F. Engels, *Revolution in Spain* (London, 1939).

[6] A. Borrego, *La revolución de julio de 1854, apreciada en sus causas y en sus consecuencias* (Madrid, 1855), p. 55.

order over revolution, and authority over the 'uncontrolled' freedom of the preceding years. Apart from political theory and rhetoric, however, the central role of the Crown had a clear party connotation. The politician and writer Juan Donoso Cortés made this brutally clear in a private letter to the Duke of Riánsares (the morganatic husband of the Queen Mother, María Cristina de Borbón):

> The Progressives do not need the Monarch in order to be strong because the basis of their support is the mob ... We Moderates do not need the mob in order to be strong because the basis of our support is the throne: but where will our strength be if we are not supported by either throne or mob? You will say it is a sorry matter to release the prey.[7]

From the outset, the Moderates saw Isabel II as a prey, a 'power that could be taken over', encouraged by the situation of personal confusion of a Queen who had only just left childhood behind. The Queen's personal weakness, combined with the strengthening of the royal prerogatives by the Constitution of 1845, provided the guarantee that the Crown which the Moderates were designing would be at the service of their interests and theirs alone.

It has become a cliché to consider that the basic limitation of Isabel's monarchy was that it was a party monarchy: the Moderate party's monarchy. This is certainly true, as it was also true of the doctrinarians in Orleanist France. Things in Spain, however, were more complex. This complexity affected the characteristics of the Moderate party and those of the monarchy itself.

The Moderate party was a party of accretion, forming a loose amalgamation of revolutionary liberals who had gradually become more moderate during the years of the breakaway from the Old Regime, sectors of absolutism in its more or less reformist facet which had opted to defend the interests of Isabel II during the civil war, and, lastly, a substantial representation of Carlism, 'co-opted' for the cause of moderatism when the war ended.

However, unlike what happened in the Belgium of King Léopold, for example, or in the France of Louis-Philippe, the political culture of the court and the Spanish royal family continued to be a culture of resistance

[7] Archivo Histórico Nacional, Madrid, *Diversos. Títulos y Familias*, leg. 3539/3.17, doc. 6, Juan Donoso Cortés to Fernando Muñoz, 29 April 1847.

to liberalism as a whole in the 1850s. Conditioned by the existence of Carlism, this distinctly anti-liberal culture found its best definition, not in the doctrinarianism of the majority of the Moderate party, but in the formulations of the so-called 'Isabelline realists', headed politically by the Marqués de Viluma and doctrinally by Juan Donoso Cortés. For them, the representative institutions, reluctantly accepted, were no more than mere limits 'to the only power in society, the power of the monarch'.[8]

In Orleanist France, the reactionary positions of legitimism barely survived as a political alternative and affected the governing doctrinarianism very little. In Spain, however, the forces of the anti-liberal reaction were not confined to the threat of Carlism but were embodied in the court itself and in a very influential sector of the governing party. The acute political and social insecurity of the Moderates had led them to tie their fortune as a party too closely to the strengthening of the power of the Crown. The practical consequences of that decision, unforeseen or unwanted by the Moderates themselves, are what I am interested in discussing here.

As some of its most lucid representatives pointed out, if the Moderate party drifted towards being a mere Court party, it could only lose authority in relation to the Crown and pass from taking over to being taken over. The consequences for the liberal system as a whole would be to convert the new representative system into a pure constitutional farce capable of smothering even the substantial liberal middle-class interests that the Moderates wanted to represent.[9]

That is exactly what happened at the end of the so-called 'Moderate Decade'. In their search for royal favour, conceived as purely and narrowly instrumental, the latent internal divisions in moderatism simply became more acute and reproduced within it the political Cainism that had characterised their relations with the Progressives until then. In turn, the disintegration of moderatism affected the Crown's position in two ways. On the one hand, it created an independent margin of power for the Crown, sustained by the maxim of *divide et impera* which had such a long tradition in Bourbon political culture. On the other hand, not necessarily in contradiction with what has just been said, it dragged the monarchy — specifically, Isabel II and her all-powerful mother — into an involvement with the internal conflict between the party's various factions. From the outset, this

---

[8] J. Donoso Cortés, *Sobre el proyecto de ley fundamental* (1837), *Obras Completas*, 1 (Madrid, 1970), p. 454.

[9] A. Borrego, *Estudios Políticos* (Madrid, 1855).

blocked any possibility that the monarchy might become an institution for regulation or arbitration in the game of politics — not so much between Moderates and Progressives as among the Moderates themselves.

Thus, because of the undesired effects of the political practice to which it gave rise, the party takeover of the monarch's power became a kind of political boomerang for the Moderate's ability to control the Crown. Like Victor Frankenstein, they had created an unpredictable monster whose desires and reactions were getting out of hand.

The *internal* crisis of the Spanish monarchy in the mid 1850s was due to at least three closely interrelated reasons. They all involved the royal family directly and combined politics, economics and morality. The first was the attempt to force a political involution, inspired by Louis Napoléon's *coup d'état*, which called even the 1845 Constitution into question. In the design of that planned involution, public opinion pointed openly to the influence of the Queen Mother, who, rightly or wrongly, was considered the person who really wielded the royal power in her daughter's name.

Secondly, the Moderates' model for economic development, extraordinarily closed and focused on the State, contributed very intensely to the growing internal division in historical moderatism. The shrinking of the game of politics (increasingly a parlour game) was a reflection of the shrinking of the game of economics, which ultimately transformed the embryo liberal State into a private financial undertaking in which all operations were carried out with a view to the profit that the partners could obtain from them. In this context, the political visibility of the royal family was echoed by its visibility in the world of business, in clear competition with other financial actors. This was a situation which, once again, basically affected María Cristina de Borbón and her husband, the Duque de Riánsares, both involved in all the business activities (whether fraudulent or not) which were carried out in that period with the use of privileged access to the resources of the State's power. Thus the concessions for the building of the railway, among others that were equally lucrative, became the centre of the political debate.

It is worth dwelling on this point. Every ruling class needs a personal ethics which (ideally) subjects it to a specific code of conduct. During those years, the actions of the Queen Mother and her family, as a nucleus of economic power which maximised the power of the State in its own favour, became a mirror and open denunciation of the whole political and economic framework constructed by the Moderates after the break with absolutism. When a family closely identified with royalty, as in the case of the Queen Mother, acted like just another bourgeois family firm, the cross-contamination of politics and business became a source of unbearable tension for the very people who had encouraged it.

Thirdly, in that great crisis of values (a harbinger of the crisis which put an end to the Isabelline monarchy in 1868), the private behaviour of Queen Isabel II became a matter for condemnation, providing political ammunition for liberalism and for broad sectors of Moderates within it, who saw power slipping out of their hands. In fact, the emissaries of the rumoured lovers of a Queen who had only just emerged from adolescence, and authors of tales of the dubious paternity of her children, were the Moderate liberals themselves.[10]

The double morality here was not just concerned with the fact that what was accepted in men (and in all kings, before and afterwards) was not accepted in that particular woman and queen. The distinction was not strictly a double morality, but a profound cultural value of the time concerning the different nature and functions of men and women. The duplicity really had to do with the fact that Isabel II's lovers acquired political visibility when their function of patronage and access to the royal will was not shared out sufficiently. The very individuals who, in situations of power or foreseeable access to power, bent like reeds at all the Queen's private eccentricities, did not hesitate to drag her name through the mud when that power slipped away from them.

The problem, therefore, was not only that Isabel II's love life clashed increasingly with middle-class cultural conventions concerning women's behaviour. The basic problem, at least at that point in the evolution of nineteenth-century Spanish society, was that the Queen's deviation from the middle-class ideal of the domestic angel (or Christian mother) became a powerful symbol, on a moral level, of the Crown's political independence. This was an independence — both perceived and constructed in terms of political, economic and personal *immorality* — that was understood as what it really was: a threat to liberalism as a whole.

It was this general threat that determined the shift towards opposition of a broad sector of the Moderates from 1851–53 onwards, the forging of an alliance with the Progressives which was created under the banner of uniting all liberals on behalf of 'regeneration of the country', and — some-

---

[10] Isabel II was married against her will, at the age of sixteen, to her cousin, Francisco de Asís. I have studied the political, social and cultural implications of Isabel II's private life in I. Burdiel, 'The Queen, the woman and the middle class: the symbolic failure of Isabel II of Spain', *Social History*, 29:3 (2004), pp. 301–19.

thing less well known — with the prominent involvement of those very Moderates in the delegitimation, not of one government or another, but of the monarchy itself. As the British ambassador in Madrid wrote a few years later:

> All the parties and factions defend themselves rather than the Crown and attack or protect it depending on whether they are in power or not … . In no party or faction is there a genuine monarchic feeling as we understand it, they all despise the royal family, and they despise it all the more the more they need it.[11]

During those months, both the British and the French ambassador reported on the approaches made to them by various political leaders in the opposition who explicitly sought the support or neutrality of their governments to force Isabel II to abdicate and replace her with some Portuguese or Italian prince.[12] Among those leaders, several were Moderates and of the highest level. In particular, there was General Ramón María Narváez, several times Prime Minister and generally considered the leading 'blade' of the Moderate party. 'The Queen should abdicate,' Narváez said to the British ambassador in January 1854, 'and Parliament should declare her children to be bastards … she is something that I shall not repeat and her mother is a monster of iniquity … it is absolutely necessary to put an end to the Bourbon dynasty in Spain.'[13]

So why did Isabel II not fall in 1848, as Louis-Philippe did? In order to answer that question it is necessary to emphasise the basic difference in the relationship between the two monarchs and their respective governing parties at the time when the two revolutions broke out.

In Spain, unlike what happened in the final stages of the Orleanist regime, and also unlike what has become a commonplace in the historiography of the period, the problem was not so much that the monarchy was identified exclusively with one party, the Moderate party, incapable of socialising the institution politically. The real problem was that the monarchy had become independent of the bulk of that party, thus subverting the party's situation of exclusive domination and drawing a

---

[11] National Archives (hereafter NA), London, Foreign Office (hereafter FO), *Spain*, 72/897, no. 235, Howden to Clarendon, 7 November 1856.

[12] A Portuguese Braganza (specifically, a son of the Queen, Maria da Glória) or the Duke of Genoa, the King of Sardinia's brother.

[13] NA, FO, *Spain*, 72/842, nos. 6 and 9, Howden to Clarendon, 1 January 1854.

substantial sector of it towards disaffection, disengagement or insurrection. In that context, the basic reasons why the monarchy did not fall with the Moderate party in 1854 are five in number, and they are closely interrelated.

The first was the impossibility of achieving the agreement, or at least neutrality, of France and England concerning a change of dynasty in Spain at a time (the beginning of the Crimean War) which was especially delicate for the balance of power in Europe. The second was the shift — half spontaneous, half organised — of public anger from Isabel II to her mother, María Cristina de Borbón. Third and fourth were the conviction of most of the liberals (including the Progressives) of strong public attachment to the monarchic form of government and the difficulty of improvising the historical legitimacy of succession to the Bourbons by another dynasty. The example of what happened to the Orleanist monarchy was still very fresh, and there was also the fear that a change of dynasty might make popular support swing towards Don Carlos. Finally came the decision of the Progressives to keep Isabel II, believing that they too could take over the monarchy, in this case by the practical exercise of national sovereignty.

In this scenario, the operation to save Isabel II as Queen was conceived as an attempt by liberalism to reappropriate the institution of monarchy, in which the Progressives took the initiative from then on.

III

It has been said repeatedly that the Progressives lacked an alternative constitutional model to the doctrinally inspired regime of double trust. This was the system which requires governments to put their trust in the Crown and Parliament simultaneously and on an equal footing. However, matters alter substantially when we leave the realm of theory and turn to practice and when we also make an effort to contextualise progressivism among other European liberal movements.

In the whole of Europe, the evolution towards the pre-eminence of Parliament over the Crown during the nineteenth century was more a matter of political practice than constitutional theory. In general, until the democratic constitutions after the First World War, constitutionalism in Europe was a dual system in which, as Martin Kirsch has shown, the King and Parliament were constantly obliged to make compromises.[14]

In the mid-nineteenth century, the response which almost the whole of

---

[14] Kirsch, *Monarch und Parlament*, p. 386.

European liberalism was providing to the structural political tension between monarchy and Parliament consisted in 'surrounding the monarchy with the nation' or, in López's terms, 'smothering' it with the liberal representative institutions, on both a state and a provincial or municipal level. Following Adolphe Thiers's formula, that meant no more than the practical imposition — not necessarily made explicit in constitutional theory — of a situation in which 'the King reigns but does not govern'.

This was the process that had been followed in the admired British model (and partly, too, in the Belgian model), without the need for specific regulation of either the role of the government as the real depositary of executive power or the monarch's exclusively 'dignified' or formally arbitral new function. The problem consisted, of course, in the fact that nobody (anywhere in Europe, in the period that we are discussing) ever gave a good definition of the precise content of the function of reigning without governing. Thiers himself had not been able to express that function beyond a vague formulation to the effect that 'reigning consists in being the truest, highest and most respected image of the country'.[15]

The Progressive tension concerning this was made explicit in the parliamentary session of 30 November 1854, in which, for the first time in Spain, there were debates about the form of government. In those debates the Progressives, confronted with the demands of the democrats and republicans and with the very considerable social agitation that had fomented the revolution, reproduced the already long historical tension within Spanish liberalism between the defence of national sovereignty and the strong identification of the monarchy with Spanish national identity. The Progressive politician Patricio de la Escosura put it thus:

> We are only legislators of a nation with an existence of its own, a nation with history; and once the Spanish nation ceases to be monarchic, it ceases to exist ... the Spanish nation is monarchic because of its history, it is monarchic because of its geography, it is monarchic because of its essence.

[15] It must be remembered that Walter Bagehot's *The English Constitution* (1867) was not translated in Spain until 1902. Also, the classic distinction that it established between 'efficient power' (in the hands of the government) and 'dignified power' (in the hands of the King) was an *a-posteriori* study of what had been happening, in practice rather than in a programmed fashion, in the relations between the Crown, the Government, the parties and the British Parliament. I am using the edition published by Fontana Press (London, 1993). The quotation from Thiers is taken from Rosanvallon, *La Monarchie impossible*, p. 157.

That identification of monarchy with the Spanish nation was there to serve order and unity against social revolution and national disintegration. Escosura recalled that Spain consisted of

> a portion of peoples with diverse, heterogeneous tendencies, dispositions and characteristics. What unity do you want there to be between them if you deny us monarchic political unity? ... Do you want a federal republic?

Another Progressive figure, Evaristo San Miguel, considered that without Isabel II's throne there would be nothing but 'ruins, anarchy and disorder', and that what the nation needed was

> something fixed and stable which does not give way to the torrent of revolution; something as a centre, around which all the wheels or parts of this social and political machine revolve and move.[16]

So what difference was there between Progressives and Moderates in their conception of the monarchy? More precisely, what specific resources were available to the Progressives to neutralise the Crown politically and at the same time use it as a symbolic element of social and national cohesion without crossing the line that divided liberalism from democracy? The progress that the Progressives visualised was in the direction of a society governed by merit, reason and work embodied in the middle classes (Progressive, of course), in which the people was a subordinated subject until it attained the status of middle class. Therefore they could never abandon their defence of the monarchy (and religion) as essential elements of Spanish identity because that identity thus became a practical limit — a cultural limit in the broadest sense — to the advance of democracy, identified by them with a (possibly federal) republic and with an autonomous, disorderly nation.

Progressivism's monarchic illusion consisted in believing that, in the Spanish situation, with no change of dynasty and without any substantial extension of suffrage, it was sufficient to surround the monarchy with the nation (an elective Congress and Senate, people's delegations, town councils,) in order to oblige it to cease being an active power in politics and force it to yield to the representative powers which (in their judgement) in a situation of free elections, would always have a Progressive majority. In

---

[16] Diario de Sesiones de Cortes, Congreso, 30 November 1854.

other situations, unfortunately for them, they worked out hardly any constitutional mechanism to solve an open conflict between the representative institutions and the Crown. For the case of an open conflict, the only resource they had was mobilisation of the national will, that is, agitation, extra-parliamentary action and revolution.

In their defence it must be said that almost all European liberals had the same problem — as is shown by the revolutionary convulsions on the continent until well into the nineteenth century, especially, but not only, in the case of France. However, in the European context of a constant struggle between Crown and Parliament, it is worth reflecting on some key points in the political practice of the Spanish Progressives. The first was their difficulty in consistently (and sincerely) conceiving and practising political plurality, and the consequent need to promote the organisation of a strong party, solidly established in society and independent of famous military 'blades'. In the case of the Progressives, the soldier in question was General Baldomero Espartero, whom the 1854 revolution had raised to the presidency of the Council of Ministers.

Progressives believed that party competition was an evil to be overcome, but while they considered themselves to be the true representatives of liberalism (expelling both the democrats and the Moderates from that field), they always had great difficulty in finding a single structure in which to fit the middle-class leaders of progressivism and a social basis which was much more mixed, popular and politicised than that of the Moderates. As a result almost all Progressives regarded Espartero as an indispensable political umbrella. Driven on by their own political and social insecurity with regard to 'radical', that is, democratic and republican liberalism, in 1854 the Progressives thus saved a monarchy in which they did not believe and which, for them, was not, as Thiers proposed, the highest and most respected institution in the country. It was also a monarchy which was openly hostile to them and was not prepared to give up the political importance which the Progressives requested (or, to be more precise, demanded) in return for its symbolic dignification.

IV

In fact, for the whole royal family, the regime that emerged from the revolution was perceived as what it really was: a violent imposition on the will of the Crown and a break with the constitutional legality of 1845, which granted the Queen complete freedom in the appointment and dismissal of governments. At the same time, the entire royal family was aware that the 1854 revolution had seriously endangered the continuity of the dynasty and that the continuance of Isabel II on the throne was the result of a consensus more negative than positive. From both viewpoints, the completely 'natural' — that is, completely internalised — response of the Crown was to resist and lay the foundations for a recovery of its lost power.

The Crown's strategy of trying to re-establish its legitimacy and engage in action on the post-revolutionary scene was organised around two assumptions, both of a moral and cultural nature but with profound political implications. Being fully aware of their loss of personal popularity, the royal couple tried to clean up its private image as publicly as possible. Isabel II's current lover was sent off to the Austro-Hungarian Empire and the royal couple began to show unprecedented signs of constituting an exemplary family. In addition, the Palace sought to influence public opinion directly by funding at least one periodical (*El Amigo del Pueblo*), several pamphlets and a biography of Queen Isabel II.[17] The message of the campaign was twofold. The first was the exculpation of Isabel II from all political responsibility for the mistakes of the 'Moderate Decade' by presenting her (not all that paradoxically) as a queen who had reigned but not governed since she came of age. The second was the strengthening of a close identification of the defence of the Catholic religion with defence of the Isabelline monarchy in the eyes of public opinion.

It is in the light of this strategy that we must understand the centrality of incidents between the government and the Crown during the *Bienio* in connection with matters that really transcended party divisions, such as the second basis of the Constitution (with its timid attempt to introduce religious tolerance) and a new sale of church property. A very efficient campaign to wear down the government was organised around these two issues, and it succeeded in unleashing a veritable religious hysteria (especially among the upper classes) which contributed considerably to the erosion of the government, presenting it as both anti-monarchic and anti-religious; in other words, as anti-Spanish.

On this matter of the religious question, Isabel II was both emblem and victim of the Palace's powerful clerical camarilla. Any possibility of an

---

[17] As far as I am aware, this was the first biography of Queen Isabel, published that year, 1854, in Paris, with the title *Isabelle de Bourbon, reine d'Espagne*. It appeared anonymously, but I have been able to confirm that the author was Eugenio Ochoa, an intimate adviser of the royal couple. Archivo Histórico Nacional, Madrid, *Diversos. Títulos y Familias*, leg. 3430/196, doc. 67, Eugenio Ochoa to Mª Cristina de Borbón, 22 October 1854.

understanding between the Queen and the Progressive government was nipped in the bud. Her purely primitive, superstitious conception of religiosity was stimulated to paroxysm, convincing her that her private sins could only be purged if she became the firmest champion of the rights of the Catholic Church. The Queen also became convinced that her sceptre would be in danger — if not from the revolution, then from the Carlism that it revived — if she did not resist Progressive pressure on matters sensitive for the Church. In both connections, the assiduous correspondence of Pope Pius IX was decisive.

The clerical pressure from the Palace was also accompanied by other changes which affected the correlation of internal forces of a royal family which had always been disunited. In the absence of María Cristina — transformed into the scapegoat of the revolution and forced to seek exile in France — the King Consort acquired a power that he had not previously possessed and had been trying to obtain for years. From the outset, his aim was to become the centre of an alliance between the Moderates and the Carlists that would put a stop to any further ripples of revolution and force a return to the monarchy as it was before the liberal revolution of the 1830s.

'What will my Cousin do,' the King Consort wondered, 'if we hoist his political banner? What would he be left with?'[18] The documentation to which I have had access allows us to conclude that Isabel II's rights were clearly put at risk in the conspiracy hatched by the King Consort, without her full knowledge. Her own husband thought of forcing her abdication and (together with Don Carlos) establishing a co-regency until their respective children, united in matrimony, came to power.

That operation failed for three closely interrelated reasons. The first was the clear, emphatic opposition of María Cristina in Paris, who even threatened to make the conspiracy public. This was accompanied by something that goes a long way towards explaining the ex-Regent's attitude: the rejection or inhibition, in broad sectors of moderatism, of a reaction that might involve substantial concessions to Carlism and a return to a pre-liberal situation. Thirdly, the Carlists feared falling into a political trap if they took part in a rising with the Moderates, whose political conservatism was liberal rather than absolutist.

With the path of insurrection blocked, Isabel II recovered part of the initiative that she had lost to her husband and she concentrated on seeking — and obtaining — the support of another general, General Leopoldo O'Donnell, who was then Minister of War. O'Donnell, who had been the

---

[18] Real Academia de la Historia, Madrid, *Colección Pirala*, leg. 9/6860.

leader of the military insurrection which unleashed the revolution of 1854, was increasingly identified with the idea of a conservative but not anti-liberal change of direction, and he was increasingly opposed to General Espartero. Most important was the recognition by both the Queen and O'Donnell of the need for the change of direction to be accompanied by an intense campaign in the press and in Parliament, which involved giving precedence to the game of politics in the institutions rather than the strategy of conspiracy and insurrection.

It is significant, however, that the monarchy itself recognized its political powerlessness if it did not have the support of some faction of liberalism. The faction concerned was that led by O'Donnell, which was seeking an alliance with the more temperate sectors of progressivism on behalf of a new party, the so-called 'Liberal Union'. This political platform, which was still in the embryonic stage, was to be the great political winner in that fluid scenario, showing itself to be capable of wearing down both the Moderates (on the left) and the Progressives (on the right), thus increasing the internal crisis — the political exhaustion — of the two great traditional parties that had emerged from the Spanish liberal revolution.

In this context, an analysis of the events of July 1856 (which brought the *Bienio Progresista* to a close) shows the extent to which the Progressives were trapped in their own monarchic illusion. Very briefly, the Queen took advantage of one of the fierce arguments between the two generals who were sharing power to replace Espartero with O'Donnell. This anti-parliamentarian but not anti-constitutional manoeuvre simply highlighted and profited politically from the profound contradiction in the Progressives' monarchism: their inability to 'smother' the Crown with the nation when the Crown used against the nation the constitutional prerogatives and historical legitimacy that they themselves had recognised in it. The result was the monarchy's recovery of the political independence which the revolution had attempted to avoid.

This political independence was almost immediately applied to achieving a reaction, including a version of the story of Judas's thirty pieces of silver in which the treacherous O'Donnell was in turn betrayed, dismissed from the government and replaced by the most reactionary Moderates. However, this outright reaction failed for various reasons. The reason subsuming them all was the fact that in the two years prior to the *Bienio* there was no unity of action either in the royal family or in the dispersed remnants of the Moderate party. For the royal family, those two years were yet again a pathetic setting for the King Consort's struggle to take over, in practice, the royal power attributed to his wife and to become the champion of a political withdrawal which implicitly included the political annulment of the sovereign and the end of any experiments with constitutional monarchy. In giving effect to this scheme the Queen's husband sought to exploit the ongoing irregularity of his wife's personal conduct to blackmail her and to play on her fear of divine punishment. Having recently taken a new lover to whom the King Consort (covertly in public and openly in private) attributed the paternity of the child who later reigned as Alfonso XII, Isabel was particularly vulnerable to such a strategy.

As far as the Moderates are concerned, I think it can be said that historical moderatism did not survive the *Bienio*. None of the governments that followed was capable of establishing sufficient links to unite the various Moderate factions, and to a large extent they exhausted themselves (paradoxically, and contrary to what has been said) in their attempts to resist the anti-liberal tide while at the same time trying to avert another revolution. The disintegration of the Moderate party was not simply an atomisation into purely personal factions with no political meaning. Seen in perspective (and the experience of the *Bienio* was also fundamental in this), the upshot was the collapse of the centrist sector of the party, the sector closest to French doctrinarianism. This collapse favoured the positions represented by the neo-Catholics, for whom even the 1854 Constitution was too advanced. On the other hand, at the opposite extreme of the conservative political arc, there was a gradual increase in the acquisition of political power by O'Donnell's 'Constitutional Monarchists' who were prepared to make a pact with the less radical progressivism under the banner of the Liberal Union.

Isabel II's apparently erratic attitude and the shuffling of ministries between 1856 and 1858 can be best understood in this context of the definitive crisis of historical moderatism and the 'internal' harassing of the Queen's personal position by her husband and the neo-absolutist sectors which went along with Francisco de Asís's aspirations. The result was the reproduction of the two basic dangers that had led to the 1854 revolution: the creation of an imprecise but very broad political area for the monarch's personal intervention and, at the same time, the chronic instability produced by the lack of unity within the major parties.

What actually happened in the two years following the *Bienio Progresista* was a kind of political entropy in which the strength of the various Moderate factions and the disagreements within the royal family itself obstructed and blocked each other, making any stable government impossible. This state of affairs has a number of important implications for our understanding of the relationship between monarchy and liberalism in mid-nineteenth-century Spain.

First, it has traditionally been considered that the Progressives' only experience of government during Isabel II's reign was a political failure. Its legacy for the future development of Isabelline society and Spanish capitalism in the nineteenth century is supposed to have resided exclusively in the economic laws produced by the Progressives which survived their fall. This is only partly true. The 1854 revolution and the experience of the *Bienio* were highly effective — not only in the short term but also in the medium and longer term — in avoiding a reactionary, authoritarian shift of the right wing of moderatism and of the Crown. In this respect, the brief occupation of power by the Progressives was fundamental for the preservation of the liberal regime in Spain.

This may not have done much for the aspirations of substantial transformation of the regime which inspired the democrats and the 'pure' Progressives and also, of course, the social and workers' demands which erupted during the *Bienio*. However, it was decisive if one considers the intensity of the reaction which might have taken place if the (apparently unspectacular) 'Spanish 1848' had not intervened. The Progressives did not succeeded in shifting the Crown towards the non-active area of politics — largely because of their own internal contradictions — but the scenario created by the 1854 revolution did avoid a reaction to a pre-constitutional or even openly anti-liberal monarchy.

Secondly, as far as Isabel II's position is concerned, the experience after the *Bienio* demonstrated the Queen's personal and political inability to exercise power directly, to reign and govern by subjecting the majority parties, and particularly the Moderate party, to the authority of the Crown. To be able to do so (to be able to give power to or take it away from political options which were so at opposition with each other), she would have had to possess a margin of symbolic authority and power which she never had, either during the *Bienio* or in the years before or after it.

Isabel II's broad margin for detailed manoeuvring was thus revealed, at a deeper level, as a substantial inability to raise herself to the status of an unquestioned and unquestionable institution, above the political parties, even above the Moderate factions and the conflicting interests of the royal family. Parties, factions and family never hesitated to use the Queen's 'private vices' to weaken her politically and, in passing, to discredit the robust monarchy that they professed they wanted to introduce.

The distinctly private, personal peculiarities of Isabel II make historical sense in the context of the more structural tension between the monarchy's broad margin for constitutional manoeuvre and the purely instrumental, party and factional function which, in practice, *everybody* foresaw for it. Thus there is value in analysing the contingency of the monarch's private personality and the effects of Isabel II's power. This power, which was not so much positive as negative, was deployed in ways that squandered the symbolic capital of monarchy. It proved especially dangerous where monarchic legitimacy was used to shield the political system from the adverse affects of a lack of significant consensus among political actors.

All this explains why, when faced with the imperative need to re-establish the Isabelline monarchy, a substantial sector of liberalism was incapable of really thinking of the circulation of power among the traditional parties. As a result, it attempted to use the Liberal Union to bring about the dissolution of the two old political formations which had emerged from the outbreak of revolution in the 1830s and which, each in its own way, had proved incapable of 'absorbing the monarchy' and neutralising it.

In this respect, the Liberal Union was not merely — as most Spanish historiography has argued — a party conceived *in order* to support Isabel II's throne and perpetuate the Moderate party in a different guise.[19] The Liberal Union was *also* a party conceived in order to offer a distinctly liberal power to *confront* a throne that was dangerous for the constitutional regime as a whole, on both a political and a moral level. To achieve this it needed to rescue the clearly liberal sectors of moderatism from the hands of the Crown and the clearly monarchic sectors of progressivism from the temptation of revolution.

Its very emergence as a party shows that Isabel's reign cannot be understood, like that of Louis-Philippe, simply as 'the reign of the Moderates'. It certainly was that, but it was also something else. As the political experience of the middle years of the reign shows, the confrontation of two liberal versions of constitutional monarchy (Moderate and Progressive) was one part of the conflict. The other, if not prior then at least contemporary and decisive, had to do with the very definition of Isabel's monarchy as a constitutional and thus liberal monarchy. Seen in this light, the uses of the monarchy in mid-nineteenth-century Spain acquire greater complexity and take their place at the heart of the mighty battle that was being waged throughout the whole of continental Europe in that century, between traditional order and modern freedom.

[19] This is the opinion of the leading expert on it, N. Durán, *La Unión Liberal y la modernización de la España isabelina. Una convivencia frustrada, 1854-1868* (Madrid, 1979).

Chapter 11

Settler Utopianism? English Ideologies of Emigration, 1815-1850

James Belich

One of the most interesting things about nineteenth-century Britain is the number of people who left it. In the long eighteenth century, 1700-1815, fewer than 500,000 people emigrated from Britain and Ireland, only a quarter of them English.[1] Between 1815 and 1914, by contrast, about 22 million left, over half of them English.[2] Naturally, this massive exodus has received considerable scholarly attention, both historical and econometric. The debate is often presented as a rather dreary ping-pong between 'push' and 'pull' theories. The classic pull theory is rational actor migration. People learned that wages were higher, and opportunities more numerous, in new societies than in old, and migrated as soon as means became available.[3] Higher wages and opportunities did exist, but only at some times in some migrant destinations, and the discrepancy in *real* wages is often exaggerated. It is hard to believe that it was in itself enough to persuade people to undertake the dangerous, difficult, traumatic and expensive act of long-term, long-distance, emigration. 'Real wage gaps will not suffice to explain emigration.'[4] Paid passages, distributed mainly by British imperial and colonial governments from 1830, helped with the expense, but the difficulty, trauma, and danger remained. In any case, only 7% of British emigrants received assisted passages.[5]

Some obvious push factors, such as population growth, were neces-

---

[1] Aaron S. Fogleman, 'From Slaves, Convicts, and Servants to Free Passengers', *Journal of American History*, 85 (1998), pp. 43-76.

[2] W. A. Carruthers, *Emigration from the British Isles* (London, 1929), p. 305; David B. Abernethy, *The Dynamics of Global Dominance* (Newhaven, 2000), p. 92. These are gross figures, and deducting returned migrants might reduce them by about 25%.

[3] Patrick J. Jobes *et al* (eds), *Community, society, and migration. Non-economic migration in America* (Lanham, MD, 1992), editors' introduction, p. 1.

[4] T. J. Hatton and J. G. Williamson, *The Age of Mass Migration. Causes and Economic Impact* (New York, 1998), p. 36. See also Avner Offer, *The First World War. An Agrarian Interpretation* (Oxford, 1989), p. 13.

[5] Eric Richards, *Britannia's Children* (London and New York, 2004), p. 138.

sary but not sufficient conditions. England's population doubled in size in the first half of the nineteenth century, but at the same time industrialization and urbanization provided alternatives to overseas emigration. Economic historians ingeniously posit a 20-year lag between the birth of a numerous generation and its oversupply of the labour market, leading to lower wage rates and hence to an increased propensity to migrate.[6] But population growth peaked in England about 1815, while English migration rates peaked about 1913, almost a century later. In between, population growth rates generally trended down, while migration growth rates trended up. 'Population size alone was never sufficient to explain emigration.'[7] The classic push factor is starvation, sheer want, which may work well enough for 1840s Ireland, but not for most parts of Britain, most of the time. Scholars accept that surges of British emigration do not correlate well with economic recessions.[8] As Tom Devine has pointed out for Scotland, there is paradox in the fact that Britain was the first country to industrialize *and* the first the engage in overseas mass migration.[9]

Another push theory stems from the agricultural 'revolution'. Enclosure and improvements in labour productivity displaced agricultural workers, so making them candidates for emigration. But, in England, enclosure came too early, and major reductions in the agricultural workforce came too late, to explain the surge of immigration in the first half of the nineteenth century. 'Whereas about seven million acres had been enclosed in England between 1760 and 1815, from 1815 to 1845 only 200,000 underwent enclosure'.[10] Mechanization, increased food imports, and a shift from arable to pastoral farming eventually decimated the agricultural labour force, but not until the second half of the century. Unemployment and unrest certainly did occur, especially in the agricultural southeast, from the Luddite outbreaks of the 1810s to the 'Captain

[6] Hatton and Williamson, *Age of Mass Migration*, p. 8.

[7] Richards, *Britannia's Children*, p. 65. See also Roger Schofield, 'British Population Change, 1700-1871', in Roderick Floud and Donald McCloskey (eds), *The Economic History of Britain since 1700* (Cambridge, 1994), second edition, pp. 69-70. For migration rates see Dudley Baines, *Emigration from Europe 1815-1930* (Basingstoke, 1991), p. 10.

[8] Richards, *Britannia's Children*, p. 180.

[9] T. M. Devine, 'The Paradox of Scottish Emigration' in *Exploring the Scottish Past: Themes in the History of Scottish Society* (East Linton, 1995).

[10] Eric Hopkins, *Industrialization and society* (London, 2000), pp. 87-88. See also Mark Overton, *Agricultural revolution in England and the transformation of the agrarian economy 1500-1800* (Cambridge, 1996), p. 148.

Swing' troubles of 1830. Yet rural labourers had suffered and rioted before without resorting to emigration, and the very poor were unable to emigrate without help. A refinement of the farm worker-displacement thesis is that agricultural wages rose in areas close to urban and industrial centres, because they had to compete with the high wages there, but fell elsewhere. The 'low-wage' counties then supplied many emigrants. Yet 'in 1827-31 only 21% of English emigrants came from agricultural low-wage counties against 55% from industrial high-wage ones'.[11] Indeed, some experts now believe that most English emigrants were not farm workers.[12] After all, displaced farm workers had the option of shifting to burgeoning industrial and urban areas.

A newer approach, which evades the push-pull dichotomy, is to see British overseas migration as an extension of internal migration.[13] It is true that, for various reasons, English rural folk had become less rooted to place than, say, their French equivalents. But internal migration was an old story; mass external migration was not. Nineteenth century rates of increase in the former were much lower than in the latter until 1890.[14] The notion of stage migration has been convincingly debunked for England, and high rates of internal migration could co-exist with low rates of external migration, as was the case in Oxfordshire.[15] Most internal moves were very short indeed — less than 60 miles, 1818-1839.[16] It is hard to see how such a shift led to one of several thousand miles to the wilds of North America or Australasia.

The best recent studies concede that an element of mystery remains about British mass migration, especially in that most difficult of historians' terrains, the inside of peoples' heads. 'Perhaps the most remarkable aspect of the phenomenon of emigration', Eric Richards argues, 'was its sheer spontaneity; it happened outside government control and beyond contemporary understanding. It was atomistic. Millions of people departed with

---

[11] Ian D. Whyte, *Migration and society in Britain: 1550-1830* (London, 2000), p. 132.

[12] W. E. Van Vugt, *Britain to America* (Urbana, 1999), p. 18; Dudley Baines, *Migration in a Mature Economy* (Cambridge, 1985), pp. 144-5.

[13] Whyte, *Migration and society*, p. 116; Richards, *Britannia's Children*, pp. 10-11; 44; Devine, 'Paradox of Scottish Emigration'.

[14] Colin G. Pooley and Jean Turnbull, *Migration and Mobility in Britain since the 18th century* (London, 1998), p. 59.

[15] Baines, *Migration in a Mature Economy*, ch. 9 and pp. 234, 247.

[16] Stephen Nicholas and Peter R. Shergold, 'Internal Migration in England, 1818-1839', *Journal of Historical Geography*, 12 (1987), pp. 155-68.

astonishingly little framework or ideology'.[17] This essay argues that, on the contrary, it is possible to detect nineteenth century English ideologies of emigration.

It is certainly possible to detect an English anti-emigration ideology, at least in elite public discourse. Much eighteenth century emigration was compulsory and disreputable, the fate of convicts and people so hopeless that they indentured themselves as temporary slaves as a last resort. 'Emigration', stated Lord Sheffield in the 1780s, 'is the natural recourse of the culprit, and those who have made themselves the objects of contempt and neglect'.[18] Canada was sarcastically known as 'the Irishman's Prize'.[19] In the early nineteenth century, the British still 'looked upon a life in the colonies as socially degrading, and having much in common with penal transportation'.[20] In 1816, a *Times* of London editorial divided emigrants into two categories: paupers and fools on the one hand and, on the other, 'malignant outcasts ... execrably base in their natures'.[21] In 1820, the same journal published with satisfaction a letter from a migrant to South Africa. 'You told me true when you said I may as well blow out my brains as come upon this expedition. Indeed, I have totally ruined myself.'[22] The prevailing British attitude was later famously summarized by Charles Buller. Emigration was 'little more than shoveling out your paupers to where they might die, without shocking their betters with the sigh or sound of their last agony'.[23]

Emigration's image problem was resolved by what contemporaries rightly saw as 'a revolution in colonial thought'.[24] It is normally attributed

---

[17] Richards, *Britannia's Children*, p. 149. See also Dudley Baines, 'European emigration, 1815-1930: looking at the emigration decision again', *Economic History Review*, 47 (1994), pp. 525-44 and Whyte, *Migration and society*, p. 103.

[18] Quoted in Doron S. Ben-Atar, *Trade Secrets; Intellectual Piracy and the Origins of the American Industrial Power* (New Haven, 2004), p. 112.

[19] Philip Lawson, '"The Irishman's Prize." Views of Canada from the British press, 1760-1774', *Historical Journal*, 28 (1985), pp. 575-96.

[20] S. C. Johnson, *A History of emigration from the United Kingdom to North America, 1763-1912* (London, 1913), p. 21.

[21] *Times*, 27 August, 1816.

[22] *Times*, 12 Sept 1820.

[23] Quoted in Peter Gray, '"Shovelling out your paupers": The British state and Irish famine migration 1846-1860', *Patterns of Prejudice*, 33 (1999) pp. 47-65.

[24] Edward Brynn, 'The Emigration Theories of Robert Wilmot Horton, 1820-1841' *Canadian Journal of History*, 4 (1969), pp. 45-65. See also *The Collected Works of Edward Gibbon Wakefield*, ed. M. F. Lloyd Prichard (Glasgow and London, 1968).

to Edward Gibbon Wakefield and his fellow 'colonial reformers', and dated to around 1830, when there was indeed a surge in emigration. Scholars have long pointed out that Wakefield had his precursors, notably Robert Wilmot Horton, Parliamentary Under-Secretary of State for the Colonies, 1822-8. Under his influence, British restrictions on emigration, nominal in any case, were repealed in 1824, a parliamentary inquiry into emigration took place in 1826-7, and six small government funded schemes moved 11,000 people to Canada and the Cape Colony by 1826.[25] But, as Wakefield pointed out, Wilmot Horton's emphasis on pauper emigration also fed public prejudice against emigration in general. Another Wakefieldian precursor has recently been suggested in the shape of Thomas Douglas, Earl of Selkirk, who published advocacies of emigration from 1805, and practiced what he preached by founding a precursor of Winnipeg in 1812.[26] But Selkirk's efforts did not correspond in time with a general surge of emigration. Wakefield's did, but historians tend to miss the fact that the 'Wakefieldian' surge of 1830 was not the first of the nineteenth century.

This actually occurred in 1815-9, but was camouflaged by the absence of official immigration statistics in the United States, the main destination, until 1820. Yet enough evidence does exist to suggest a British and Irish emigration of about 150,000 between 1815-1820 – the highest annual average rate ever up to that time.[27] Unlike eighteenth century emigration, the great bulk was voluntary. Furthermore, a small government scheme for settlement in South Africa in 1819 accepted 4,000 emigrants, but was over-subscribed by 80,000, which 'strongly suggests a large pent-up demand for emigration'.[28] There was a corresponding surge of emigration literature. In 1810-4, according to the British Library Integrated Catalogue, the number of books published in Britain with the words 'emigration', 'emigrants' or 'settlers' in their title was precisely nil. In the next five years, 1815-19, there were twenty such publications. This is a conservative proxy for the total number of emigration books, since it excludes such titles as Morris Birkbeck's *Notes on a Journey in America* (1817) and William Cobbett's

---

[25] H. J. M. Johnston, *British Emigration Policy 1815-1830: 'Shovelling out paupers'* (Oxford, 1972).

[26] Alexander Murdoch, *British Emigration, 1603-1914* (Basingstoke, 2004), p. 85.

[27] Hans-Jurgen Grabbe, 'European immigration to the United States in the early national period, 1783-1820', *Proceedings of the American Philosophical Society*, 133 (1989), pp. 190-214; P. D. McClelland and R. J. Zeckhauser, *Demographic dimensions of the new republic: American interregional migration, vital statistics, and manumissions, 1800-1860* (Cambridge, 2004), pp. 96-112.

[28] Richards, *Britannia's Children*, p. 112.

Journal of a Year's Residence in the United States (1819). These early nineteenth century emigration books, an important source for this essay,[29] noted a shift in the quality as well as the quantity of emigration after 1815. 'Emigration assumed a totally new character; it was no longer merely the poor, the idle, the profligate, or the wildly speculative, who were proposing to quit their native country.' 'The mania for emigration is not now, as formerly, confined to the poorer class and such as could not gain a living at home.'[30]

We know what Wakefield thought of emigration, but what of the mass of the people? The problem of the silent majority is, of course, endemic in the social history of ideas. The standard solution, one not to be despised in the absence of alternatives, is to pile up available examples of opinions in the vague hope that these are typical. One possible refinement is the analysis of the conceptual language of substantial groups of lesser writers who are trying to persuade their still-larger target audience to do something. Such people play their various tunes on chords they believe to already exist in the minds of their readers. Their guess is more likely to be right than ours, especially when it was consistent, persistent, and widespread, and when the relevant campaign of persuasion had some success. The conceptual language of large-scale, long-term, campaigns of persuasion can therefore permit tentative deductions about popular ideology. The discourse of Protestant evangelism is one example that flowered in the early nineteenth century; the discourse of emigration is another. A third approach to the problem of the silent majority, or at least a section of it, is to trace changes in conceptual language through the newly available digitally searchable newspaper databases. Of course, there are pitfalls. A colleague discovered an astonishingly early use of the term 'Lesbian' only to find she was a ship. Advertising campaigns or political controversies that happen to use the chosen concept can distort the picture, and the growing use of a concept might simply reflect the growth in size of the relevant serial publication. One can sometimes cater for this, however, by

---

[29] In addition to those cited below, see Anon, *The American traveller and emigrant's guide* (Shrewsbury, 1817); British Traveller, *The colonial policy of Great Britain reconsidered...* (London, 1816); Anon, *The Emigrant's guide to the British settlements in Upper Canada and the USA* (London, 1820); E. Dana, *Geographical Sketch of the Western Country, designed for Emigrants and Settlers* (Cincinnati, 1819); Francis Hall, *Travels in Canada and the United States in 1816 and 1817*, second edition (London 1819); Anon, *The emigrants guide, or, A picture of America...* (London, 1816).

[30] Henry Bradshaw Fearon, *Sketches of America...*, third edition (London, 1819), xi; A. J. Christie, *The emigrants' assistant* (Montreal, 1821), pp. 21-22.

eliminating advertising from the search and by looking at the relative frequency of use of two or more concepts. I do not claim that this produces good evidence of the history of mass ideology, but simply that it produces better evidence.

In understanding the discourse of emigration, it is helpful to distinguish between a 'formal' variety, produced by the upper and middle classes for themselves and the lower classes, and an 'informal' variety, produced by the lower classes for themselves alone. The vehicles of the formal version were books, pamphlets, and lectures, as well as periodical and newspaper articles. These tracts regularly claimed objectivity, but were notoriously exaggerated and polemical, and prone to trip each other up by denigrating rival emigrant destinations. They were often mocked at the time, and dismissed as self-interested 'puffery'. Yet this can also be said of highly successful 20th century advertising campaigns. As with twentieth century mass advertising, the scale of nineteenth century emigration literature was vast enough to over-ride or outflank qualms and contradictions through the sheer volume of volumes. The score or more titles of 1815-19 were the beginning of an avalanche. A further 338-plus such titles followed between 1820 and 1850, and many American publications did not make it to the British Library. Broadly defined, 'booster books' must be one of the largest genres of nineteenth century English-language literature, up there with religious tracts.[31]

Informal emigration literature was produced by common folk for common folk. It included the oral communications of sailors, sojourners and returned migrants but this is hard to access. Migrant letters to those back home survived better, and over the years thousands have been fully or partly published, both by contemporaries and historians. Boosters selected letters that supported their case. But the informal letter writers knew their audience better, and had a somewhat different appreciation of what types of persuasion would work for them. 'Tell little Adam', wrote Alice Barlow to her English mother from the United States in 1818, 'if he was here, he would get puddings and pies every day'.[32] It is reasonable to conclude from this that little Adam, and perhaps others like him, actually did like puddings and pies, and that he aspired to puddings and

---

[31] J. M. Powell, *Mirrors of the New World* (Folkestone, 1977); Stephen Fender, *Sea changes. British emigration and American literature* (Cambridge, 1992); David M. Wrobel, *Promised Lands. Promotion, memory, and the creation of the American West* (Lawrence, KS, 2002).

[32] Letter extract in John Knight, *Important Extracts from Original and Recent letters written by Englishmen in the United States of America*, second series (Manchester, 1818), pp. 20-21.

pies every day.

The 1815 shift can be traced in the conceptual language of formal emigration discourse, as represented by the digitally searchable database of the *Times* newspaper. The *Times*, of course, was not necessarily typical even of the elite, but the people who used its pages were trying to convince fellow-members of the middle-class with what they considered to be the appropriate language of the day. 'Emigrant' was the standard term for out-migrant, but in the early nineteenth century, two rivals emerged. One was 'immigrant', a more welcoming variant, which was coined in the United States about 1790 and had entered common usage there by 1820.[33] Unlike the US, Britain was primarily a source of migrants, rather than a destination, and 'immigrant' was slower to take off. It was first used in the *Times* in 1835. The second alternative to 'emigrant' was 'settler'. This word was used with its current meaning at least as far back as the seventeenth century, but it was used infrequently. By the nineteenth century it had connotations of a higher status than 'emigrant'. Settlers were distinct from sojourners, slave or convict emigrants, and initially even from lower-class free emigrants. In Australia, 'settlers' were men of capital and, in the 1820s, regarded as the true colonists, to be distinguished from mere labouring '"immigrant" ... though eventually all Australia's immigrants were termed "settlers"'.[34] 'Settler' was used very rarely in the *Times* before 1810, but surged thereafter — actually outnumbering usages of the much better established word 'emigrant' in the 1820s. 'Settler' fell back thereafter, but only to between half and two-thirds of 'emigrant' usage, where it remained until 1890. The *Times* was editorially antagonistic to emigration, at least until the 1830s. It was semantically easing the stigma of emigration despite itself. *Blackwood's Edinburgh Magazine*, fully searchable between 1843 and 1863, used emigrant and settler equally in these years (124 usages to 126).[35]

---

[33] David Hackett Fischer and James C. Kelly, *Away, I'm bound away. Virginia and the Westward Movement* (Richmond, 1993), p. 65.

[34] Richards, *Britannia's Children*, p. 109.

[35] Internet Library of Early Journals.

Usage of words in Times (advertisements excluded):[36]

Decade	'settlers'	'emigrants'
1785-9	2	27
1790s	7	870*
1800s	22	149
1810s	110	192
1820s	280	272
1830s	336	639
1840s	539	1105
1850s	599	1735
1860s	936	1480

*Probably references to French and other Continental émigrés fleeing French Wars.

A revival in the relative usage of 'emigrant' in the 1840s and 1850s may stem from negative English perceptions of the massive Catholic Irish diaspora of those decades. Irish and others might be emigrants, but Britons were *settlers*. This transition from low-status emigrant to higher-status settler, it is suggested, was a key factor in the English exodus dating from 1815.

The new retention of standing despite emigration was buttressed by relatively easy access to legal and political rights in the emigrant destinations. For white males, the western states of America were notoriously democratic and provided easy access to full citizenship. Fully responsible self-government in the British settler colonies did not arrive until the 1840s and 1850s, but settler representation of some kind dated back to 1758 in Nova Scotia. Booster books emphasized that colonial laws and constitutions were similar to those of Britain, as in Upper Canada in 1819. 'Consequently, an Englishman, coming to this province, gives up nothing.'[37] By the 1820s, even the convict colonies of New South Wales and Van Diemen's Land had an element of (unelected) settler representation, as well as cherished legal rights for non-convicts such as trial by jury, and they made the most of it in their booster literature.[38] English advocates of emigration tried explicitly to 'remove from the minds of persons of all

---

[36] *The Times Digital Archive, 1785-1985*, Thomson Gale Databases.

[37] John Strachan, *A visit to the province of Upper Canada in 1819* (Aberdeen, 1820), pp. 137-9.

[38] e.g. Henry Melville, *Van Diemen's Land...* (London, 1833); Henry Walter Parker, *Van Diemen's Land, its rise, progress and present state with advice to emigrants* (London, 1834).

classes that emigration to Canada is banishment ... it is only removal from a part of the British Empire ... to another'.[39] But the status at issue here was not national. English potential settlers in the early to mid nineteenth century might be prejudiced against the Irish, among others, but it is not clear, *pace* Linda Colley, that they were yet British patriots. Around 1820, a brief radical phase in English booster literature, epitomized by the works of William Cobbett, encouraged co-nationals to immigrate to the United States and so escape the oppressions of pre-1832 Britain. This generated a counter-current in its own day, which later became increasingly strong, or at least loud. Why go to the slave-owning madly democratic United States to be mocked, formal British boosters pleaded, when there were much better British-ruled destinations such as Canada or New Zealand? Yet the United States 'captured the great majority of British migrants and capital throughout the nineteenth century'.[40] Informally, what seems to have concerned settlers was not so much their flag but their standing as full citizens, as central members of a central society rather than marginal members of a marginal one. This *settler transition* involved a transfer of metropolitan-ness as well as British-ness, and at first the former outranked the latter.

To briefly place the settler transition in its context, the year 1815 was also a watershed in several other respects. The end of a quarter-century of world war — and of almost 150 years of endemic maritime warfare — suddenly reduced the risk and cost of trans-oceanic travel. Considerable risk remained, as noted above. But after 1815 English ships were not going to be captured by French or American warships or privateers. Insurance rates, crew numbers, and the cost of shipbuilding fell dramatically, and the regularity and reliability of shipping rose through packet services. Coupled with this, the Napoleonic Wars had forced Britain to substitute New Brunswick for its traditional Baltic source of timber. Between 1805 and 1812, British North America's timber exports shot up from 5,000 to 100,000 tons. The new trade not only survived the Peace in 1815, but also profited from it. By 1819, the flow of timber to Britain weighed 240,000 tons, and a massive 417,000 tons by 1825.[41] This probably matched the volume of all trans-Atlantic trade 50 years earlier. As generations of Canadian historians have observed, timber ships returning from Britain in

[39] Quoted in Cowan, *British Emigration to British North America*, p. 205.
[40] Richards, *Britannia's Children*. p.119.
[41] Graeme Wynn, *Timber Colony: A Historical Geography of early nineteenth century New Brunswick* (Toronto, 1981), p. 33.

ballast greatly lowered the cost of emigration. This sudden rise of mass transfer from 1815 extended to money. British overseas investment is estimated to have totaled only £10 million in 1815. In 1816 alone, this total was increased 150% by an outflow of £14.6 million, especially to the United States. By 1850, the total was £208 million, about $US one billion and twenty times the 1815 figure.[42] It was not Wakefield who initiated the alchemy of migrants *plus* money.

There was also a marked rise in the mass transfer of ideas and information. The early nineteenth century in Britain witnessed a 'print revolution'. Technological advances included all-metal presses from 1795, mechanized paper-making from 1803, and steam-powered printing presses, first used in London in 1814 and extended to American newspapers by 1823.[43] Cheap chapbooks, cheap or free religious tracts, and cheap periodicals, the 'penny press', also proliferated from about 1805. 'The phenomenon of the unsought mass audience ... first appeared in the early nineteenth century'.[44] The number of newspapers in Britain burgeoned from 1800, and its only rival in this field was the United States. In 1810, about 21 million individual newspaper issues a year were produced in the British Isles; and roughly the same number in the United States. By 1821, the figures were 56 million and 80 million respectively.[45] There was also a huge rise in postal services, especially in English-speaking countries. In the United States, post offices multiplied like amoeba from 75 in 1790 to 13,500 in 1840 — twice as many as Britain and five times as many as France.[46]

Accessing all this, of course, required literacy, and this was a time when literacy rates in England were increasing. 'The present consensus is ... that by 1840 between 67% and 75% of the British working class had

---

[42] Lance E. Davis and Robert E. Gallman, *Evolving Financial Markets and international capital flows; Britain, the Americas, and Australia, 1865-1914* (Cambridge, 2001), pp. 55, 64.

[43] Patricia Anderson, *The Printed Image and the Transformation of Popular Culture, 1790-1860* (Oxford, 1991), p. 2; Francis Sheppard, *London 1808-1870: The Infernal Wen* (London, 1971), p. 181; Allan Pred, 'Manufacturing in the American Mercantile City, 1800-1840', *Annals of the Association of American Geographers*, 56 (1966) pp. 307-38.

[44] John P. Klanchard, *The Making of English Reading Audiences, 1790-1832* (Madison, Wisc., 1987), p. 172.

[45] Charles G. Steffen, 'Newspapers for free; the economics of newspaper circulation in the early republic', *Journal of the Early Republic*, 23 (2003), pp. 381-419.

[46] Daniel R. Headrick, *When Information came of age: technologies of knowledge in the age of reason and revolution, 1700-1850* (New York, 2000), p. 190.

achieved rudimentary literacy... [with] a particularly rapid growth in the first few decades of the nineteenth century.'[47] This consensus is convenient for this essay, but unfortunately not convincing. Scholars still tend to use the signing of marriage registers as a proxy for literacy, and being able to sign your name did not mean you could read or write well. On the other hand, the study of literacy as a means of information transfer is not the same as the study of literacy for itself, or as a proxy for social capital. Literacy as mass communication does not require universal or even majority literacy. There is abundant evidence of letters and printed matter being read *to* people in the early nineteenth century. Sergeant-Major William Cobbett, a pioneer of literature for the working-class from 1816, was 'intensely aware [that] his writings were likely to be more often read aloud than silently', and designed his text accordingly.[48] One immigrant letter was 'read at the village inn and at the Methodist Chapel every Sunday until it was nearly worn out'.[49] It may be that this moment of intersection between literacy and orality was particularly fertile ground for change in folk ideology. Parsons and preachers had long given the lower classes indirect access to literacy, but from the early nineteenth century virtually all lower class communities, neighbourhoods, and even families had literati of their own.

After the rise of mass transfer around 1815, people and money, things and thoughts, all ceased to trickle across oceans and began to flow. The discourse of emigration could now reach far more people, but how precisely did it manage to move them, and does its effort reveal a mass ideology of emigration? Formal emigration literature varied greatly in many ways, but as Robert Grant has recently observed it also displayed a 'curious consistency'.[50] Booster books normally portrayed themselves as guides, manuals, or handbooks, works of information specializing in hard fact, replete with gazetteers, and lists of statistics, wages and prices. But this was usually interwoven with attempts to capture the imaginations of their readers. The trick was to attach emigration to pre-existing hopes and

---

[47] R. S. Schofield, 'Dimensions of illiteracy in England. 1750-1850' in Harvey J. Graff, *Literacy and Social Development in the West. A Reader* (Cambridge, 1981), p. 201. See also David Vincent, *Literacy and Popular Culture in England, 1750-1914* (Cambridge, 1989) and *The Rise of Mass literacy: reading and writing in modern Europe* (Malden, MD, 2000).

[48] Vincent, *Literacy and Popular Culture*, p. 243. See also Klanchard, *English Reading Audiences*, p. 122.

[49] Michael Krause, 'Across the Western Sea', *Journal of British Studies*, 1 (1962) pp. 91-114.

[50] Robert D. Grant, *Representations of British Emigration* (Basingstoke, 2005).

to detach it from pre-existing fears. On the fearful front, we have seen that emigration was successfully detached from its low-status 'emigrant' past and attached to a higher-status 'settler' future. Emigrants no longer needed to fear being seen as part of an 'excrementitious mass'.[51] Settler status, standing as a proper person, a full citizen, was among the mass transfers rising from 1815. Success on the hopeful front is less easy to measure, but attempts to appeal to pre-existing images of hope were made.

Utopian or paradise imagery, which invoked a linked cluster of aspirations, was very common. Writers did not portray destinations as heaven above, but they did regularly invoke the Biblical heaven on earth, the Promised Land of Canaan, flowing with milk and honey, complete with natives to dispossess. In formal booster literature, this fused with more secular ideas of Arcadia, fertile virgin lands in which lower class emigrants would become self-sufficient yeomen farmers through hard work and self-restraint. Utopias proper overlapped with this, but allowed more room for the higher classes and the healthy city, as in the organized colonization leading to instant civilization proposed by Wakefield. Just how influential this nominal utopianism was is hard to say, but it did seek to exploit the spirit of the age. Some looked upward to heaven for their promised land; some looked backward to an idealized 'world we have lost'. Others looked forward, to a religious millennium or a socialist paradise on earth. Emigration literature encouraged a people prone to seek promised lands to look *outward* for them — to the English-speaking new societies.

At the more specific level, formal and informal settler literature, or settlerism for short, agreed that emigration would enhance the lives of common folk through better wages, and provide them with opportunities for social promotion. Formal versions consistently emphasized one type of promotion: becoming a yeoman freeholder, owner-operator of a small-medium farm. The yeoman, of course, had a special status in British and American thought from the late eighteenth century if not before. Historians today accept that becoming a yeoman, acquiring a freehold farm, was the leading motivation for nineteenth century British emigration.[52] It certainly was one key motivation, but exclusive emphasis on it may be misplaced. Emigration was higher in frontier booms, when land was expensive, and lower in busts, when it was cheap. Land-ownership,

---

[51] James Payne, quoted in Ken Lewandowski, '"A new transportation for the penitentiary era"; some Household Words on free emigration', *Victorian Periodicals Review*, 26 (1993), pp. 8-18.

[52] e. g. Charlotte Erickson, *Invisible Immigrants* (London, 1973), p. 27; Richards, *Britannia's Children*, pp. 44, 62.

which was indeed widespread on settler frontiers, is too readily conflated with possession of a viable farm. Land might be urban, and rural land owned might be undeveloped or semi-developed, or too small or isolated for full-time farming. Occupational fluidity was the rule, especially in booms; 'farmers' were often just as much foresters, or contractors, or labourers on roads, canals, and railroads. Formal settlerism emphasized self-sufficiency and the sanctity of freehold, and held that all working emigrants could hardly wait to hew their yeoman-hold from the wilderness. Informally, settlers were often willing to compromise with leasehold and tenancy, which freed capital to develop the farm.

They did not care much about self-sufficiency — the alleged 'desire to make their own consumer goods'[53] — but sought independence from masters, not markets. Informally, independence could come from a tavern, a store, or a carting business as well as from a farm. The potential yeoman was sometimes reluctant to fling himself into the wilderness if conditions were not prime. Formal settlement literature often complained about migrants hanging about in ports and cities, leaking virtue. When conditions were prime, aspirant yeomen were *more* impatient than formal settlerism prescribed. Wakefield wanted migrants to serve a substantial term as wage labourers and servants while saving to obtain farms, hence his high price for land. Even in the Wakefieldian settlements of South Australia and New Zealand, migrants failed to oblige him. The yeoman motive was by no means absent in informal settlerism, but it was renegotiated, diluted, and coupled with other motivations less recognized by the historiography.

An intense but qualified egalitarianism pervades letters back. Class, the existence of masters and men, was accepted; but deference and condescension were emphatically rejected. Manual workers were more valued; labour had more dignity. There were far fewer of the trappings of inequality, though not necessarily much more of equality itself. 'Jack was as good as his master' in dress and address. Caps were less doffed; forelocks less tugged. 'Sirs' were rare; 'Misters' were mutual. 'Workmen are not afraid of their masters, they all seem as equals.'[54] 'You feel as good as your employer and on a par with them, saying what you like … every one is alike, master and man.'[55] 'Jack is as good as his master here.

---

[53] Charlotte Erickson, *Leaving England* (Ithaca, 1994), pp. 50-52.

[54] William Cobbett, *The Emigrants Guide in ten letters addressed to the Tax-Payers of England* (London, 1829), p. 66.

[55] Quoted in Van Vugt, *Britain to America*, p. 12.

Masters are glad to get servants, and come to hire them; no running after masters.'[56]

Much was made of the fact that masters worked with their men and mistresses with their maids. This might lead to closer supervision and therefore harder work, but it also raised the status of manual labour. 'The working class call no man master — indeed, they are all the working class — it is no uncommon thing to see a judge ploughing, or a general getting potatoes'.[57] 'An extraordinary degree of social equalitarianism is perceptible everywhere. The squire yoking his oxen, the major of militia selling turkeys.'[58] This was not a matter of full equality.

> Here no man thinks himself your superior. There is no disgusting and improper equality, for character has its weight and influence, and the man who is really your superior does not plume himself on being so.[59]

At least one formal booster hoped, in 1819, that this change was merely nominal. 'Servants, let me observe, are called "helps": if you call them servants they will leave you without notice.' This, like the use of 'boss' for 'master', was 'the alteration of *names* while *things* remain the same'.[60] But this was wishful thinking. Perhaps the most consistent *cri de coeur* of the settler gentry, from North America in 1815 to Australasia in 1914, was the difficulty of obtaining and keeping deferential domestic servants. William Cobbett suggested that the aversion to the world 'servant' was peculiarly American, resulting from its association with slaves.[61] But the aversion was just as strong in New Zealand, where there had never been slavery — or convicts for that matter. There, as in North America, the English practice of calling permanent farm labourers 'farm

---

[56] In Wendy Cameron *et al* (eds), *English Immigrant Voices. Labourer's Letters from Upper Canada in the 1830s* (Montreal, 2000), p. 167.

[57] In John Knight, *Important Extracts from … letters written by Englishmen in the United States of America* (Manchester, 1818), pp. 42-43.

[58] Quoted in W. S. MacNutt, *New Brunswick. A history 1784-1867* (Toronto, 1963), pp. 213, 280-1, 281.

[59] *Noble's Instructions to Emigrants. An attempt to give a correct account of the United States of America* (Boston, 1819), pp. 75-6.

[60] Henry Bradshaw Fearon, *Sketches of America…*, third edition (London, 1819), p. 31.

[61] William Cobbett, *Journal of a year's residence in the United States of America* (Fontwell, Sussex, 1964), (original 1819), p. 188.

servants' was quickly ditched.[62] Aversion to domestic service was not gradually acquired, but instant, and Cobbett was right about this. 'Imagine not that you will find English servants more submissive; liberty and equality are in the *atmosphere*: the English catch them, the moment they land.'[63]

Informal settlerism also stressed equality of dress, at least on Sundays; access to home ownership (not necessarily farm ownership); and access to riding horses, which were much more numerous in proportion to people in settler destinations than in Britain. The right and capacity to hunt, shoot, and fish was another theme of letters back.[64] 'This is a fine country, and a free country; you can go where you like here, and no one to hinder; shoot anything as you see'.[65] 'We have nobody to run over us here, and to order us out of their fields. We can take our gun, and go a deer hunting, when we likes; so we hope all that can come, will have heart enough'.[66] 'My son James goes a hunting and shooting, and I can eat partridge as well as any knave in England'.[67] Formal settlerism also alluded to the fact that 'the sports of the field are free to all' but without anything like the same frequency or relish.[68]

Letters back also placed great emphasis on the abundance of food, especially meat. This was not a merely a matter of more food, the absence of hunger, but something deeper. Meat was a high status food in many societies, and this was especially so in Britain, where 'Britons, roast beef and liberty' had long been associated.[69] 'Dear sister you know that we could hardly get a taste of meat in England, but now we can roast a quarter of meat'. 'We have roast meat twice in one day'. 'We always buy a quarter or a half of meat, instead of a pound or two'.[70] 'We bought a QUARTER OF A COW at three farthings a pound.'[71] One might think that the prevalence

---

[62] James Belich, *Making Peoples* (Auckland, 1996), p. 331.

[63] Cobbett, *Emigrants Guide*, p. 101.

[64] In Horst Rossler 'The dream of Independence: The "America" of England's North Staffordshire potters', in Dirk Hoerder and Horst Rossler (eds), *Distant Magnets: Expectations and Realities in the Immigrant Experience* (New York and London, 1993), p. 143.

[65] In Cameron *et al*, *Immigrant Voices*, p. 67.

[66] *Ibid.*, p. 115.

[67] In Knight, *Important Extracts*, second series, p. 47.

[68] Charles F. Grece, *Facts and Observations respecting Canada and the United States of America* (London, 1819), xiii.

[69] Ben Rogers, *Beef and Liberty. Roast beef, John Bull, and the English nation* (London, 2003).

[70] In Cameron *et al*, *Immigrant Voices*, pp. 41, 172, 231.

[71] In Rossler, 'The "America" of England's North Staffordshire potters', p. 138.

of hunting made game the meat of choice; instead the emphasis was usually on prime cuts of butcher's meat, with cheaper cuts discarded. Emigrants to Canada in 1820 'gave meat to their cats and dogs that they once would have been happy to eat themselves'.[72] Emigrants to Australia in the 1850s played the same tune. 'Here is very great waste of beef and mutton, it being cheap and everyone wants the best joints.'[73] 'While I write, I have a fat sheep hanging up in my back place, and we actually throw to the dogs enough meat that would keep a family in England.'[74] The symbolism was not lost on Lord Dalhousie, Governor of Canada in the 1820s, who bemoaned the workers habit of eating 'beef steaks at breakfast, dinner, & supper', and linked it to the 'utmost American impudence. Every man ... is laird here'.[75]

There was also the matter of how the meat was eaten. 'We do not have to take a piece of dry bread, in our pockets, and go to our 6d a day work here; but we go to eat with our master and mistress; and have the best the world can afford.' 'We do not sit under the hedge to eat a bit of bread and cheese, but go in doors, and have the best that the country affords.'[76] 'When I go to work for a man, I sit at the table with the family and Jack is as good as his master.'[77]

> They don't put up dinners in this Country, but they dine along with masters and the mistresses as you call them in England, but they will not be called so here, they are equals-like and if hired to anybody they call them their employers.[78]
>
> It is no use of high spirited farmers wishing to come out to this country; for they will not get their servants to wait upon them as at home, and to sit down at second table to eat their crumbs. The servant is made equal with his master, in all respects of that kind, and not treated ... as dogs.[79]

---

[72] Johnston, *British Emigration Policy*, p. 55.

[73] James Jupp, *The English in Australia* (Cambridge, 2004), p. 177.

[74] Dennis, Hitch, 'Cambridgeshire emigrants to Australia, 1842-1874: a family and community perspective', *Family and Community*, 5 (2002), pp. 85-97, 92.

[75] Quoted in D. A. Sutherland, '1810-1820. War and Peace' in Phillip A. Buckner and John G. Reid (eds), *The Atlantic Region to Confederation* (Toronto, 1994), p. 240.

[76] In Cameron *et al*, *Immigrant Voices*, pp. 87, 123.

[77] Quoted in Cobbett, *Emigrants Guide*, p. 75.

[78] Cameron *et al*, *Immigrant Voices*, pp. 40-41.

[79] *Ibid.*, p. 148.

This informal settlerism echoed some elements of a well-known English folk utopianism generally labelled 'Merrie England', or 'the world we have lost'. Both Merrie England and the settler destinations were alleged to deliver good food, contentment, and mutual respect between master and man. The two diverged on the acceptance of hierarchy. The exchange of paternalism for deference between master and man, was prominent in at least middle class constructions of Merrie England, but absent in informal settlerism.[80] The settler utopia seems more akin to that amorphous and egalitarian English folk Eden identified by Patrick Joyce. 'What is evident in English popular culture', argues Joyce, 'is the extraordinary force and longevity of the vision of a lost Eden'. Joyce examined a wide range of popular songs, verses and the like, and noted 'a utopianism that irradiates the whole literature'. It aspired to 'justice and reconciliation', and was willing to tolerate 'high ups' as long as they 'do not put on airs and act as ordinary, decent folk'. Decent food, including prime meat, was a major symbol.[81] Other sources confirm that folk literature emphasized 'equal rights and equal laws'.[82]

This utopian myth may have had a kernel of truth, much more recent than Merrie England's hazy dating to before the Norman Yoke. It is widely, though not universally, accepted among British social historians that the early nineteenth century was a time of 'a widening gulf between masters and men'.[83] The attitudes of gentry and farmers to the poor 'increasingly included the rejection of the paternalistic code of previous centuries in favour of market and individualistic values'.[84] Contemporaries noted the shift. In 1819, one wrote 'we take the most alarming signs of the times to be, that separation of the upper and middle classes of the community from the lower, which is now daily and visibly

[80] 'Merrie England', Jacqueline Simpson & Steve Roud (eds), *A Dictionary of English Folklore* (Oxford, 2000), *Oxford Reference Online*.

[81] Patrick Joyce, *Visions of the People* (Cambridge, 1991), pp. 283, 297-8.

[82] Robert D. Storch, 'Please to remember the 5th of November. Conflict, solidarity and public order in southern England, 1815-1860' in Storch (ed.), *Popular Culture and Custom in 19th Century England* (1982), p. 79.

[83] David Vincent, 'The decline of oral tradition in popular culture' in Storch (ed.), *Popular Culture*, p. 38.

[84] John E. Archer, *Social unrest and popular protest in England 1780-1840* (Cambridge, 2000). See also W. A. Armstrong, 'The countryside', in F. M. L. Thompson (ed.), *The Cambridge Social History of Britain, 1750-1950*, 3 vols (Cambridge, 1990), 1; Lenore Davidoff, 'The Family in Britain' in *ibid.*, 2.

increasing'.[85] The following year, another noted the decline of 'kindly and immediate dependence' of the lower orders on the upper, and Thomas Carlyle famously alleged an 'abdication on the part of the governors'.[86] Servants were still eating with their masters in 1853, but it had become rare, and the fact was resented in folk ballads.[87] My own guess is that it was not so much the paternalism or the 'kindly dependence' that common folk missed as the sense of being respected or at least valued. Emigrants might ask for help from their betters, but were not polite when it was declined. When a Devonshire carpenter's request for an assisted passage for his wife was rejected by his local poor law commissioners, he responded: 'You Can Just kiss my Ass. I am now in America living in the land of the free.'[88]

There was also, it seems, an increasing constriction of lower class living conditions. It appears that yeomen increased in numbers in the seventeenth century, especially if copyholders with cheap and secure tenancies are included, then declined in the later eighteenth century. The policing of poaching is well known to have increased massively through the nineteenth century.[89] It seems that English working people had indeed once been big meat eaters. 'Circumstantial evidence from the period between 1670 and 1760 suggest that meat eating was widespread and commonplace among English people of virtually every class.'[90] It then fell sharply, especially between 1795 and 1820, though this does not necessarily apply to the availability of food in general. There was therefore substance in the legendary land of lost content, much more than many historians' versions concede. Truth and legend mixed were more potent than either alone.

Formal settlerism could handle workers enjoying prime cuts and hunting. It was less comfortable with the paucity of deference and patriotism. But most subversive of all informal settlerism's themes was the idea of abundance without work. Formal settlerism always stressed the need

---

[85] Klancher, *Making of English Reading Audiences*, p. 49.

[86] Quoted in Harold Perkin, *The Origins of Modern English Society, 1780-1880* (London, 1969), pp. 180, 183.

[87] Alun Howkins, *Reshaping Rural England 1850-1925* (Harper Collins, 1991), p. 43.

[88] Quoted in Barry Reay, *Rural Englands* (Basingstoke, 2004), p. 159.

[89] Robert C. Allen, *Enclosure and the Yeoman. The Agricultural Development of the South Midlands 1450-1850* (Oxford, 1992); Overton, *Agricultural Revolution in England*.

[90] B. A. Holderness 'Prices, Productivity, and Output' in G. E. Mingay (ed.), *The Agrarian History of England and Wales, 1750-1850* (Cambridge, 1989), 6, p 157. See also K. G. Fenelon, *Britain's Food Supplies* (London, 1952), pp. 4-6.

for hard work; informal settlerism emphasized that fertility and abundance diminished it. 'I cannot describe to you the ease in which every one seems to live.'[91] 'People get rich here without much trouble or exertion.' 'Every laboring man's house abounds with plenty.' 'The farmer reckons to work three months in the year'.[92] 'The people will not work, they can live with the greatest of ease and don't want to be rich.'[93] This was anathema to formal settlerism. In 1819, an emigrant's guide indignantly repudiated a periodical article which claimed that, on Prince Edward Island, 'industry is not required'; 'amusement is the sole duty of the farmer'; 'the poorest families will set down to a roast pig, wild ducks, and salmon, every day'.[94]

Here again, there was an element of the 'world we have lost'. 'Immigrants hoped they would find the leisure on American farms they believed their forefathers had enjoyed in Britain.'[95] A recent study suggests a big increase in English working hours 1760-1800, and a smaller increase 1800-1830.[96] This was accompanied by a well-known decline in traditional holidays. Both were part of an 'industrious revolution' which increased family incomes, but the loss of freedom was resented. On the settler frontier, virgin land, especially forested land freshly cleared by fire, was very fertile for the first few years. It did yield abundant crops and one encounters numerous references to giant vegetables. Moreover, most frontier farms were surrounded by unoccupied land — a vast informal common — and livestock could make a good if semi-feral living on this. In Illinois in 1818, claimed one letter back, most settlers 'cultivate but little land, but live principally on hunting, and breeding cattle and hogs; this is done with the greatest of ease, they being surrounded by land possessed of no-one'.[97] Samuel Crabtree wrote to his brother from Virginia in the same year along similar lines,

> I believe I saw more peaches and apples rotting on the ground than would sink the British fleet. I was at many plantations where

---

[91] In Noble's *Instructions to Emigrants*, p. 73.

[92] In Knight, *Important Extracts*, pp. 20-21 30, 32.

[93] In Knight, *Important Extracts*, second series, pp. 28, 47.

[94] Anon., *Information to emigrants: an account of the island of Prince Edward...* (London, [c1819]), pp. 10-17.

[95] Charlotte Erickson, *Invisible Immigrants*, pp. 28-29.

[96] Hans-Joachim Voth, 'New Estimates of Labor Input in England, 1760-1830', *Journal of Economic History*, 61(2001), pp. 1065-82.

[97] In Knight, *Important Extracts*, Second Series, p. 28.

they no more know the number of their hogs than myself. Sometimes a sow, having been two or three months in the woods, returns home with ten or twelve pigs.[98]

There is, it seems to me, more here than a folk memory of the extra few hours of leisure available in the eighteenth century. There is an echo of that oldest, most amorphous and fantastic, and most lower class of utopias — the Land of Cockaygne, '*the* popular or folk utopia', where omelets grew on trees and spit-roast pigs begged to be eaten. Here, abundance did not require work; consumption was not moderated by self-restraint. All were equal because everyone had all they wanted but, just in case, lords had to do seven years penance in a pigsty before being permitted entry. 'It was a penance that the peasant had already performed'. Life in Cockaygne was 'like a perpetual wedding day'.[99] In Crabtree's Virginia, 'there is enough and to spare of everything a person could desire ... the poorest families adorn the table three times a day like a wedding dinner'.[100]

This essay suggests that there was an English ideology of migration, articulated from 1815 and corresponding with the actual rise of English emigration, with each probably helping cause the other in chicken-egg fashion. For higher and lower classes alike, this 'settlerism' removed or at least alleviated the old stigma attached to emigration. Formal and informal versions alike offered workers better wages and more opportunities for promotion to middle class independence, with the former stressing yeoman freeholds more than the latter. Formal and informal versions diverged more on the other alleged benefits of emigration. The informal stressed egalitarianism, though not equality, the enhanced dignity of manual labour, and the capacity to hunt, consume prime meat, and possess leisure through abundance. Formal settlerism could compromise on much of this, though with less enthusiasm, especially bemoaning the dislike of domestic service. Where it could hardly compromise at all was on the leisure issue. It shared a wider middle-class concern to promote the work ethic among the lower orders, and plenty acquired with ease was subversive of this. Still more tentatively, I suggest that this informal settlerism was intimately connected to a secular English folk utopianism. This contained elements of 'Merrie England', but was less sentimental and

---

[98] *Ibid.*, pp. 36-8 (Samuel Crabtree to brother, from Wheeling, Virginia, 10 April 1818).
[99] Krishnan Kumar, *Utopia and anti-utopia in modern times* (Oxford, 1987), pp. 7-8; J. C. Davis, *Utopia and the ideal society* (Cambridge, 1981), pp. 20-22.
[100] In Knight, *Important Extracts*, second series, pp. 36-38.

romantic than later (more middle-class?) constructions. In particular, paternalism and at least the appearance of hierarchy were unceremoniously ditched. A more subversive folk utopia was also invoked: the Land of Cockayne, which delivered ease as well as plenty.

This essay, part of a wider study of Anglo-American settlement, raises at least as many questions as it answers. Did a settler transition, entwined with folk utopianism, occur among non-English mass migrants? What happened to settler utopianism in the destination lands — are there echoes of it in American and British colonial populism and folk constructions of 'national character'? There might also be echoes in late nineteenth and twentieth century Britain. British ruling elites increasingly had to compete with settler destinations to keep someone to rule, by broadening suffrage, providing welfare, compromising with unionism and facilitating wider home and farm ownership — all characteristics of the settler societies. Might settler utopianism have further developed in the new worlds, then ricocheted back to sender in the old? How did settlerism interact with the other 'isms' of the day — racism, radicalism, socialism and religious evangelism? These questions cannot be answered if British history is located solely in Old Britain. Historians of the English common people in the nineteenth century need to pay more attention to their subjects' most dramatic mass action: emigration. You cannot tell the history of the nineteenth century British Isles, let alone that of the British and Irish peoples, without the twenty million who got out.

Chapter 12

A Colonial Way with Welfare?

David Thomson

Arguments over reform of the poor law periodically convulsed large sectors of British society across the nineteenth century. The questions who had a right to what assistance, when and under which conditions, attracted enormous attention as debate and agitation intensified and eased across the years, with the 1790s, 1810s, 1860s and 1890s being decades of especial activity. But most critically, the 1830s and 1840s saw the triumph of classical economics and evangelical values, as substantial reform of the poor law — 'reform' of public welfare always means cutting spending and entitlements — took place after very public inquiries in England (1834), Ireland (1838) and Scotland (1845).

In these same decades, too, new British settler societies were being established, in Australia and New Zealand in particular, and self-government soon followed. It is no surprise therefore that the poor law debates of 'Home' carried into these new settlements, their tiny governments and early legislative acts. Standard poor law issues soon arose — people fell sick, had accidents, lost jobs or deserted families in the New World just as in the Old. Colonial arguments about public support for the needy went to the heart of how new settlers saw themselves, their emerging states and their futures. And they have gained a modest place in the subsequent historiographies, though perhaps a lesser place than is their due.

But what strikes the reader of these national tales is how blind each remains to its fellows. Each looks inward most of all; then to Britain and its poor laws to varying extents, largely ignoring developments elsewhere. That provides our starting point — how much did New Zealand, Australia or others share or not share, as they set their paths on public welfare, that is on balancing individual, family and wider communal responsibilities for the needy? In Britain the answers were structured around the long-standing Poor Law — what would happen in new lands?

Comparative history is never easy, and of public welfare is made doubly difficult because its historians tend to impressions and rhetoric, rather than counting or measuring. Friendly societies are said to have 'flourished wondrously' in Australia, poor relief in early nineteenth century Upper Canada is rated loosely against that in England, or charity in Australia is described as being like or not like relief back Home, with little attempt to weigh what actually got done anywhere. Ambitions here must be modest.[1] By focusing on England and New Zealand in particular, I want to suggest a possible wider 'model' of New World welfare arrangements. Just where New Zealand might sit among nineteenth settler societies is speculated upon, but remains to be tested more rigorously.

We might expect the new British colonies to have followed similar paths, for they had much in common. The timings of settlement were close. Institutions of colonial then of self-government were copied. Key personnel were shared, an excellent example being George Grey who was successively governor of South Australia, New Zealand, the Cape Colony, and New Zealand for a second time, leaving his stamp on welfare legislation and practice in each place. Technological developments — steam shipping, the telegraph, railways — eased the exchange of goods, persons and ideas. Settler capitalism, quickly binding the farthest new settlements into a global economy centred upon London, shaped each of them powerfully. And the origins and character of the settlers were similar, with the exception perhaps of the early convict era in parts of Australia. A few more Irish and Roman Catholics went to Eastern Australia than elsewhere, a few more Scots and Presbyterians to New Zealand and parts of Canada, and more of the poorest made the shorter and cheaper passage to North America than further afield. But there was not a lot in it. Let us start, then, by noting a few shared welfare patterns.

One, perhaps inevitably, was the pervasive influence of the English poor law. It was referred to repeatedly, as a marker of what should or should not be repeated. Quite simply, we cannot make sense of colonial welfare debates without close attention to the English poor law of the 1830s and 1840s in particular. The Scottish poor law, perhaps more unexpectedly, was seldom referred to even though it was different from the

---

[1] The phrase is from J. Hirst, 'Keeping colonial history colonial: the Hartz thesis revisited', *Historical Studies*, 21 (1984), p. 85; R. Baehre, 'Paupers and poor relief in Upper Canada', *Canadian Historical Association: Historical Papers* (1981), pp. 57-80. Among the many who have considered how similar/dissimilar were Australian relief efforts and the English poor law are Hirst; R. Bereen, '"And thereby to discountenance mendacity". Practices of charity in early nineteenth century Australia', in M. Wearing and R. Bereen (eds), *Welfare and Social Policy in Australia: the distribution of advantage* (Sydney, 1994), pp. 3-22; B. Dickey, *No Charity There. A Short History of Social Welfare in Australia* (Melbourne, 1980).

English and was the more direct Home experience of substantial fractions of settlers.[2] It had been the focus of much favourable attention from English poor law reformers through the first decades of the nineteenth century. Scotland, in the eyes of many, had the better welfare balance (that is, more self-reliance, less public and more family and charitable assistance), and its leading advocate of a minimal poor law, Rev. Thomas Chalmers, was often described as the most influential man in all Britain on welfare matters.[3] Yet while overt references to Scottish practices were few in colonial debates, key 'lessons' from it were perhaps learned nevertheless, for as we shall see something closer to a Scottish way with welfare than an English one did emerge in the New World. The Irish poor law seemed not to figure in any new world discussions, perhaps because the Irish were relatively poor and powerless, an Irish poor law was a very recent development, it was remembered unhappily by the Irish abroad as a harsh and hated imposition by English rulers, and because Irish poverty, famine and land laws were seen as peculiar and so of little wider relevance.

Opposition to a poor law appears widespread among settlers in both North America and Australasia, though the insistence that there be no poor law at all was perhaps heard loudest in the southern hemisphere. To settlers the cry of 'no poor law' meant primarily that there must be no legal right to public assistance, and no compulsory taxes or rates to fund such a thing. The objections were moral above all — a legal right to aid would encourage idleness, loss of self-respect and irresponsibility, as well as bring economic ruin to those who had to pay for it all. A New Zealand Minister of Immigration voiced the standard objections in an 1877 debate as

> the class requiring assistance would begin to consider that they had a right to demand the money, which was collected by means of a poor rate, whereas they ought rather to feel that any assistance they obtained was given as charity.[4]

A future Premier and Chief Justice put it more bluntly as 'I consider [a right to public assistance] to be a most dangerous principle for any state

---

[2] Good introductions to the Scottish poor law are R. A. Cage, *The Scottish Poor Law, 1745-1845* (Edinburgh, 1981); and R. Mitchison, *The Old Poor Law in Scotland* (Edinburgh, 2000).
[3] An excellent introduction to arguments about poverty and poor relief in that era remains J. R. Poynter, *Society and Pauperism: English Ideas on Poor Relief, 1795-1834* (London, 1969).
[4] *New Zealand Parliamentary Debates*, 24 (27 July 1877), pp. 73-74.

to affirm'.⁵ When assistance was absolutely necessary, as all conceded would happen from time to time, it must be met by family first of all, then by the informal and local charity of friends and neighbours. Any assistance would be short-term, controlled, meagre, and designed to get the temporary unfortunate back on his or her own feet quickly.

Things seldom worked out so neatly of course. In the early years in Australasia colonial governors or emigration companies often had to give direct assistance to large numbers to meet unemployment, bankruptcy, even starvation, since private resources were so few. By the second and third decades of settlement, as populations and wealth grew, assistance typically became more organised: governments built hospitals and lunatic asylums with wider sheltering functions than their namesakes back home, churches established charities, and concerned citizens founded benevolent associations to channel aid-giving and receiving. All were soon government-supported, with pound-for-pound subsidies and the like, but the emphasis upon 'charity' rather than 'right' remained central. Institutional titles invariably included the words 'Benevolent' or 'Charitable' to stress this very point, governments were kept out of management, poor law terminology was studiously avoided, and no legislation granted entitlements to anything. The result was an untidy mix called 'Charitable Aid' in parts of Australia and in New Zealand, or 'Benevolence' elsewhere. It was definitely not the poor law as the English understood it. Nor was it Scottish, though in its muddle, miserliness, and emphasis upon church, family and charity, it did look more Scottish than English.⁶

In Canada, as in much of the United States too, things looked similarly muddled though the patterns were more complex and in some respects closer to those of the Old World. Most importantly, a number of the eastern settlements there had been founded rather earlier, when the poor law was more accepted and less reviled, and it had migrated across the Atlantic as a normal part of the transfer of British (and French) peoples and institutions. Formal poor laws had been legislated in the seventeenth and eighteenth centuries in many of the eastern settlements that would form the new United States, while Canada got a real mix. Nova Scotia formalised a poor law in legislation in 1763 and New Brunswick in 1786 for example, but Upper Canada (Ontario) pointedly did not when legis-

---

⁵ *Ibid.*, p. 75.

⁶ Good surveys of these early years include M. Tennant, *Paupers and Providers. Charitable Aid in New Zealand* (Wellington, 1989); and Dickey, *No Charity There*.

lating on relief in the 1790s.[7] Ontario later instituted elements of a statutory poor law, for example when it passed a House of Industry Act in 1837 to establish government-run relief institutions, but there was never a fuller English-style poor law there.[8] The expectation that public assistance would be minimal, and secondary to family support and charity, was deep-rooted across nineteenth century North America. But a formal poor law, once in place, proved difficult to dislodge, and it remained in large parts of the continent as the frame around which communities met their obligations to the needy, even as they retrenched on these in the later nineteenth century. The poor law also migrated westward, with western states and provinces in turn adapting the legal codes of older eastern ones.

In short, there seems to have been a shared New World experiment with minimal formal public welfare in the nineteenth century, but it took two broad forms largely as a result of the different timing of settlement. The Australasian version was perhaps the more 'pure' and extreme, because less fettered by the past.[9]

Another New World feature was that everywhere the rhetoric seemed harsher and the handouts fewer than in post-1834 England. There were various reasons for this. Many settler leaders were imbued with anti-poor law ideas to an unusual degree — it was part of what drove them to emigrate. This was true, too, of the mass of migrants, who evinced a strong belief in 'getting on', in self-help and self-responsibility in new lands of freedom and opportunity. New Zealand, and Australia after the convict era, gained almost no involuntary or 'desperation' migrants, for the costs of the lengthy trip remained high throughout the century. Canada did perhaps receive more of the poorest, but there too a respectable, upwardly-striving working class and lower middle class settler ethos predominated. Receiving public assistance themselves, or paying taxes to give it to others, was just not part of the settlers' vision for a new life.

There was, too, the apparent feasibility of an anti-welfare stance, given the demographic peculiarities of the first few decades of a new settlement. At Home arguments against public welfare might be all the

[7] The Canadian experience is outlined in D. Guest, *The Emergence of Social Security in Canada* (Vancouver, 1980), pp. 1-38. On Ontario see R. Splane, *Social Welfare in Ontario, 1791-1893: a study in public welfare administration* (Toronto, 1965).

[8] See Baehre, 'Paupers'; and E. A. Montigny, *Foisted Upon the Government? State Responsibilities, Family Obligations and the Care of the Dependent Aged in Late Nineteenth Century Ontario* (Montreal, 1997).

[9] A number of Australian authors make a similar point, including Cage and Hirst.

rage, but it was still hard to cut back when so many depended on it: across broad swathes of South and East England at mid century, for example, half and more of all persons aged 70 or above were Poor Law pensioners, being sustained with regular weekly cash payments and medical supplements, alongside smaller fractions of younger cohorts.[10] These constraints or 'reality checks' did not apply with the same force in the mid-century settlements. Settlers enjoyed relatively high wages and good employment opportunities, and they included few of the elderly, long-term impaired or fatherless families — the expensive claimants of public assistance in all eras — because the very process of long-distance migration tended to keep the most indigent and feeble at home. Britons on the frontier could indulge anti-welfare urges with an ease that older communities simply could not.

The New Zealand experience will help illustrate the vigour of the colonial drive to limit public assistance. Public spending on charitable aid was about 2.4 shillings per annum per head of population around 1890, the first date for which the estimate is possible: in England it had been 10 to 12 shillings early in the century, six to seven shillings at the mid-century low, and about eight in the 1890s. Relative to average earnings or prices or national income, the Old World/New World spending contrast was considerably greater still — about 10 times as much per capita in early nineteenth century England for instance as in late-century New Zealand.[11]

This gulf is clear, equally tellingly, when we look closer at assistance given to specific groups, such as the elderly. In New Zealand's Otago province in the late nineteenth century, for example, charitable aid was more highly organised and widespread than in the rest of the country. Yet even there the fractions of the elderly who were assisted were tiny. Just three percent of Otago men and women over age 70, for instance, received regular outdoor relief in the early 1890s (the earliest records available). Comparisons with England are not simple, because few returns of poor law recipients were published by age, but a few local examples will point up the contrasts. In Bedfordshire in the early 1840s — that is, after the post-

---

[10] Explored further in D. Thomson, 'Provision for the Elderly in England, 1830 to 1908' (unpublished PhD dissertation, University of Cambridge, 1981), and in D. Thomson, 'The Decline of Social Welfare: Falling State Support for the Elderly since early Victorian times', *Ageing and Society*, 4 (1984), pp. 451-82.

[11] Evidence presented more fully in Thomson, *World Without Welfare*, pp. 83-103, and in D. Thomson, 'Workhouse to Nursing Home: Residential Care of Elderly Persons in England since 1840', *Ageing and Society*, 3 (1983), pp. 43-69.

1834 purges — 50-55 percent of all men and women aged 70 or more appear to have been regular poor law pensioners (and a few percent more were 'in care' in the workhouses). The figures were about 40 percent in rural areas of Essex around 1840, 50 percent across the whole of Cambridge county and city around 1870, and even in the notoriously more parsimonious West Midlands and Lancashire could be at 40 percent and more.[12] Following a second severe 'crusade against outdoor relief' in the 1870s and 1880s, the percentages were still 20-25 across Cambridgeshire, rural Essex and industrial and mining Staffordshire, though a few cities elsewhere reported figures down towards the New Zealand levels.

Nor did institutions provide indoor relief to many of the Otago aged, as a possible counter to the lack of outdoor assistance. About four percent of all Otago men over 65 were in the public Benevolent Institution in the 1890s, one half of the English proportion at that date, while for Otago elderly women the proportions indoors were around one in 100, a quarter of the English rate. This meant a new balance of indoor and outdoor relief in New Zealand, in line with the demands of poor law reformers everywhere that if relief must be granted it be so unattractively, even punitively, through incarceration in an institution. Assistance in an institution would always cost more, but that was to be borne for the greater, moral good. In England at mid century nine elderly men were assisted outdoors for every one taken into an institution, or three to one by century's end; in Otago the ratios were reversed, at two indoors for every one out.

One further trademark of poor law reformers everywhere was the insistence that if outrelief had to be granted, it should be given not as cash but in kind — as direct rent payment to a landlord, items of clothing or fuel, or chits for certain approved (non-luxury) foods at specified stores, so as to increase the inconvenience and indignity of it all, and with that the individual's struggle to avoid a request for public assistance. But although routinely deplored, cash payments remained standard in England even at the height of the late-century crusade against outdoor relief: among other things, English officials found relief in kind cumbersome to administer, and the hostility of the poor to it and themselves unrelenting. Yet despite similar pressures in new societies, charitable aid in New Zealand was given in kind rather than as cash — what little was given to the few came in unwelcome forms.[13] In short, by all the familiar yardsticks of nineteenth century anti-poor law rigour, the new colony stood well to the reform

---

[12] Thomson, 'Provision for the Elderly', chs 1 and 6.
[13] Explored more fully in Tennant, ch. 5.

extreme, and continued to do so to century's end.

We have been looking thus far at things which the settlers did and did not take up from Britain. But perhaps more important were their new ventures, which went beyond anything tried at Home, and fell under two headings — new family responsibilities, and the wider 'settlement agenda' within which the 'no poor law' push was embedded.

English law, as many have observed, placed remarkably few obligations upon individuals to assist their relatives, other than their spouses and dependant children.[14] Nor had it done so for a very long time — a situation unusual in Europe, where legal obligations upon kin were typically more specific and enforced.[15] The English Common Law was largely silent on the subject, and the famous Elizabethan Poor Law Act of 1601, the basis of English welfare law down to 1948, gave more the appearance than the substance of familial legal obligation. That long statute set out the rights of destitute citizens to rate-funded public assistance, and it included just one short, late clause on the obligations of family in return. It stated, in effect, that once a person was receiving public assistance, poor law officials might seek through the local courts to recover some of the costs from children and grandchildren, if they were 'of sufficient means'. A series of higher court judgements through the seventeenth and eighteenth centuries had limited even these few obligations quite severely, to mean that only in exceptional circumstances might a very few sons and the extremely rare unmarried daughter be forced to repay the poor law authorities anything.[16]

Poor Law reformers routinely deplored this apparent lack of natural feeling and filial duty — it offended their religious values, indicated a serious lack of personal responsibility or family bonding, and cost the ratepayers far more than was right. But little happened, and reformers always stepped carefully in this delicate area. The authors of the 1832-4 Royal Commission Report on the English poor laws, for example, merely remarked in passing that few parishes anywhere reported support for the elderly from families, regretted that this was so and that so much cost thus wrongly fell to the Poor Law, and left it at that.[17] A few years later, when

---

[14] See e.g. W. W. Garrett, 'Filial Responsibility Laws', *Journal of Family Law*, 18 (1979-80), pp. 793-818.

[15] A short summary of the legal duties of children to support parents in various European countries is given in M. Rheinstein, 'The Duty of Children to Support Parents' in E. W. Burgess (ed.), *Ageing in Western Societies* (Chicago, 1960).

[16] Discussed more fully in D. Thomson, 'I am not my father's keeper: families and the elderly in nineteenth century England', *Law and History Review*, 2 (1984), pp. 265-86.

some enthusiastic post-1834 local poor law officers in England started cutting outrelief to the elderly, pushing more into the new workhouses and pressuring children to pay up as the law allowed, they were reined in by London and told in effect to leave well alone. My analysis of a range of local English poor law and court records suggests that prosecutions for recovery of maintenance costs of elders remained very rare, outside of a few years in the 1870s and 1880s when the campaign against outrelief was at its height. And no changes to the limited laws of family liability were attempted, apart from a late and short-lived 1890 Maintenance of Destitute Parents Act.

But not so in the new settlements. There the legal balance of responsibilities — community or family? — was reversed from the outset, in ways without precedent back in England. In the United States this was achieved through crucial amendments to the poor laws which had been inherited from England, or via explicit additions to their legal codes that specified family obligations beyond just poor law cases. These made clear that in law family support would come first, and public assistance second.[18] In Australasia, of course, legal changes concerning family responsibility could not be bedded in a modified poor law — there was to be no poor law. Family obligation instead entered the law codes through a series of ordinances and acts for the Maintenance of Destitute Persons. Tasmania passed such an ordinance in 1837, New South Wales in 1840, South Australia in 1842, West Australia in 1845, and New Zealand in 1846. The New Zealand example will serve as our illustration here. Its typicality remains to be tested. West Australia and South Australia both passed laws on destitute persons that were very close to New Zealand's in title, purpose, structure and wording, and they passed comparable amendments through the century to extend and strengthen the laws' reach. But the former convict colonies in the East did not, and the enforcement of these laws anywhere in Australian courts has still to be studied. It may be that late-founded New Zealand, the clearest 'child of the 1830s', went to an extreme in its determination to uphold family rather than collective responsibility.[19]

---

[17] S. G. and E. O. A. Checkland (eds), *The Poor Law Report of 1834* (Harmondsworth, 1974), p. 115.

[18] See, e.g. D. R. Mandelker, 'Family Responsibility under the American poor laws', *Michigan Law Review*, 54 (1956), pp. 497-532 and pp. 607-32; S. A. Riesenfeld, 'The formative era of American public assistance law', *California Law Review*, 43 (1955), pp. 175-233.

[19] Commentators on this include P. Gunn, 'Legislating filial piety: the Australian experience', *Ageing and Society*, 6 (1986), pp. 135-167; or Kewley, ch. 1.

The 1846 New Zealand Ordinance for the Support of Destitute Families and Illegitimate Children gave 'any respectable householder' the right to begin action before the Justices on behalf of any 'destitute' person who appeared to have 'near relatives' who could give support. Those relatives could be ordered by the courts to make weekly cash payments direct to the needy person, under threat of fine or imprisonment. 'Destitute' was not specified, but Justices could order payments of up to 20 shillings a week — half to three-quarters of a labouring wage. This indicates that relatives were obliged not merely to meet the most basic of needs, but to sustain a reasonable lifestyle. 'Near relatives' were restricted at this stage to the 'father and grandfather, mother and grandmother, and children', but as the century advanced a series of amendments extended the net to take in stepfathers, stepmothers, brothers, sisters and grandchildren. Uncles, aunts, nieces and nephews were also considered by parliament for inclusion as liable relatives, but these were deemed steps too far.[20]

Powers of investigation and enforcement were extended repeatedly over time, and my research on local court records indicates that these were employed fairly frequently. Sons and some daughters (but no others, except in support of lunatics in an asylum) were ordered by the courts to pay weekly sums of 2/- or 3/- and up to 5/- a week each (up to 20/- a week total per parent) direct to a parent. These maintenance orders ran for many years and even decades, were backed up with fines and imprisonment with hard labour, and continued well into the twentieth century, often with numerous returns to the courts as personal circumstances changed or family members fought amongst themselves.[21] Such a direct right to sue relatives for support, not just for subsistence, simply had no precedent in Britain. It put into law some of the most radical principles underlying anti-poor law thinking in nineteenth century Britain — Thomas Charmers would have been proud, and amazed — and formed a central

---

[20] Discussed more fully in Thomson, *World Without Welfare*, pp. 22-27. South Australia expanded the definition of 'near relative' similarly, but not to include brothers and sisters — in this New Zealand seems to have been at the extreme. The relevant South Australian statute was the Destitute Persons Act, 1881 (44 & 45 *Vic* No. 20), clause 5. The extension of responsibility to siblings and grandchildren occurred also in many states of the United States: see, e.g. J. tenBroek, 'California's dual system of family law: its origins, development and present status', *Stanford Law Review*, 16 (1964), pp. 257-317; R. J. Levy, 'Supporting the aged: the problem of family responsibility' in J. Eekelaar and D. Pearl (eds), *An Aging World: Dilemmas and Challenges for Law and Social Policy* (Oxford, 1989), pp. 253-80.

[21] Thomson, *World Without Welfare*, pp. 144-8.

and distinguishing feature of the colonial experiment in doing without a public welfare system.

But of course, 'no poor law' would only prove viable if alternative means of support were put in place. Individuals and families, if they were to live and thrive in a 'world without welfare', must have the resources to do so. In England in the early nineteenth century, calls for a minimal public welfare ran alongside *laissez-faire* arguments for less rather than more active government: the poor law burden was seen by reformers as a product of governments being too interfering in the free market. But in the new settlements opposition to a poor law was linked inextricably to an expectation of more rather than less interventionist government. 'No poor law' would work, in the settler view, so long as governments did many other things to help make it possible. The settlers felt entitled to this, as a quid pro quo for not having poor law rights as a protective fallback.[22]

Their demands led to the unusually active governments that became a distinguishing feature of new settlements in the nineteenth century.[23] Governments, whether at first the Imperial government in London and its colonial officers, or later the representative and responsible governments of the colonists themselves, were expected to lead and push development in a host of ways. There is little sign of a conscious or consistent plan or ideology behind it all, and no one spoke in favour of 'pump-priming' 'big government', as later ages might call it. Rather, government-led development arose piecemeal, an accumulation of responses to calls for help, investment, regulation, protection and promotion, as settler desires to 'get on' and 'gain a competency' ran up against colonial realities. These included many things — vast distances, hostile native peoples, difficult terrains, tiny numbers, scattered settlements, huge capital costs — and the lack of institutions other than government to organise the settlement effort.

Governments were, first, to acquire large stocks of land for the settlers from the indigenous peoples, quickly, cheaply, ruthlessly, and brutally if necessary. Governments were then to manage the migration process care-

---

[22] The following summarises arguments developed more fully in *ibid.*, pp. 107-28. A similar argument has been outlined for Australia in Hirst, 'Keeping colonial history colonial'.

[23] An early and perceptive observer of this, and one still well worth reading, was W. P. Reeves, *State Experiments in Australia and New Zealand*, 2 vols (London, 1902). Reeves contrasted the 'free play of private enterprise' which characterised the settlement of eighteenth century North America, with the government-managed settlement of nineteenth century Australia and New Zealand, and it is a theme that has been widely accepted in the subsequent historiography.

fully, so as to maintain healthy labour markets in the new settlements — to create 'workingmen's paradises' of high wages, full employment, limited hours, and ready job mobility. To this end, they were to regulate and monitor shipping, so that the long journey out was not too dangerous or unpleasant or off-putting to a steady flow of good migrants. They were to 'select' migrants to ensure a superior colonial stock, by keeping out undesirables — the sick, very poor, characters of low morals, non-British, and non-whites — and by enticing in desirables — young families, rural workers, women, Britons, people of some means. Colonial governments ran a host of recruitment campaigns and subsidy schemes to this end, with agents operating throughout Britain, talking up the benefits of emigrating, meeting prospective settlers, paying their fares, and arranging their departure to the docks. Once in the new country emigrants were met by further government officers, housed in temporary immigrant barracks, helped find jobs, paid passage money to inland districts, or engaged on government public works. And, of greatest importance, governments were expected to control the flows, by speeding up and slowing down immigration as far as was possible given the slow communications and limited government machinery of the day, all so as to maintain full employment and good wages for the settlers.

Further, colonial governments were expected to ease the flow of settlers onto the land and into private ownership. They paid for surveying and land registration, built roads and railways into new districts, gave land away free or sold it at low prices and on deferred terms, and crafted a complex of land laws that favoured new owner-occupiers. The whole process was rather messier than this might suggest, but the result nevertheless was a striking and rapid (if ecologically unsound) transformation of the landscape, and a spread of property ownership that was simply unimaginable back Home. Various studies suggest that half and more of all men owned real estate in nineteenth century New Zealand or Eastern Australia, and that this was similar to levels in North America.[24] Another indicator of wide ownership was the large numbers of nineteenth century men (many fewer women) who were able to retire in middle age or early old age, on the strength of their savings in property primarily.[25] By compar-

---

[24] See Thomson, *World Without Welfare*, pp. 67-80. A summary of a number of these studies appears in M. Fairburn, *The Ideal Society and Its Enemies. The Foundations of Modern New Zealand Society, 1850-1900* (Auckland, 1989), ch. 4.

[25] The best studies of this have been done in the United States. See, e.g. R. Ransom and R. Sutch, 'The labor of older Americans: retirement of men on and off the job, 1870-1937',

ison the settlers cared little for alternative means of saving — banks, friendly societies, life insurance, building societies or annuities. They expected some legal protection for these, even some direct government involvement through state banks or insurance companies, and they probably used these means of thrift to a greater degree than happened back in Britain.[26] But there was no special enthusiasm for these saving instruments — by contrast with the passion for real estate.

And beyond all that lay the broader expectation that governments would promote colonial growth and hence private wealth. Governments were to borrow in London to fund the road building, rail laying, harbour construction, bridging and more that would make land clearing and local industries both possible and profitable. In other words, the infrastructure needed for a new society and economy was a state priority, and governments were often involved very directly in both funding and operation. They ran railways, harbours and shipping lines. They had public works departments, to build and maintain roads, bridges, dams and water schemes — and to soak up surplus labour on relief schemes when private employment was insufficient. The examples could be multiplied — state pensions for soldiers and civilians, government agencies to control pests and promote farmer training, cheap state loans to farmers, protection of local industries through tariffs, government housing and more. It cost a great deal, and settler governments (like settler societies) were heavily in debt, borrowing in London and hoping that the sought-after economic growth would generate the means to repay in time — or at least, the means to go on borrowing. Revenues came from high import duties, land sales, and government trading operations such as running the railways, but there was little enthusiasm for an income tax.

The central point here should be clear. Doing away with formal poor relief was part of a larger new expectation of government. The colonial welfare experiment was buttressed by vigorous governments, which actively promoted settlement, employment and property ownership. Demeaning, demoralising poor law hand-outs were to be replaced with energising, re-moralising hand-ups into independence. It was a social

Journal of Economic History, 46 (1986), pp. 1-30; and 'The decline of retirement in the years before social security: United States retirement patterns, 1870-1940' in R. Campbell and E. Lazear (eds), *Issues in Contemporary Retirement* (Stanford, 1988), pp. 3-37. Canadian evidence points to similar conclusions: see Montigny, *Foisted Upon the Government?*, pp. 26ff.

[26] That was true in New Zealand at least: explored further in Thomson, *World Without Welfare*, pp. 34-67.

vision built around notions of work, property and self-reliance — of a rather blinkered sort, for colonists demanded a great deal of help in their 'self-made' 'independence'.

What became of this colonial welfare experiment? In many respects it succeeded, though in ways perhaps not envisioned by anyone. Viable, lasting, prosperous, healthy, orderly and relatively peaceable societies emerged, though things did not look so good for their aboriginal minorities. Patchy systems of public relief were created to assist the most unfortunate, but in generosity or reach they were kept well short of the English or even the Scottish poor laws, Old or New. Individuals and families were required to, themselves expected to, and did indeed have the resources to care for their own to a degree not seen in nineteenth century Britain. Settlers joined friendly societies, took out life insurance, and accumulated bank savings to a greater degree than back at Home, and held private property to an extent without compare. And charity, of a fairly controlled and controlling nature, became the guiding principle for relief, when own and family resources failed. The proponents of early nineteenth century poor law reform might have been pleased.

But if this was a world without welfare, a child of the 'principles of 1834', it was not what poor law reformers had dreamed of, and they would have been shocked by the dependence upon government that was central to it all. Nor did the experiment really outlast the nineteenth century, even though it continued to shape the welfare states which emerged in the twentieth. Quite quickly, from the 1890s various features of the poor law — though never the name — were reintroduced across New Zealand and Australia. New laws now gave rights to cash benefits via a language of pensions and citizen's rights — to the elderly first of all, then to widows, orphans, some industrial survivors such as miners, later to the unemployed. Rights to handouts returned, and with that the whole debate about 'demoralisation' and 'welfare dependence'.

Critical to this end-of-century turn, at least in Australasia, was prolonged economic depression, bringing the collapse of prices and property values and wide unemployment. This was coupled with rapid population ageing, which saw the proportions of the elderly rise swiftly from the 1870s to about Old World levels by 1900. These developments together revealed major limitations to the colonial welfare experiment. It had run seemingly well for a time, but in peculiarly favourable new-settlement conditions when it was never really tested. Demographic ageing and economic downturn exposed the weaknesses, revealing big numbers without savings or relatives or much to contribute in the labour market, and with families unable or unwilling to support large numbers of elders or other dependants. Twentieth century societies, Old World and New, would once again resort to poor law-like relief practices, and grapple again with long-standing dilemmas of balancing individual, family and wider collective responsibilities in support of the needy.

Conclusion

Chapter 13

Why *Homo Sapiens* had to be Saved by Culture

Peter Munz

As far back as we know and almost certainly much further back, *homo sapiens* has had what we call 'culture'. According to the researches of Kroeber and Kluckhohn the term 'culture' can be understood in about 165 different ways.[1] Most conventionally it is used to refer to those habits and beliefs which are not genetically programmed, but which have to be learnt and taught in every generation.[2] This usage of the term is doubtful because there are many non-human primates who have this kind of culture.[3] I propose to use it in a more stringent way, specifically to refer to all those non-genetic practices and beliefs which are irrational and non-verifiable and which serve to identify a particular group. Culture, in this sense, is unique to *homo sapiens* and can serve as one of the terms defining its sapiential nature. This culture is not the sum total of useful habits, skills and beliefs which are present even in the most primitive societies and which have to be taught and learnt because they are not transmitted genetically. Nor am I thinking of those extremely important and edifying voluntary tail-ends of traditional culture such as literature, poetry, chamber music and opera. Rather I am thinking of 'culture' as the sum of irrational and unverifiable beliefs which serve the purpose of defining a given community in a way which makes it separate and distinct from all other communities. The only feature these traits have in common with what is conventionally called 'culture' is that they, too, are not transmitted genetically.

We have known ever since the Enlightenment that culture in this narrow sense is economically wasteful and a handicap. For example, why do humans build cathedrals rather than simply till fields? Why do they fast from time to time rather than consume more food so that the production of food is encouraged and investors tempted to put more money into it to

---

[1] A. L. Kroeber and C. Kluckhohn, *Culture* (New York, 1952).
[2] Peter J. Richerson and Robert Boyd, *Not by Genes Alone* (Chicago, 2005), p. 5.
[3] S. Kawamura, 'The Process of Sub-Culture Propagation among Japanese Macaques', *Primates*, 2 (1959), pp. 43-60.

create more employment? In general terms, the disadvantages of culture can be summed up under three headings. In the first place there is a cognitive disadvantage, because culturally constrained beliefs are dogmatic and do not allow themselves to be replaced by criticism and rationally founded knowledge. Secondly there is an economic disadvantage, because culturally prescribed habits are wasteful and condemn a large part of the population to poverty, or at least to a standard of living which is lower than necessary. Finally there is a political disadvantage because people outside the confines of a culture are considered to be strangers, that is, potential enemies to be guarded against. Why, then, have humans saddled themselves with culture when they could have improved their lives so much without it? Why have all people always inflicted the self-denying ordinance of culture on themselves?

The conventional answer to these and many similar questions has been that since humans cannot understand the universe and grasp why they exist and how it is that there is a universe in which they are living, they have used their brains to *invent* stories about the universe and their existence in order to make their lives more tolerable. Given the cognitive, economic and political disadvantages of culture, one must comment that the small comfort that might be derived from such make-believe stories about the universe and our existence in it, was a very high and, I would argue, an intolerable price to pay. Without denying the iota of truth which may be in this explanation, I propose to take the problem further. It is not only the universe and our existence in it which we cannot understand, but, more immediately, we cannot understand our own selves, let alone the selves of our fellow men unless we are living in a culture which furnishes the language and, up to a point, the beliefs and premises which that kind of language is capable of inventing.

With this insight we are faced with the crucial question why it is that the human brain cannot understand its own, so called, 'self' and the 'selves' of our fellow men. It has been a convention for many millennia that there is a difference between one's own self — which one can understand very well by introspection — and the selves of others, which, obviously, one cannot understand by introspection. But this distinction between the possibility, let alone the certainty of introspection and whatever it is one has to do to understand others, breaks down when one pays closer attention to the process of introspection. It will then appear that when one is introspecting, one is doing something which is not at all different from what one is doing when one is hypothesising about the inner feelings of others. When so called introspection is recognised not to be different from inspection, one is faced by the question raised above: what is the matter with our human brains which can ask questions about our own and other peoples' selves, but are unable to answer them, unless there is some assistance from the outside in the form of what I have called culture?

The answer must be that the human brain is in several ways maladapted. This premise will seem strange because most people who have thought about this matter have gone with the simple Darwinian conclusion, seemingly following from the doctrine of natural selection, that whatever has evolved must be adapted. If it were not adapted, it would not have been selected for survival. When one comes across specific examples of such alleged adaptation of the human brain, one will find that scientists and thinkers are fairly arbitrary in their description of what constitutes the human brain's adaptation. Thus we have been told recently by Tooby and Cosmides that the human brain is well adapted because it can detect social free-riders and cheats.[4] Alternately, we have been told by Humphrey that the human brain is well adapted because it is able to cheat other members of one's society and thus get a free-ride.[5] Since these and similar conflicting theories of adaptation point to a certain vagueness, not to say downright ignorance, I propose to take a closer look at what neuroscientists have come up with. But first a question about the problematic nature of the view that the brain *is* well adapted. If it is well adapted, why do we find that humans have always surrounded themselves by cultures which are cognitively, economically and politically disabling? It is inexplicable why a well adapted and well functioning brain should engage in the sort of self-denial that is required when it enmeshes itself in a culture.

As one might expect, the advocates of the view that the brain is well adapted tend to make short shrift of the ubiquitous presence of cultures. Toby and Cosmides are inclined to the view that the presence of culture is an illusion and that one can best explain human behaviour without reference to culture.[6] Others, like Steven Pinker, accept that cultures are ubiquitously present, but maintain that such presence is like the icing on the cake,[7] which makes life a bit sweeter, but is not essential. Ernest Gellner, in

---

[4] J. Tooby and Leda Cosmides, 'Psychological Foundations of Culture', in J. H. Barkow *et al.* (eds), *The Adapted Mind* (New York, 1995).

[5] R. Byrne and A. Whiten (eds), *Machiavellian Intelligence. Social Expertise, and the Evolution of Intellect in Monkeys, Apes and Humans* (Oxford, 1988).

[6] J. Tooby and Leda Cosmides, 'The Past explains the Present: Emotional Adaptations and the Structure of Ancestral Environments', *Ethnology and Sociobiology*, 11 (1995), pp. 375-424.

[7] S. Pinker, *How The Mind Works* (London, 1998), p. 522.

his posthumous *Language and Solitude* of 1998,[8] took the bull by the horns. He explained blandly that if it is true that the brain is well adapted enough to allow a use of language which does no more than 'picture' the world we are living in, as Wittgenstein had argued in his *Tractatus*, there would have been no cultures. He suggests that, since there are cultures, we must ask how bad the brain must be to make it necessary to have cultures.

It takes only a little genuine Darwinian thinking to understand that there must be something wrong with the high-handed dismissal of the crucial role of culture. If culture played no vital part, Darwinian thinking forces one to conclude that culture, though it could well have emerged, would not have been universally selected for survival. On Darwinian premises — and I assume that there are no others — there must be a reason not necessarily for the emergence of culture but for its selective retention. Cultures must serve a purpose. I will argue that they serve to compensate for the maladaptations of the human brain.

The human brain is considerably larger than the brain of non-human primates, even of those primates which are closely related to us and with whom we appear to share as much as 94% of genes. Primate brains are well adapted because they are programmed to learn only those things that are available in their niches.[9] This shows that the size of their brains and the complexity of their brains are closely related to what those primates require for survival.[10] The human brain, by contrast, is very large and it seems that its size and its consequent complexity has not developed in response to the niche in which humans are living, but that it has grown spontaneously, driven by its own built-in structure.[11] If this is so, one cannot take it for granted that it is well adapted. On the contrary, one must suppose that it has not been selected because it gave its bearers a better chance of survival. Let me detail two major maladaptations and define the damage they cause.

First, Semir Zeki's *A Vision of the Brain*, shows that the old belief on which so called scientific knowledge used to be founded, namely that one can get correct and certain information about the world by looking at it, cannot stand up to neuroscientific findings. This simple view used to be

---

[8] E. Gellner, *Language and Solitude* (Cambridge, 1998), p. 68.

[9] Katherine Nelson, *Language in Cognitive Development* (Cambridge, 1998), p. 38.

[10] R. Dunbar, 'Coevolution of neocortical size, group size and language in humans', *Behavioral and Brain Sciences*, 16 (1993), pp. 681-735.

[11] B. L. Finlay, R. B. Darlington and N. Nicastro 'Developmental Structure in Brain Evolution', *Behavioral and Brain Sciences*, 24 (2001), pp. 263-78.

salutary when people were used to reading books about the world rather than observing it. But neuroscience has discovered that simply looking or staring does not yield the desired information. There has to be something in addition. The fact is that when we are observing, each aspect or feature of what we are seeing is registered in a different part of the brain. The brain's size and its accompanying complexity have led to a cerebral division of labour.

> The problem is that of determining that it is the same (or a different) stimulus which is activating different cells in a given visual area or in different visual areas. Suppose that three cells in area V3, all responsive to the horizontal orientation ... are activated by the same horizontal stimulus, for example the upper edge of a fence gate. Suppose further that these three cells receive inputs from twelve cells in area VI with corresponding orientation which, in turn, are responding to the same stimulus. The task is here to ascertain that the three cells in V3 and the twelve cells in VI are all responding to the same, and not to different stimuli.[12]

What Zeki is saying is that something more than reliance on or recourse to observation is needed. Simply staring at the world will not yield much information. There has to be an ability to decide which registrations belong together and which registrations belong somewhere else.

Neuroscientists have endeavoured to solve this problem and to show how the brain itself is sufficiently adapted to achieve the binding of these separate registrations in different and unconnected parts of the brain. There are many different suggestions by famous people like Francis Crick and Gerald Edelman and Roger Penrose — but in the end we are left with the laconic conclusion by Edelman in his recent book *Wider than the Sky* that there simply is no organ in the brain which is able to achieve the binding.[13] Others have commented that at present there is a gap in our knowledge, because since the binding is achieved there must be a cerebral operation to achieve it. After all, we *do* 'see' a chair when we are looking at one and are not left with the noted division of labour and the separate registrations of its length, height, location, colour and shape. Steven Rose writes that the

---

[12] S. Zeki, *A Vision of the Brain* (Oxford, 1993), p. 321.

[13] Francis Crick, *The Astonishing Hypothesis* (London, 1993), p. 208; Gerald M. Edelman and Giulio Tononi, *Consciousness* (London, 2001), p. 106; Roger Penrose, *The Emperor's New Mind* (London, 1989), pp. 516-8; Gerald M. Edelman, *Wider than the Sky* (London, 2004), p. 36.

solution of this problem is the foremost task of twenty-first century neuroscience.[14] In this kind of thinking it is assumed that the brain is adapted and that the solution of the binding problem must come from inside the brain, that is, from a function or a part of the brain which we have not yet been able to detect. But if we are willing to entertain the possibility that the brain is not well adapted, then the discovery of the gap in our knowledge of the brain is not something negative, but a positive contribution. It indicates that, since binding is achieved, it must come from the outside. There must be something in the lives of humans to control the damage.

Antonio Damasio has shown that, among other things, the operations of the cerebral neurons do not yield the emotions we are experiencing. The process which leads to our knowledge of our emotions is much more complex. The neurons generate what Damasio has called 'somatic markers' or 'raw feels'. They are felt or are productive of awareness as visceral events or as the tingling of our skins or an increased heart-beat or similar purely bodily sensations. The point is that we are aware of these somatic markers but as they stand, they have no name, no meaning, and no character. In short, they do not carry enough information to indicate what word we ought to use to name them and to give them a local habitation. Nevertheless, eventually they turn into emotions of which we are fully conscious. Being fully conscious implies that we can say what they are — love, hatred, jealousy, ambition and so forth.

Damasio is a neuroscientist and not given much to philosophical analysis. He therefore does not hesitate to say that once the somatic markers are present, they can be seen and, seen, they can be named. He takes it that somatic markers can readily be identified and he would probably argue, if pressed, that their presence is not a maladaptation. All one has to do is to look at them and name them. If one objects that those markers cannot be 'looked' at, he would say that one has to 'see' what they feel like in order to identify them verbally. He states without hesitation that 'humans … can engender verbal narratives out of nonverbal ones'.[15] In his major work *The Feeling of What Happens* he states explicitly, but erroneously, that 'language gives us names for things' and that those things are known identifiably before language.[16] This picture theory of language is

---

[14] Steven Rose, *The 21st Century Brain* (London, 2005), p. 157.

[15] A. R. Damasio and H. Damasio, 'Images and Subjectivity: Neurological Trials and Tribulations' in R. N. McCauley (ed.), *The Churchlands and their Critics* (Oxford, 1996), pp. 169, 173.

[16] A. R. Damasio, *The Feeling of What Happens* (New York, 1999), p. 108.

the view expressed in Wittgenstein's *Tractatus*, and rejected in Wittgenstein's later work, the *Philosophical Investigations*. Surprisingly, Damasio states, nearly fifty years after the appearance of Wittgenstein's *Philosophical Investigations*, the fact that we can say 'I' proves that there exists a non-verbal self of which the word 'I' is a picture.[17] But only a little philosophy is required to understand that the use of the word 'see' when one is vaguely aware of a feeling or somatic marker, is a metaphor and that the feeling stands as it is being *felt* — no more and no less. Most certainly, it cannot be 'seen' any more than the use and intelligibility of the word 'I' proves that there is a pre-lingual 'self' which we should name 'I'. The ready assumption that somatic markers do not pose an identity problem because they can be named if one looks at them, is, I would suggest, Damasio's error, which replaces what Damasio has called Descartes' error.[18] As soon as one understands that the somatic marker cannot readily be identified verbally, one must conclude that the appearance of those markers is, in the first instance, a disadvantage, that is, a maladaptation. As they stand or are being felt, they are a disorienting disturbance.

To summarise, the brain's division of labour when we are observing something, and the brain's production of somatic markers when its neurons are churning, are maladaptations because they impair and even damage our ability to orient ourselves in the world. Since *homo sapiens* has survived, that damage must have been controlled by something. I would like to nominate human culture as the prime candidate for the control of that damage. To repeat, 'culture' in this sense is the sum of wasteful, superfluous, irrational, traits and beliefs and practices which inflict cognitive, economic and political damage. This means that cultures by themselves are not well adapted either. My point is that it is precisely those maladapted cultures which have come to the rescue of the maladapted brain of *homo sapiens* and that it is their very maladaptation which has been able to control the damage inflicted by the maladapted brain. In short, here is a case where, against all proverbial expectations, two wrongs make one right. It is the maladaptation of the human brain which explains why maladapted cultures are ubiquitous. Humans, with their over-sized brains, have not been able to survive without those maladapted cultures. Those humans who failed to invent those cultures did not survive for long. It remains now to explain in which way such cultures were able to control the damage.

---

[17] *Ibid.*

[18] Peter Munz, 'The Evolution of Consciousness — Silent Neurons and Eloquent Mind', *Journal of Social and Evolutionary Systems*, 20 (1997), 4, p. xvi.

The reason why culture is able to control the damage is that it defines a circumscribed group of people which form a speech community or, better, what Wittgenstein called a 'Form of Life'. By 'Form of Life' Wittgenstein did not mean amoebas or giraffes or *homo sapiens*, but culturally discrete entities of humans. The damage is not controlled — and this is worth stressing — by the idiosyncratic, unverifiable, irrational beliefs and practices which constitute culture. The damage is controlled by the special language which is spoken and understood in every particular Form of Life defined by and identifiable as a culture.

Before I explain how this language is functioning and why it can function only in a community constituted as a Form of Life, let me look briefly at current theories about the origin or evolution of such groups. A Form of Life, capable of generating and practicing the special kind of language required to control the damage resulting from the over-sized brain, must have a boundary and be different from all other Forms of Life so that whatever lies beyond the boundary is 'the Other', something strange, incomprehensible and alien. The 'Other' is an essential ingredient in the identifiability of a Form of Life by the people *in* that Form of Life. To identify themselves, they must know, among other things, what they are not. The current theories about group formation all fail to account for that kind of boundary.

According to Trivers, groups are formed by people who practice reciprocal altruism. Such altruism, is in many important ways, the dictate of reason.[19] But if groups are formed by such practice, there is no necessary boundary, because there is no reason whatever why altruism suddenly should stop at a particular point. Next comes the view of Hamilton according to which groups are formed by the practice of 'inclusive fitness' — which means that people who are altruistic are not, in the struggle for survival and the selection of the fittest, at a disadvantage because their genes are handed down to their kin and often enough well beyond their immediate kin, by marriage.[20] In this way the genes of altruistic people survive successfully, or at least as successfully as selfish people, in the struggle for survival. Again there is no explanation why groups with a specific culture which designates a boundary beyond which altruism must not and cannot be practiced, should ever have emerged.

---

[19] R. L. Trivers, 'The Evolution of Reciprocal Altruism', *Quarterly Review of Biology*, 46 (1971), pp. 35-57.

[20] William D. Hamilton, 'Genetic Evolution of Social Behaviour', *Journal of Theoretical Biology*, 7, (1964), pp. 1-52.

Next comes the theory of group selection. It used to be favoured and popular and, after a longish period of decline, it has been revived by the writings of Elliott Sober and Sloane Wilson.[21] In their view, group selection is *sui generis* and takes priority. Once the group is formed, altruisms and cooperation inside the group are bound to develop. Here we get an explanation of the existence of boundaries because the emergence of a group implies the presence of a boundary; but there is no explanation why groups have to differ from one another and why whatever is beyond the boundary must be different for each group to function as a Form of Life.

As against all these theories, I propose that Forms of Life are human groups which are defined by their specific cultural practices, so that there are boundaries where the group ends, and whatever lies beyond such boundaries is 'the Other'. Such Forms of Life have emerged and been selected for retention because it is only inside such Forms that the special language which can control the damage can function. In contrast to practically all current theories about the origins of communal or group life, this theory suggests that group life started because people grouped themselves around sets of myths and rituals. The practices of altruism and cooperation developed once these Forms of Life had emerged. Altruism and cooperation, though their advantages are undoubted, were secondary and must not be taken to have been the prime movers. The reason for the retention of these Forms of Life — in spite of their obvious economic, cognitive and political disadvantages — was that they were able to supply the kind of language which was able to control the damage inflicted by the over-sized human brain.

It is clear that these Forms of Life inside which non-ostensively defined communication is possible, were, in the first place, what Karl Popper called 'closed societies'.[22] Popper was wrong in thinking that the formation of closed societies in very early days in the history of mankind was either a mistake or the result of sinister political intrigues. Given the problems presented by the large human brain, they were, on the contrary, an iron necessity because they promoted the development of the kind of language needed to control the damage caused by the over-sized brain. As time went by and as this kind of language had come to be firmly practiced and ensconced, it became gradually possible to soften the closedness and to attend to the cognitive, economic and political disadvantages brought

---

[21] Elliott Sober and D. S. Wilson, *'Unto Others'. The Evolution and Selection of Unselfish Behavior* (Cambridge, Mass., 1998).

[22] K. R. Popper, *The Open Society and its Enemies*, 2 vols (London, 1945), 1, p. 151.

about by original closeness. But this part of human history, desirable as it obviously is, is an after-thought. We owe it to Wittgenstein's diagnosis of the functioning of non-ostensively defined language that we have come to understand why, in the first place and since earliest times, Forms of Life rather than freely agreed upon associations, had to be the rule.

It is worth noting, though not strictly relevant, that such Forms of Life resemble biological species. Biological species are groups the members of which are infertile if they interbreed with members of other species. When members of a species breed with each other, their offspring always will be 'true', that is, they will have the same characteristics as the other members of the species. Finally all members of other species are available as prey – to be eaten or enslaved, as the case may be. The same characteristics apply to the Forms of Life. Sexual intercourse with members of other Forms of Life is prohibited, or at least discouraged – which assures artificially, for practical purposes, the same as biological infertility. The offspring of members of the Form of Life are brought up educationally to ensure that they continue in the same Form of Life – which corresponds to what in biology we call 'true breeding'. Finally members of other Forms of Life are considered to be enemies and treated with suspicion – which comes near enough to taking them to be available for food or enslavement. Although these similarities are not strictly relevant to the present argument they are worth noting if one wants to understand the quality and character of a Form of Life.

What then, precisely, is the kind of language which can control the damage caused by the somatic markers and the binding problem? The idea that a Form of Life furnishes a special way in which we understand what we are saying was first put forward by the later Wittgenstein. The best way to grasp the role of the Form of Life is to follow Wittgenstein's own thought processes. At the time of writing his *Tractatus* he had taken it that when we say 'chair', we are painting a sort of verbal 'picture' of the chair and we know that other people will understand what we mean by saying 'chair' because we can simply point at the chair, that is, we can give the verbal picture an ostensive definition. After many years, Wittgenstein thought better of it. He came to realise that when we are pointing, we are pointing silently and, in doing so, there is no telling whether by pointing at the chair we mean the whole chair or the colour of the chair we are pointing at, or the shape of the chair or its beauty, or, for that matter, its ugliness or usefulness. In short, he came to understand that ostensive definitions cannot work to make people understand what precisely we mean when we are saying 'chair'. Hence he concluded that there must be a different explanation why people understand what we mean when we are saying 'chair'.

The different explanation is that, in spite of the fact that ostensive definitions do not work, we understand what is meant by saying 'chair' because we as well as our listeners, are members of a speech community or Form of Life in which there is a verbal usage which governs the employment of the word 'chair'. In a given Form of Life people will understand what we are saying even though we cannot provide an ostensive definition of the word we are using. It is this kind of language the meanings of which do not depend on observation but on the usage which prevails in a speech community or Form of Life, rather than the picture theory of language, which is able to control the damage. But Wittgenstein merely reasoned that since we cannot define the meaning of what we are saying ostensively — that is, by pointing at what we think we have in mind[23] — we can understand what we are saying only because we are saying it in a social context we are sharing with other members of our Form of Life.[24]

To flesh out this reasoning, I want to quote three psychological descriptions of what such context in a Form of Life amounts to. These descriptions are designed to show how the connection between words and things is mediated by patterns of social interaction rather than by simple observation of what it is we are referring to when we are speaking.[25] These psychological reflections have given teeth to Wittgenstein's abstract reasoning. Thus Jerome Bruner wrote, following Wittgenstein, that a child acquires the conventional use of a linguistic symbol by learning to participate in an interactive format (form of life, joint attentional scene) that she understands, first, non linguistically so that the adult's language can be grounded in shared experiences whose social significance she already appreciates.[26] In order to learn how to follow the rule which happens to be in vogue in the community of which he or she is a member, the child has

---

[23] Peter Munz, *Beyond Wittgenstein's Poker* (Aldershot, 2004), p. 141.

[24] Ludwig Wittgenstein, *Philosophical Investigations*, p. 226e. See also David Bloor, 'Linguistic Idealism Revisited' in H. Sluga and D. G. Stern (eds), *The Cambridge Companion to Wittgenstein* (Cambridge, 1996), p. 371.

[25] David Bloor, 'Linguistic Idealism', p. 367.

[26] Cf. J. S. Bruner, 'From Communication to Language', *Cognition*, 3 (1974-5), pp. 255-76; J. S. Bruner, *Child's Talk* (Oxford, 1983), especially pp. 17-19; R. Worden, 'The Evolution of Language from Social Intelligence' in J. R. Hurford *et al.* (eds), *Approaches to the Evolution of Language* (Cambridge, 1998), p. 152; R. Burling, 'Comprehension, Production, and Conventionalisation in the Origins of Language' in Chris Knight *et al.* (eds), *The Evolutionary Emergence of Language* (Cambridge, 2000), p. 37.

to appreciate other people as intentional beings.[27]

> We learn and teach words in certain contexts, and then we are expected and expect others, to be able to project them into further contexts. Nothing insures that this projection will take place ... just as nothing insures that we will make, and understand, the same projections. That on the whole we do, is a matter of our sharing routes of interest and feeling, senses of humour and of significance and of fulfilment, of what is outrageous, of what is similar to what else, what a rebuke, and what forgiveness, of when an utterance is an assertion, when an appeal, when an explanation... .[28]

People living in a community which is a Form of Life can understand what they are saying to one another without having prior and *independent* knowledge of what it is the words are referring to. They repeat what they or their ancestors have heard before. For example, in Christian communities people are apt to quote the Bible. They are doing so in the mistaken belief that they are quoting an authority which validates their beliefs. In reality they are merely using turns of phrase which have been used before and to which people are accustomed and which people understand. Or take other, less religious examples, here is how Mme de Staël put it in the early nineteenth century: 'novels ... have all too well discovered to us the most secret recesses of sentiment. Nothing can be experienced that we do not remember to have read before, and all the veils of the heart have been rent'.[29] This is from Thomas Mann, in the middle of the twentieth century: 'I am inclined — and I am by no means alone in this — to view all life in the shape of mythic clichés and to prefer quotation to independent invention.'[30] This is how Patrick White's publisher explained the workings of Carson McCullers' fertile mind to him: 'The year I arrived in New York, was the year Carson McCullers made her mark with *The Heart is a Lonely*

---

[27] See M. Tomasello, *The Cultural Origins of Human Cognition* (Cambridge, Mass., 1999), pp. 109, 116.

[28] S. Cavell, *Must We Mean What We Say?* (New York, 1969), p. 52. See also Marie McGinn, *Wittgenstein and the Philosophical Investigations* (London, 1997), p. 58: 'Language is essentially embedded in structured activities that constitute a "form of life"'. Cf. Tim Ingold, *Perception of the Environment* (London, 2000), pp. 167-8.

[29] Mme de Staël, *Germany* (London, 1813), 2, pp. 320-1.

[30] Thomas Mann, *Die Entstehung des Doktor Faustus* (Amsterdam, 1949), p. 137.

Hunter and those New Yorkers who read reviews, if not the book under review, were agog with the event. 'How could a young girl know, etc ... ?' Ben's quiet reply to their admiring incredulity was: 'surely, she can read, can't she?'[31] Finally this is how Oscar Wilde hit the nail on the head: 'Literature always anticipates life. It does not copy it, but moulds it to its purpose ... . We are merely carrying out, with footnotes and unnecessary additions, the whim or fancy of a great novelist.'[32]

Our use and our understanding of language is essentially a communal activity. For a long time — precisely from the days of the Royal Society in the seventeenth century[33] right down to the age of the early Wittgenstein's *Tractatus* — this had not been understood. It had been assumed that we understand language because we can point at what we mean to be referring to. We first look at what we mean and then report, as soberly and without adornment as possible, what it is we have seen. There was special stress on the importance of the absence of 'adornment', lest figures of speech or emotional stresses distort the 'picture'. In this view, language is simply a verbal repetition of the activity of our senses. The first to raise a doubt was Swift who satirised this view in *Gulliver's Travels*, Book III, chapter v. He wrote that if it were true that language is nothing but a report of what we observe, and if it is true that we understand what anybody is saying because we can *look* at what is being reported, then it would be possible to dispense with language. We could then, more efficiently and to avoid all misunderstanding, carry in bags the objects we are seeing and reporting about. Instead of speaking, we could reach for the object and parade it in front of the person we are talking to and, for the rest, remain silent.

Unfortunately the force of Swift's satire was pushed aside. Right down to the time of the Vienna Circle's insistence that only those sentences are meaningful (that is, can be understood) which are protocols of experiences, the view of the Royal Society prevailed. We mean what we can point at and other people understand what we mean because what we are saying is nothing but an unadorned report of what we have been looking at. To understand, all they have to do is to look at the same object or situation. In this way, the use and nature of language was merely a matter of our neurons and had nothing to do with, let alone dependent upon, the society

---

[31] Patrick White, *Flaws in the Glass: A Self-Portrait* (London, 1998), pp. 75-76.

[32] R. Ellmann, 'The Decay of Lying', *The Artist as Critic* (London, 1970), p. 309.

[33] Thomas Sprat, *History of the Royal Society*, ed. J. I. Cope and H. W. Jones, (London, 1959), p. 113.

we are living in. It took the later Wittgenstein's *Philosophical Investigations* to undermine this simplistic view and to explain that, above all, the use of language is a communal enterprise. It is dependent on the Form of Life people are living in and sharing, rather than on their individual sense experiences. In essence, Wittgenstein did no more than repeat as a logical argument Swift's insight.

Let me illustrate this with the help of a famous argument advanced over two hundred years ago by David Hume. Hume was solidly convinced that the reason why we understand what people are saying is that we can, independently of what is being said, put our finger on the thing they are talking about. Thus he reasoned that he himself could never think of having or being a 'self'.[34] This was due to the fact that whenever he thought about himself, he could never strike anything other than 'being cold' or 'being angry' or 'loving somebody' and so forth. Wherever he turned, he could never see anything that could be called a 'self'. He concluded, therefore, that the self of David Hume did not exist. This shows that with his reasoning mind he was in thrall to the Royal Society view that we understand what is being said because it is a report of something we or somebody else has seen or experienced. But now take a closer look at this reasoning and read between the lines. Hume did not hesitate to use the words 'self' and 'I' even though he was logically satisfied that they did not refer to anything. In using these words he was completely confident that he and his readers would understand what he was talking about, even though he was reasoning that these words did not refer to anything and that, therefore, they ought to have been unintelligible.

We have here a curious spectacle. In his conscious, upper mind, Hume adhered to the view of the Royal Society and, for that matter, to the views of the twentieth century Vienna circle as well as to the views stated in Wittgenstein's *Tractatus*, that the only intelligible words are those that are pictures of reality. But in his unthinking, contextually oriented mind, Hume did not hesitate to use words which were *not* pictures of reality and he was completely confident that both he and his readers would understand them even though they were neither pictures of reality nor the Vienna Circle's protocol sentences nor the 'unadorned reports' of his experience demanded by the Royal Society. It looks as if Hume was intellectually schizophrenic. When conscious, Hume thought like a follower or, rather, precursor of Wittgenstein's *Tractatus*; and in his unconscious behaviour, he wrote like a follower of Wittgenstein's *Philosophical*

---

[34] David Hume, *A Treatise of Human Nature*, part IV, section vi.

Investigations. Above all, Hume's thinking demonstrates that he took it for granted that even his uncompromising critical rationalism could only be pursued intelligibly in a Form of Life in which both he and his readers were completely familiar with the usage of such words as 'I' and 'Self', even though he managed, to his own satisfaction, to demonstrate that these words had no meaning. Paradoxically — or should one say ironically? — Hume's very demonstration of the lack of meaning of these words could only be carried out convincingly in a culture in which people understood what they meant and to what they were referring.

This revised understanding of language enables us to see why our language, dependent as it is on a specific Form of Life, can control the damage caused by our partially maladapted brain. If the meanings expressed in our language are not derived from what our language is supposed to be referring to, we can understand what we are saying even though we cannot point at what we are referring to or at what we have in mind. It is precisely this quality of language which is needed to control the damage caused by both somatic markers and the binding problem. In the first place the somatic marker is an awareness of a raw feel, 'a violent disturbance at the base of our brain', as Baudelaire had put it.[35] As it is being felt, it is disorienting and disturbing. In order to bring it into full consciousness and make out what precisely it is we are feeling, it has to be turned into a full blown, identifiable emotion. In a Form of Life we have a language which is able to do this. We can talk about the raw feel or the somatic markers even though we cannot point at it, let alone say in so many words what it is. It cannot be observed. But the kind of language furnished by a Form of Life can make a meaningful statement about it in spite of the fact that it cannot be observed. It can invent an interpretation of it and, because it is operating in a speech community or a Form of Life, people will understand what we are saying about the somatic marker even though neither we nor our listening fellow-men are *first* able to identify and name it *after* the identification. The language we are using about it can be understood in the absence of a prior knowledge of what it is it is referring to.

Secondly, the binding problem arises because our brain registers the several aspects or properties of an object we are looking at in different parts. The brain's labour is divided. In spite of such division of labour, we have no difficulty in stating that we are seeing, for example, a chair. Since

---

[35] Quoted by R. Snell, 'The Folly of Allegory and Interpretation', *Times Literary Supplement* (18 April, 1997), p. 17, col. 2.

there is no part or organ or neuronal circuit which achieves such binding, we are pushed back on our language.[36] Since the language we are using in our Form of Life does not depend for its intelligibility on a prior ascertainment of what it is we are referring to or what it is we have in mind, we can talk about a chair and bind the several registrations together and ascertain that, though separate, they all belong to the same object. If our language was the sort of communication system envisaged by the Royal Society in the seventeenth century or by the Vienna Circle and the early Wittgenstein of the *Tractatus* in the twentieth century, such binding could not be achieved by language.

The conclusion is now obvious. The deficiencies of our brains are controlled by human cultures which define societies as Forms of Life inside which we can practice a language which is intelligible because of the communal context rather than because it is a picture of reality or a protocol of experiences. On the view of the *Tractatus* we would have to remain silent about our somatic markers and the several cerebral registrations of one single object, because we would have to be silent about the things 'whereof one cannot *speak*'.[37] Language conceived as a mere protocol of experiences or an unadorned report of observations, would be helpless and useless when confronted by nothing more than separate neuronal registrations of the several properties and qualities of a chair or those somatic markers some of which Baudelaire called 'a violent disturbance at the base of our brain'.

But language as it really is — a method of communication which depends on the context furnished by the community we are living in rather than on our individual ability to observe what that language is supposed to be referring to — is able to bind the disparate registrations together and provide a name for somatic markers so that they can be experienced as identifiable and articulated emotions. Forms of Life or cultures which give a distinct and recognisable shape to a human society, no matter how economically, cognitively and politically disadvantageous they are, allow us to continue life with a maladapted brain. Though this may not be the way the world ends, it is the way *homo sapiens* was rescued by culture.

---

[36] Edelman, *Wider than the Sky*, p. 36.

[37] Ludwig Wittgenstein, *Tractatus*, trans. C. K. Ogden, introduction by Bertrand Russell (London, 1955), proposition 7, my italics.

A Bibliography of the Publications of J. C. Davis, 1968-2007

Jocelyn Gamble

BOOKS

Utopia and the ideal society: A study of English utopian writing 1516-1700 (Cambridge: Cambridge University Press, 1981); paperback edition 1983; transl *Utopía y la sociedad ideal: studio de la literature utópica inglesa 1516-1700* (Mexico, Fondo de Cultura Económica, 1985).

Fear, Myth and History: The Ranters and the Historians (Cambridge, Cambridge University Press, 1986).

Edited with Peter Lineham, *The Future of the Past : themes in New Zealand History* (Palmerston North, Massey University Press, 1991).

Oliver Cromwell (London, Edward Arnold; New York, Oxford University Press, 2001).

ARTICLES & CHAPTERS

'The Levellers and Democracy', *Past and Present*, 40 (1968), pp. 174-80.

'Utopia and History', *Historical Studies*, 13:50, (1968), pp. 165-76.

'Thomas More, Cardinal Morton and the Politics of Accommodation', *Journal of British Studies*, 9:2 (1970), pp. 27-49.

'The Levellers and Christianity', in B. S. Manning (ed.), *Politics, Religion and the English Civil War* (London, Edward Arnold, 1974), pp. 223-50.

'The Levellers and Democracy', in C. Webster (ed.), *The Intellectual Revolution of the Seventeenth Century*, (London, Routledge, 1974), pp. 70-78.

'Gerrard Winstanley and the Restoration of True Magistracy', *Past and Present*, 70 (1976), pp. 76-93.

'Pocock's Harrington: Grace, Nature and Art in the Classical Republicanism of James Harrington', *Historical Journal*, 24:3 (1981), pp. 683-97.

'Radicalism in a Traditional Society: The Evaluation of Radical Thought in the English Commonwealth 1649-1600', *History of Political Thought*, 3:2 (1982), pp. 193-213.

'Science and Utopia: The History of a Dilemma', in E. Mendelsohn and H. Nowotny (eds), *Nineteen Eighty-Four: Science Between Utopia and Dystopia, Sociology of the Sciences Yearbook Publication*, 8 (Dordrecht, Reidel 1984), pp. 21-48.

'The History of Utopia: the Chronology of Nowhere', in P. Alexander and R. Gill (eds), *Utopias* (London, Duckworth, 1984), pp. 1-18.

'Utopia and Political Science', *Political Science*, 36:1 (1984), pp. 77-83.

'Abiezer Coppe and the well-favoured Harlot: The Ranters and the English Revolution', *The Turnbull Library Record*, 20:1 (1987), pp. 17-30.

'Utopia Science and Social Science', in E. Kamenka (ed.), *Utopias* (Oxford, Oxford University Press, 1987), pp. 83-100.

'Cromwell's Religion', in J. Morrill (ed.), *Oliver Cromwell and the English Revolution* (London, Longman, 1990), pp. 181-208.

'Fear, Myth and Furore: Reappraising the Ranters', *Past and Present*, 129 (1990), pp. 79-103.

'Puritanism and Revolution: Themes, Categories, Methods and Conclusions', *Historical Journal*, 33:3 (1990), pp. 693-704.

'The Significance of the Ranters', *Early Modern History*, 1:1 (1991), pp. 30-32.

'Utopianism', in J. H. Burns and M. Goldie (eds), *The Cambridge History of Political Thought 1450-1700* (Cambridge, Cambridge University Press, 1991), pp. 329-44; transl., *Histoire de la pensée politique moderne* (Paris, Presses Universitaires de France), (1997), pp. 298-311.

'Religion and the struggle for freedom in the English revolution', *Historical Journal*, 35:3 (1992), pp. 507-30.

'Against Formality : One Aspect of the English Revolution', *Transactions of the Royal Historical Society*, Sixth Series, III (1993), pp. 265-288.

'Formal Utopia/Informal Millennium: The struggle between form and substance as context for Seventeenth-century Utopianism', in K. Kumar and S. Bann (eds), *Utopias and Millennium* (London, Reaktion Books, 1993), pp. 17-32.

'Reply' in 'Debate : Fear, Myth and Furore: Reappraising the Ranters', *Past and Present*, 140 (1993), pp. 194-210.

'An historian's view: colleagues on Harvey Franklin', *Pacific Viewpoint*, 35:1 (1994), pp. 29-31.

'A Short Course of Discourse: Studies in Early Modern Conscience, Duty and the English Protestant Interest', *Journal of Ecclesiastical History*, 46:2 (1995), pp. 302-9.

'Backing into Modernity: The Dilemma of Richard Hooker', M. Fairburn and W. H. Oliver (eds), *The Certainty of Doubt: Tributes to Peter Munz*, (Wellington, Victoria University Press, 1996), pp. 157-179.

'The millennium as the anti-Utopia of seventeenth century political thought', *Anglophonia; French Journal of English Studies*, 3 (1998) pp. 298-311.

'Equality in an unequal Commonwealth: James Harrington's republicanism and the meaning of equality', in I. Gentles, J. Morrill, and B. Worden (eds), *Soldiers, Writers and Statesmen of the English Revolution* (Cambridge, Cambridge University Press, 1998), pp. 229-242.

'Oliver Cromwell: Peacemaker', *Cromwelliana* (1998), pp. 2-7.

'La igualdad de derechos en la revolución inglesa: el republicanismo de James Harrington y el significado de la igualdad', in *Derechos y Libertades*, 4:7(1999), pp. 189-205.

'New World/Old World: The theatre of interests and Sir Thomas More's Utopia', in J. M. Maguin and C. Whitworth (eds), *Thomas More 'Utopia' : Nouvelles Perspectives critiques* (Montpellier, Centre d'Etudes et de Recherches sur la Renaissance Anglaise, 1999), pp. 105-120.

'Utopias', in Paul F. Grendler (ed.), *The Encyclopaedia of the Renaissance*, 6 vols (New York, Charles Scribner: for the Renaissance Society of America, 1999), 6, pp. 200-4.

'L'Utopia et le Nouveau Monde 1500-1700', in P. Crouzet (ed.), *Utopia : La Quête de la sociétié idéale en Occident*, (Paris, Biblothèque Nationale de France/Fayard), (2000), pp. 104-125; transl 'Utopia and the new world 1500-1700', in R. Schaer, G. Claeys and L. Tower Sargeant (eds), *Utopia: The Search for the Ideal Society in the Western World* (New York, New York Public Library/Oxford University Press, 2000), pp. 95-118.

'The Levellers and Christianity', in Peter Gaunt (ed.), *The English Civil War: Essential Readings* (Oxford, Blackwell, 2000), pp. 279-302.

'Political Thought 1640-1660', in Barry Coward (ed.), *The Blackwell Companion to Stuart Britain*, (Oxford, Blackwell, 2002), pp. 374-96.

'Conquering the conquest: the limits of non-violence in Gerrard Winstanley's Thought', *Le Joug Normande*, (2004), pp. 71-88.

'Gerrard Winstanley', *Oxford Dictionary of National Biography* (Oxford, Oxford University Press, 2004), vol. 59, pp. 762-70.

Scholarly Reviews

Theodore Olsen, *Millennialism, Utopianism, and Progress; Journal of Ecclesiastical History*, 34:3 (1983), pp. 446-48.

Richard L. Greaves & Robert Zaller (eds) *Biographical Dictionary of British Radicals in the Seventeenth Century; Political Science*, 37:1 (1985), pp. 166-72.

James Holstun, *A Rational Millennium: Puritan Utopias of Seventeenth-Century England and America; History of Political Thought*, 8:1 (1988), pp. 175-80.

Timothy Kenyon, *Utopian Communism and Political Thought in Early Modern English; History of Political Thought*, 11:2 (1990), pp. 360-2.

Conal Condren, *George Lawson's Political Thought and the English Revolution; Parliamentary History*, 2:2 (1992), pp. 305-6.

J. A. I. Champion, *The Pillars of Priestcraft Shaken; Albion*, 25:1 (1993), pp. 103-4.

Stephen Baskerville, *Not Peace but a Sword: The Political Theology of the English Revolution; Parliamentary History*, 13:3 (1994), pp. 372-374.

The Dictionary of New Zealand Biography, 1769-1869, 1; *The Dictionary of New Zealand Biography 1870-1900*, 2; *The New Zealand Journal of History*, 28:2 (1994), pp. 214-16.

Gregory Claeys (ed.), *Utopias of the British Enlightenment; Utopian Studies*, 6:1 (1995), pp. 131-2.

B. H. G. Wormald, *Francis Bacon: History, Politics and Science, 1561-1626; History*, 80 (1995), p. 258.

Roger A. Mason (ed.), *Scots and Britons. Scottish political thought and the union of 1603; Journal of Ecclesiastical History*, 46:4 (1995), pp. 746-7.

J. G. A. Pocock, Gorden J. Schochet, Lois G Schwoerer (eds), *The Varieties of British Thought, 1500-1800; Parliamentary History*, 14:2 (1995), pp. 200-2.

David Fausett, *Images of the Antipodes in the Eighteenth Century: A Study in Stereotyping; Utopian Studies*, 7:2 (1996), p. 253.

Glenn Burgess, *Absolute Monarchy and the Stuart Constitution; Parliamentary History*, 16:2 (1997), pp. 234-6.

Amy Boesky, *Founding Fictions: Utopias in Early Modern England; Utopian Studies*, 9:2 (1998), p. 237.

Sarah Barber, *Regicide and Republicanism: Politics and Ethics in the English Revolution 1646-1659; Parliamentary History*, 18:2 (1999), pp. 213-5.

Marina Leslie, *Renaissance Utopias and the Problem of History; Utopian Studies* (1999), p. 236.

Keith Lindley, *Popular Politics and Religion in Civil War London; History*, 84:2 (1999), pp. 162-4.

Andrew Sharp (ed.), *The English Levellers, Parliamentary History*, 18:1 (1999), pp. 87-89.

Perez Zagorin, *The English Revolution, Politics, Events, Ideas; Parliamentary History*, 19:2 (2000), pp. 293-294.

Donald R. Dickson, *The Tessera of Antilia: Utopian Brotherhoods and Secret Societies in the Early Seventeenth Century; Utopian Studies*, 11:2 (2000), pp. 253-5.

Peter Matheson, *The Imaginative View of the Reformation; Utopian Studies*, 12:1 (2001), pp. 217-8.

Robert Appelbaum, *Literature and Utopian Politics in Seventeenth-Century England; Utopian Studies* (2002), pp. 98-100.

Raymond John Howgego (ed.), *Encyclopedia of Exploration to 1800; Utopian Studies*, 14:2 (2003), pp. 173-6.

D. Alan Orr, *Treason and the State: Law, Politics and Ideology in the English Civil War; History of Political Thought*, 25:1 (2004), pp. 178-181.

Jan Waszink (ed.), *Justus Lipsius: Politica, Six Books of Politics or Political Instruction; Journal of Early Modern History*, 1090 (2005), pp. 222-4.

David R. Como, *Blown by the Spirit : Puritanism and the Emergence of an Antinomian Underground in Pre-Civil War England; American Historical Review*, 110:1 (2005), p. 214.

Bronwen Price (ed.), *Francis Bacon's New Atlantis: New interdisciplinary Essays; Modern Language Review*, 100:4 (2005) pp. 1088-1090 (3).

Patrick Little, *Lord Broghill and the Cromwellian Union with Ireland and Scotland; American Historical Review*, 110:5 (2005), p. 1590.

Philip Withington, *The Politics of Commonwealth, Citizens and Freemen in Early Modern England; Parliamentary History*, 25:2 (2006), pp. 272-274.

Nicholas McDowell, *The English Radical Imagination: Culture, Religion and Revolution, 1630-1660; English Historical Review*, 122 (2007), pp. 191-2.

Ann Hughes, *Gangraena and the Struggle for the English Revolution; Milton Quarterly*, 41:1 (2007), pp. 54-58.

Contributors

James Belich is Research Professor of History at Victoria University of Wellington.

Michael Braddick is Professor of History at the University of Sheffield.

Isabel Burdiel is Professor of Modern Spanish History at the Universitat de València.

Glenn Burgess is Professor of History at the University of Hull.

Dr Dámaso de Lario is the Spanish Ambassador to Venezuela.

Dr Mark Goldie is University Senoir Lecturer in History in the University of Cambridge and a Fellow of Churchill College.

Mark Knights is Professor of History at the University of Warwick.

William Lamont is Professor Emeritus of History at the University of Sussex.

Dr Gaby Mahlberg has recently completed graduate studies in History at the University of East Anglia.

John Morrill is Professor of the History of Great Britain and Ireland in the University of Cambridge and a Fellow of Selwyn College.

John Morrow is Professor of Political Studies and Dean of Arts at The University of Auckland.

The late Peter Munz was Professor Emeritus of History at Victoria University of Wellington.

Jonathan Scott is Carroll Amundson Professor of British History at the University of Pittsburgh.

David Thomson was formerly Professor of History and is now a Research Associate in the School of History, Philosophy and Politics at Massey University.

Index

Adam 142-5, 148
Agreement of the People 34
Allegiance 175
Anglican (ism) 12, 27, 46, 55, 63
Apostles, Acts of 93, 96, 100
Asís, Francisco de, King Consort 201, 208, 209-10
Astrology 188-89, 192
Aubrey, John 9
Australia 235, 236, 248
Authorial intention 113, 125-30
Authority 4, 10-11, 13, 15-16, 21, 27, 155-7, 165, 176, 197
   absolute 11-12, 195, 210
   arbitrary 11-12, 50, 95
   clerical 2, 27
   divine 17-18
   kingly 11, 57-59
   religious 24-25

Baptists 33, 45, 46, 63, 64
Baxter, Richard 2, 32, 35, 45, 59, 60, 62, 64-65
Belief 154-6, 163-5
Bible, the Holy 4, 5, 23-5, 89-111, 134, 139, 140, 143-5, 146, 147, 152
   Geneva 94, 97
   King James 94, 97
Bienio Progresista 196, 207, 209-11
Blount, Thomas 78-80
Bolingbroke, Lord 129, 154
Book of Common Prayer 178-80
Borbón, Mária Cristina de, Queen Mother 198, 199, 203, 208
Brain, binding functions and 257-59
Brain, apparent maladaption of 255, 256, 259
Brenner, Robert 191

Buckingham, Duke of 46, 55
Burnet, Gilbert 49-51, 55, 81

Calvin (ism) 22, 42, 43, 177, 183
Canada 216, 217, 221-2, 236, 238-40
Cape Colony 217, 236
Catholic (ism) 3, 15, 46, 50, 52, 57, 68, 70, 71-73, 80-82, 92, 93, 98, 103, 141, 163, 179 (See also: Popery)
Carlyle, Thomas 4, 153-72 (See also: Forms; Leadership)
Cavendish family 9, 25-6, 28
Charles I (of England) 5, 10-11, 13, 69, 77, 84, 91-2, 100, 102, 133, 141, 147, 148, 165, 169, 176, 183, 184
Charles II (of England) 3, 27, 43, 52, 55, 58, 67-86, 113, 116, 138, 149, 144, 147
Charles X (of France) 162
Carlism (ist) 198, 199, 208
Civil War, English 148
'Church-clothes' 155, 162
Church government 187
Church, of England 12-13, 25, 28-9, 46, 53-54, 65, 66, 74, 81, 146, 178, 184
Church, of Rome 14, 56, 64, 81
Church, National 32, 37-41, 63, 64
Church, Spanish 207-8
Clarendon, Earl of 46, 74, 85
Clergy 22, 27
Cobbett, William 224, 226-28
Colonisation; *see* emigration, migration
Commerce 34-35, 36, 42
Commonwealth, English 29, 35-36, 40, 101, 138, 167-8
Commonwealth, Holy 37-39

276

Conventicle Act (1670) 46, 154-5
Constitution (alism) 149-50, 159-60, 167, 185, 203-4
Cortés, Juan Donaso 200, 201
Crisp, Tobias 44
Cromwell, Oliver 1, 4, 5, 33, 34, 35, 36, 37, 54, 56, 89-111, 114, 133, 164, 166-8
Cromwell, Richard 33, 35, 38, 39, 40, 99, 133
Crown (in Spain) 196, 197, 198, 199, 203-4, 205, 211
Corinthians, Letter to 94
Culture 253-68 (See also: Form of Life)
 apparent dysfunction of 253-4
 language and 263-8

Danby, Lord 82
Darwinism 255, 256
Davis J. C. (Colin) 1, 10, 27, 33-34, 42, 89, 153, 176
Democracy 204, 205
Digges, Dudley 11
Discipline, Godly 10, 33-34
Divine right 11, 15, 142, 143, 146, 152
Dover, Treaty of 69, 75, 76, 79
Du Moulin, Louis 60
Dunbar, Battle of 108
Dutch, the 29, 35, 70, 73, 75, 85, 132, 135, 136, 138, 146, 150, 151
Dutch War 46, 48, 76, 138

Elizabeth I (of England) 14, 56, 135, 147
Emigration, ideology of 216-34 (See also: migration)
 abundance in 230, 231-2
 advertising and 218-19
 anti-paternalism in 231, 234
 discourses of 220, 224-5
 formal and informal 219, 226
 independence in 226-7, 247-8
 literature of 217-18, 224-5
 pauperism and 216-17
 'settlers' in 220-1
 utopianism in 230, 232, 233
 working conditions and 232-3
 yeoman ideal in 225-6
Engagement, political 175, 177, 182
Enlightenment, the 59, 134, 152, 154, 158, 253
Episcopacy 13
Escosura, Patricola de la 204-5
Esparto, Baldomero 206, 209
Evelyn, John 53-4
Exclusion Crisis, the 76, 133

Ferne, Henry 11
Filmer, Sir Robert 141-4
France 49, 68, 76, 82-4, 157-62
Fisher, Samuel 32
Fleetwood, Charles 99-100
'Form of life' 260-68
Forms (formality) 6, 89, 109, 153-72
 authority and 169-70
 false 155-6, 158-60, 163
 puritanism and 163-4 166, 167, 170
 reality and, 159, 161, 165
 religion and 157, 163-4
 self-consciousness and 156, 165-66
Fullwood, Charles 53-54
Fullwood, Frances 62-63

Girondins 160-1, 162, 170
Government 21, 28, 48-50, 60, 157, 160, 167-8, 171
Goffe, Colonel 91-92, 93

Grey, Sir George 236
Grosse, Robert 17
Grotius, Hugo 20, 40, 61

Halifax, Marquis of 81-82, 85
Hammond, Henry 12-13
Hammond, Robert 95, 100
Harrington, James 133, 146, 150
Hartlib, Samuel 188-91, 192
Hebrews, Epistle to 107
Heroism 167-8, 171
Hobbes, Thomas 2, 9-10, 23-8, 29-34, 43-44, 48-49, 59, 73 110, 149
Hollis, Thomas 131, 152
House of Commons 45, 49, 69, 70, 76, 95, 83 143
Huddleston, Father John 80, 84
Hudson, Michael 15-18
Humphrey, John 40-41, 48-49, 54-55, 60-61, 63-64
Hyde, Sir Edward 11

Impersonation 121
Independents (Independency) 2, 12, 28-9, 30, 33, 43, 46, 48, 57, 61, 145
Indulgence, Declaration of (1672) 45-60, 63-65, 70, 71, 74, 75, 81
Instrument of Government 34
Ireland (Irish) 96, 99, 101, 103, 153, 170, 235
Isabel II (of Spain) 5-6, 195-212
   1848 revolutions and 202-3
   personal morality and 201, 207-8, 210, 211
   religiosity of 207-8
Isaiah, book of 94, 102, 108, 109

Jacobins 160-1, 162, 170

James I and VI (of England and Scotland) 28, 82, 98, 140, 147, 165, 169
James II (of England) 15, 47-48, 59, 63, 70, 72, 85, 133
James, Epistle of 95
John, Gospel of 96, 98

King (ship) 70, 77, 91, 92, 105-6, 158, 169 (see also: monarchy)
Knox, John 163

Laud, Archbishop William 163, 169, 184
Law 11, 20, 21, 49, 51-52, 145, 149, 185
   moral 15-16
   natural 47, 134-5, 148-9
   of God 17-20, 164, 165
Leadership 157, 164, 167-8, 172
Legitimacy 176, 177
L'Estrange, Roger 4-5, 113-30
Liberalism, in Spain 195, 196, 198, 199, 201, 203, 207, 210-11
Liberal Union (in Spain) 209, 210, 212
Liberty (freedom) 1, 10, 16, 20, 29-30, 31, 32-35, 39, 42-43, 67, 142-3, 164, 177
   of conscience 16, 22, 27, 30, 334-35, 45-47, 166
Lilburne, John 175, 190
Lilly, William 188
Leviathan 16-17, 26, 27, 29, 31, 43
Levellers, the 16-17, 31, 169
Locke, John 16, 47, 57, 134, 146, 149, 152, 190
Lockyer, Nicholas 54-55, 69, 74, 77, 83, 93

London, City of 69, 74, 77, 83, 93, 115, 118, 120, 176-7
Long Parliament, the 97, 167, 170
López, Joaquín Maria 195-6, 204
Louis XIV (of France) 3, 68, 71, 75, 76, 83, 84
Louis XV (of France) 157-8
Luther, Martin 165, 165

Magistracy 10, 21, 37-38, 57
Marvell, Andrew 45-46, 47, 50, 57
Massachusetts 41, 137
Mayne, Jasper 9, 16-26
Migration 6, 213-34, 246 (See also: Australia; Canada; Cape Colony; Emigration; New Zealand)
   agricultural development and 214-15
   economic conditions and 214-15
   internal 215
   population growth and 213-14
   sea transport and 222-3, 236
Milton, John 47, 132, 146, 148
Mobilisation 5, 117, 175-7, 181-4, 187-93
Moderate Party (in Spain) 196, 197, 198, 199, 201-2, 205, 206, 210, 211-12
Monarchy 5, 11, 132, 134, 140-1, 203-4 (See also: kingship)
   absolute 195, 210
   constitutional 195, 210, 212
Monmouth, duke of 137, 138
More, Thomas 137, 138
Mylius, Hermann 90-1
Muggletonians 42, 43

Napoleon Bonaparte 161-2
Narváez, Ramon Maŕia 202
Navigation Act 190-1

Neville, Henry 4-5, 77, 131-152 (See also: Patriarchalism)
New South Wales 221
New Zealand 222, 227, 235, 236, 237-38, 240-1, 248
Newcastle, Duke of 27, 28
New Model Army 84, 93, 97, 109
Numbers, Book of 92, 101, 109
Nye, Philip 57, 58

Oates, Titus 70, 80
O'Donnell, Leopoldo 208-9
Obedience 13, 155
Orleanist monarchy 198, 199, 202
Orwell, George 30
Owen, John 2, 29, 32-4, 40, 46, 53, 54, 64

Parker, Henry 180, 190
Parker, Samuel 29-30, 34, 47, 50, 60
Parliament, English 18, 46, 47, 56, 76-76, 83, 93, 95, 97, 100, 106-7, 109, 119, 141, 143, 176, 177, 179, 180, 184
Parliament, Spanish 196
Progressive Party (in Spain) 195-6, 197, 199, 201, 203-4, 208, 209, 211
Psalms, Book of 97, 106-7, 108
Patriarchalism 132, 134-5, 138, 139-43, 145-7, 14950, 151-2
Penn, William 47
Pepys, Samuel 67, 77
Peters, Hugh 98
Petitions 113-29, 181, 190, 248-9
Poor Law (s) 6, 235
   active government and 245-48
   colonial opposition to 237-38, 248-9
   English 236, 242-3, 248
   Irish 237

Scottish 236-7, 248
Prerogative, royal 45, 50, 51, 69, 76, 141, 184
Pocock, J. G. A. 127-8
Pope, the 91
Popery 14, 18, 40, 49-50, 64, 70-71, 74, 80, 178-80, 184
Power, civil 18-19, 104
Power, ecclesiastical 18-19, 21-2
Presbyterian (ism) 2, 3, 12, 27, 32, 48, 61-64, 117, 121, 166,
Preston, Battle of 95
Print 180, 184,187
Protestant (ism) 18, 50, 61-64, 124, 163, 178
Protestant Dissenters 3, 45, 46, 51-55, 59, 62-64, 70
Protestant Reformation 163-6
Puritan (ism), English 34, 42, 45, 48, 57, 59, 61, 110, 162-8, 169-71, 178
Putney Debates 34, 91-92, 95-96, 102
Pym, John 179, 184

Quakers 32, 42, 46, 47, 60, 63, 64

Radicalism 185-6
Ranters, the 176, 178
Regicide 97, 98, 100, 102, 103
Religious belief 28, 30
Republicanism 115, 131, 132, 134-5, 148-50
Resistance theory 17-19, 177, 183
Revolution, Conventing 182-4, 193
Revolution, English 20, 26, 153, 157, 162-72, 176, 177, 192-3
Revolution, French (1789) 153, 157-62, 164, 165, 169
Revolution, French (1848) 162, 211
Revolution, Spanish (1854) 196, 197, 203, 207, 211

Restoration 82, 85, 95, 113
Revelation, Book of 91, 92
Robespierre 160-1
Romans, Epistle to the 95
Royal family, Spanish 198, 200, 206-7
Royalism 2, 3, 11, 12, 22, 27-8, 113, 119, 175, 176
Rump Parliament 119-20, 128, 168

Saints, the 38, 166-7, 189
Samuel, Book of 96
Sansculotte 159, 160-1, 169, 170
Scotland 82, 95, 103-4, 182-3, 185, 186, 236-7
Sectarianism 179-80
Selden, John 59-60
Settler societies 236-49
Shaftesbury, Earl of 46, 50, 51 55-56
Shere, Sir Henry 75
Sidney, Algernon 73, 74, 132, 152
Skepticism 153, 158
Skinner, Quentin 10, 125, 128-9
Solemn League and Covenant 13, 177, 182-3, 187
Spelman, Sir John 11
Spain 5-6, 195-212
Spinoza, Benedict de 134, 146
State, colonial 247-8
State Formation 191-3
St. John, Oliver 94-95, 96, 99-100, 103
St. Paul 95
Stubbe, Henry 32, 48-49, 58, 59

Talbot, Peter 81
Taylor, Martha 30
Tawney, R. H. 36, 38-40
Tew Circle, the 11
Tomkinson Thomas 43
Toleration 13-14, 29, 32, 38, 45-65, 121, 207

Toleration Act (1689) 45, 51-53

United Provinces 71, 72, 151
United States of America 217, 220, 239
Utopia 6, 138, 189, 225

Van Dieman's Land 221
Vane, Sir Henry 31, 38, 41

Wakefield, Edward Gibbon 216-7, 223, 225
Walwyn, William 16, 32-32, 111, 190
War 21, 191
Weldon, Anthony 17
Welfare provisions 235-49 (See also: Poor Law)
    Australasian patter of 239
    Dependence and 248
    English 240-1, 242-3
    Family responsibility and 238
    Full employment and 246
    Institutional 241
    New Zealand 242-2, 243-5
    North American pattern of 239
    Property ownership and 246-7
Westminster Assembly 12, 33, 48, 110
Wharton, Philip 101-2
Whitehall Debates 33
Whitelocke, Bustrode 47, 48-49, 51, 57-59, 180
Wild, Robert 52, 55
William III (of England) 35, 39, 82
Williams, Griffith 11, 13-14
Winstanley, Gerrard 111
Wittgenstein, Ludwig 259, 260, 262-3, 265, 266
Wood, Anthony 138-9

Worcester, Battle of 3, 67-68, 78, 84, 96
Worden, Blair 105-6
Worsley, Benjamin 190-1